A History

MYANMAR

since Ancient Times

Traditions and Transformations

MICHAEL AUNG-THWIN
and
MAITRII AUNG-THWIN

SECOND UPDATED AND EXPANDED EDITION

REAKTION BOOKS

To Pwap and Shan, Grandmother and Grandson

Published by Reaktion Books Ltd
Unit 32, Waterside
44–48 Wharf Road
London N1 7UX

www.reaktionbooks.co.uk

First published 2012, reprinted 2012
Second updated and expanded edition, first published in paperback,
with a revised chapter Twelve 2013
Transferred to digital printing 2024
Copyright © Michael Aung-Thwin and Maitrii Aung-Thwin, 2012, 2013

Printed and bound in Great Britain by CPI Group (UK) Ltd, Croydon CRO 1YY

A catalogue record for this book is available from the British Library

ISBN 978 1 78023 172 3

CONTENTS

Timeline

40,000–3,000 BC Stone Cultures

3,000–500 BC Metal Cultures

500 BC–AD 800 Urban ('Pyu') Period

800–1300 'Classical' Myanmar – the Pagan Dynasty and Kingdom

1364–1527 Post-'Classical' – First Ava Dynasty and Kingdom

1358–1539 First Pegu Dynasty and Kingdom

1539–1599 Second Pegu / Toungoo Dynasty and Kingdom

1597–1752 Second Ava Dynasty and Kingdom

1752–1886 Konbaung Dynasty and Kingdom

1824–1942 British Colonial Period

1942–1948 The Second World War, the Japanese, and Independence

1948–1962 Civil War and the 'Parliamentary' Experiment

1962–1974 The Revolutionary Government and the 'Burmese Way to Socialism'

1974–1988 The Burma Socialist Programme Party

1988–2010 Transition to a Multi-party System

2011–present 'Disciplined Democracy'

Preface

The term 'Myanmar' needs some clarification. First, spelled *Mranma* and *Myanma* in Old and Modern Burmese script respectively, it is not a noun but an adjective that modifies the noun that follows it, so that *Myanma Pyay* (or *Pyi*) is a reference to the country, *Myanma Lu Myo* to the people and *Myanma Saga* to the language. To use the term 'Myanmar' as a noun is, in Burmese, tantamount to using the word 'American' for 'America', so that one would be saying 'I am going back to American' rather than 'I am going back to America'. Nevertheless, Myanmar, used as a noun, is now the legal English term for the country recognized by the United Nations.

Second, Myanmar is *not* a new word coined only in 1989 by the military Government to replace the term 'Burma' as often contended by the 'international' media (and even some 'scholarly' works). On the contrary, its Old Burmese equivalent (*Mranma*) has been used for the state and country in much the same way since at least the early twelfth century if not earlier. Similarly, the country's place-names; 'Yangon' was only much later anglicized as 'Rangoon' by the British, 'Pyi' as 'Prome' and 'Muttama' as 'Martaban'. To Burmese speakers, who currently represent well over 87 per cent of the population, the Burmese versions have always been known and used as such.

Indeed, it is 'Burma' that is actually the new (and foreign) term, likely created only in the nineteenth century and the British period. It is certainly *not* an indigenous word and cannot be found as such in either the national language or any minority languages of the country prior to that era. Although the word 'Burma' may have been phonetically derived from the Burmese word *Bama* (the colloquial equivalent of *Myanma*), 'Burma' per se is still English, and still a colonial term imposed on the country's people without their knowledge and/or consent.

Even during the height of the colonial period when English was the official language of state, if one were to ask ordinary Burmese speakers who did not speak English (which constituted the vast majority of the

7

population) what the name of the country was, they surely would have replied 'Myanma Pyi', not 'Burma', and if asked the name of the capital at the time, would have said 'Yangon', not 'Rangoon'. It was only amongst the very small English-language-speaking elite circles that their anglicized equivalents were used.

Third, many ex-colonies since independence have returned to using indigenous place-names, understandably after humiliating colonial experiences. Sri Lanka and Myanmar are just two examples while in India Bombay is once again Mumbai, Calcutta is Kolkata and Madras, Chennai. Yet whereas Sri Lanka and India are not ostracized for doing this, Myanmar is, indicating that the reason a few rogue nations continue to insist on using the term 'Burma' rather than 'Myanmar' is obviously political. The word 'Burma' has no legal standing internationally, is clearly exogenous, and only perpetuates rather than resolves current tensions.

To clarify further, in American academic usage, the word 'Burman' refers to the ethno-linguistic group and 'Burmese' to citizens of the nation. In British academia, however, the two are reversed. Yet neither is correct, for there is no such distinction made in Burmese itself between the ethno-linguistic and the national group; both are *Myanma* (or *Bama*). That distinction between 'Burman' and 'Burmese' (like the word 'Burma') is also a colonial creation that appears to have followed the differences perceived between 'British' and 'English' so important to the British colonial power. And, of course, there is no such thing as 'Myanmarese'.

For the sake of convenience this book uses the current internationally recognized legal term 'Myanmar' for the country, 'Burmese' for the national group and language, and 'Burma' when the context dictates; that is, usually for references made during the colonial period when official statements or records are cited or proper names in English that use the term 'Burma'. We also retain the former English spellings of well-known words such as Upper and Lower Burma, Irrawaddy, Salween, Ava, Pagan, Moulmein, Martaban, Pegu, Mandalay and Arakan to minimize confusion.

Prologue:
A Synthesis of Old and New

As the Silk Air jet from Singapore lands at the small new modern Yangon International Airport – where tall grass rather than concrete and urban sprawl meets the runway – one is a bit puzzled. Has time stood still or moved forward in Myanmar? The ambiguity is warranted, for both observations are accurate. The country today is struggling to accommodate its past with its present, attempting to integrate long-standing cultural traditions and historical trends with more immediate, short-term, mainly externally generated economic and geo-political realities, resulting in both a 'fusion' and a 'tension' between old and new. Thus, while this Prologue introduces the reader to present day Myanmar, the following chapters in 'flashback' fashion explain how it got there.

Once inside the clean, air-conditioned and orderly terminal, legal entry to the country is quick and easy. Immigration is staffed mainly by women wearing Western-style uniforms but with traditional *thanakha* paste on their faces, and what was once a manual affair with long lines, many sheets of paper being stamped, scrutinized and approved by many different people is now done with a few clicks of the keyboard on computers (even 'visa-on-arrival' is now available.)[1]

After Immigration, luggage is quite painlessly collected from actually functioning carousels, after which we surprisingly waltz through Customs without any fuss. There is no longer that bottleneck behind (usually Burmese) nationals whose suitcases have been opened, everything spilling out, threats (by the owners of the suitcases) of reporting to someone higher up that they know, and counter-reprimands, or thinly veiled extortion attempts to garner cigarettes and/or alcohol by customs officials; the kinds of things in the past that made entry into Myanmar a nightmare. One realizes then and there how much things have changed from just ten years ago.

Outside the airport there is no longer a noisy throng of people all clamouring to get customers by grabbing one's suitcases towards rickety taxis. Instead, everyone on the kerb officially 'belongs' there (with uniforms and badges to prove it!), the process is orderly if not down-right calm, and soon one is on the way to the hotel amid relatively clean, still tree-lined streets. Unfortunately, many of the oldest trees that used to provide shade to these streets and their pavements no longer grace them today, having been uprooted by Cyclone Nargis, which hit the Delta and Yangon in early May 2008.

The cyclone had suddenly and unexpectedly changed course east-wards towards the Myanmar Delta from its annual northerly direction towards Bangladesh, catching everyone unprepared. Even the more than 32 warnings given by the Government within the 36 hours or so it had, would not have done much good.[2] Most Delta people do not have tele-phones (certainly not mobile phones) and usually travel by boat (as the roads are inadequate for transporting goods and people on a large scale even in normal times), while the farming and fishing villages, constructed mainly of bamboo and thatch, are located right on the coasts or close to irrigation streams and rivers.

As the entire Irrawaddy Delta is barely above sea level, neither people nor houses could have survived the 150-mph winds and the 20-foot ocean surge that hit it. The cyclone took an estimated 138,000 lives; most, probably, by drowning. The surge also inundated the low-lying rice-lands, although no rice would have been planted that early. Resettlement and reconstruction continues in the devastated areas today, and the 2009 rice crop was already in when we arrived. (Some estimate that only about 5 per cent of the money that was promised by outside sources has actually materialized.)

On the road from the airport to our hotel is the old American ambas-sador's residence, which at the time of the cyclone housed the US *chargé d'affaires*. It still commands one of the best views and prime real estate locations in Yangon. Set on Inya Lake, it has its own tennis court, servant quarters and boat dock. Yangon University, a bit further down the road from it, and now meant for graduate rather than undergraduate studies, still occupies many wooded acres, with its distinctive colonial period-style architecture that can be found throughout Southeast Asia. The most conspicuous building on campus remains imposing Judson Chapel tower of what was, prior to Independence in 1948, Judson College (named after the renowned American Baptist missionary). Yangon Uni-versity was well known for its political activities, most notably during the nationalist and post-Independence periods.

Between the airport and city centre traffic is hardly the quagmire found in most Southeast Asian capitals, especially Bangkok, although the Burmese jaywalkers (likely the best in the world) are quite conspicuous. If this is the visitor's first time in the country, one immediately notices both men and women still proudly donning their national dress: the

Burmese version of the Southeast Asian *sarong*, unlike most people in other urban areas of Asia nowadays who have opted for Western-style clothing despite the heat and humidity of the region. Yangon has the feel of an overgrown town attempting to adjust to new growth within a limited old space. The same is true of the composition of the vehicles on the road: a mix of old Second World War vintage trucks alongside new Toyota and Kia SUVs from Japan and Korea.

As the taxi makes its way to the hotel on one of the main arteries leading into the city centre, one cannot miss the majestic Shwedagon Pagoda that stands atop the highest hill in Yangon. It is, for the predominantly Buddhist population, the city's sacral epicentre. But it has also served as a symbolic staging area for political resistance during both the colonial and nationalist periods and the location of massive rallies. Religion and politics in Myanmar has always had both an explosive and cosy relationship.

The hundreds of acres of tax-exempt glebe property that belong to the Shwedagon's estate also reflect the intimate *economic* relationship between church and state since the eleventh century. It must be one of the most valuable pieces of property in the country. On it are located many monasteries, in which reside devout monks who have taken their vows seriously to renounce this material world. They belong to the supreme national ecclesiastical organization in the land, the Sangha, recognized by the state as the official 'church', which (at last count) includes nine distinct Orders with approximately 400,000 monks and novices (larger than the Tatmadaw, the armed forces, with approximately 280,000 soldiers).

Monks on their morning rounds for alms at Pagan, 2007.

Novices on their morning rounds for alms in Yangon, 2007.

The national Sangha has its own elected hierarchy of officials and elders who oversee the organization, conduct qualifying exams, enforce discipline, defrock the unworthy and insure the integrity of the religion.

At the same time there exist marginalized 'outlaw' monasteries in Yangon and elsewhere whose monks do not belong to the official Sangha. These 'humans in yellow robes' (as U Nu, the first premier of the Independent Myanmar, once referred to them) have little or no serious commitment to a life of renunciation, have not passed the requisite entrance examinations or served the required number of *wa* (rainy seasons) as monks. They are, for the most part, ignorant of scripture beyond the most simple of doctrines and, as a result, not recognized by the national Sangha as bona fide, and do not accept the decrees passed by that body.

They live a life of leisure in their monasteries without the rigours of study and discipline expected and required of the orthodox clergy. But having taken sanctuary from, and escaped the usual hardships of secular life – including personal problems, debts, taxes and even the law – they are often a law unto themselves. And because they still don the saffron robe and shave their heads, they are visually indistinguishable from genuine monks and thus continue to receive homage and respect from most lay people. That fact was manipulated during the so-called 'saffron revolution' of 2007 whereby members of the political opposition shaved their heads and donned saffron robes, and after infiltrating and usurping the leadership role, turned what had initially been a peaceful protest into a violent one.[3] (This event will be more fully described in chapter Twelve.)

Once we arrive at the hotel the taxi is greeted by the friendly doorman who handles the luggage. At the registration desk attractive young men and women who speak good English welcome the visitor with cool wet towels and a local fruit drink. They handle the reservations that have been made via internet expeditiously and politely. One can pay either in Burmese currency or US $, as the latter can be changed in the hotel itself for Burmese kyats at the current market rates without any problems.[4] Except for the intense scrutiny of the notes for newness, crispness and microscopic tears, there is no fuss: no bargaining over rates, no looking over one's shoulder, signing this or that form, presenting one's passport, as was the case in earlier decades.

The hotels used to take American credit cards until economic sanctions were imposed on the country by several Western nations led by the United States. No longer are they readily accepted, at least not without a 'laundering' process via different currencies and agents which add considerably to the costs. More important, the sanctions in general and the American credit card in particular have had a negative affect on the people least able to afford it. In our case, without the cushion provided by our credit cards, we tended to be more careful with cash. The tip we gave the young man who brought the luggage up to our room would have been doubled had our Visa credit card been accepted at the hotel, for we would have been much freer with our money. There are other unintended consequences of the sanctions on Myanmar that have made the rich even richer. And as for the intent of the sanctions – to bring the Government to its knees – it has, not surprisingly, not worked, as Myanmar can buy what it wants from its neighbours, including arms and ammunition from China and training and advice from allies of the United States such as Israel.

Our hotel room at the 'four-star' Summit Parkview contains the amenities one has come to expect in modern travel: air-conditioning, refrigerator, private bath with towels, shampoo, soap, even a new toothbrush. Of course, there is TV that features broadcasts by CNN, BBC, Myanmar TV and numerous other European (French, German, Italian) and Australian channels, as well as regional broadcasts from India, China, Malaysia and Thailand. In the refrigerator are the all-important complimentary bottles of safe drinking water. An electric hot-water dispenser, some instant tea and coffee packets and a bowl of seasonal fruit are also standard. A buffet breakfast of Asian and European fare is inclusive of the (off-season) hotel rate of approximately US $29 per night. As many of the tourist hotels in the country are financed and designed by Singapore, even the fixtures in the room are reminiscent of those we have found there.

There is also a swimming pool, a well-equipped gym and locker rooms with sauna and steam, dance-aerobics studio and a (genuine) massage parlour. The hotel also has a bar for the public that usually features Filipino bands, although the one we encountered consisted of a Kachin, Burmese and Karen female vocal group, with Burmese and Karen males playing back-up on electric guitar and keyboards. (None of them spoke, although they can sing in, English.) There is also an internet room in the lobby, and for US $1 a person can have a half-hour access to Google, hence to virtually everything else on the web, most importantly our email. This is not the Yangon of even a decade ago.

Once outside the hotel one can patronize ordinary roadside tea shops where the gossip flows freely and conversations (in Burmese, of course) are hardly muted or politically circumspect. One can also visit food courts whose prices are mid-range, or more expensive upscale restaurants that feature very good Western food. The surprise here is the latter are being patronized mainly by local (mostly Westernized) Burmese, not foreigners. Ten years ago, we would not have seen a single Burmese face amongst the diners; all would have been foreigners. There is obviously now a class of Burmese (and *not* necessarily military) who can afford to eat at these places. And when they climb into their new Land Rovers or Toyota SUVs after dinner the initial observation is confirmed.

The larger 'dry markets' are stocked to the ceiling, especially the famous Bogyoke Ze in Yangon and Zegyo in Mandalay. The 'wet markets' are also well supplied with fresh vegetables, fruits, fish, poultry, where, of course, hawkers sell what some of us consider the only 'authentic' Burmese food in the country. But that is not the case; one can get relatively 'authentic' indigenous food now in the fanciest hotels as well; it just costs more, is 'safer' to eat (for those of us who have lost their immunities) and can be enjoyed in clean air-conditioned comfort.

Another hotel we stayed in, the Sedona, overlooks the city side of Inya Lake on whose banks is the recently constructed, fortress-like United States Embassy built on what was once called 'Washington Park', an exclusive residential area for American diplomats and their families. Nearby is Aung San Suu Kyi's house, to which the Mormon from Missouri swam and remained for two days. Unfortunately, that event set back what had appeared to be (finally) a change of policy in Washington on Myanmar, hinted at by Secretary of State Hilary Clinton in Indonesia a few weeks theretofore. But the swimmer 'incident' stopped dead any move towards reconciliation. Indeed, similar 'incidents' have occurred almost like clockwork during the past twenty years whenever there was a hint of reconciliation in the air.[5] One wonders if there is any relationship between these incidents and certain dissident organizations that materially benefit handsomely from the *failure* of reconciliation, as success would surely turn off their cash spigots.

But what was interesting to us about this particular incident (and apropos to one of the approaches of this book) is that it was *not* the subject of much conversation in Yangon itself, although it was a relentless topic in the English-language media of the region, especially Thailand and Singapore. It confirmed our long-held contention that a quite different and largely *imaginary* Myanmar exists in the *cyberspace* of foreign countries with little or no correlation to the 'real' Myanmar we were visiting on the ground. In other words, the concerns and priorities of the foreign press almost never reflect those of the majority of the people of Myanmar. To find those priorities and concerns, we must travel to Upper Myanmar, the traditional 'heartland' of the country.

One can get there by car, train, bus, plane or boat. Most international visitors take the Dutch Fokker jets now servicing Pagan and Mandalay. The circular route includes other points of interest before returning to Yangon. Just 30 years ago, there were only two (at most, three) scheduled flights per week with UBA (Union of Burma Airways) and only two hotels in Pagan; now, there are dozens of flights and hotels with the usual amenities. Most of these are now located outside the designated archaeological site itself, given plots of land and motorized tube wells to continue their businesses. (The cost for a room in one of the more modest hotels during the early 1990s, including breakfast and a bicycle to tour the temples, was only US $4.)

Earlier, the airport at Nyaung-U which served Pagan had a dirt runway and only one of the roads in the ancient capital was paved. Foreign visitors were not usually able to see temples such as the Dhammazayika for it was considered 'too far' and difficult to get to. (Now, it is a major stop for tourists.) Nearly 2,900 temples still dot the approximately 16 square miles of Pagan, under the charge of the Department of Archaeology, although some of its endowed lands still belong to the Sangha. A large museum has been built to replace a very tiny one in order to display many of Pagan's most important treasures. New offices and housing quarters for the staff of the archaeological service have also been built. Despite the meagre budget the Archaeological Department has tried to preserve the ancient ruins by using period-style materials and original designs taken from still standing structures and existing wall paintings.

From Pagan one can continue by air, boat, or road to Mandalay, located on the mighty Irrawaddy, on a vast and strategic plain where several ancient routes to China and India converge. Mandalay is also a crossroads for important domestic routes. It is only a day trip to Shwebo, the original seat of the last dynasty, located across the Irrawaddy to the northwest.

It once controlled the upper entrance to the Mu River valley and its vast irrigated fields whose perennial supply of water still flows today in canals dug by Myanmar's kings back in the twelfth century. When quizzed about the annual tax on (state) canal water that the farmers using it are charged for their privately owned rice fields, one laughed and said, 'twelve kyats' (approximately 12 US cents). Although he could choose not to, he sells his rice to the Government at a little below market prices but, in return, gets discounted prices on next year's fertilizer (along with canal water).

One can also go in the opposite direction, southeast to the Kyaukse valley, where several large perennial streams run north towards the Myitnge (literally 'Little River' but quite sizeable), thence to the Irrawaddy. They originate in, and are fed by, the Shan Hills to their east where the rainfall is much higher, turning Kyaukse into the most productive rice-producing region in pre-colonial times. Many of the canals and weirs constructed during Pagan times still operate and provide some of the most varied agricultural products in the country. For millennia this region fed the entire population of the country until the British turned the Irrawaddy Delta into the premier rice bowl of the colony by the first half of the twentieth century. With that, the centre of gravity moved to Lower Myanmar, until in 2005–6 the capital, Naypyidaw, was built adjacent to Pyinmana, returning the centre of power to the Dry Zone.

Because the farming and/or farming-related classes still constitute approximately 70 per cent of the population of the country, since Independence the Government (both civilian and military) has placed its priorities on agriculture and rural Myanmar. As a result it paid less attention to the urban sectors, from where, not surprisingly, most of the protests of the modern era, their leaders, their followers and their issues have come.

Mandalay is also the 'gateway' to the Shan Hills on its east, where the Shan (or T'ai) speakers largely live and currently make up about 9 per cent of the present population of Myanmar. Yet everywhere we went in the Shan Hills, the national language, Burmese, is also spoken, in some cases with a 'Shan accent'. Buddhism is evident in every nook and cranny as well. Religion and language have been two of the most important integrators of the state.

The British, attracted by this cool and elevated region, built their most famous summer resort at nearby Pyin Oo Lwin, known as May Myo to English speakers. Its higher elevation provided a respite for the northern hemisphere conquerors who otherwise would have suffered in Mandalay during the summer heat, 'mad dogs and Englishmen' notwithstanding. Today Pyin Oo Lwin's Victorian houses, Anglican churches and an English Tea Garden provide historic charm to those nostalgic about and/or those who benefited from the colonial period. But other than that, and a few similar 'artefacts' and certain institutions – such as the descendants of people with whom some of the colonizers inter-married and decaying colonial architecture seen here and there along with some components of the Indian Penal Code still intact – it seems today as if the British never even set foot in Myanmar. The vaunted 'legacy' of the British exists largely in the minds and books of historians.

Travelling up-country by car is also a safe and pleasant experience now. In the late 1950s and early 1960s, one could not have travelled far outside Yangon, as insurgents and dacoits (bandits) controlled much of the rural areas. Train travel was also risky as rail tracks and bridges were blown up regularly. Since the 1970s, however, the country had become much more secure and even though the insurgents were still active in the remoter areas, banditry was all but gone elsewhere and one could visit places not possible earlier.

In 2009 the drive on a four-lane super highway to the new capital Naypyidaw was somewhat reminiscent of taking Interstate 90 in the US Midwest: long and rather boring. Although the Yangon–Naypyidaw highway was not yet complete at the time, already probably more con-crete has been laid there than in all of Myanmar put together. And the trip that used to take about twelve hours took us about six even with only two lanes operating as of spring 2009. Currently, it is said to take less than four hours.

Naypyidaw – which can be translated in numerous overlapping ways as 'capital', 'royal abode' or 'royal city of the sun' (to which Myanmar's kings traced their cosmological ancestry) – is a new city, reminiscent of Brasilia when it was first being built. As noted above, it is adjacent to Pyinmana, an old prehistoric and historic urban settlement, and an important governorship since the Pagan era. It is part of the ancestral

Yangon–Naypyidaw highway, 2009.

'heartland' of the country, the Dry Zone, where most of its people lived and much of its history was made.

In the modern era, as well, Pyinmana has symbolic importance: it is considered the place from where Aung San and the Burma National Army first turned against the Japanese en masse by the spring of 1945, ahead of the Allies' counter-attack. Thus it has the same sort of historic importance in the country's military history that (say) Trenton, New Jersey, and 'crossing the Delaware' on Christmas Eve by George Washington has in military American history.

Apart from these historic, cultural and psychological reasons, building the new capital has strategic and other practical value. Naypyidaw sits between Yangon and Mandalay on the Sittaung Valley's important north–south axis, with quick access to the Shan Hills on its east and Prome on its west, for long part of the domestic and international network of overland routes that still serve Myanmar today. It is also central and closer to the natural resources of the country, particularly precious stones (such as ruby and jade), teak forests and minerals. The capital also lies close to new hydro-electric projects that supply electricity 24 hours a day (unheard of in Yangon) along with other amenities expected of any modern capital city.

Neither Yangon's space nor infrastructure could have possibly sustained the kinds of improvements needed or envisioned for a twenty-first-century capital city in Asia. At Naypyidaw everything is built anew: roads, sewers, water supply, the electric grid, telecommunications, government buildings, hospitals, homes for the aged, power plants, schools and even the central bazaar. The city is sprawling, government buildings are large, with spacious compounds set a good distance from the main roads, which are also spacious with often six lanes (or more) for traffic to move both ways.

Housing for civil servants was said to have been free at one time, though this is said to be no longer the case. But garden plots are allotted to each tenant nonetheless, a much valued accessory. Hotels are more reminiscent of motels in the Midwest United States; spread out rather than up. It is a city in which one currently needs a car (or taxi), as public transportation is not yet very conspicuous for the still growing population. (As of 2010, the population of Naypyidaw is reported to be close to a million – perhaps including Pyinmana's population as well – making it the third largest city in the country after Yangon and Mandalay.) An international airport is being built, to where flights from Yangon take about half an hour while a new train station was recently completed at Naypyidaw, connecting it to the old Yangon–Mandalay line. The plots for the various embassies have already been allotted, the largest taken by China, although the newly built United States Embassy will probably remain in Yangon.

Shwedagon Pagoda, Yangon, present form 15th century.

In traditional times any legitimate capital had to have seven requisites, one of which was the main temple, considered the palladium of the state built at one of the auspicious corners of the city. Naypyidaw's new 'capital temple' called the Uppatatheinti (also spelled Uppatasanti, meaning 'protection from calamity') is, not accidentally, built in virtually the same style as the holy Shwedagon in Yangon. However, the *anda* (dome structure from the platform upward) is said to be one foot *lower* than that of the Shwedagon in Yangon. The reason for that, we have been told by numerous scholars and monks, is that no replica can be larger than the original. Its public consecration ceremony included Sangha and state participation at the highest levels.

The imposing buildings in 'traditional' style built to house the Hlutdaw ('Parliament') after the 2010 elections on 7 November, were still being constructed as of Spring 2009, but are now finished. They stand at the end of a broad avenue, up which important rituals of state are to be re-enacted, much like New Delhi's broad, awe-inspiring avenue that moves majestically from the Gateway of India to Parliament.

Although enmeshed in the past in numerous ways, Naypyidaw also represents the present by breaking with some traditions regarding capital cities in Southeast Asia. In earlier times the political centre was also the economic, cultural, religious and social centre of the kingdom. Now with Naypyidaw as political centre, Yangon as economic (also perhaps religious) centre, and Mandalay and Pagan as cultural centres, the *integrated nature* of the pre-colonial capital has been broken. In other words, the political centre is no longer *concurrently* the religious, cultural and economic centre,

The Hlutdaw (parliament) complex, Naypyidaw.

much the pattern found in many *new* nations. The building of Naypyidaw, therefore, is not only a *physical* but a *structural and conceptual transition*, representing both a return to oldness and a step towards newness: the prevailing pattern in the modern history of Myanmar.

The return journey from Naypyidaw was more interesting as we decided to take the old Toungoo road back to Yangon rather than the new super highway. It runs through many historic towns and villages, including Toungoo, the original home of one of the most important dynasties in Myanmar's history. As one enters the city from the north a new larger-than-life statue of the famous king Bayinnaung in traditional military uniform with sword partially drawn, guards entry to the city. He represents Toungoo's tutelary 'deity', in much the same way Abraham Lincoln, sitting larger-than-life and calmly observing the goings-on at the Capitol from his throne-like seat at the Memorial, is also guardian 'deity' of that nation and its capital.

As the most militarily accomplished king in Myanmar's history, Bayinnaung today is a major hero, along with two others: Aniruddha and Alaungpaya. All three reunified their respective kingdoms after periods of destruction and anarchy, returning them to their previous preeminent positions in the region, in the throes of what were relentless external and internal attacks. Bogyoke Aung San, the 'father' of modern Burma, and his military successor General Ne Win, are perceived to have done much the same thing after the anarchy and chaos of the Second World War and Independence, and therefore have become part of the unwritten 'pantheon' of Myanmar's unifying heroes. These themes – of reunification,

restoration of identity, self-reliance and return to preeminence – still
resonate with both ruler and ruled.

The old Toungoo road has been improved, on which nearly every
fifteen minutes or so during a seven and a half-hour trip back, we passed
huge Nissan Diesels loaded to the brim. There is obviously much economic activity going on, the likes of which neither we nor probably any UN
statistician has heretofore seen in Myanmar. We even saw a semi-tractor

Modern statue of King Bayinnaung (*reg.* 1551–1581) at Toungoo,
completed in 2009.

trailer for the first time, which could never have navigated Myanmar's roads even a decade ago. The infrastructural development of rural Myanmar between 1988 and 2010 has been remarkable, yet barely (if at all) reported in the 'international' press.

There are many places to eat in the towns we passed through, obviously a response to the increase in traffic. They looked and felt the same as any in rural Myanmar, and the one at which we stopped had refrigerated bottled water and Coke (from Thailand) but also a dirt floor. Indeed, when one stops at these and other ordinary villages, things seemed to have remained much the same as before. In such calm and relaxed settings one is made acutely aware of what Burmese hospitality and friendliness are really like. Yet these rural situations and the less friendly urban ones are both authentic, no less than (say) Crete, Nebraska and Chicago are also authentically American, even if they seem to belong to different worlds. Nevertheless, one should be reminded that while urban areas hold only about 25 per cent of the country's population today, the rest of Myanmar's 59 million plus people live and die in rural Myanmar.

In short, and in stark contrast to the image evoked whenever one reads about the country in Western-language accounts, a visitor to Myanmar would have been surprised *not* to find the armed soldiers, tanks, armoured cars or barbed-wire surrounded machine-gun nests at street corners that typify military rule. And although the words 'brutal' and 'repressive' are the *sine qua non* of nearly every journalistic account about the previous Government, when one comes in personal contact with ordinary people there is no hint of fear or oppression in their faces or behaviour as implied by these accounts. Indeed, it is just the opposite: the warmth,

Girls of Ava, 2007.

hospitality, sense of humour, spirit, spunk and pride of ordinary Burmese people that one invariably encounters defy the police-state image of the country perpetrated by the self-appointed 'international community' and its media during the past twenty years.

There is a real dissonance, then, between what one expects to find and what one really finds, between the *actual* Myanmar and the *virtual* Myanmar, the country as experienced 'on the ground' in 'real time' (and changing) and the one seen in cyberspace on one's computer screen (forever frozen in time). If the reader is serious about understanding and knowing Myanmar better, he or she should visit the country with an open mind, not with the intention of confirming their prejudices.

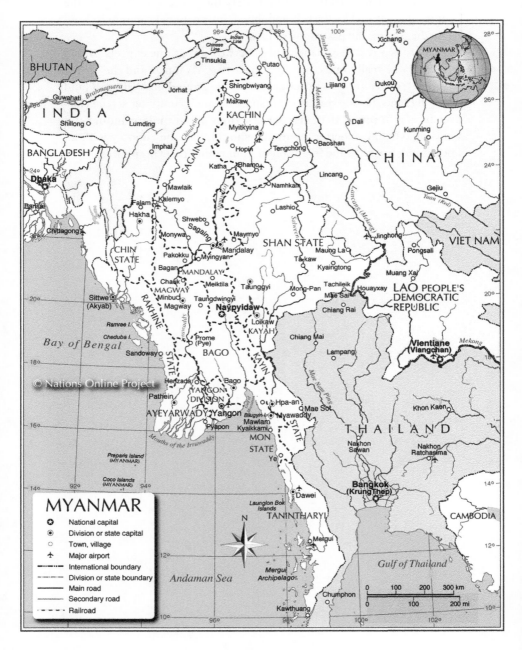

Political map of Myanmar, 2011.

Introduction:
A Different Perspective

This book is a history focused on 'the state' and covers a long period of time, from prehistory to March 2011. However, although the demographic, technological, artistic and habitation record of the land itself goes back at least 40,000 years (to the Palaeolithic period), the origins of the 'state' in Myanmar can be taken back not much earlier than the last 1,200, to the mid-ninth century and the first integrated kingdom in the country, Pagan, which ruled between the ninth and early fourteenth centuries AD. Thus our history begins there and ends with the current Republic of the Union of Myanmar, highlighting the most pivotal individuals, groups, events, institutions, places and patterns to 2011.

Focusing on the last 1,200 years admittedly gives 'agency' to the Burmese speakers: *their* leaders, *their* history, *their* ideas, *their* institutions, *their* culture and *their* space. But that emphasis stems less from design than from the historical record. For, after all, the Burmese speakers *did* dominate the history of the last 1,200 years, and that history, in turn, directly led to the 'making' of modern Myanmar, so that *their* story, to a large degree, is also the story of the country.

Remove *it*, and 95 per cent of the country's verifiable history must also be discarded. Remove *them*, and 70 per cent of the country's actors and nearly all the most historically important leaders must also be excluded. Remove their *institutions and ideas*, and only pre-state forms of society remain. Remove *their space*, and the most productive regions that have sustained the peoples and cultures of the country for over a millennium, along with most of the evidence for 'civilization' must be cast out as well. In other words, any attempt to reconstruct the history of the country without the central role played by the Burmese speakers not only would be nearly impossible in an empirical sense but, if deliberate, intellectually dishonest as well.

By 'Burmese speakers' we are referring to the dominant *cultural* group that shares the same language and identity, shaped by numerous components: a virtually universal religion and related belief system undergirding notions of power, legitimacy and authority; a common (even if contested) history, literature and mythology; a similar habitat and livelihood; and a familiar set of social customs, values and law. In other words we are referring to the vast majority of the population who, in the past and today, consider Myanmar their home and its prevailing culture theirs.

It was that majority who 'made' the history of Myanmar, as much as the English, French, German, Thai and Vietnamese speakers also 'made' the histories of England, France, Germany, Thailand and Vietnam. The Burmese speakers are the (present) 'winners' in this 'contest' for the nation-state, the primary objective of nearly all majority ethno-linguistic groups in much of the world during the nineteenth and twentieth centuries. They 'won' this contest primarily because they were able to maintain their demographic, material, political, military and cultural dominance for over a millennium, and did so at some of the most crucial moments in the country's history. As a result, the individuals, events, institutions, ideas and places most important in *their* history are also, and have come to be identified with, those of Myanmar.

Obviously, that is not to say that minority peoples and cultures (the 'supporting cast' so to speak) did not contribute to or are unimportant in the making of the country's history. They did and they were. Centres *and* peripheries, agrarian *and* maritime regions, hill tribes *and* lowland villages, rural *and* urban sectors, Buddhists *and* non-Buddhists are all part of the analysis and their role acknowledged in the present book when applicable, even if at times it has been much exaggerated.

In fact, we need to be extremely careful when seeking 'balance' for its own sake, for giving 'equal weight' to people and events when empirically unwarranted can actually distort history. A clear distinction must be made, therefore, between the academic desire for attaining 'balance' on the one hand and historical accuracy (our priority) on the other. Whereas the former is essentially a moral (political) concern, the latter is an empirical (historiographic) one. They are *not* alternative approaches of equal value to a common goal – the reconstruction of history – for both their ends and means are quite different.

Therefore we do not automatically 'give voice' to the 'unheard voices' simply to 'balance' unequal historical situations or help rectify the unfairness of the world. We do so only when the evidence dictates. (Besides, if the scope and scale of the verbiage in the 'international' media about Myanmar were criteria to determine whose 'voice' is heard *less* during the past twenty years, it is actually that of the majority, not the minority.)

Providing 'balance' also does not mean turning everything on its head, where exceptions become rules, and rules, exceptions, distorting history even more and creating a worse *imbalance*. Thus, for example, a 'state-less' history of Southeast Asia has been suggested recently, that 'privileges' non-state entities (such as hill tribes and other 'interstices') as a different way of looking at the problem.[1] But such a topsy-turvy perspective is not only empirically untenable but, without the state, there is little outside it that can be demonstrated (with original evidence) to have even existed.[2] In terms of hard evidence, the history of pre-modern Southeast Asia *is* a history of the state.

Even the way in which historians often organize their histories of Myanmar can create imbalance. For example, most general histories of the country published in English disproportionately give the largest number of chapters to the most recent century (representing less than 5 per cent of the country's total history), while giving the smallest number to the 21 centuries that preceded it (representing over 95 per cent), thereby 'privileging' the much shorter (modern) period over the much longer (pre-modern) one and all that that emphasis implies.

And yet, what best defines Myanmar today – its religion, language and literature, customs and civil law, performing and other arts, agrarian socio-economic and 'patron–client' political values – derives almost solely from the pre-modern not the modern period. This means the above *quantitative* imbalance given to the short modern period is further compounded by creating a *qualitative* imbalance that 'de-privileges' the pre-modern era, so that the 'tail wags the dog'. Such an approach not only distorts the history of Myanmar, it implicitly acknowledges that things *external and recent* are more important than things *indigenous and ancient*. Such exogenous 'present-centrism' continues to shape the way the history of the country is perceived, understood and written today.

In part as a response to that imbalance and distortion of the country's history, this book has reduced the number of chapters conventionally allotted to the modern era and has given more to the pre-modern, although not nearly by as much as their vast difference in time and import actually warrants. Even so, this modest change can and has altered interpretations and conclusions regarding modern Myanmar history, as we shall see in subsequent chapters.

In addition to giving more space disproportionately to a (desired) 'period' in history, simply shortening or lengthening 'periods' also affects the way history is presented and understood. For example, the British 'period' in conventional histories is 'ended' in 1948 with formal Independence. Yet the Japanese invasion of the country in 1942 is what effectively terminated British rule and hence the reason for our 'ending' it then. Both dates have more to do with the importance given to events and individuals by historians than to the 'objective' role these events and individuals themselves played, which has been and continues to be highly subjective.

Our approach in such cases is to give back 'agency' to things indigenous. That means, to paraphrase a historian of Indonesia, we have returned the

Burmese speakers to 'the centre of their own history' and have once more placed the bulk of that history in the (active) *foreground* where it belongs rather than in the (passive) *background* where it has been relegated.[3]

More specifically, and vis-à-vis the external world, that means the main cultural and technological contributions that India, China and the west have historically bestowed on the country no longer occupy centre-stage or the entire 'play'; only parts of certain 'scenes' and specific 'acts'. Indigenous data – literatures, myths, epigraphs, chronicles, edicts, law codes, census records – receive priority in our reconstruction (especially) of the country's pre-colonial history. Myanmar's beliefs concerning power, authority and legitimacy – about 'man' and 'his' world – also receive emphasis in our analysis and conclusions about the country's history and politics, rather than (or less than) exogenous ones that are either poorly understood by or demonstrated to have been of low priority for the majority of the people.

Vis-à-vis the internal (domestic) scene, such an approach also puts agriculture (and agrarian values) back in the foreground where it belongs – the prevailing and dominant way of life for most of the people of the country for most of its history – rather than the conventional emphasis given to 'international' trade and commerce, an exogenous perspective now relegated to the background. The Dry Zone of the major river valleys, where the state and its capitals were almost always (and are still) centred, thus regains its preeminent role in the country's history, culture and politics.

This approach returns 'balance' to the 'imbalance' that currently exists and gives back the country's history to its most historically significant peoples and cultures, about whom this book is written. It is part of our contribution to the 'autonomous' historiography of Southeast Asia.[4]

We also emphasize *narrative* history – what the Annales School calls '*l'histoire événementeille*' (the history of events) – rather than *institutional* history. However, that is not meant to imply that the former is more important than the latter. On the contrary, we feel that '*l'histoire événementeille*' has meaning only (or largely) when it occurs within a particular context, a long-term 'constant' – in this case, the geo-demographic environment of Myanmar – that spawned its socio-political and cultural institutions. The latter, in other words, has shaped the significance of events and individuals as much as the former has shaped it. This interaction between 'change' and 'constancy' – or put another way, between linear and cyclic history – has produced a 'spiralling' historical pattern in which much of Myanmar history has moved.[5]

Finally, and whatever one's conceptualization of history, its reconstruction must be based on the best available evidence. One cannot begin with a notion or theory – worse, a political philosophy or agenda – then

28

find the 'facts' to fit it, a method unfortunately used rather profusely in recent years with Myanmar. The sources used for this book are many and varied, and focused on primary (original and contemporary) data. By and large, the history of the pre-colonial period has been based on contemporary or near-contemporary archaeological, epigraphic and literary sources of various kinds, while that of the colonial and post-colonial periods largely on government (British and Myanmar) as well as non-government sources. Citations are intentionally kept to a minimum although the sources used in this book are relatively large and fairly well represented by the bibliography.

Chapter One, 'The Setting', describes the material (physical) and human environment: the unchanging geographic and intermittently changing demographic foundations on which the history of Myanmar has been made, and by which it has been shaped. The importance of those invariable and persistent foundations is often minimized by historians, since our discipline emphasizes individuals and events that are always changing over time (the 'software', so to speak). Yet, as we shall see, the physical setting (the 'hardware') has been as much a factor in the development of Myanmar's history and the institutions and 'structures' it has created.

Chapter Two deals with the prehistory of Myanmar dated approximately from around 40,000 years ago to 500 BC. It is focused on the Palaeolithic, Neolithic and Chalcolithic ages, including the bronze and iron cultures that followed. These were part of or had links to a much broader prehistoric and early historic Southeast Asia pattern, stretching from Yunnan and India to the Malay and Indonesian archipelagos. Within the country itself, the earliest and largest number of sites are located in the river valleys of the Irrawaddy, Chindwin, Mu, Myitnge, Sittaung and Samon (essentially the Dry Zone of Myanmar) with a few settlements found on and/or near the coasts. The peoples and cultures of these prehistoric and early historic eras were the ones who laid the foundations for the Urban Age that followed.

The subject matter of chapter Three concerns that Urban Age, Myanmar's formative period. Although by about the eighth century BC there is evidence of settlements in the Dry Zone of people using bronze and iron artefacts, it is only by the second century BC that reliable scientific evidence emerges of true urban society. With it is associated a Tibeto-Burman speaking people conventionally called 'the Pyu' whose culture was pervasive until the mid-ninth century AD. It was this urban culture that laid the foundations for the 'classical' age that followed, Myanmar's 'golden age'.

Chapter Four describes that 'classical' period. Centred at the walled city of Pagan on the east bank of the Irrawaddy, the Kingdom of Pagan was to last more than four centuries – from the mid-ninth to the beginning of the fourteenth – and was to become the exemplary model, the 'template' so to speak, for the country. The scope and scale of its religious devotion, wealth, power, authority, cultural sophistication and grandeur was never again surpassed, while its basic structure became the quintessential model for subsequent ages. Led and dominated by Burmese speakers, their culture over time came to be associated with the 'national' culture as it spread to the far reaches of the country in all directions over the next several centuries, although its core remained in the wide valleys of the Chindwin, Irrawaddy and Sittaung rivers.

The kingdom began to show signs of weakness by the end of the thirteenth and the first decade of the fourteenth centuries when externally generated events accelerated and exacerbated internal long-term problems of a structural nature that finally led to its decline. This was, to use the terminology of the Annales School, a classic 'conjuncture' of '*l'histoire événementeille*' and '*longue durée*' – that is, where 'incidents of the moment' and long-term patterns in society and history come together to create structural change – in this case the disintegration of Pagan. And it was just that: *an end to integration*, not a decay or disappearance of the elements that made Pagan. The padi fields, the irrigation systems, the cultivators, the soldiers, the scribes, the monks, the monasteries, the temples, the villages, the towns, the teak forests, the ruby, silver and gold mines, the forest products, continued to exist; only they were no longer integrated under one centre.

When Pagan ceased to be that integrator, the remnants of its royal family and their descendants (real as well as fictive) separated into three smaller centres of power that had been governorships earlier. After half a century of this situation, the dispersed human and material resources that were still present were once again reintegrated and reunited in 1364 under the First Inwa (Ava) Dynasty, whose capital was a new city by that name.

Ava used the same *structure* that Pagan had used, perpetuating the latter's institutions. Contrary to long-held convention, the Ava kingdom (and period) was *not* a 'dark age of Shan barbarism' that destroyed everything that preceded it. Recent research shows that Ava was not only a Burmese-speaking kingdom but a mini-renaissance of Pagan, resurrecting and preserving its 'classical' traditions for posterity; some of them until the twenty-first century.

In the meantime a maritime kingdom had emerged in Lower Myanmar. Formally called Hamsavati, its centre was locally known in Old Burmese as Payku (anglicized as Pegu and pronounced Bago in Middle Mon) apparently led by Mon speakers who had been migrating into Lower Myanmar for several centuries. The kingdom was only much later named Ramannadesa (the 'Realm of the Rman') whose mythical origins were pushed back to the most exemplary of Buddhist times (India under King Asoka) to become, in the hagiography of the Myanmar Mon, their 'Camelot'. Predictably, dismantling this myth has stoked the fires of modern Mon nationalism, once again bringing the past into the present. It was also during the late Pegu period that Europeans as a group first entered Myanmar's history. Chapter Five, then, concerns the origins and development of, and relationship between Upper and Lower Myanmar during the 'post-classical' period, which covers part of the fourteenth, the entire fifteenth and the first quarter of the sixteenth centuries.

Chapter Six describes one of the most important periods in Myanmar's history. It spans the first quarter of the sixteenth century to its end – part of what historians call the 'Early Modern' era – of which the mid-sixteenth century particularly is notable. It is the story of the Second Pegu Dynasty centred at Pegu (also called the First Toungoo Dynasty), which unified all of Myanmar once again and proceeded to conquer the major centres of western and central mainland Southeast Asia, nuclei of what were to later become Thailand and Laos.

Yet it was also the shortest-lived dynasty in Myanmar's history and was to last no more than 60 years. Nonetheless, indigenous historians consider this period to be the 'second reunification' in Myanmar's history (the first being Pagan) and to have attained its highest military achievements, a theme not easily forgotten today in a country whose cultural identity, domestic order, territorial integrity and political sovereignty has been sustained in modern times largely by a series of military leaders and governments.

By the very end of the sixteenth century a newly arisen maritime centre and power, Mrauk-U, located in what is now Arakan province on the West coasts of the country and Toungoo, which lay at the edge of the Dry Zone on the Sittaung River, destroyed Pegu, the capital of this vast even if short-lived empire. Surviving members of the dynasty, already ensconced in Upper Myanmar, capitalized on the power vacuum and created a new dynasty there, the story of chapter Seven. This new dynasty and period is known to indigenous histories and historians as Dutiya Inwa Minset, the Second Inwa Dynasty (1599–1752), although it is also called the 'Later' and 'Restored Toungoo Dynasty' by Western historians.

Returning to the 'heartland' and resurrecting the old city of Ava as its capital, the leaders of the Second Ava Dynasty first consolidated its human and material resources. They then moved downstream to pacify an anarchic, chaotic and fragmented Lower Myanmar in large part created by the destruction of 1599. Soon the country was looking more and more like Pagan, particularly in terms of its size and composition, although not in terms of wealth or grandeur.

The material foundations of the Second Ava Dynasty consisted basically of the same resources of Upper Myanmar that Pagan and the First

Ava Dynasty had enjoyed, now irregularly supplemented by Lower Myanmar's trade revenues. The new dynasty also restored the conceptual system of Pagan and First Ava, along with their legal and administrative structures, holding on to traditional principles of the patron–client *myosa* ('town eater') system. New dynasties in Myanmar rose and survived because they reinstituted old institutions and ways, less because they created entirely new ones. But that meant old problems would also be resolved in old ways, leading to predictable outcomes.

The Second Ava Dynasty was destroyed in 1752 by one of its own vassals: a revived Pegu, the centre of an economically rejuvenated Lower Myanmar with a new cycle of growth and expansion in trade and commerce in Asia, a second 'Age of Commerce' stimulated not only by a resurgent India and China, but also by the arrival of the British and Dutch who had replaced the Portuguese. Pegu left a governor at Ava, took the booty, including all the members of the Ava court along with its archives, and returned home.

As others before them, they did not reunify the country under their own aegis, neither considering it their destiny nor part of their political vision. Thus it was the act of a mere 'spoiler' who left with the spoils of war, not that of a leadership with a broader vision beyond itself. Indeed, it appears that in Myanmar the destruction of reigning dynasties by those not in power (even though they were part of the same royal family) was as much to prevent the former from succeeding than for the latter to itself succeed, an attitude that has been played out time and again not only in the country's pre-modern but modern history as well.

Chapter Eight is the story of the last dynasty of the Myanmar monarchy (the Konbaung), which ruled between the mid-eighteenth and late nineteenth centuries. Its genesis was the result of Pegu's cavalier attitude to Upper Myanmar, leaving it relatively untouched, conducting only formal oaths of loyalty with important centres and their leaders. It was only a matter of time before another charismatic leader with a broader vision of unity would capitalize on the power vacuum and reunite the country. Originally centred at a militarily important town called Shwebo, the last dynasty subsequently moved its capital to Ava, thence to Amarapura just north of it, finally ending at Mandalay a few miles further north. Indigenous historians consider this period to be the 'third reunification' of Myanmar.

The Konbaung Dynasty survived until the end of 1885 when British forces, having already taken large segments of the lower country in successive increments after three wars – in 1824, 1852 and 1885 – finally conquered and looted Mandalay. After formal surrender on 29 November 1885, that very same evening at 6:30 pm the king and his chief queen were exiled to India where he died in 1916. (His queen returned to her homeland in 1919 as a private citizen.) On 1 January 1886, when 'Burma' formally became a province of British India, Lord Randolph Churchill gave it as a 'New Year's present' to Her Majesty the Queen of England. The circumstances surrounding and the consequences of the British conquest and annexation of Myanmar is the topic of chapter Nine.

Fierce armed resistance to British rule ensued and continued for more than a decade. But by about 1900 the last groups had been brutally crushed and Myanmar 'pacified', at least in terms of overt and explicitly articulated resistance. In terms of 'everyday forms of passive resistance' to foreign rule, however, Myanmar was never pacified.[6] With the monarchy eliminated (and its religious counterpart, the head of the Sangha – the Buddhist 'church' – about to be), society had been decapitated. With its 'head' removed, 'the body' went into convulsions. And on that 'convulsing body' was imposed a totally foreign ideological, socio-economic, legal and political system, creating a 'hybrid' of the worst kind.

The remaining support structure – of hereditary village headmen born locally with local loyalties who had maintained rural society for over 900 years – was also destroyed. It was replaced by salaried agents of the British Government loyal only to it and recruited from outside the area they governed. Although it was a 'rational' system and provided general order/equilibrium to colonial 'Burma', it had little or no meaning for the majority of the people; hence our phrase 'order without meaning' to describe the colonial period. It is exemplified by the Saya San Rebellion of 1930–32, the only genuine peasant rebellion in the country's entire history. That story of colonial 'Burma' is the subject of chapter Ten.

'Burma' remained under de facto British rule until the Japanese invasion of 1942. From then to 1962 is the subject of chapter Eleven, an unconventional periodization scheme that removes the 'agency' given to Britain and its post-war role in Myanmar, and returns it to the Burmese and, in some respects, to the Japanese as well. However, this approach is not simply a matter of changing perspectives, for the evidence makes clear the war years between 1942 and 1945 were instrumental not only in determining Myanmar's future leaders, but also in establishing a genuinely representative national political party (the Anti-Fascist People's Freedom League, AFPFL) and the creation of a truly national army (the Burma National Army, BNA). Thus, although Japanese rule did not last much longer than three years, its impact on Myanmar's post-war history has been very important, particularly in shaping the political and military character of modern Myanmar thereafter.

We consider this entire period (1942–62) one of 'disorder with meaning', replacing the previous era of 'order without meaning'. It was meaningful in that the bulk of this period allowed the people of the country to once again determine their own destiny. Yet it was also an era marked by extreme disorder, when civil war and lawlessness engulfed the countryside and crime pervaded the cities. The situation was reminiscent of the period of anarchy prior to King Alaungpaya's reunification of the country in the mid-eighteenth century, when, lamented the chronicles, 'mothers could not find their children, and children, their mothers'.

The period was also marked by ineffective and weak civilian government, a situation that continued through the 1950s until the potential disintegration of the Union became a reality by the beginning of the next decade. On 2 March 1962, therefore, General Ne Win – a wartime hero and confidant of Aung San, the 'father of modern Burma' – whose army had saved the capital from being overrun by insurgents just a decade earlier, finally carried out a near bloodless *coup d'état* and took over the Government.[7] His Revolutionary Council, backed by a loyal and disciplined army, maintained the integrity of the Union, thereby preserving the nation, the highest priority of Government. Law and order was also restored to an anarchic and fissiparous civilian society.

Social order, the most important concern of the people of Myanmar throughout their history, and union solidarity, the primary objective of the modern Burmese state, were re-established. Both priorities (with intermittent outbursts) have remained generally viable until today. Anarchy, lawlessness, banditry, insurgency and other serious urban crime have been greatly reduced since the 1950s. The decentralism, chaos and anarchy of state and society during that time (under a 'parliamentary democracy') – which gave the country the dubious distinction of having one of the highest homicide rates in the world – is now only a bad dream. Hence the period from 1962 to the present, part of chapter Twelve, we have characterized as one of 'order with meaning'.

To be sure, however, while social order was restored, the economy of most urban areas failed miserably, especially during the first decade of this period, driven as it was by the main ideology of the 1962 Revolutionary Council, called the Burmese Way to Socialism. As one astute observer put it, that ideology was Marxist in inspiration, Leninist in implementation and Buddhist in its goals.[8] Consequently, the main *economic* goal of the subsequent two governments since 1962 has been attempting to 'play catch-up' with the most developed nations of Southeast Asia by a process of incremental introduction of market principles to what is still a controlled economy.

Yet, despite this history – of the Second World War, civil war and reconstruction – the *external* perspective of Myanmar today is based on a single event – the 'crisis' of 1988 – to which is then attributed a single cause – the desire for democracy, virtually ignoring the history of the country's past 50 years. Framed in a binary analysis of 'good and evil' – therefore, taking a moral position – that view has come to dominate the

English-language media. It defines what Myanmar is and is not, dictates what it should be and should not be and determines what it should do and should not do.

In contrast is our *internal* perspective based not on any moral position but a historically empirical one which takes into account Myanmar's recent history of reconstruction following a half-century of civil war, in which the 1988 crisis, though important, was just one event. Having returned the Burmese 'to the center of their own history' and given 'agency' back to the indigenous, it is they who should define what Myanmar is and is not, decide what it should be and should not be and determine what it should do and should not do.[9] Whatever these are, and however imperfect and contested they may be, they nonetheless represent the values and emotions, issues and concerns, priorities and prejudices of the people of Myanmar. And it is these that should matter (and be 'privileged'), not those claimed as 'universal' by exogenous forces.

From that (indigenous) 'angle of vision' the past two decades in Myanmar turn out *not* to be a (moral) struggle between democracy and authoritarianism, freedom and tyranny, the masses and the elite, but an (empirical) one between effective and ineffective rule, order and disorder, elites and other elites – in short, a contest between the forces of strength and the forces of weakness. This simple shift in perspective turns the recent story of Myanmar from an emotional 'morality play' into a sober historical account.

We end the book with a short conclusion that raises questions about Myanmar's future. Given the country's 'objective' demographic, geographic, political, economic, religious and historical context – in other words, removing the *moral component* imposed on them – what might Myanmar look like? What will change, how much, and what will remain the same? In this process, what Southeast Asian country might Myanmar model itself after, if at all, and why? In other words will the Myanmar we know today still be recognizable a generation from now, 100 years from now? Our bet is that much of it will be.

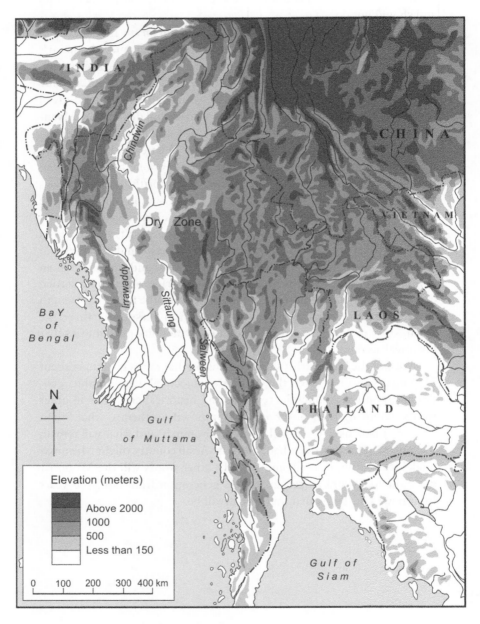

Physical map of Myanmar

I

The Setting

THE LAND

About the size of Texas and nearly three times the size of the UK itself, Myanmar – also known by its colonial term 'Burma' – occupies approximately 261,552 square miles, the largest nation in Southeast Asia in terms of contiguous land mass. Longer than it is wide, the country's major mountain chains – the Arakan, Pegu, Chin and Shan *Yoma* (meaning 'main bone', as in one's spine, a common metaphor for mountain ranges) – lie north to south and slope east to west, while its major rivers – the Irrawaddy, Chindwin, Sittaung and Thanlwin (Salween) – run largely parallel to and in between them. The country is thus divided into long and wide plains areas, extremely conducive to north–south movement but more difficult when moving east–west, a configuration that has significantly shaped the country's history and culture.

Among these large plains areas, the one belonging to the Irrawaddy River runs right down the country's middle, and was (and still is) the most fertile and agriculturally productive region yielding the most variety of crops. It had (and still has) the greatest population density in the country, providing it with the wherewithal not only for the earliest but also the longest prehistoric and historic record, from which the country's 'classical' civilization, its golden age, originates. It boasts the earliest, most sacred and largest number of the holiest shrines in the country, the most 'orthodox' of monasteries and the most learned of ecclesiastics in the country. It was (and is) also the country's centre for producing the best of the fine arts and crafts, the most renowned masters of the theatrical arts and the most accomplished literary traditions and literature. And it was, for the greatest length of time, the most politically dominant region.

It is no surprise, then, that the names of places such as Pagan, Ava, Kyaukse, Minbu, Mandalay, Meiktila-Yamethin, Pyinmana, Pyi, Shwebo – all representing the country's heart and soul, its ancient and earliest history, traditions and cultures, power and authority, in short, its civilization – recur time and again throughout the centuries until today. They evoke the same kinds of images and sentiments as when Kyoto and the Kyoto Plain of Japan, Delhi and the Yamuna-Ganges valley of India, Beijing and the Hwang Ho and Yangtze river valleys of China, Baghdad and the Tigris-Euphrates in Iraq, Mohenjo Daro and the Indus, and of course, Cairo and the great Nile are mentioned. In the same way the Irrawaddy River valley of Upper Myanmar is (and was) the 'heartland' of the country.

The general centre of this 'heartland' lies at the 'Y' created by the confluence of the Irrawaddy and Chindwin rivers, extending south as far as Prome (Pyi) on the Irrawaddy, and to Toungoo, on the Sittaung. It is a large area that has come to be known as the Dry Zone, receiving on average only 45 inches of rain a year.

However, immediately north, west and east of it, especially in the hills, rainfall is abundant. These areas of much heavier rainfall are drained by hundreds of streams and rivers, most of which flow into the Dry Zone and into the major perennial rivers – the Chindwin, Irrawaddy and Sittaung – so that although the Dry Zone itself does not directly receive the kind of rainfall adequate for growing the most important annual cereal in the country – rice – it is nevertheless well watered.

In order to harness these rain-fed perennial streams and rivers flowing into the Dry Zone, sophisticated irrigation works were built and/or administered by the state (as well as non-state peoples) since ancient times. During the monsoons low-lying watersheds and flood plains in the middle of the Dry Zone inundate vast areas of land where catchment basins were dammed to store water during the dry season. The natural activity of the major rivers as well as the man-made canals and sluices for irrigation continuously enrich the central region with silt, turning the Dry Zone into a veritable oasis despite its appellation.

In fact, many parts of the Dry Zone such as the Mu, Kyaukse and Minbu valleys contain the most fertile land in the country, producing (for millennia) the largest variety of crops in addition to the staple: rice. That, along with more than the 150 days of sunshine needed to ripen this most important annual cereal ensured the regularity and predictability of a bountiful yearly harvest. Because there was a predictable food supply, which more often than not yielded a surplus, Upper Myanmar in general and the Dry Zone in particular throughout the history of the country attracted the most valuable asset in early Southeast Asia: people.

It comes as no surprise, then, that the earliest evidence of humans and human habitation can be found in these river valleys. Human settlements date back at least to the Palaeolithic Age (if not earlier), while the majority of the settlements belonging to the Neolithic and subsequent metal ages are also located mainly in sites nestled along, next (or with access) to, these rivers and their tributaries.

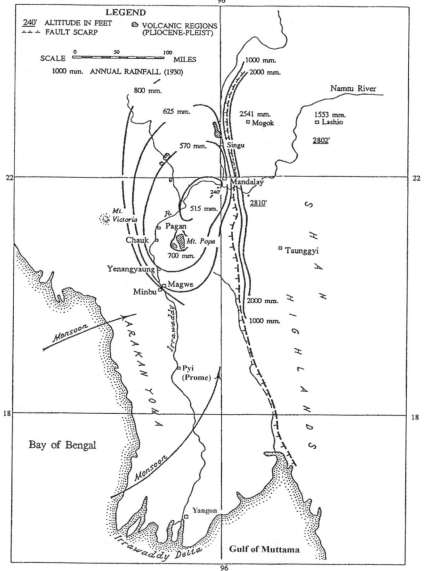

Climate and geological map.

Not surprisingly, the origins of the state lay in the Dry Zone of Upper Myanmar. Of the half dozen capitals of monarchical Myanmar, all except one were located here.[1] The region retained that attraction for people throughout the country's history until the very late nineteenth and early twentieth centuries when the British developed the Lower Myanmar Delta to become a new frontier and the new 'rice bowl' which finally began to draw people away from Upper Myanmar.[2] Only then was there a shift in population density from Upper to Lower Myanmar, although the Irrawaddy River valley as a whole still contains the bulk of the population today. Population density was a *sine qua non* for state formation in labour-scarce Southeast Asia, so that whoever controlled the Irrawaddy River valley and its human and material resources, particularly of Upper Myanmar, nearly always also controlled the rest of the country.

All these factors led to a historical pattern in Myanmar history we have called 'Dry Zone Paramountcy' – the control of and/or hegemony over the whole country for most of its history from the Dry Zone. Only once, when Lower Myanmar's Pegu in the mid-sixteenth century became the country's capital did the centre of economic and political gravity shift to the south. Even then, it was temporary, lasting approximately 60 years before the capital moved back to the Dry Zone to remain there for another 300 years until the British conquered the country in the late-nineteenth century and re-established Lower Myanmar as the country's seat by making Yangon (anglicized as Rangoon) their colonial capital. But as the capital of an *independent political* entity, Yangon (and Lower Myanmar) was to last even less than 60 years, for in 2005 a new capital (Naypyidaw) was built in the Dry Zone, adjacent to Pyinmana, an old governorship since the 'classical' period.[3]

Thus the conceptual and physical centre of the country has nearly always been associated with Upper not Lower Myanmar. Such 'constancy of place' *preserved* rather than *changed* that way of life. This phenomenon is seen by geographers as the ability of a particular geographic area to sustain a stable economic and political environment over a long period of time.[4] It offered certain advantages, but produced analogous problems. Whereas it provides a predictable and dependable resource base (hence, a familiar and comfortable socio-psychological setting), it also tends to constrain the system from expanding beyond a certain limit, a kind of 'braking mechanism' that discourages society from leaving that comfortable situation for the unknown. It creates a conservative mind-set that resists fundamental (structural) change, one of the major themes in the history of Myanmar. Yet the role Upper Myanmar has played in the history, politics, economy, religion, society and overall mainstream culture of the country has been understated or minimized by present political concerns which attempt to trivialize that historical principle, 'privileging' instead the exceptions: the modern, the urban, the western, the coasts.

The geography of Myanmar had other kinds of effects on the country's history. The rivers of these valleys provided an easy mode of transporting troops, peoples, goods and culture; they still do today. Exploiting the north to south flow of the current and the south to north movement of the wind made travel on the Irrawaddy River relatively fast both ways. A relay of war-boats that changed crews along riverine towns built precisely for that purpose could go from the Dry Zone (say Ava) to Dagon (modern day Yangon) in about five days. In pre-modern times in Southeast Asia, that was extremely fast. The trip up-river, of course, took longer, but even in 2004 an ordinary local sailboat going upstream, against the current but with the wind, moved faster than, and overtook the diesel powered tourist boat we were on in about half an hour.

On the west, east and north of these river valleys stands a wall of dense forests and relatively high mountains which contain rich natural resources. They include teak and numerous hardwoods as well as other forest products, along with valuable precious stones such as rubies and jade along with gold and silver. But these forests and mountains also act as physical barriers to invasion while encouraging economic self-sufficiency and relatively unfettered indigenous cultural development. In Myanmar, therefore, whereas mountain ranges have been dividers more than unifiers, rivers have been more unifiers than dividers.

Several hundred miles south of the Dry Zone is Lower Myanmar and the deltas of the Irrawaddy, Sittaung and Thanlyin (Salween). These are relatively recent geographic phenomena, attaining their present form only by or around the sixteenth century (and are still growing each day). And until the mid- to late nineteenth century, when the British drained, cleared and began cultivating the Irrawaddy Delta, it was largely mangrove swamps or otherwise unsuitable for cultivation. That was the reason the area was not well populated until the twentieth century when migration from the interior and immigration from British India and coastal China swelled the population density to levels we see today.

That natural geographic difference between Upper and Lower Myanmar was expressed conceptually in the Burmese terms *anya* ('upstream') and *akye* (literally, 'the lower part of a river', hence, 'downstream'). 'Downstream' was usually a reference to the region south of Pyi (Prome) and Toungoo, the 'gateways' between Upper and Lower Myanmar. Pyi was the most important fortified city amongst Upper Myanmar's kingdoms on the Irrawaddy and, situated at the southern end of the Dry Zone, it was also the staging area to points west, such as Rakhaing state (anglicized as Arakan) with its coasts on the Bay of Bengal. Toungoo, on the Sittaung River valley, assumed the same role on the east, with access points to the Shan states. The terms *anya* and *akye* had a cultural meaning beyond their geographic distinction: each depicted a particular way of life, attitude and behaviour without being considered foreign, much like the terms 'Midwest' or 'East Coast' do in the United States.

Although Lower Myanmar receives an inordinate amount of rain compared to the Dry Zone, because it is largely low lying, newly formed (or still forming) delta, its production of annual cereals was very minimal until the late nineteenth and early twentieth centuries. Only after the first quarter of the twentieth century did the Irrawaddy Delta unequivocally become the 'rice bowl' of British Burma. Even today large portions of the Irrawaddy and Sittaung deltas are still in the process of forming, much barely above sea level, and thus a difficult place to settle; while those areas that have been cleared and drained are suited mainly for monocrop production: rice.

As a result of all these factors Lower Myanmar has been less important politically in the country's approximately 2,200-year pre-colonial history. The first distinct kingdom (or state, polity) there emerged only by the late thirteenth century, and had little or no impact on the country's history and culture until more than two centuries later. Its historical development was also secondary, not primary, while its culture was derivative, not original. Indeed, Lower Myanmar as a region held sway over the entire country in pre-colonial times only once, and when it did, its dynasty came from the Dry Zone.

Buttressing coastal Myanmar are two major bodies of water that linked it to international and regional trade: the Gulf of Muttama (Martaban) and the Bay of Bengal. These were the major highways for external stimuli and influences: trade and commerce, culture and ideas. Lower Myanmar was thus a window to the maritime world and its international trade and cultural contacts, and also home to a mixture of different peoples and cultures, domestic and foreign. This was where the culture of the marketplace took root, with direct links to the outside world and its ideas, products and ways of life.

As a result people and society in Lower Myanmar were demographically and perhaps culturally more cosmopolitan, outward looking, changeable and flexible, and less homogeneous ethno-linguistically. They were more adaptable to sudden changes elsewhere in the external world, as their livelihood depended on that ability to change. Yet the causes for that strength were also the reasons for its weakness, for such a commercial society was vulnerable to outside events, disallowing long-term economic and political stability.

In contrast, Upper Myanmar's agriculture was based largely on internally controllable factors – the maintenance of irrigation systems on perennial rivers, the administration of cultivator classes, the ability to clear and cultivate virgin land. As a result food production was also more regular and predictable than the uncontrollable international market situation of Lower Myanmar, thereby encouraging retention of the population, making Upper Myanmar society much more stable demographically, therefore, politically and socially as well.

It also had a conceptual and quantitative advantage: civilization there emerged centuries earlier (hence, its claim to the country's origins and ultimate legitimacy), its population comprised the majority (hence, its superiority in numbers), and it controlled the country's food supplies (hence, maintained its political power for most of the country's history). Indeed, it was the interaction between these two varied ways of life that provided the country much of its dynamism, a topic to be discussed in chapter Four.

For too long the role of geography in the shaping of modern Myanmar, particularly of the inland agrarian interior, has been minimized and underestimated by historians while reified ethnicity, spectacular political events (often mere 'incidents of the moment') and trade and commerce have been 'privileged'. We hope to change that perspective in this book.

NATURAL RESOURCES

In much the same way that pre-colonial society built its civilization on the geographic foundations given it, modern Myanmar has built upon the well-endowed natural resources that, until today, have remained largely untapped. It is still one of the least densely populated countries in Asia with 69.9 persons per square kilometre and an annual population growth of only 0.78 per cent. It produces more than enough food internally to feed its relatively low population of 59 million individuals. Approximately 41 per cent of its total habitat is still covered by woodlands and forests (with the second lowest rate of deforestation in Southeast Asia) and most of its natural resources are still intact. There is a plentiful supply of fresh water that far exceeds that available for India or China per capita, not to mention Africa.

The country is also known for its gems (primarily its rubies, considered the finest in the world, along with sapphires and jade), oil and natural gas (with 50 million barrels of proven oil reserves and 10 trillion cubic feet of natural gas reserves), and minerals such as tin, tungsten, lead, silver, copper and zinc. Its teak and other hardwoods remain some of the largest unexploited resources in the world.

The higher reaches of the country are covered with laterite (red soil leached of silica but containing iron oxides and hydroxide of aluminum) and the lower regions, especially the river valleys, with alluvial soil, mainly silt and clay. In the central Dry Zone the alluvial soil is black, rich in calcium and magnesium, but when the clay content is low it becomes saline under higher evaporation rates and turns yellow or brown.

It has a long coastline that provides ample marine products. Myanmar's coastal waters are full of fish and shrimp, which still yield a bountiful harvest. Several points on the coasts of Myanmar, which comprise nearly 40 per cent of its boundaries, are natural harbours on the main trade routes to and from Asia. Although a few of these located at the mouths of rivers, such as Bago and Pathein (anglicized as Pegu and Bassein), have now silted up and are no longer as crucial as they once were as ports, most remain on or are close enough to the ocean to be important points for trade, while their hinterlands have become increasingly more important in the growing of rice.

The Myanmar Delta, where the Irrawaddy River splits into approximately nine channels that run into the Gulf of Muttama, is a continuously expanding area that grows by approximately ten feet per year. Much of the drained area is now under padi (rice) cultivation, much of it begun during the early colonial period, as noted above, until by the beginning of the Second World War it had surpassed central Myanmar as the rice granary of the country. This attracted people from the interior as well as overseas, so that by the middle of the twentieth century Yangon and Lower Myanmar was one of the most populated regions in the country.[5]

THE PEOPLES

It is upon these material foundations – the eco-demographic setting – that the peoples and cultures of Myanmar made and shaped their histories. Today, approximately seven major and many more minor ethno-linguistic groups occupy Myanmar, nearly all of whom belong to three of the four main language families of Southeast Asia: Tibeto-Burman, T'ai-Kadai, Austro-Asiatic and Austronesian.

Tibeto-Burman speakers comprise the largest number with nearly 85 per cent, of which between 69 and 70 per cent claim Burmese as their 'mother-tongue'. Karen speakers follow with about 6 to 7 per cent, then Arakanese, the dialect closest to Burmese, with about 4 per cent. The rest of this language family belongs to smaller minorities such as the Kachin, Chin, Lisu, Akha, Lahu and Naga.

The second largest language family is T'ai-Kadai, represented by the Shan speakers who make up about 9 per cent of the population today. The Austro-Asiatic family represents the smallest number, with Mon speakers comprising about 2 per cent of today's population, while the percentage of Palaung and Wa speakers is even smaller. There are even fewer Austronesian speakers in Myanmar, represented by the so-called 'sea-gypsies' (Moken/Solen) of the Mergui archipelago who live off the western coasts of southern Tenasserim, and also by those living in the southernmost sections of that same province who speak a kind of Austronesian.[6]

Today, of course, nearly everyone speaks Burmese, the national language, so that unless one's 'mother-tongue' in a minority language is steadfastly maintained in the family, the next generation may no longer know it. But prior to nation-building and the establishment of national languages for purposes of state integration, such problems of losing one's 'mother- tongue' presumably would have been rare, as ethno-linguistic groups had few reasons not to maintain it, other than learning the dominant group's language for purposes of upward socio-economic and political mobility.

The map provided represents the general location of Myanmar's ethno-linguistic groups found in nineteenth-century British ethnographies, and although migrations of some of these groups have occurred in the twentieth century for socio-economic and political reasons, nonetheless it probably depicts a fairly accurate picture of the regions they inhabited in the recent past and the ones they still mainly occupy today.

What is more difficult to determine is *when* they actually appeared in these places. Of course, we know more about the majority people, the Burmese speakers, who left the largest number of early written records and politically and culturally dominated the country since at least the Pagan period (ninth to fourteenth centuries). With the exception of the fifteen or so inscriptions in the 'Pyu' language that belonged to another group of Tibeto-Burman speakers who preceded the Burmese speakers, more than a thousand Old Burmese language inscriptions survive, representing the next oldest written indigenous language in the country, going back at least to the tenth century if not earlier. Thus the oldest inhabitants in Myanmar to be documented by the earliest written records were Tibeto-Burman speakers. (Obviously, no one knows the ethno-linguistic background of the Palaeolithic and Neolithic people and their immediate successors, for they left no writing.)

Next to Tibeto-Burman, the second oldest documented language family in Myanmar is Austro-Asiatic, represented by Old Mon. The earliest records in Old Mon date to the 1090s in Lower Myanmar and used the Old Burmese script, by then already present and used in Upper Myanmar for nearly a century. Yet these earliest records written in Old Mon consist of royal inscriptions that were the product of a single Upper Myanmar king, who for some reason wrote in a language that did not represent the majority of the people living in his kingdom. In other words, the earliest written Old Mon language in Myanmar appears solely

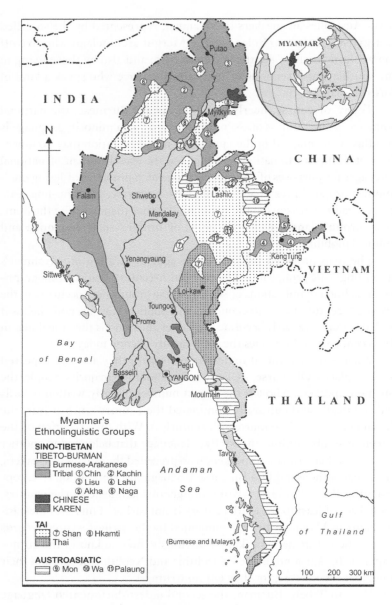

Ethno-linguistic groups of Myanmar.

(or almost solely) in elite circles, whose impact was largely felt at the
court level, while no evidence of Mon written by (or for) commoners
appears until several hundred years later in Lower Myanmar. In any case,
because the 'original' homeland of the Mon speakers is said to be located
in what is now Thailand, they must have migrated to Myanmar sometime
around the late eleventh century.

The next language family to appear in the written evidence of the country is T'ai-Kadai, represented by the T'ai (or Shan) language speakers. Although the people who spoke T'ai-Kadai are mentioned in Old Burmese sources by the twelfth century if not earlier, this largest minority group in Myanmar did not leave a single stone inscription in its own language in pre-eighteenth-century Upper Myanmar. Only two, whose dates are unknown, have been found in the southernmost extremity of the country at Mergui, across the border from Thailand and are thought to belong to that country when Mergui was under its sway after the thirteenth or fourteenth century. Probably the Myanmar Shan had no written script until much later, perhaps the eighteenth or even nineteenth century when their first chronicles appear.[7] As for the Austronesian language family, there is no evidence of their written language in the country before the colonial era.

Not only does this data suggest a general time frame for the appearance of the most prominent ethno-linguistic groups in the country, it also provides evidence for *where* some of them were located. Many of these minorities, even without a writing system to record their presence, were already present in the country, for they are mentioned in the majority language (Old Burmese) of twelfth and thirteenth-century Pagan, as well as fourteenth and fifteenth-century Ava. That means they were already living in the central plains amongst the Burmese speakers by then.

What the written evidence suggests, then, is that by the Pagan period the Tibeto-Burman language speakers can be found inhabiting the entire country, within whose population lived other minority ethno-linguistic groups. In Upper Myanmar in the river valleys of the Irrawaddy, lower Chindwin and Sittaung, where the bulk of the Burmese speakers lived, can also be found the Chin, Kachin, Karen, Mon, Shan, Arakanese, Wa, Lawa and others. Tibeto-Burman speakers can be found early on the western shores of Myanmar (in Arakan) and dominated the Kaladan River valley, perhaps from about the eleventh century onward, likely making the journey from the Dry Zone via the three passes in the Arakan Yomas.

Only subsequently, after the fifteenth and sixteenth centuries, did their economic and cultural ties shift towards Muslim India and the Bay of Bengal, but only temporarily. And although popularly considered a Muslim province, nearly 88 per cent of Arakanese are Buddhists, and much of their historical, religious and political links before and after the fifteenth and sixteenth-century hiatus are with the interior Burmese culture. Their language, to reiterate, is essentially Burmese, as close as, or closer than, Lao is to T'ai. Arakanese is probably the only language spoken today in the country (perhaps along with certain words in Burmese spoken in Tavoy and regions south of it) that has retained some of the older pronunciations found in Old Burmese. North of the Arakanese lived other Tibeto-Burman speakers such as the Chin, on whose north and northeast were the Kachin speakers.

In Lower Myanmar as well, the Burmese language can be found amongst the Karen of the Sittaung River valley in eastern Myanmar, although there is no evidence of that in Karen sources, for they did not have a written language until the early nineteenth century and the arrival of American Baptist missionaries. The Burmese speakers had migrated even farther south to settle on the Lower Myanmar coasts and the Tenasserim Peninsular, at Tavoy (Dawei) and Mergui, probably as early as the second half of the eleventh century. This had to have occurred *before* the Mon speakers migrated to Lower Myanmar by the end of the eleventh century, as demonstrated by the linguistic 'wedge' they drove between the Burmese speakers north and south of them near the delta of the Salween River. In part that explains the 'archaic' nature of eighteenth-century Tavoy Burmese, having been cut off from the northern (and main) branch of Burmese speakers by that Mon speaking wedge, thereby preserving the older forms that existed prior to that while the Burmese north of it continued to change.[8]

The T'ai-Kadai speakers represented by the Shan of Myanmar were already living in the country by the middle and end of the twelfth and thirteenth centuries. They inhabited the areas north and northeast of the Dry Zone, mainly in the highlands, except for those who had integrated into lowland Burmese society. And, as noted above, although the Shan left no contemporary stone inscriptions, there is enough evidence in later chronicles, both Chinese and Burmese, to place them in the general area they live today.

The other minority groups in the country such as the Kachin (who are mentioned in Old Burmese inscriptions), Naga, Lahu (also found in Laos and Northern Thailand), the Lisu (found in Yunnan as well) and Akha (in northeast Myanmar but also in northwest Laos) appear to have generally remained where they were located.

The role played by the prominent minority ethno-linguistic groups in Myanmar varied. The Shan speakers on the north and east, the Arakanese on the west and the Mons in the south periodically and to different degrees asserted their influence in the shaping of Myanmar's history. But most of these influences, particularly the political ones, were temporary, or if cultural, had been absorbed and synthesized by the dominant culture and group, so that it is often difficult to separate the different ingredients that went into the pot, except for the linguistic ones.

Some – such as the Shan, Arakanese and Mon – are mentioned in important positions in the Burmese state while others were at the bottom of society, so that their contributions to social and political history as well as to the culture of the country at the 'national' level also varied. Groups such as the Karen and Wa who are mentioned in Burmese sources appear not to have contributed as much to that 'national' culture, at least not that early. Most, however, were part of the historical scene nonetheless, whether or not they were the main players in it.

SOCIO-ECONOMIC LIFE

The socio-economic life of most of the people in Myanmar, regardless of ethno-linguistic background, revolved (and still revolves) around agriculture (and occupations related to it), consisting of both *sawah* (wet-rice) and *swidden* ('slash and burn') cultivation, the majority using the former. A not insignificant minority, however, engaged (and still engages) in trade and commerce as its main livelihood.

The two major immigrant groups, Indians and Chinese, came to the country in large numbers primarily during the late nineteenth and early twentieth centuries as part of British colonialism. Many of them emigrated as part of the British colonial labour force, and lived in colonial cities such as Rangoon. They served the British need for manual as well as clerical labour to run the colonial administrative and economic apparatus.

However, the stone inscriptions and other art historical and textual evidence demonstrate that much earlier, both Indian and (though somewhat fewer) Chinese peoples and cultures were already present and well entrenched in early Myanmar, so that the celebrated 'plural society' of Southeast Asia usually attributed to colonialism is not entirely as late a phenomenon as often thought.

As noted, the population of Myanmar today is estimated to be 59 million, making it the country with the lowest population density in Asia, with a ratio of men to women that is nearly equal. Total life expectancy is 63.4 years; 65.7 for females and 61.2 for males. In terms of demographic distribution, Yangon (until 2005–6, the capital) had a population of between three and four million, Mandalay about one million, and Maulmain more than 200,000. (The current population of Naypyidaw, the new capital is said to be approximately 926,250 people, perhaps including Pyinmana. If correct, it is now the third largest city in the country.)

The above statistics mean the large majority of Myanmar's population, nearly 70 per cent, does not reside in urban but in rural areas, and Myanmar today is still largely an agrarian country. That in part explains why over 57 per cent of its labour force is found in the agricultural sectors (including forestry and fishing) and agriculture accounts for over half of the country's GDP), while industry accounts for a little less than 10 per cent with approximately 33 per cent in services, a growing sector. Of the latter, about 6 per cent is in government, and 3 to 4 per cent in 'other' occupations.

Despite this rural focus general literacy rates are relatively high (86.2 per cent), with male literacy rates estimated at 89.6 per cent and female rates at 82.8 per cent. Part of the reason for these high rates in Myanmar is monastic education, which for centuries had taught children how to read and write, thereby establishing a solid infrastructural and conceptual foundation on which independent Myanmar could and did build.

The majority of the population is Theravada Buddhist (about 89 per cent), while Christians and Muslims each make up about 3 to 4 per cent, Hindus comprise less than 1 per cent, and 'animists' and 'others' total about 2.2 per cent. However, the latter statistic can be a bit misleading, for whatever the religion one claims to profess, most indigenous people, including Christians, believe in the spirits of 'animism', the *nats*.[9]

Both in practice and in principle Myanmar is one of the most tolerant countries in the world in terms of religious freedom, and Buddhism one of the religions most open to those of other persuasions, claiming no exclusive 'god' belonging only to a chosen group of people who will determine 'salvation' for the entire world. Rather, it professes a universal law of karma (the moral law of cause and effect) whereby everyone reaps whatever he or she sows.

ADMINISTRATION

The modern nation of Myanmar is organized into fourteen major administrative units, with seven 'states' and seven 'regions' (previously called 'divisions') with equal legal status and over 500 townships divided into wards and tracts. (Several minor 'self-administered areas' have been added in the 2008 Constitution, in order to categorize some of the remotest, mainly ex-insurgent areas located at the true 'peripheries' of the nation.)[10]

The seven 'regions' (*taing desa*) consisting of Magwe, Sagaing, Irrawaddy, Yangon, Mandalay, Bago and Taninthayi (anglicized as Tenasserim) have been historically and are currently home to the majority of the country's population. Although most of the *taing desa* originally consisted of Burmese speakers, it is also the primary region into which people of various ethno-linguistic backgrounds have regularly migrated. The *taing desa*, therefore, represent not so much an ethno-linguistic locale as they do the nuclei of the state in Myanmar, of which five are also the oldest settled areas in the country, while two, Bago and Tenasserim, were settled relatively late: only by the late twelfth century.

In contrast the seven 'states' (*pyi nay*) are organized around and named for the seven major ethnic groups (Karen, Mon, Shan, Arakanese, Chin, Kachin, Kayah), which also, by and large, reflect the territory in which they now reside (and historically have probably resided). *Pyi nay* without their ethnic designation means something approximating 'countryside', that is, outside the *taing desa*, and were once regions considered distant from the capital. These, when conquered, became tributary states (*nuinnam* or 'conquered areas' in Old Burmese, and *naingam*, or 'nation' in Modern Burmese). If the *pyi nay* were not conquered they remained autonomous centres of culture and sometimes power.

Only when the British claimed as their territory the areas that are now represented by the *pyi nay* did the latter become de facto permanent territorial fixtures of the modern Burmese nation-state so that, in this sense, one could argue that the British in the last phases of colonial rule helped in the 'making' of modern Myanmar Pyay, a process that had been going on for at least a millennium.

With the departure of the British and the country formally independent by 1948, both these categories of territories were reconsolidated into the new Union of Burma. In doing so the Government reinstituted rather than discarded what was, in practice and principle, colonial notions and policies dealing with reified ethnicity, along with, of course, the territories held by them. Ethnic *identity*, an abstract idea, was once again (as under the British) reified; that is, regarded as a concrete entity in Independent Myanmar, so that colonial notions of ethnicity as an *ascribed* attribute were retained while traditional, indigenous notions of ethnicity as a *relational* attribute were lost.

Because the former (colonial) notion implies instinctive and primordial antagonisms between different ethnic groups, it is almost directly contrary to the notion of national unity and the nation. But whereas it was a useful strategy and ideology during the colonial period of 'divide and rule', it was not so subsequently when consensual political unity was the paramount concern. In other words the notion of reified ethnicity, the modern contentiousness over the creation of 'autonomous' ethnic states and the 60-year civil war that followed Independence were ironically the result of having readopted rather than rejected British Burma's conceptualizations and policies.

The relatively recent cease-fire agreements between the Government and nearly all the major ethnic groups once clamouring for autonomous status of one sort or another, therefore, marks an important milestone in the modern history of the country, suggesting (finally) the successful implementation of the modern nation-state. Whatever holdouts are left represent only a few select politicized communities whose agenda had been shaped by a variety of domestic historical, political and economic factors, most based on old vendettas and outmoded ideologies, and encouraged and financed by external groups and governments for a variety of personal, political, economic and ideological reasons, a subject to be discussed in subsequent chapters.

However the pre-modern and modern history of Myanmar is interpreted, it is clear that the country's geography, demography and ethno-linguistic underpinnings – its basic material and human foundations – have shaped that history.

2

Prehistory

Although historians normally define 'prehistory' as the era prior to the appearance of writing to distinguish it from 'history', it is not as if there were no people, places and pasts before writing appeared in Myanmar with Indic culture, most likely with Buddhism, during the last half of the millennium BC. Thus the line between prehistory and history is rather thin and fuzzy (if not arbitrary), whereby things move almost imperceptibly from one to the other. For scholars actually looking for change – as most Western-trained scholars in virtually every field of the social sciences are wont to do – that kind of analytical distinction may be helpful, but the actual situation 'on the ground' is no less ambiguous.

Perhaps the discipline of history can be persuaded to move its line in the sand farther back in time to the advent of humans, their settlements and their material culture – better analysed now with new technology – than to the first appearance of writing. After all, some societies still do not have writing (or acquired it relatively recently) although their history is not entirely irretrievable. Of course, the reason for that is less the advent of writing than using methods that allow disciplines to do more. At the same time we sometimes lose sight of the fact that these artificial lines drawn between and amongst disciplines are just that: heuristic devices that do not exist 'out there' in the past but in the classroom or the research laboratory. For these and other reasons we do not always follow convention in our organization of Myanmar's 'prehistory' and include eras in it and information pertinent to it based both on written and unwritten sources.

MYANMAR'S PREHISTORY

During the last two glacial periods, the first occurring around 40,000 and the second 18,000 years ago, several important things occurred. The water levels dropped considerably in what is now insular Southeast Asia so that much of the archipelago was connected to the mainland by land bridges. The lower sea levels varied between 430 and 165 ft, when large sections of both hemispheres iced over, drawing large amounts of water from the sea. Fauna and flora, along with *Homo sapiens* (modern humans) migrated farther than they had (or could have) theretofore, taking with them their culture, technology, plants and animals.[1]

Issues surrounding *Homo sapiens* are not so much of a problem in Myanmar Studies; it is *Homo erectus* that is more of a hot topic, along with those dealing with the so-called 'missing link' anthropoids. As we are neither palaeontologists nor prehistorians, we tread with caution when discussing such issues. Yet we still wish to summarize for the reader what some of the important debates and issues are with regard to those subjects as they pertain to Myanmar.

Homo erectus, once thought to be a distinct precursor to *Homo sapiens*, is now said to be a possible contemporary of *H. sapiens* during the latter's earlier stages of evolution. *H. erectus* is known to have existed in Asia between 1.5 million and 0.5 million years ago, well before the last two glacial periods mentioned above when *H. sapiens* roamed the area. The most well-known specimens of *H. erectus* are Java and Peking Man and another specimen found in Vietnam. But 'he' has never before been found in Myanmar; that is, until 1981, if the data and analysis are viable, which at the present time are still being studied.

In that year a fossilized fragment of the right maxillary bone with the first molar and second premolars intact of what the excavators are convinced is *H. erectus*, was found in Upper Myanmar. It was discovered near Nwe Gwe village, Budalin township, in the basin of the Chindwin River that runs through the Dry Zone and where evidence of bronze has also been found recently. The former site lies in a gravel deposit and red earth belonging to the Late Pleistocene era. Although this raises some questions about the age of the mandible – since most scholars in the field tend to place *H. sapiens* rather than *H. erectus* in the Late Pleistocene – from dental analysis, the Myanmar scholars are fairly certain, perhaps hopeful, that the specimen is *H. erectus*.[2] And if it is, it is important because it is the first such specimen to be uncovered in Myanmar, and adds another piece to the puzzle of *H. erectus* in mainland Southeast Asia.

The continuity or replacement of hominids is another important issue being debated by palaeontologists and prehistorians. Simply put, did the *H. sapiens* of Southeast Asia evolve directly from the *H. erectus* species found in Southeast Asia, or was *H. erectus* of Southeast Asia replaced by *H. sapiens* that evolved ultimately 'out of Africa'? In other words, what happened to *H. erectus* in Southeast Asia; did he/she 'become' *H. sapiens* naturally by evolution or was he/she replaced by outside *H. sapiens*? (Of course, there is also the issue of whether *H. erectus* was a direct precursor of *H. sapiens* rather than a 'dead-end' path.)

Also problematic is the issue regarding the culture left by humans in general. The Old Stone Age (Palaeolithic), New Stone Age (Neolithic), the Copper Age (Chalcolithic) and the Iron Age – broad periods into which Western prehistory has been organized – seem to have had their counterparts in Southeast Asia and perhaps Myanmar as well. But in Myanmar and Southeast Asia there is not so clear-cut a sequence, for one often overlapped with another in indistinguishable fashion. That may be a consequence of the paucity of research conducted so far, but Southeast Asia scholars nonetheless wonder if it is justifiable to use categories of analysis meant for European and other cultures for those of Southeast Asia, for instance the categories 'Renaissance' and/or 'Enlightenment' as historical periods in Southeast Asia.

And although it is usually accepted that the Neolithic (and subsequent) cultures were certainly the work of *H. sapiens*, *H. erectus* seems to have had a hand in fashioning parts of the Palaeolithic. One has to be therefore careful not to conflate the issues and problems surrounding the *cultural remains* left by humans with those regarding the evolution of *hominids* per se. In this chapter it is not so much the issues surrounding the origins and dispersal of *H. erectus* and *H. sapiens* in Southeast Asia that is important, but the *culture* left behind by humans in the region now defined as Myanmar.

THE STATUS OF THE FIELD IN MYANMAR

Comparatively speaking, very little archaeological and even less palaeontological work has been done in Myanmar to provide the reader with the kind of information available in studies of long-established sites such as those in Meso-America and the Middle East. Even within Asia, Southeast Asian archaeology lags far behind that of China and Japan. And in Southeast Asia itself, Myanmar's archaeology is relatively underdeveloped when compared to that of Thailand, Vietnam and the Philippines.

The major reason for this is the lack of internal and external funding as well as the priorities placed on stability, security issues and infrastructural development that one finds in any developing country, some more compelling than in others. Training and expertise in archaeology are also lacking, as most students who have opportunities to study abroad choose scientific and technical subjects that promise a quicker and larger economic return while the handful of the country's trained archaeologists are deceased or retired. Although there are archaeologists outside Myanmar interested in, and who have contributed importantly to, its prehistory, other kinds of problems inhibit long-term sustained work in the field. Most of these scholars, for example, are focused on the urban period that followed the prehistoric era, even if some have made serious attempts to reconstruct aspects of the latter.

Part of the problem too is that since many ancient remains that need critical assessment (and repair) are above ground and receive priority (as they are invariably Buddhist in character), it is simply easier to address those concerns than to conduct long-term, laborious and expensive excavations for which professional human and material resources are already scarce. Thus the data produced during the past century by the Archaeological Survey of India and its successor, the Myanmar Archaeological Department, along with that belonging to the handful of indigenous archaeologists trained overseas and a few foreign-led and funded projects, have been the field's mainstay.

Despite this handicap there is no lack of interest and enthusiasm for archaeology in Myanmar, and the country does what it can with what little it has. Considering the fact that the total annual budget for the Department of Archaeology was until recently smaller than each of the annual graduate student fellowships the authors of this book received at Michigan, it is amazing what has been accomplished. The present chapter therefore provides a general picture of the country's prehistory based not only within the above practical context, but on what has been done during the past century, gleaned from both published and unpublished sources, Burmese as well as English.[3]

ANYATHIAN MAN

Very little work has been done on the 'stone age' culture of Myanmar, either Palaeolithic or Neolithic. The only scientific study of the former (and aspects of the latter) whose data has been published in English was conducted in the 1930s and 1940s by two Western specialists.[4] Their research showed that the valley of the Irrawaddy in and around the Dry Zone was inhabited by humans who made hand tools of stone, and lived by hunting and gathering wild fruits and vegetables and other root crops. They seemed to have been part of a more general culture found in mainland and insular Southeast Asia where evidence of similar remains has been discovered.

The Palaeolithic period is conventionally distinguished from the Neolithic by the latter's domestication of agriculture and animals amongst other things. One of the consequences of this was the settling down of its people in communities and the creation of occupations that suited settled life. In Southeast Asia the early phases of the Neolithic have been called the Hoabinhian by some, after a site in Vietnam at Hoabinh whose culture resembles the Neolithic elsewhere in the region, and seems to have been widespread throughout mainland and certain parts of island Southeast Asia.[5]

This 'stone age' culture in Myanmar has been named Anyathian, from the Burmese term *anyatha*, or 'offspring of the upstream region' (that is, Upper Myanmar), in turn divided into 'early', 'middle' and 'late' phases.[6] At the time, there were about fourteen sites thought to be Anyathian, spread over Upper Myanmar. All of them are located in the Dry Zone, in and around the most important capitals that emerged during the historic period. The Anyathian culture used several different kinds of stone tools: the faceted, shouldered and splayed axe; the wedge; the chisel and the hand adze; indeed, about 80 per cent of the tools found are adzes. They are made by chipping, edge-grounding and complete grounding methods.

The earliest evidence of a 'Neolithic Age' in Myanmar to date has been found in the Shan hills near Taunggyi, in three caves: Tin Ein, Maung Pa and, most famous, Padhalin. Their remains have been dated to a period between 10,000/6,000–4,000 BC.[7] Stone tools belonging to this

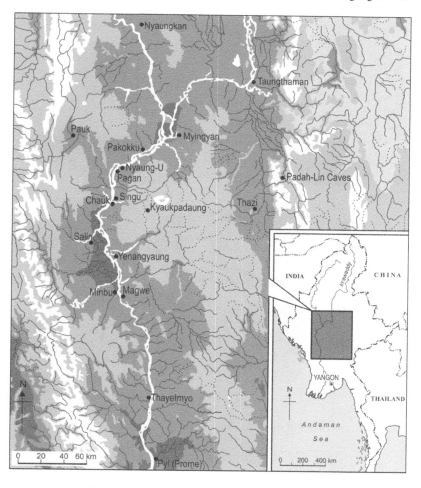

Stone Age sites of Myanmar, 40,000–3,000 BC.

Stone axes and chisels of the 'Neolithic' of Myanmar, dating from 3000–1500 BC.

culture have been discovered in abundance, along with charcoal and bone collagen; the latter dated to about 11,000 BP (Before Present, calibrated to 1958). Moreover, aesthetically pleasing pictures painted on the walls of one of the caves with red ochre, reminiscent of, but not nearly as sophisticated or aesthetically appealing as the Lascaux and Altamira caves in France and Spain, have nonetheless placed the Myanmar site in an international 'Neolithic' context.

Southeast Asia's Neolithic also produced what is thought to have been domesticated agriculture, particularly the remains excavated at Spirit Cave near the Thai-Myanmar border as well as others such as Non Nok Tha and Ban Chiang, also in Thailand. Probable beans, possible peas, water chestnut, bottle gourd, butternut, almond and other vegetable remains are said to have been discovered in Spirit Cave, which itself is dated to about 10,000 BC.

But what is most important to the region as a whole as well as to individual communities in terms of the development, ultimately, of 'the state' is the discovery of domesticated rice, the all important annual cereal that would have affected the demography of its users, enough to make the transition from *swidden* ('slash and burn') to *sawah* (wet-rice) agriculture, thence, to the development of towns, cities and states. What is thought to be a grain of domesticated rice in Southeast Asia (found at Non Nok Tha) has been dated by association with other implements to about 4,000 BC, and therefore said to have *preceded* specimens found in both India and China.

There has been passionate and intense debate over this issue, not so much over the provenance, testing methods or even the date of the rice specimen, but over whether it was domesticated or wild. Some scholars have rejected outright its domesticated status. Others have classified the rice specimen a 'transitional' type, while still others have said it is definitely domesticated. These (essentially) scientific issues have been complicated further by the national, cultural and academic background of the scholars involved in the debate.

The most recent assessment regarding the dates surrounding the domestication of rice in Southeast Asia has revised the earlier date of 4,000 BC and suggested a much later one of around 1,500 BC. This places the domestication of rice in Southeast Asia *later*, not *earlier*, than in both India and China.[8] While it tempers Southeast Asia-centric perspectives that were in fact responses to earlier Sino and Indo-centric views regarding the development of Southeast Asia, the issue has not been resolved entirely. In Myanmar itself, perhaps towards the middle but certainly by the end of the Anyathian period and the last millennium BC, it appears domesticated rice might have been present. But there has been no scientific study of this particular issue to date.[9]

THE METAL CULTURES OF MYANMAR

There does not appear to have been a clear-cut Chalcolithic (copper) Age distinct from the 'Bronze Age' in Southeast Asia. In Myanmar recent excavations and international workshops have uncovered a bronze culture in Myanmar's Budalin Township and elsewhere, but no solid dates based on scientific tests have yet been provided from the site. Stylistically this culture seems to have been built on the remains of the stone culture that preceded and continued with it, for the bronze implements closely resemble those of stone whenever possible.

What evidence there is on these bronze sites suggests that the people inhabiting them likely continued the general economic culture of the previous inhabitants simply by remaining in the same locations.[10] This metal culture is wide ranging and found throughout the country, although nearly 90 per cent of its finds are from Upper Myanmar, focused in the Dry Zone. The settlements themselves from which the material cultural remains have been excavated cluster around the most important river valleys, large and small, mainly Upper, but also include some in Lower Myanmar: the Irrawaddy, Chindwin, Myitnge, Samon and the Mu, along with the Sittaung and the southern sections of the Irrawaddy respectively.[11] The former areas are also the same general locations where much of the Palaeolithic and Neolithic remains have been uncovered.

Called the Samon Valley Culture by scholars (named after what appears to be the heart of this culture around the Samon River in the Dry Zone), their earliest dated and, in some ways, most profound artistic links are with the Dian culture of Yunnan in Western China. The Samon culture also shares some of its artistic styles with other parts of Southeast Asia, particularly its beads and works of art in semi-precious stones. These cultural artefacts, scientifically dated to about the eighth century BC, show no links to Buddhist or other forms of Indic influences from India. These make their first dated appearance sometime in the last half of the millennium BC.[12]

That the Samon Valley Culture appears to be pre-or non-Buddhist, but with cultural links to the Dian culture of Yunnan and other regions of Southeast Asia where bronze has been uncovered, provides historians of Southeast Asia concerned with the phenomenon called 'localization' – adaptation by indigenous people of external influences – a much broader range of evidence, analysis and issues with which to work. Not least it removes the fulcrum of debate from the nation-state inherent in the terms 'Indianization' and 'Sinification' (that is, 'India' and 'China' before either emerged as such) and instead puts emphasis on communities in the region with no international boundaries that shared certain technologies and artistic sentiments and ideas, if not goods and services as well.

Heretofore Indic influences have been given much 'agency' in early Southeast Asian history and prehistory. But the research currently being done on this period by a handful of scholars has appreciably changed our perspectives and understanding of it, so that we can say with some aplomb that it was pre-Indic. Its material, social and possibly conceptual foundations seem to have been a mixture of both indigenous and northeastern (central and northern mainland Southeast Asian) influences.

At the same time, however, there is a concern with some of the recent interpretations that these River Valley Cultures, because of their perceived variety, reflect heterogeneity and suggest more than a single or dominant culture. One simply cannot prove from differences found primarily in their art that the society that produced it was either homogeneous *or* heterogeneous, especially without the evidence of writing, which at least, though not inevitably, suggests a common language and ethno-linguistic group. The penchant, perhaps even fetish, amongst Western academics for privileging differences, variety, heterogeneity, individuals – in other words, an anti-monolithic sentiment and favouritism shown currently for 'populous' values – has, in part, been responsible for this sort of interpretation of ancient society. But it must not become the framework of analysis for assessing state and society of two millennia ago in Myanmar.

In any case, what is important to the history of Myanmar is that the areas in which these bronze (and other metals) cultures are found, are

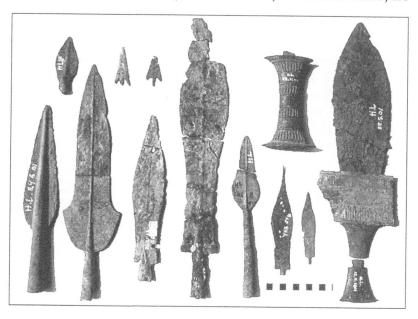

Bronze Age weapons found in Myanmar, dating from 1500–500 BC.

also virtually the same as those occupied in historic times. That is not to say that the people were of the same genetic or linguistic stock, for there is neither DNA evidence nor written records to indicate that. But it is to say that the geography of Upper Myanmar was as crucial in prehistoric as it was in historic times. In other words there is good reason for historic peoples to settle in or take over the same areas that for centuries had also sustained prehistoric peoples and cultures rather well.

A point that should be reiterated is that most of the earliest, largest and most complex prehistoric settlements are found in Upper Myanmar. Not that there are none in Lower Myanmar, but they are far fewer (and shown to be less archaeologically significant) than those found in Upper Myanmar. The quantitative difference cannot simply be passed off as a matter of wetter weather destroying artefacts (particularly of stone). Rather, it might be one of Upper Myanmar's climate and soil conditions being more suitable for complex agriculture. These sites are located in a temperate not tropical zone, with alluvial soil replenished annually by the silt of the major rivers, and sufficient number of sunny days to ripen annual cereals properly. These factors were what attracted humans to settle there in the first place, so that 'civilization', in both the general and technical sense of the term (from '*civitas*' or 'city'), moved from Upper to Lower Myanmar, rather than the other way around as convention (with its trade-centric view) has it. It is this mix of environment and humans that set the stage for the urban era that was to follow, which in turn had tremendous consequences for the formation of the state in Myanmar subsequently.

By about 200 BC, iron was already in use for daily practical purposes and fortified brick-walled cities had begun to emerge, later scattered over most of the Dry Zone and even reaching the coasts, ushering in the age of urbanism that convention attributes to people exogenously referred to as the 'Pyu', the topic of the next chapter.

3

The Urban Period

The prehistoric period in Myanmar's history was finally 'superseded' by what is conventionally known as the 'Pyu' period, dated approximately between 200 BC and the ninth century AD. Although the time frame itself, particularly the beginning of the period (which could have been earlier and therefore left open and flexible) poses no serious problems amongst scholars, using the name of a *presumed* ethno-linguistic group to characterize an entire millennium, does. It creates several problems, not least in the way the period has been consequently interpreted heretofore. At the root of the problem is the *assumption* that the Chinese term 'P'iao' and the Burmese term 'Pyu' are the same, which is flawed in terms of both evidence and analysis.

First, the term 'P'iao' is based on approximately three Chinese texts of varying provenance and chronology spanning several hundred years, so that the characters used for the term are different in at least two of the Chinese texts with two entirely different meanings, neither of them indicating any relationship to ethnicity per se. At the same time, the Old Burmese term 'Pyu' appears in Old Burmese inscriptions not only much later (the thirteenth and fourteenth centuries AD) but not necessarily in reference to 'ethno-linguisticity' but to individuals distinguished by occupation, gender and location. In other words there is nothing in the early Chinese texts or the later Burmese evidence to suggest a historical or etymological link between the two terms.

What has linked them is that they sound alike to modern ears: the twentieth-century English pronunciation of the Romanized version of the twentieth-century Cantonese pronunciation of the written character 'P'iao' and the English pronunciation of the Romanized version of the modern Burmese pronunciation of the Old Burmese word 'Pyu'. This is hardly compelling evidence that the two are etymologically connected.

Second, most scholars of Myanmar have nevertheless assumed that 'P'iao' and 'Pyu' were references to an ethno-linguistic group rather than some other category of identification. Actually the Chinese used the word 'P'iao' to identify a particular *kingdom* located in a particular place and inhabited by a particular people they call 'P'iao'. But there is no indication in the Chinese characters used for the word – one meant 'bandit' and the other 'cavalry' – that they were references to a *single* ethnic group. There could have been many different ethnic groups living in that 'P'iao king-dom', but dominated by the 'P'iao', hence the name given to it by the Chinese as they were often wont to do. They did the same, for example, with their term *kun-lun*, a reference to coastal peoples nearly everywhere in Southeast Asia of *various* ethno-linguistic backgrounds, just as the term 'American' is a reference to various ethno-linguistic groups.

Third, the term 'P'iao' is an exogenous one *given* to a people, not an ethnonym; that is, the term by which these people called themselves. The word 'P'iao', then, is much like the term 'Burmese', a term *given* to the people of Myanmar by outsiders, not what the people call themselves in their own language (*Myanma Lu Myo*). Indeed, according to the same Chinese texts, these 'P'iao' people already had an ethnonym, calling them-selves 'T'u-lo-chu'. This was thought to have been a reference to 'Tircul', found in Pagan epigraphs of the early twelfth century, written in Old Mon. But here also, both 'T'u-lo-chu' and 'Tircul' (like 'P'iao' and 'Pyu') are twentieth-century English pronunciations of the Romanized versions of two old words, one Chinese and one Old Mon.

Fourth, whether or not 'P'iao' and 'Pyu' in fact refer to the same group (ethno-linguistic or otherwise), it still has not been established that they were the same people who inhabited and ruled the urban culture in Myan-mar under discussion, particularly since the Old Burmese inscriptions in which we find the word 'Pyu' appear centuries later. Of course, there is another option: the people who inhabited and dominated the Urban Period in Myanmar during these centuries were indeed the 'P'iao' of the Chinese texts, but they may or may not have anything to do with the thirteenth and fourteenth-century 'Pyu' of the Burmese texts.

Finally, whoever these people may have been and whatever others (or they) called themselves – 'P'iao', 'Pyu', 'T'u-lo-chu' or 'Tircul' – to mark an entire historical period with an ethno-linguistic term gives un-necessary 'agency' to ethno-linguistic categories, as well as to a group of people to which it has been only ambiguously linked. Not that ethno-linguistic groups do not deserve a historical period named after them (such as Anglo-Saxon England, Khmer Angkor or Burmese Pagan) when it is warranted. But when there is no proven reason for privileging reified ethnicity over other much more important historical factors (such as urbanism) for which there *is* concrete evidence, and when that attribution is being done nearly two millennia later by nineteenth and early twentieth-century colonial scholars influenced by a host of ideas belonging to their age, there is reason enough to reconsider the name given to this period in Myanmar's history; hence our phrase 'Urban Period' instead.

Unfortunately, convention is often stronger than compelling critiques of it, and convenience less onerous than conviction, so that in casual as well as academic conversation, this period continues to be called 'Pyu', if for no other reason as an identifier of a particular era. We, however, would like to terminate the use of this label (even if more convenient) and continue one begun in 1982–3 by one of the authors of this book – namely, the 'Urban Period' in Myanmar's history – thereby giving 'agency' not to (unsubstantiated) reified ethnicity but to substantiated historical phenomena.

URBANIZATION AS A PHENOMENON

The historical phenomenon that defines and characterizes this period is the emergence and development of urban society (along with all that it implies), not only distinguishing the period from the prehistoric and 'River Valley Cultures' that preceded it, but also from those that succeeded it, giving it special significance in the long-term history of the country. What the earlier pre-urban Neolithic and Metal Ages could not do, the Urban Period could do, and well. That is not to trivialize or minimize the importance of the previous periods, without which the Urban Period could not have done what it did. But it is to identify certain patterns and accomplishments that can be attributed to the urbanized period that can be considered 'firsts' in the history of the country, on which were based many of the developments that made up Myanmar state and society thereafter.

Thus the Urban Period, as the term urbanism itself implies, is the first in Myanmar history where the walled city, in some cases symbolically representing the Buddhist-Hindu universe with its architectural features, is ubiquitous and becomes standard.[1] Furthermore, the Urban Period saw the beginning of 'Dry Zone Paramountcy', an overall continuous historical pattern of Upper Myanmar hegemony over Lower Myanmar that remains viable even today with the recent shift of the country's capital back to the Dry Zone 'heartland'. The urban age also witnessed the origins of writing in Myanmar whose original Sanskrit alphabet remains the basis for today's national script. Moreover, the first evidence of large-scale irrigation systems able to serve social and political entities larger and more complex than simpler village society dates to the Urban Period. In addition the first Buddhist *stupas* (temples with solid cores) in the country were built during this period, as were the first hollow temples and *stupa*-temples (combination of solid and hollow temples), which became templates for those of succeeding ages, especially the 'classical' period. In certain areas of the arts and crafts – gold and silver ornaments, silver coinage, semi and precious stone artefacts, ceramics – this period was another 'first'. Finally, and perhaps most important, the first evidence of an Indic 'conceptual system', including 'Theravada' and other sects of Buddhism and their related ideologies appears in this period.

If urbanism is the critical feature of this period – as we are arguing – how does one define it? Were there not sizeable human settlements before it? Following the (late) eminent scholar Paul Wheatley, urbanism can be defined as the degree of socio-cultural integration relative to what preceded it, rather than relative to what lay 'outside' it. Urbanized society is not to be contrasted with its surrounding countryside, but with pre- or non-urbanized society. It is a phenomenon of type *in time*, not just one of type *in space*. Urbanism, therefore, is more than a *quantitative* phenomenon about the degree of physical space involved; it is also very much a *qualitative* phenomenon.

Urban living features a significantly different and distinctive manner of life from one that precedes it. This is, in turn, expressed in built forms, so that the city itself can be seen as an arena for acting out that lifestyle. Yet because those who do not live in the city proper nevertheless come under the influence and control of its institutions, the definition of urban must include its rural components as well. As Wheatley so well put it, people may not *live in* the city but must *live in terms* of it. The city proper is the critical nexus in which are located the institutions of society, so that the structure of the city itself epitomizes the pattern of society at large. Urbanism, therefore, is a behavioural, structural and processual phenomenon that reveals a systemic transformation from one distinct level of socio-cultural integration into another, higher degree of complexity.[2]

THE URBAN PERIOD IN MYANMAR'S HISTORY

Over a dozen urban settlements belonging to the period between the first two centuries BC and the first millennium AD have been discovered in Myanmar. As noted, many, if not most, are built near or on the country's Palaeolithic, Neolithic and metal sites, therefore suggesting a geographic and technological if not also basic cultural continuity with the prehistoric ages. Needless to say, that does not necessarily imply an ethno-linguistic continuity between the people of this Urban Period and those of the 'River Valley Cultures' that preceded it, especially when we are not certain of the background of either group.

Most of the walled sites are located in the great plains created by the Irrawaddy River and its tributaries. Some are found as far north as its upper reaches, some as far south as the northern reaches of the coasts of Tenasserim. This urban culture stretched from the walled city of Halin in Upper Myanmar's Dry Zone (close to the site where the possible *Homo erectus* mandible mentioned in chapter Two was found), to Winka, another city in the far south on the coasts bordering the Gulf of Muttama with similar cultural remains but no scientifically confirmed dates that it too belonged to this age.[3]

This urban phenomenon, however, was not unique to Myanmar. It was also part of what appears to have been a larger process of transform-ation occurring roughly during the same first millennium, particularly in socio-political entities that we know as Funan and Champa (in what is now Cambodia and Vietnam), Dvaravati (in modern day Thailand), Tambralinga and Takuapa (which lay on or near the Isthmus of Kra) and Sri Vijaya (which we think was centred at Palembang in southeast Suma-tra). Urbanism can also be found in central and east Java, examples of which were contemporaries or near-contemporaries of that in Myanmar. And, as in the latter, foundations were being laid throughout the region during this period that would subsequently give rise to Southeast Asia's magnificent 'classical' states (such as Pagan and Angkor), a period that can be considered the 'golden age' of Southeast Asian history. Urbanism, in other words, was a precursor of, and a necessary phase in, the formation of the state in Southeast Asia.[4]

The largest of these cities during the Urban Period in Myanmar were Binnaka, Mong Mao, Beikthano, Halin and Sri Ksetra, all located in the Dry Zone. The last two probably served as political centres in sequence or in conjunction, although that is not certain. What we do know is that the best dates for both centres, derived from art historical, epigraphic and radio-carbon evidence suggests they overlapped and survived from the early centuries AD to about the ninth.

These brick-walled cities are usually circular, rhomboid or rect-angular and rather large compared to later cities.[5] They are fortified with (sometimes double) moats and walls. At least two of the most prominent ones contained the standard twelve symbolic gates, one at each of the four cardinal points, flanked by two minor gates on either side, a design meant to represent Buddhist conceptions of time and space based on the twelve Zodiac signs, a concept and design that was carried into nineteenth-century Mandalay.[6] Within and around each of these are palaces, temples, storage facilities, burial grounds and irrigation systems; demonstrating the existence of communities that were quantitatively and qualitatively different from the chiefdoms and pre-urban settlements that preceded them.[7] The urban culture used well-burned, large bricks of mainly uni-form size, and in one case, either Halin or Sri Ksetra, the city walls were said (by the Chinese) to have been covered with green ceramic glaze.

Artefacts discovered throughout this urban culture, especially in Upper Myanmar, are thought to have belonged to a period between the

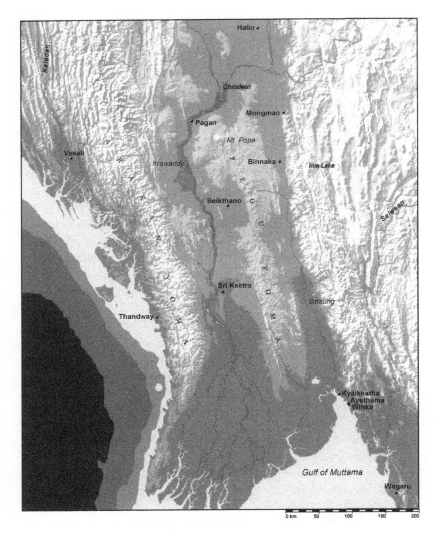

Major urban sites in Myanmar, 200 BC–AD 900.

first century BC and AD and resemble products manufactured in Rome, northwest India or south India. Carnelian and onyx beads similar to those of Hastinapura and Brahmapuri of second-century AD India have also been excavated. Sprinkler vessels of Roman style, either made in Rome or in its factory in south India at Arikamedu have been unearthed. And the kind of rouletted black ware found in western Java and other parts of Southeast Asia has also been discovered at Beikthano in interior Myanmar.[8]

Four urban sites with very similar, in some cases identical cultural artefacts were discovered near the coasts east of the Gulf of Muttama, north of where the Thanlyin (Salween) empties into the sea. They are Winka, Hsindat, Wagaru and Ayethema.[9] Their location suggests that they had direct access to and participated in the trade between South India, Anuradhapura, Dvaravati, Island Southeast Asia, Funan and points farther east. Even though no thermoluminescence or radio-carbon dates have so far shown them to have been contemporary to those of Upper Myanmar, most scholars of this period in Myanmar's history are nonetheless agreed that they were the maritime appendages of the urban culture of the interior. If these coastal towns did in fact exist during the earlier part of the general Urban Period, they apparently took advantage of the Rome–India–China trade in which Southeast Asia at the time had become a valuable crossroads and *entrepôt*.

In contrast to this maritime focus on commerce by the coastal cities, the interior ones depended on rice as their economic wherewithal, with perhaps some overland trade with India and China playing a subordinate role. There is certainly evidence of tank (reservoir), if not weir-and-canal irrigation in nearly all of these interior cities. The data on the chronology

Satellite photograph of the city of Sri Ksetra and its circular walls, 5th–9th centuries.

of the latter type of irrigation, however, is not conclusive; it may have belonged to a later age although weir irrigation is so structurally tied to canal irrigation in Myanmar that it is difficult to imagine one without the other.

These cities had also developed a local coinage based on Indic styles which may have been used for commercial purposes, and is found as far away as present day Saigon. The *Yin Tang Shu*, a Chinese history of the time, stated that 'they take gold and silver to make it into coin. It is like a halfmoon in appearance, called *dengchietue* [*dinga*] and *zudantuo*.'[10] The people of this Urban Period continued their cultural contacts with China, sending, in AD 800 and 801–2, troupes of about 34 musicians to the T'ang capital where their instruments and songs were recorded in fairly good detail.[11]

One of these interior cities in Upper Myanmar grew powerful enough to attempt integration of the others under its rule, forming what might be construed as a real kingdom or city-state of some sort. There is contemporary written evidence of kings, queens and their dynasties, so that its political system was probably centred on a monarchy based on a royal family with Indic titles.[12] The largest and most politically and militarily important of these settlements may have been, either in succession or contemporaneously, the culture's exemplary centres, so that at one time its rulers may have integrated the territory between the central plains and the coasts.

The evidence between the seventh and ninth centuries AD shows a *cultural* and *technological* homogeneity, manifest in art styles, political and religious beliefs, rituals, language, writing system and ordinary ways of life. Their coins, burial jars, pottery, beads, gold and silver jewellery, temples and especially script appear to belong to the same or similar culture. Some of those cultural links reveal ties to India's Nagarjunakonda (in south-central India) and also Sri Lanka's Anuradhapura, some of whose architectural characteristics are found in Beikthano's *stupas* (solid-core temples)

Bronze figurines of performing artists, 9th century.

and 'moon-stones' (semi-circular carved stone thresholds of doorways) of the first to second century AD among other things.[13]

The people of this urban culture are said to have spoken a Tibeto-Burman language written in a common alphabet (the earliest found in Myanmar) based on Sanskrit that had previously been adapted by the Kadamba of Vanavasi and/or the Pallava of Andhra in south India. Two gold plates and a manuscript of gold leaves have been found, palaeographically datable to the fifth century AD, consisting of excerpts from the *Abhidhamma* and *Vinaya*, two of the three main sections of the Buddhist scriptures attributed to the Theravada sect. A stone slab containing Pali excerpts from the *Mangala Sutta*, the *Ratna Sutta* and the *Mora Sutta* found recently is datable to the sixth or seventh century, and also attributed to the Theravada sect.

Clay votive tablets with Buddha figures, inscribed with Buddhist sayings, have also been uncovered. A square pedestal holding the statue of a Buddha in stone with a Sanskrit inscription and interlinear 'Pyu' words has been found. The Sarvastivadins, a Hinayana sect that wrote in Sanskrit, seems to have been present at Sri Ksetra relatively early as well.

However, one should not make too much of some of the analytical distinctions amongst religious sects, as some are actually the creation of much later colonial scholarship of the nineteenth and twentieth centuries rather than differences found amongst the various groups during the period under discussion. Nonetheless, this evidence is important in that it shows Theravada Buddhism was actually well embedded in the country several centuries earlier than eleventh-century Pagan, to which it has been conventionally attributed.

Some social customs of this urban culture resemble those of other contemporary areas of Southeast Asia as reported in Chinese accounts. The people of Funan and Champa were said to have cremated their dead, placed the ashes in earthen, silver or gold urns, and cast them into rivers. The people of Myanmar's Urban Period also placed their dead in stone urns after secondary burial and stored them in mausoleums. The urns were often embedded in a layer of white pebbles. Valuables were buried with the deceased: gold rings or star-shaped flowers, gold and silver leaves with writing, silver coins, jadeite, bracelets of various materials, and also iron nails, pins, hooks, knife-blades and rods, barbed or carved at one end, resembling the point of the spear from a modern spear gun. Two caltrops, each with a large six-sided iron plate studded with 43 nails, 7–11 inches in length, and a large knobbed pin at the centre of the plate have been found. These are thought to have been used as weapons, thrown on the ground when pursued by enemies on foot, horses or elephants.

In terms of religious architecture the people of this urban culture of Myanmar may have been the first to use the distinctive vaulting and

Silver reliquary depicting the four Buddhas of this kalpa (age), found at Sri
Ksetra, dating from the 5th–7th centuries.

keystone arching techniques that later made Pagan famous, although evidence of this among its sites cannot be dated unequivocally to their era and may instead belong to Pagan, where the dates are not only secure but the samples plentiful.[14] There is some evidence of this particular kind of vaulting in eastern India, although the dates for this are relatively late or unknown, and samples extremely paltry, making one reluctant to see it as the ultimate source. The Chinese, it is said, had the keystone arching technique as well.

Most of the monuments that remain of this urban culture, in any case, are *stupas*: solid brick structures with usually no interior space that required vaulting. The significance of these edifices is that the design that began here with the Urban Period became the basic style in the Kingdom of Pagan, the classical Burmese state, whence it passed to succeeding generations, until today. That style is represented by the quintessential *stupa*, the Shwedagon (and more recently, the Uppatatheinti at the new capital, Naypyidaw). Much of the art of the Urban Period points to the end of the Gupta Age in India, about the seventh century AD.

The doctrine of the future Buddha, Maitreya, the saviour who is to descend to earth after 5,000 years of the religion has elapsed was also a major ideology during this Urban Period. It became, at Pagan later, one of the most important concepts underlying state and society, and remains important today. The doctrine of the four Hinayana Buddhas of this *kalpa* (the present cosmic age) was also an important principle in the temple architecture of the urban culture, reflected in the arrangement of the court and ideology of kingship. Some of the most important 'Mahayanist' deities, such as Avalokitesvara (who became Kwanyin in China and Canon in Japan), can be found during this period; along with two of the most important Brahmanic deities: Indra and Vishnu.

Thus the religious beliefs of Myanmar's urban culture in which lay conceptions of state and king, authority and legitimacy, power and acquiescence, derive from a variety of sources – Brahmanism, Hinayana Buddhism of the Sarvastivardin Sect, Theravada and Mahayana (even Tantric) Buddhism, and later Hinduism – and were present rather early, to become crucial in the conceptual system of the 'classical' state in Burma: the Kingdom of Pagan.[15]

THE HISTORICAL SIGNIFICANCE OF THE URBAN PERIOD

We have called the Urban Period the 'formative age of Myanmar', for it began a process that led to the first integrated polity in the land, the Kingdom of Pagan, the 'classical' Burmese state upon which the foundations of modern Myanmar rest. Those urban age foundations were conceptual, material, political, technological and demographic in nature, and the Kingdom of Pagan took them and refashioned them for itself, whose principles then became the bases for state and society thereafter. Indeed, because the Urban Period laid the foundations of the 'classical' state, and the 'classical' state was, in turn, the origins of the state in Myanmar, one could say that the Urban Period was crucial in the making of Myanmar.

At the same time that the Urban Period laid the foundations for the future it also set itself apart from its immediate past: the River Valley Cultures. It had gone beyond these pre-Indic and pre-urban societies, presumably organized around chiefdoms based on villages (or similar settlements) to become a truly urban society, a vital transition that set the stage for what was to come. In this process certain geo–political, technological, structural and perhaps conceptual continuities remained between the pre-urban and the Urban Periods. That, of course, does not mean that earlier village communities ceased to exist, no more than stone tools, bronze and iron weapons, copper implements or gold and silver handicrafts that belonged to the 'River Valley Cultures' of Myanmar disappeared.

It does mean, however, that the form that became the most dominant politically, economically and socially, whose principles had become paramount in society, was urbanism, so that the development of cities must be considered the most important qualitative and quantitative departure from what preceded. The Urban Period, in other words, is the first documented example of what it meant to be both old and new.

Another characteristic of this Urban Period important to the history of Myanmar is the geographic *direction* in which this urbanization process moved: from 'upstream' to 'downstream' rather than the other way around, as conventionally presented. The earliest, most complex, as well as the most numerous examples of urban society in all its manifestations can be found in the interior, not the coasts, a pattern also of its prehistoric sites. One can say, then, that 'civilization' in Myanmar began in the interior, most notably in the Dry Zone and moved towards the coasts: from river valley to delta, hinterland to sea, dry zone to wet zone, temperate to tropical. But it was more than a directional and spatial movement of 'civilization'; it was also a qualitative development and growth: political, socio–economic, conceptual, cultural and demographic. It ultimately resulted in a synthesis of the two regions.

The urban culture at its height was not just an isolated and parochial interior one; it was quite extensive and found in nearly all of the country's main river valleys where the bulk of its population lived and, in many cases, still live. It stretched from the current northern borders of today's Myanmar to nearly its southernmost regions on its north–south axis, and as far west as Arakan and the Bay of Bengal to the foot of the Shan Hills on its east–west axis. (This widespread distribution, although of course not to the same degree everywhere, is also true of the pre-urban settlements so far identified in the country.) In short, much of the present land has been occupied since ancient times.

Our understanding of the Urban Period also contributes importantly to an old academic issue called 'Indianization', particularly in terms of its chronology. Recent research on both the pre-urban and Urban Periods now shows that only by the last few centuries of the millennium BC did society in what is now Myanmar no longer face northeastwards towards 'China' (at least not as much as it had done previously) but more intently westwards towards 'India'. It is only in the Urban Period that the first evidence of 'Indianization' in Myanmar appears, which in turn suggests that it was a crucial component in the genesis and development of urban society and, by extension of that argument, also to the development of an Indic-style state and monarchy. And in this development of the state the evidence for 'Indianization' appears *much earlier* in the interior than on the coasts (by as much as a millennium), contrary to long-held convention that *reversed* the scenario and gave 'agency' to trade and commerce of the coasts instead.

One of the most important and interesting features of this urban culture, on which all of its scholars are agreed, is its longevity. Although the span of time currently given to the period can be lengthened or shortened according to the criterion one wishes to emphasize (although not by much), it survived just over a millennium, from (at latest) the second century BC to the third quarter of the ninth century AD, a feat no other single entity (polity, kingdom or dynasty) managed to accomplish in the history of Myanmar thereafter *except* that of the Burmese speakers, who have been present and dominant now in the country for twelve nearly consecutive centuries.

That longevity of culture, when combined with what the geographers call 'constancy of place' created conditions that tend to provide those communities with certain advantages. 'Constancy of place' refers to the ability of a particular geographic area to sustain a stable economic and political environment over a long period of time. Although it offers certain advantages – such as a predictable and dependable resource base, hence a familiar and comfortable socio-psychological setting – it can also constrain a system from expanding beyond a certain limit in any significant way, a kind of 'braking mechanism', to use a phrase from the historians of the Annales School. This means that until and unless society is willing and able to move away permanently or substantively from the agrarian heartland – thereby changing its emotional, physical and structural attachment to it – the relationships between that society and its environment would continue to reproduce themselves over and over again, so that the same or similar problems would tend to be resolved by the same or similar solutions. The system was self-perpetuating and self-regulating.

Such constancy of place and longevity of culture led to the development of a cumulative tradition in Myanmar, a strong continuity not only between the period of urbanism and its predecessors but also its successors. This continuity has often been missed (or neglected), particularly by those trained in Western academia where change rather than continuity, differences rather than similarities, individuals rather than groups, exceptions rather than norms are usually sought and given 'agency'. When one values change and actively seeks it, phenomena such as longevity, 'constancy of place' and cumulative traditions become virtually invisible.

Of course, the presence of a cumulative tradition in no way implies that important, fundamental changes did not occur in the 2,000 years of Myanmar's history. Indeed, this entire chapter has emphasized the importance of a structural transformation from pre-urban to urban forms, and the consequences of the latter on the development of states and kingdoms. The point being made here, therefore, is that despite such transformations, because the Urban Period survived in more or less the same general region over a long period of time, it was able to develop a cumulative tradition that otherwise might not have materialized.

This amalgam of change and continuity can best be depicted as a 'punctuated equilibrium' (to borrow a phrase from Palaeontology), where change is an infrequent but transformative feature of a longer and more stable process of continuity. The concept is applicable not only to the pre-urban and urban phases, but to all of Myanmar's long history.

4

Pagan:
The Golden Age of Myanmar

The roots of modern Myanmar go back to the great Kingdom of Pagan, the country's 'golden age', its 'classical state'. It emerged in the mid-ninth century AD and endured for four and a half centuries.[1] By the time it appeared the Burmese speakers were already the ruling group, structured around a monarchy that was to become the Pagan Dynasty. The factors responsible for the rise, development and decline of that dynasty and kingdom, along with a synopsis of the nature of state and society are the foci of this chapter.

THE ADVENT OF THE BURMESE SPEAKERS AND THE GROWTH OF PAGAN: MID-NINTH TO THE MID-ELEVENTH CENTURIES AD

In AD 832 the powerful Kingdom of Nanchao, which ruled between the seventh and mid-thirteenth centuries the area that is now approximately Yunnan in Western China, reportedly attacked a 'P'iao Kingdom' thought to be located in Upper Myanmar, taking some 3,000 of its people. Earlier Myanmar scholars concluded that this attack was the event that first brought the Burmese speakers into the plains of the Irrawaddy, for among the Nanchao troops, it was believed, were people called the 'Mien' (or Mian), a term the Chinese used to refer to the people that inhabited the same general region later occupied by the Burmese speakers. These 'Mien' were ostensibly an 'ethnic tribe' under the hegemony of the Kingdom of Nanchao, which was said to have used them on this conquest. But once in the Irrawaddy valley, and having tasted 'independence' and 'freedom', so the story goes, the Burmese speakers broke away from the Nanchao kingdom and decided to remain in 'Myanmar', ultimately founding their own kingdom there.[2]

In contrast is our view that the Burmese speakers may have been living in the plains of the Irrawaddy River valley all along, among the people the Chinese called the 'P'iao'. The Burmese speakers probably lived in the legendary 'Nineteen Villages' east of Pagan where tradition places them, and from where the founders of the Pagan Dynasty likely came. If correct, the origins of the Burmese speakers in Myanmar may well be earlier than, and had nothing to do with, the Nanchao raid of AD 832.

If the conquest of a 'P'iao Kingdom' by Nanchao and the removal of a sizeable number of its people is historical – regardless of whether the Burmese speakers were part of the Nanchao forces or already part of 'P'iao' society – a power vacuum was created nonetheless, into which the Burmese speakers moved. Around 849, just 17 years after the Nanchao raid, they had built a walled fortress at a place later called Pagan, which was to become the centre of one of the great kingdoms of Southeast Asia.

Located around the 'bend' in the Irrawaddy, on its eastern bank, the fortified town of Pagan was built on a pre-existing (perhaps 'P'iao') settlement. It had easy water and land access to what became the three most productive and fertile regions in Upper Myanmar during pre-colonial times – Kyaukse, Minbu and the Mu River valley.

The walled citadel of Pagan, with thick and high balustrades built of brick, measured only 355 acres, a little more than a half-mile square, small compared to the much larger walled cities of the previous Urban Period. Sri Ksetra was fourteen times larger, and Halin, Mongmao and Beithano were each seven times larger. The small size of Pagan suggests that only the royal family, senior ministers of the court and crown troops sufficient to guard them lived within the walled area itself.

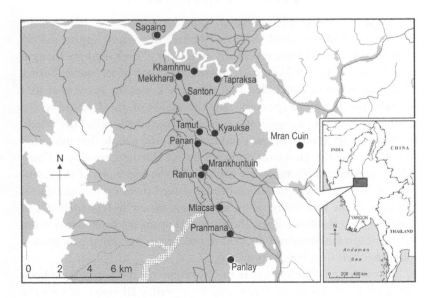

Kyaukse Valley, Pagan period, 9th–13th centuries.

However, one need not assume that the size of the centre is an indication of the size of the kingdom. In fact it was just the opposite during the Urban Period, whose much larger centres did not necessarily reflect a larger kingdom – if indeed they were an integrated kingdom at all. Whereas most of their population, cultivated fields, irrigation works, palaces, temples, monasteries, royal mausolea, houses and animals are found *inside* their larger walled cities, at Pagan all these were located

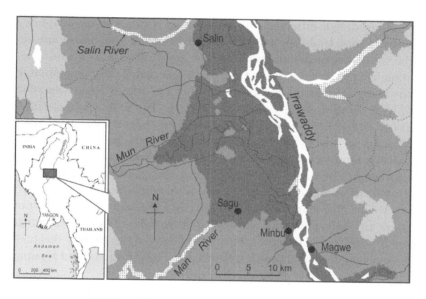

Minbu Valley, Pagan period, 11th–13th centuries.

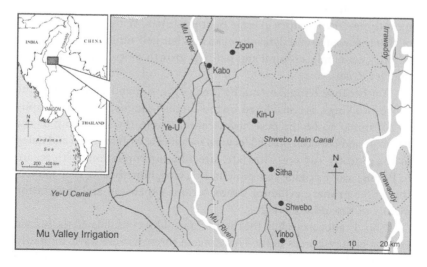

Mu Valley, Pagan period, 12th–13th centuries.

79

outside the centre itself. This suggests that during the Urban Period the countryside was sparsely populated and *unsecured*, while during the Pagan period the countryside was more densely populated and *secured* with all its 'valuables' *outside* the walled capital. (In fact, having the king-dom's wealth outside the walled citadel itself may have been one of the major reasons for Pagan's longevity, as we shall see below.) The configur-ation certainly suggests a larger and safer entity, and one that was better administered and integrated.

Indeed, that difference in configuration between an un-integrated Urban Period landscape and an integrated Pagan Period one recaptures the two phases in state-formation: its *inception* and *zenith*. A transform-ation had clearly taken place from an un-integrated conglomeration of city-states to an integrated kingdom; from a politically loose federation of large autonomous city-states of the Urban Period to a far more inte-grated and perhaps even centralized kingdom under the Pagan Dynasty, the latter secured by more than 45 strategically arranged provincial cap-itals representing central authority. This transformation, then, was more than simply a matter of *quantitative* change (in size and scope); it was also a matter of *qualitative* change (in structure and character).

By the mid-tenth century a monarchy was already in place, part of whose city walls and palace remains have been radio–carbon–dated to that century and later.[3] We know the names and dates of two kings of that time from epigraphy and chronicles: Saw Rahan (*reg.* 956–1001) and Kyaung Phyu Min (1001–21), heretofore considered legendary.

By 1004, during the latter's reign, a Chinese source recorded an embassy that visited the Sung capital from the 'P'u-kan kingdom' seeking recognition from the superpower of the region, the standard protocol for recently emerged polities in early Southeast Asia. With the development of this new capital and dynasty began another half millennium of demo-graphic, economic, cultural and political growth centred in the plains of the Dry Zone.

Yet because King Aniruddha (1044–77), son and grandson of the above two kings, is considered by the English-language historiography of Myanmar to be the first historical monarch, the beginning of the Pagan period has been pushed forward to coincide with his reign and dated to 1044, nearly 195 years too late, affecting interpretations with regard to Pagan's early origins and growth. It is true, nonetheless, that some of the better primary evidence shows serious expansion and integration mainly in Aniruddha's reign.

Shortly after ascending the throne Aniruddha consolidated the human and material resources in the Dry Zone in three discrete ways: militarily, economically and ideologically. His grandfather and father seemed to have begun the process, especially of ideological integration, when the former purified the Sangha (Buddhist church) and the latter symbolically linked the capital city with the Buddhist universe. Continuing that tradition found earlier during the Urban Period, Pagan's city walls were also punctuated by twelve gates – four main ones at the cardinal directions with two minor ones flanking each – representing the twelve signs of the Zodiac and Buddhist cosmic time and space.[4]

For Aniruddha, however, military concerns were higher priority. He secured the northern frontier early, the traditional direction of invasion and the 'front door' of Myanmar, by building (or restoring) 43 forts northward along the Irrawaddy. Their settlement pattern reveals his intention to protect the fertile plains of Kyaukse from northern invasion, creating a line of defence all the way to a most strategically located city, Bhamo, near the current China border. Next, he fortified over a dozen well-placed towns in the Kyaukse valley itself, all arranged to ensure the protection and security of this important agricultural region. He then constructed anew (and/or repaired old) irrigation works that exploited the numerous perennial rivers of the Kyaukse valley that flowed into it from the higher and wetter surrounding mountain. As the soil in the Dry Zone came from river silt that had been deposited annually there for millennia it was very fertile, requiring only water to begin the chemical reaction that nourished crops. As the region had been cultivated earlier, his focus was on harnessing these perennial rivers more effectively, thereby improving the wherewithal for agriculture in the region.

Success in that endeavour subsequently enabled Pagan to reap at least two crops of *sawah* (wet-rice) a year, which became and remained the economic mainstay of the Kingdom for centuries thereafter. During Aniruddha's reign itself, however, Kyaukse did not yet produce sufficient wealth to integrate the entire country, his ultimate goal. As he had already integrated much of the dispersed population of Upper Myanmar, he now looked to conquering Lower Myanmar and doing the same thing there, using the easiest manner in which to move a large contingent of troops – down the Irrawaddy River. It had taken about thirteen years to integrate Upper Myanmar between his accession in 1044 and his conquests of the coasts, perhaps in 1057, as tradition asserts. As he moved downriver he subdued the populated and strategic towns that had been part of the old Urban Period landscape, particularly the most important 'gateway' to Upper and Lower Myanmar and an important centre of that time: Pyi (Prome).

In Southeast Asian history most inland agrarian states tended *not* to destroy or eliminate coastal and maritime areas. Rather, they exerted their hegemony and control over them, since the maritime regions provided trade revenues, luxury goods, manpower, a market for the interior's products and new knowledge from the outside world. In exchange the inland agrarian world supplied the all-important food staples, particularly rice, forest products such as teak, precious stones (jade, rubies) of the interior and Dry Zone crops (pulses, palm sugar, sesame and so on). Thus it was not in either's interest to 'kill' the proverbial 'golden goose', so that the relationship evolved into a symbiotic one between inland agrarian and maritime commercial societies. This 'upstream–downstream' paradigm was often repeated not only in Myanmar's but Southeast Asian history, a pattern most clearly revealed in the post-Pagan period, as we shall see in chapter Five.

At the time of Aniruddha's expansion in the mid-eleventh century Lower Myanmar was the 'frontier' of the kingdom with no polities yet evident. Thus his integration of people and resources there, particularly the scattered port-towns, invariably enhanced their commercial potential and enlarged Pagan's coffers. And as long as those maritime centres remained under Pagan's control – and they did for another two and a half centuries – the kingdom continued to enjoy these trade revenues as surplus without much initial outlay in labour or money. Just some provincial governors stationed there with several garrisons of soldiers to maintain central authority in the region, all paid for by its own revenues, sufficed.

Aniruddha was said to have brought back both human and material resources from his Lower Myanmar campaign. If true, that had important economic and political consequences for the state in both the short and long term. New labour would have increased the number of crown-service people (*kyun-taw*) for state use immediately, particularly in military and provincial administration, while their resettlement on cultivable (or cultivated) land would have increased agricultural production shortly thereafter, raising the 'GDP' of Pagan for many more generations to come as *kyun-taw* status was hereditary.

Even drought had little effect on the production of padi from crown lands, as irrigated regions such as Kyaukse and other similar areas were fed by perennial rivers and streams, including the Irrawaddy and Chindwin. Padi also stores well, so that surplus from annual yields tend to accumulate rather than diminish unless there were extraordinary circumstances to offset it. And since padi was tied in value to the silver kyat, the standard medium of exchange, 'money' was always at hand. Wealth obtained in liquid assets, of course, could be used for anything, although much went into the promotion of the religion. It was an economic (and political) investment with tremendous returns for both state and society initially, as we shall see below.

Aniruddha's expansion to Lower Myanmar for essentially these political and economic reasons, however, has been depicted by late Burmese chronicles of the eighteenth and nineteenth centuries as religious activity: the ultimate Buddhist king conducting a traditional 'righteous conquest' resulting in a 'righteous victory' (*dharmavijaya*), much like the Crusades of thirteenth-century Europe. The late chronicles record that Aniruddha marched downstream in 1056–7 to secure the 'pure' version of the Theravada Buddhist scriptures thought to be in the possession of one Manuha, king of a Mon kingdom called Ramannadesa, centred at his capital city, Thaton. With the conquest of this kingdom, capital and king, the 'orthodox' version of the Theravada Buddhist scriptures along with the entire court and population of Mon speakers were said to have been taken back to Pagan. And along with them came the (assumed) superior culture of the Mon, which was believed to have begun the 'civilizing' of Burmese state and society at Pagan (hence the country itself) with a writing system, orthodox religion, conceptions of state and king, technical knowledge of the arts and crafts, literature and a host of other contributions.

But it is all myth. None of the above assertions – the event itself, a kingdom called Ramannadesa, a Mon king named Manuha, 'his' city of Thaton and the civilizing of Pagan society – can withstand serious scrutiny or be verified by any contemporary evidence. Indeed, there is no proof of *any* political entity in Lower Myanmar remotely resembling a kingdom at any time during the first millennium BC and early centuries AD, much less a capital and king. The earliest polity in Lower Myanmar to appear in original sources dates to the late thirteenth century AD, well after Pagan had reached its apogee and begun to decline. Hence, the convention that Ramannadesa civilized Pagan is not only untenable but an anachronism.5 In fact, as noted in an earlier chapter, the whole 'civilizing' process of state development and its accoutrements 'moved' in exactly the opposite direction, from Upper to Lower Myanmar, and is found first in Upper Myanmar over a millennium before they appeared in Lower Myanmar. The only historically viable event in the entire convention is Pagan's expansion to Lower Myanmar sometime during the mid-eleventh century.

Yet 'the Mon Paradigm' (as this myth is now called) has been the basis for interpreting the growth and development of Pagan (hence, of Myanmar also) for about a century now, and unfortunately remains so for understanding (actually misunderstanding) much of early (especially mainland) Southeast Asian history and culture; this has important consequences for *current* political problems and issues in the region related to Mon independence.

Be that as it may, the third strategy that Aniruddha used to integrate the Pagan kingdom was ideological; that is, connecting religion and state. More specifically, he linked the well-being of Theravada Buddhism with the legitimacy of state and society, manifest in the orthodoxy and preservation of the Sangha. The mechanism that insured this process was the ubiquitous religious donation that also linked state and church economically. The belief behind the religious donation is called the 'merit-path to salvation' or kammatic Buddhism, which allowed ordinary people without the money, leisure or mental resolve to gain merit simply by doing 'good deeds'.[6] These could be as modest as feeding monks, giving robes, providing oil lamps for monasteries and temples, and as extravagant as building temples, monasteries, rest houses and libraries for the Sangha. The acquisition of merit, in turn, enhanced one's rebirths until one is finally reborn as a monk with the mental wherewithal to attain nirvana.

Indeed, such was the zeal and devotion for nirvana in Pagan via the merit-path that over its four centuries of existence thousands of kyats of gold and silver, hundreds of thousands of acres of padi-land and tens of thousands of people were donated to the Sangha. Some devotees even gave themselves to the Religion: one high-ranking minister of the court donated himself and his entire family to the church in perpetuity. (This donating oneself to the service of the Religion, whether in time or labour, continues today.) The 'merit-path to salvation' was a if not *the* central ideology in the practice of Burmese Theravada Buddhism.

Kammatic Buddhism was not just an ideology amongst the masses but was very much a part of established state ideology at the highest levels, especially when kings participated and led in its promotion. And since they donated the most to the Sangha in terms of money and resources they also accrued the most merit. Yet as righteous leaders (*dhammaraja*) they could not (and did not) simply keep that bounty to themselves but, as the inscriptions state, shared it with 'all creatures', thereby helping everyone else along the path to nirvana. In effect that made them saviours, bodhi-sattvas (incipient Buddhas) who temporarily forego nirvana in order to 'save' humankind.

The notion of messianism inherent in the idea of the bodhisattva was therefore incorporated into conceptions of Burmese Buddhist king-ship. It can be found in the term *hpayalaung*, meaning 'embryo' or 'immanent Buddha'. Burmese kings adopted titles with this word *alaung* in them, such as 'Alaungpaya' or 'Alaungsithu' (one of Aniruddha's succes-sors), to suggest that they were avatars (incarnations) of future Buddhas who they will become at death.

As Theravada Buddhists also believe that four of the five Buddhas in this universe have already appeared, only one was left: Maitreya. And if the present king is a bodhisattva (future Buddha), he 'must' also be Maitreya. Doctrine states that he will arrive in '5,000 years', when the world is luxuriant, the kingdom powerful, the Sangha pure and the people moral and righteous. Moreover, Maitreya will descend only to Jambudipa, the 'Southern Island' in Buddhist cosmogony where Buddhas are born and *cakravartins* ('world conquerors') rule; in other words, *this* world. Pagan kings thus attempted to create conditions during their reigns that allowed them to claim – all at the same time – that Myanmar was Jambudipa, and they *cakravartins* as well as future Buddhas.

Conquest and 'pacification' of new territories not only confirmed *cakravartin* status but provided the material resources for ensuring those ideal conditions of Jambudipa. Such actions were justified in a circular manner with the concept of *dharmavijaya* ('righteous victory'), almost always the purview of *cakravartins*. Although the notion of the future Buddha was probably more a religious than political idea to most people, it was nonetheless linked to the current monarch or (if he were intolerable) a future one who would replace him.

By the time of Aniruddha and the reigns of his immediate successors, the notion that Myanmar was Jambudipa and its kings *cakravartins* (and bodhisattvas) had been well established, continuing throughout the country's pre-modern history to become part of its self-image. In short, the spiritual and temporal salvation of society was inexorably tied to the political stature of state and king and the social and religious conditions of the religion.

The main beneficiary of this link between Theravada Buddhism and state was the Sangha, in economic, social and political ways. Kammatic Buddhism generated a sustained flow of wealth to the church that initially stimulated the economic development of the kingdom and made the Sangha rich, enhancing its social and political influence while legitimating the state. But several hundred years of taxable wealth shifting to the tax-exempt sector created a situation that would become a problem not only for Pagan, but for succeeding kingdoms throughout Myanmar's history, a topic discussed below.

Another key religious idea from Theravada Buddhism that was politicized early in the Pagan period was the notion of karma. When a member of the royal family successfully attained the throne by defeating other legitimate members of the royal family (as Aniruddha was believed to have done), *both* the concept of royal hereditary succession and successful action irrespective of heredity were being acknowledged as legitimate. However, this was a double-edged sword, for now any rebel, usurper or pretender could make a claim to the throne as long as he or she were successful, justifying it *ex post facto*. It is what the field of Southeast Asian studies (partly tongue-in-cheek) has called 'retroactive karma'. In effect, then, the ideology of hereditary succession had created its own countervailing principle: that success without the correct heredity was also legitimate.

Concurrent to politicizing Theravada Buddhist principles with the state and king, Aniruddha and some of his successors also integrated indigenous beliefs of spirit (*nat*) worship into it, creating what became known as the Cult of the 37 *Nats*. This is a pantheon of historical and legendary ancestors, most of whom were either past royalty, associated with it, or folk heroes, all (or most) of whom had been violently killed, usually unjustly at the hands of or by instigation of royalty. When people die violent deaths before their time they become *nat sein* ('green spirits') as their deaths are unripe. They are invariably malevolent and hover around the vicinity of the incident that becomes their domain. One needs to propitiate and placate them whenever their territory is transgressed.

If these were spirits of ordinary folk they would be propitiated with small spirit shrines, food, lights and flowers in their respective locale. But if the persons killed violently had 'national' or provincial stature (such as a king or governor), their spirits must then be appeased on a national or provincial scale. Such spirits are given 'fiefs' by the reigning king in the supernatural world, domains over which they are lords. Local ancestral spirits in the locality then became their 'vassals' in the same way that headmen of villages and towns accepted the authority of provincial governors appointed by the centre over their domains.

At the top of the Pantheon of 37 *Nats* is Thagya Min, the Burmese equivalent of Indra, the Vedic deity who best epitomizes kingship. Under him are Mahagiri ('Lord of the Mountain') and his sister Shwemyethna ('golden face'), said to have died violent deaths at the hands of a king of the legendary first Burmese dynasty. As supernatural counterparts to the king and chief queen (who was ideally his half-sister), they guard and protect the supernatural realm in the same way the human king and queen guard and protect the terrestrial realm. Their shrines still flank the main (east) entrance to the capital city of Pagan, making them, by extension, protectors of the kingdom itself. (Indeed, 37 *nat* figures are carved on the frame of the Lion throne of Burmese kings, a clear indication of their role as guardians of the institution of monarchy.) Both Mahagiri and Shwemyethna are also the household guardian spirits of each home in the kingdom, suggesting that state ideology and local beliefs had become well integrated.

The fear surrounding the wrath of the 'green spirit' was harnessed to ensure that those who had died unjustly at the hands or instigation of royalty were at least rewarded with a place on the Pantheon. It was perhaps an attempt to placate the victim's followers, but more to control ideology that condoned and rationalized the use of power with impunity. That such rationalization was even needed acknowledged the idea that justice must be attained in *this life* without having to wait endless cycles of rebirth implied by karmic retribution. Kings also performed many 'good deeds', particularly building magnificent temples, in part to atone for the 'bad deeds' they were compelled to commit as monarchs in a system that legitimated success *ex post facto*.

Ultimately Pagan leadership created the Cult of the 37 *Nats* to help unify the kingdom ideologically by infusing and integrating local spirits and beliefs with national ones, diverse and dispersed components of society with the centre (and thereby) with each other, minority ethnic and political groups and their local beliefs with those of the majority, past leaders with present ones, regional loyalties with 'national' ones, unsuccessful members of the royal family with successful ones, rebels with legitimate princes, and the rulers with the ruled, who otherwise would have been disconnected by culture, place, time and structure from one another.

In short, not only had Aniruddha consolidated and integrated concretely the military and economic resources of the kingdom, he had also harnessed abstract spiritual and conceptual elements. As human king, latent ancestral spirit and embryonic Buddha, he linked the present, past and future while unifying the terrestrial, celestial and supernatural realms.

DEVELOPMENT AND EFFLORESCENCE OF PAGAN: MID-ELEVENTH TO THE THIRD QUARTER OF THE THIRTEENTH CENTURIES

The crucial foundations that Aniruddha laid were institutionalized and developed even further by his able successors, notably Kyanzittha (*reg.* 1084–1111), Alaungsithu (1111–67) and Narapatisithu (1173–1210). These three especially took the kingdom to greater heights in both quantitative and qualitative ways: size and scale, power and wealth, stature and influence.

More specifically, Aniruddha's initial thrust of central authority over Lower Myanmar had given Pagan access to strategic towns such as Prome from where Arakan (and its trade connections to India and the Bay of Bengal) were within reach. His son and successor Kyanzittha continued that policy and placed governors as town 'eaters' (*myosa*) in Lower Myanmar as well. Alaungsithu, the latter's grandson, was known for the state's standardization of weights and measures. His reign also witnessed the institutionalization of a semi-bureaucratic structure composed of tax collectors, land surveyors, provincial governors and village and township headmen (*myo* and *ywathugyi*) responsible to the crown. As for Narapatisithu, he not only refined the organization of the military but pacified most of the country by the end of the twelfth century, a demonstration of Pagan's political prowess. For the first time in its history all of the north–south and much of the east–west axes of the kingdom were administered by (or under the hegemony of) town and provincial governors responsible to the Pagan monarchy centred in the Dry Zone. But pacification meant more than just military hegemony; it also meant a degree of socio-cultural and political integration.

Yet that need not imply absolute homogeneity either. To say that the Kingdom of Pagan was ethno-linguistically Burmese is to speak only of the rulers and the majority population; to label it Mon exaggerates both their size and role well beyond what the evidence warrants; to call it 'Pyu' minimizes the effects of substantial change; to declare it Theravadin over-simplifies the religious milieu. The Kingdom of Pagan at its height was all these things in various proportions.

The whole process of growth, development and efflorescence took several hundred years. Underlying this transformation was a demographic growth which was invariably a stimulus for other forms of developments. Indeed – and despite the lack of hard census data of the kind modern historical demographers have come to expect – in Pagan's case, one must assume a significant increase in population over these centuries, not just to explain the obvious physical expansion of habitat but also its socio-economic, political, cultural and religious growth, for which there is abundant evidence. And in labour-scarce Southeast Asia any increase in population would have immediately given Pagan an economic, military and political edge.

Demographic growth in Pagan was not just a matter of natural pop-ulation increase, but also the acquisition of involuntary labour, more effective integration of existing scattered communities and, most impor-tantly, *voluntary immigration*, a pattern not ordinarily recognized by scholars of early Southeast Asia. Yet it is obvious that as centres such as Pagan grew more prosperous people from surrounding areas tended to migrate towards 'civilization' and its 'bright lights' rather than flee from

Dhammayazika Pagoda of King Narapatisithu, Pagan, built in the 12th century.

it. For here education was free, literacy widespread, culture sophisticated and the religion resplendent. The most excellent literary figures, the best masters of the fine arts, the holiest shrines, the most highly revered monks and sacred relics, were all here. The grandest of religious festivals along with the most spectacular of cultural performances could be found only here, not in the periphery. The capital of Pagan was the premier pilgrimage site for devotees of Theravada Buddhism, acknowledged even by Sri Lanka, once the bastion of Theravada Buddhism.

Included in these 'pull' factors was Pagan's job market, which probably paid one of the highest wage rates in all of mainland Southeast Asia at the time. Contrary to convention and current belief Pagan had *paid*, *not slave* labour, particularly for skilled artists and craftsmen in the booming temple construction industry, which did not abate until the very end of the thirteenth century. Indeed the situation was such that under normal conditions people rather than fleeing the centres of the lowland valleys (as some popular academic paradigms have suggested

Dolomite carving of 'The Eight Scenes' in Buddha's life, 13th century.

recently), most often gravitated towards them. In early Southeast Asia centres tended to *attract* rather than *repel* people.[7]

The population of artisans and craftsmen must have grown, as approximately 3,000 temples were built during the span of three centuries between Aniruddha's reign and the late thirteenth century in the capital city itself. This building programme has been tracked by radio-carbon dating and in other ways. Masons, carpenters, sculptors, turners (lathe operators), gold and silver smiths, paid in cash (silver and gold) or kind (padi, rights to the produce of land, animals) are not only ubiquitous in the inscriptions but mentioned with increasing frequency as the centuries progressed. Even haulers of firewood and plasterers of temple walls were paid while commoners had the means to donate substantially to the religion as well as to have servants (*kyun*) of their own.

The increase in numbers of artisans and craftsmen must have stimulated the growth of other groups whose occupations supported and were dependent on the arts and crafts. The masons needed brick makers, who required clay suppliers and firewood sellers to make the millions of kiln-fired bricks needed to build the temples at Pagan. (According to estimates of modern engineers from UNESCO who have studied and repaired Pagan's temples, the Dhammayazika, one of the many temples built by King Narapatisithu in the late twelfth century, alone used six million bricks.) Considering the fact that approximately 3,000 kiln-fired brick temples were built during the Pagan period, the brick industry had to be a major one. The inscription that commemorates the building of the Dhammayazika survives, in which is also recorded the costs of the temple in silver, land and wages.

According to other inscriptions the plaster that covered the walls of *stupa*-temples (those with interior space) was made with sand, lime, milk and honey. If not hyperbole, the latter two ingredients imply a cattle and bee industry of tremendous size, especially since approximately a third of the 3,000 temples built during these centuries were *stupa*-temples in which plaster was used extensively, both inside and outside. Even if the 'milk and honey' were hyperbole, mortar (the same word as 'plaster' in Burmese without a suffix) was still needed to bind the millions of bricks in all 3,000 temples whose ingredients would have generated the creation of a huge industry.

Still other people were needed to mine and haul the marble and dolomite used in the thousands of Buddha statues sculpted by the master sculptors, either placed in temples and monasteries or sold to pilgrims. As the best-known marble quarries in Upper Myanmar were over a hundred miles distant from Pagan, there had to have been a transport industry to ship either the raw material or the finished product to Pagan. Even if only the raw material were shipped, the economy of villages and towns where the marble and dolomite were extracted and sculpted would have benefited from temple-building in distant Pagan. In other words the temple construction industry at Pagan was not just confined to the capital; it had an economic impact on the entire kingdom.

There was surely a huge demand for teak and other hardwoods growing in the surrounding forested hills for the building of hundreds of monasteries (2,004 were recorded by the late eleventh century), not to mention the houses of ministers, official buildings of the crown, the dozens of fortified outposts throughout the kingdom and the royal palaces that all used teak as their main building material. The inscriptions testify to the presence of carpenters and woodcarvers who built these buildings, decorated their countless number of doors and windows and sculpted thousands of Buddha statues for private and institutional use.

Such ubiquitous use of teak suggests a sizeable lumber industry that extracted thousands of logs, most sawed into planks for floors, doors, windows, along with the many teak logs pared by turners for use as foundational pillars in monasteries and palaces. The presence of a lumber industry in turn means a 'heavy equipment' industry must have also existed; that is, the capturing, taming and training of elephants used in that industry. (Elephants are still used in the lumber industry today.)

Since kiln-fired roofing tiles were used for the roofs of many of these teak edifices – bronze tiles were used for the palaces – there was a demand for the production of these materials and their craftsmen, another industry that added to the growth in the population, especially as the urban area grew. And we know that happened, for the capital city of Pagan expanded from a small fortress hugging the banks of the Irrawaddy in the ninth and tenth centuries under Aniruddha's father and grandfather to an urban area that was more than 40 square miles by the early thirteenth century. An architectural historian has even suggested that Pagan's urban growth showed signs of conscious town-planning, an indication of urban population pressure.[8]

In tandem with the capital city the kingdom also expanded, from a relatively small Dry Zone nucleus in the eleventh century whose reach remained mostly in Upper Myanmar along the Irrawaddy River valley northward, to nearly the size of Myanmar today by the late twelfth century, occupying most if not all of if its current north–south axis, including the Tenasserim Peninsular down to Mergui. Neither development could have occurred without a corresponding increase in the total population of the kingdom.

Demographic growth in the general populace would have a proportionate effect on the clergy needed to tend their flock. An inscription of the eleventh century during King Kyanzittha's reign mentioned 4,108 monks at the capital while another during the same century, as noted above, records a rather precise 2,004 monasteries in and around the capital. If the ratio of monks to monasteries is one in twenty (a conservative average over the centuries), there could have been nearly 40,000 monks by the twelfth century at the kingdom's core. If the ratio of monks to 'civilians' during the Pagan period was similar to what it is today – about 1 per cent of the population – the Upper Myanmar nucleus of the kingdom may have had as many as 400,000 people.

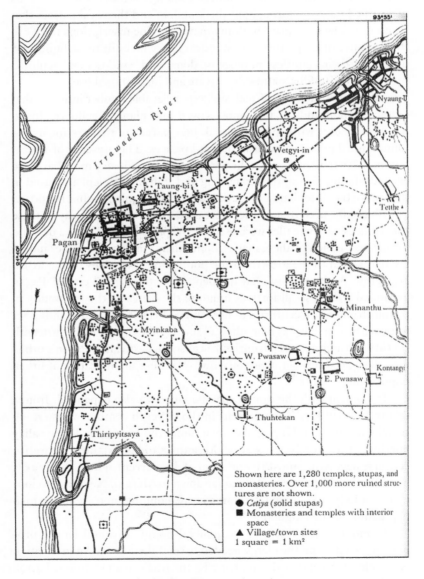

City and suburbs of Pagan, 9th–13th centuries.

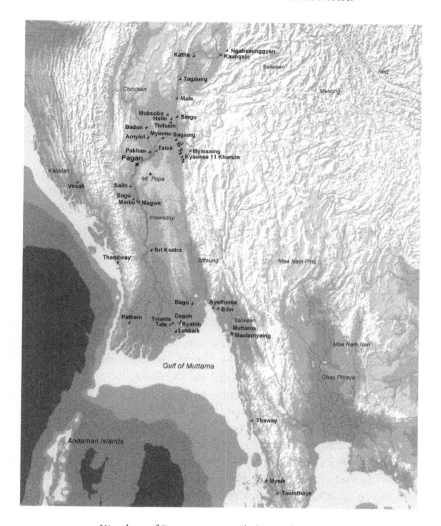

Kingdom of Pagan at its zenith, late 13th century.

Whatever the exact numbers, members of the Sangha were integral components of all new settlements, however distant they might have been from the capital. The clergy brought literacy, morality, ethics and potential for 'salvation' to the people in these new areas, a process (in medieval Europe) that has been called the 'pacification of the masses', whereby the church functioned as a socio-cultural arm of the state. The Sangha was also an avenue for upward spiritual and socio-economic mobility for many young men (and women) who saw the religion as their calling. It was a life of abstinence from the world of secular attractions, but it also provided a haven from stress, want, war, corvee labour, taxes and politics.

For the maintenance of monasteries and their clergy a variety of specialists and non-specialists was donated by state and society, some as permanent parts of religious endowments. The inscriptions mention scribes who not only copied the scriptures and other religious texts for monastic libraries but also maintained secular records of monastic property, including income from endowed lands and the allotment of produce given to each cook, sweeper, cultivator, carpenter and mason working for the Sangha. Even singers and dancers who performed on festive occasions were paid in cash or kind for their services by the donor.

There was also a constant demand for crown-service people known as *kyun-taw* ('royal subject' or 'servant') especially in the military. They were provided with many 'perks': the best irrigated land, high social status and avenues for upward political mobility. Recruitment to, as well as retention for *kyun-taw* would have been relatively easy, for they all received premium irrigated padi land to 'eat', 'work' and 'live on' (*samye, lokmye, nemye*) as payment for their services, while in the maritime port cities and towns they were likely paid from the trade revenues garnered.

The military population must have increased as the size of the kingdom grew nearly six-fold over two centuries. Beginning with Aniruddha in the eleventh century, garrisoned troops were stationed in dozens of forts that hugged the Irrawaddy River all the way to the northern reaches of the kingdom; indeed, by the late twelfth century one of these forts (Ngahsaungyan) was located inside the current China border. By the mid-twelfth century also, fortified towns had been built in and around the other two major irrigated river valleys (the Mu Valley and Minbu) that became the economic mainstay of the Kingdom. Strategic towns were garrisoned with 'marines' and supplied with war-boats all along the Irrawaddy southward. Even as early as the late eleventh century, during King Kyanzittha's reign, Tavoy in the far south of today's Myanmar was administered by governors appointed by the king. By the late twelfth century and Narapatisithu's reign, Muttama (Martaban) and Myeik (Mergui), located at the tip of the country's southern border today was under Pagan's hegemony if not suzerainty. By the late twelfth and early thirteenth centuries the Kingdom of Pagan was more or less the size of what is today the state in Myanmar.

King Narapatisithu's reign, particularly, is well known for the development of the military. An inscription of his mentions 30,000 cavalry, a large number for those days anywhere, along with a precise 17,645 soldiers (called 'braves'), perhaps representing the standing army at the capital, and clearly not the entire military that lived on their lands until called to duty. The inscriptions struck during and after his reign also record an increasing number and variety of military functions, from infantry and cavalry to elephantry and 'marines'. The military apparently also had police duties wherever they resided, maintaining law and order throughout the kingdom.

Perhaps most important, there had to have been demographic growth in the number of crown and private cultivators, for how else could the burgeoning population be fed? The ultimate proof of this is the approximately three-fold increase in the acreage of Pagan's cultivated padi lands in the kingdom of Pagan between the eleventh and thirteenth centuries. During the reigns of Aniruddha and Kyanzittha the Kyaukse valley had been the kingdom's mainstay. By the twelfth and thirteenth centuries, during the height of the Pagan period, Kyaukse had likely increased its productive capacity to approximately 119,500 acres of padi, irrigated by fourteen major canals running a total of 183 miles, sixteen major weirs (dams) and four major tanks (reservoirs). The best irrigated land there yielded approximately 1.4 tonnes per acre per harvest. That produced, on average, about 167,300 tonnes of padi per year, not counting the second (sometimes, a third) padi crop.

The Mu Valley north of Pagan was likely settled and developed during King Narapatisithu's reign, largely during the late twelfth century. He placed thousands of cultivators, soldiers, monks and *hpaya-kyun* (servants of the Sangha, Buddha, temple) to live and work there, the latter for the maintenance of his grand temple, the Dhammayazika (the one with the 6 million bricks noted above). The Mu River valley had three major canals totaling approximately 90 miles, 86 auxiliary canals, 40 weirs (dams), 31 tanks (reservoirs) and 73 sluices, altogether numbering approximately 232 pieces of irrigation works commanding nearly 230,000 acres when fully operative.

The Minbu valley south of Pagan may also have been settled during the twelfth and early thirteenth centuries. Minbu was smaller, but nonetheless harnessed 70,250 acres of cultivated land using three or four major canals and 34 subordinate ones that totalled nearly 67 miles, along with several weirs and many sluices. All told, then, the Pagan kingdom by the early to mid-thirteenth century was under the plough of Pagan's crown, private and Sangha cultivators, who tilled approximately 400,000–500,000 acres of mostly padi land.[9]

Although the general yield must have varied, the best irrigated padi land from the three prized regions ordinarily produced between 1.2 and 2 tonnes per hectare per harvest. And there was more than one harvest per annum, usually two, but sometimes three, although the second and third crops would likely yield a lower tonnage. Using figures of rice consumption in pre-colonial Asia (approximately six to seven persons ate 1 tonne per year prior to the Second World War), the above yields could have easily fed over a million people annually. Since the estimated population of Upper Myanmar was around 400,000 during the height of the Pagan period, there was clearly a large annual surplus. Indeed, one must assume a large surplus in order to explain the financing and maintenance of the massive temple construction industry for four centuries without abating. The evidence suggests that the majority of the population was free from want in terms of life's basic necessities, and the standard of living in Pagan must have been one of the highest in Southeast Asia.

Although there is no evidence with regard to life expectancy and infant mortality, there are indications that kings, queens and monks lived to ripe old ages, while no contemporary evidence exists during the four and a half centuries of the Pagan kingdom of famine or other suggestions of impoverished living conditions and inadequate food supplies. Since the Sangha functioned as the 'social services' arm of the state, even orphans, widows, the aged and the poor would have been cared for, as is the case still today in the country.

After feeding the population and promoting the religion, the surplus was obviously used for maintaining the state: the building and upkeep of royal palaces and official buildings, houses of ministers and purchase of luxury goods from foreign countries. Much surplus went towards the military: 'wages', construction of fortifications throughout the kingdom, repair and maintenance of the riverine fleet, supplying the horses for the cavalry and elephants for the elephantry, the cost of weapons, uniforms, housing and so on. Similarly the administration of the provinces was based on Pagan's surplus: stipends for governors, their housing, military support, and assistants, preservation of law and order, fortifications of provincial capitals and myriad other similar expenses.

Demographic growth and economic development invariably had social and cultural consequences. Any increase in population especially from outside the core area meant an infusion of different cultures. The inscriptions mention Indians, Sri Lankans, Chinese, Khmer, T'ai (Shan), Karen, Lawa, Chin, Mon and numerous other ethno-linguistic groups (including one 'white Indian') who resided and worked in the Kingdom of Pagan. The epigraphs also record the presence of musicians, dancers, singers and even bankers (*banda*), whose etymology suggests south Indian links. The mainstream conceptual system (and its cosmogony) was, of course, Indic, but as shown above, integrated to indigenous supernaturalism. Although the Old Burmese writing system was derived from the (Indo-European) Sanskrit alphabet via a south Indian adaptation, the language itself belonged to the tonal Tibeto-Burman family. The writing system apparently became 'standardized' by the mid-twelfth century in certain elite circles; and, of course, continues in Myanmar today as its modern script.

Achievements were made at Pagan during these centuries in Pali literature, considered the classical language used to write the Theravada

Buddhist scriptures, which even Sri Lanka, then bastion of Pali, acknowledged as superior.[10] Cultural festivities and activities were Buddhist in content and form, but shared the stage with indigenous rituals that celebrated agrarian society's seasonal activities. The names of musicians and musical instruments, of dancers and techniques of dancing were mainly south Indian, again much 'localized'. Clothes and foods were influenced by Indian, Sinic and local culture.

While much of the inspiration for art and architecture of religious edifices came from Indic culture 'localization' had rendered much of it unrecognizable even at its source. There were no equivalents in India, for example, of Pagan's *stupa*-temples and its magnificent vaulting: that was a local adaptation whose original influence is still unknown. There were also other indigenous influences on Pagan culture that can be attributed to the earlier 'Pyu' and to local minority ethno-linguistic groups, particularly in language and customs. Sinic culture contributed to Pagan's mix, but mainly at the elite level: in court attire and protocol, perhaps also military tactics and weaponry, although this appears only after the end of the Kingdom of Pagan. Pagan society had become culturally 'plural' although politically dominated by the Burmese speakers.

In order to manage this influx of peoples of different cultures, and as hierarchy was already the prevailing organizational principle of society in the kingdom, distinctions between and amongst these groups became even more pronounced and complex. There developed at Pagan a several-tiered system. Royalty was at the top, under which at the court level was an elite (both religious and secular), a higher officialdom at the provincial level, a lower officialdom at the township and village levels (again both religious and secular), supported by a large commoner class arranged according to a patron–client system of 'attachment' and 'non-attachment' (to the crown, church and individuals). Attachment was identified with the suffix *kyun*, non-attachment with the word *thi*. These were not 'slave' and 'free' categories, as convention erroneously still has it. Rather, these were indicators of socio-economic place in a patron–client based society: who one's patron was (that is, one's social identity revealed by one's patron) and whether or not one were attached at all. As noted, those attached to the crown were called *kyun-taw*; to the Sangha, *hpaya-kyun*; and those to private individuals rather than institutions, simply *kyun*.

The condition of these attached groups was either temporary or permanent, and although most became *kyun* voluntarily some did so involuntarily (as captives in war or because of debt). The status of some was hereditary, some not, but most were paid in cash or kind. Those attached to the Sangha were exempt from state taxes (corvée or produce) and had a relatively easy life, while those attached to the crown (akin to the civil servants of today's Myanmar) were liable for military duty but enjoyed some of the best 'perks', choicest of lands and a high status, as noted above. Those attached to individuals were usually ordinary household servants.

People who were *not* attached to institutions or individuals were called *athi*. Sometimes, the word *thi* was simply added to the word denoting their occupation, equivalent to the 'er' in 'baker', 'teacher' or 'fletcher'. Nothing in the word *athi* or in the actual condition of the people who were called that suggests they were 'freeborn', as so often asserted by early twentieth-century scholars attempting to find an equivalent in Pagan of the binary construct of 'free' and 'slave' labour that was the framework of analysis in Western history.

Historically, then, *athi* were simply common people who were not attached to a patron. Their economic status appeared to be relatively good, although as unattached people they would not have had the protection and support of more powerful patrons. Their unattached status would be tantamount to that of the Japanese *ronin* (masterless samurai) or, for that matter, of being untenured in today's academia. In both cases having a patron and attached status would have been preferable.

The growth in complexity of hierarchy can be found at the highest levels as well. Laws of succession had to be created as the number of princes eligible for the throne increased with the growth of the royal family. Rank and titles had to differentiate the now numerous and various levels of princes and princesses, chief queens and lesser queens, chief ministers and subordinate ministers, along with their functions. Protocol, seating arrangements, insignia and clothing of rank worn at court, appropriate vocabulary and proper etiquette, all became part of that world. In provincial centres, as well, the same or similar procedures and formalities attempted to reproduce the exemplary centre, albeit on a smaller scale.

Pagan society also witnessed the promulgation of codified law, both criminal and civil, notably during Narapatisithu's reign. Justice at Pagan was not only the preserve of the rich and famous; common people sued and won against them. There were attorneys called *shene* (literally, 'one who stands in front of', that is, an 'advocate'). Witnesses swore on the Scriptures (the *Abhidhamma*) 'to tell the whole truth', testifying for either the defence or prosecution. Judges (*thinphama*) pronounced their 'judicial decisions' from 'the Bench'. A standard legal process was followed based on evidence and witness testimony, although in rare cases trial by ordeal was resorted to as an atavistic remnant of an older age and custom. Even the punishments meted were not arbitrary but based on a written legal code divided into criminal and civil categories (*rajathat* and *dhammathat* respectively). The system even had primary and appellate levels.[11]

Such a legal system could have flourished only in a literate society. Commoners as well as the elite, monks as well as women, children as well as adults knew how to read and write. From a young age children were taught the 'three Rs' in monasteries. Donors provided fellowships for students that covered instruction as well as room and board, financed by permanent land and labour endowments. There was a good job market for literate people, what with all the written records kept kingdom-wide by state, church and private individuals during the nearly half millennium when Pagan thrived.

The kingdom was probably at its wealthiest at the beginning of the thirteenth century, by then controlling (or with hegemony over) nearly all of what is Myanmar today. Pagan was considered the most exemplary centre in the Theravada Buddhist world at that time, one of two superpowers (along with Angkor) on mainland Southeast Asia. Three of Pagan's most important kings during this time were Natonmya (*reg.* 1210–34), Kyaswa (1234–49) and Narathihapade (1254–87). Yet what they did, essentially, was to reap the benefits their predecessors had sown, maintain the institutions built by them – changing nothing of consequence – and in general perpetuating the system they inherited. They took their wealth for granted, often enjoying it carelessly, including, of course, heaping largesse on the Sangha for legitimacy.

Natonmya ('king with many earrings') was known for his extravagance. Kyaswa was known for his piety and attempted to deal with difficult problems by moral suasion rather than by exerting strong leadership. Narathihapade became the scapegoat for the 'fall' of the Pagan kingdom, therefore given the epithet 'the king who fled the Chinese' by later chronicles. It is true that his reign sustained the three Mongol invasions of the kingdom but they neither reached the capital nor actually destroyed the kingdom itself. Rather, it declined for other, internal structural reasons, which the Mongols only accelerated and exacerbated, as discussed below.

The development of Pagan as a kingdom did not go unnoticed by its contemporaries. An inscription of Angkor called Pagan 'Narapati Pura', the 'kingdom' (or capital) of Narapati (Narapatisithu). Pagan was also well known in India, as religious missions were periodically sent to Bodhgaya, the 'holy land' where the Lord Buddha attained enlightenment. There land was purchased and permanent servants hired to maintain the Mahabodhi Temple, the site that commemorated the latter event (reproduced at Pagan during Natonmya's reign). There were also contacts with Sri Lanka, the preserver and protector of Buddha's religion and its texts when India had become largely Hindu and, subsequently, Muslim. Aniruddha's reputation was legendary in Sri Lanka, whose king in the mid-eleventh century requested and received from the former a 'pure' set of the scriptures and a legitimate community of orthodox monks to purify the monkhood and the religion there. This was unprecedented,

Mingalazedi Pagoda of King Narathihapade, Pagan, built in the 13th century.

for it was usually the other way round, whereby the Theravada Buddhist world went to Sri Lanka for the pure scriptures and orthodoxy.

Even China recognized Pagan's growth and development. As noted above, Aniruddha's father had sent envoys to the Sung court in 1004 to obtain recognition from the superpower of Asia. Such diplomatic missions are recorded at least twice more: once in 1106 during King Kyanzittha's reign and again in 1178 during Narapatisithu's. Of the latter, the Sung court stated that, it 'cannot look down on [Pagan] as an ordinary little dependent kingdom' any longer. And although the imperial decree sent to Pagan in 1004 had been written on 'thick-backed paper, and enclosed in box and wrapper', now, 'we desire to follow the same ritual as in the case of the Ta-shih [Arabs], Chiao-shih [Annam], and other kingdoms' in which case the imperial decrees are to be 'written on white-backed, gold-flowered, damask paper, and stored in a partly gold-gilt tube with key, and forwarded in a brocade silk double wrapper as sealing envelope'. Quite clearly Pagan and its stature had grown, even in the eyes of the Chinese who ordinarily considered all Southeast Asian kingdoms 'barbaric'.

The Religion was certainly resplendent and several of the most sacred temples believed to hold important bodily relics of the Buddha are located in Pagan, most notably the Shwezigon and Shwesandaw both built by Aniruddha. Pagan's religious stature attracted pilgrims from all over the kingdom and abroad, infusing even more money into the kingdom. The capital city was often compared to *Tavatimsa* (the most favoured of Buddhist heavens) and considered the exemplary Buddhist site to visit while on earth. The landscape was covered with thousands of magnificent temples that pierced the skyline, whose gilded towers glistened in the sunlight while at sunset they cast dark silhouettes on a crimson horizon. Pagan was clearly perceived as the preeminent place, and the period the finest era in the entire history of the country during which only the luckiest persons could have hoped to live.

Of all the above factors that contributed to the strength and longevity of Pagan its physical configuration was most crucial. As noted above the kingdom's centre was quite distant from the bulk of its landed wealth, while the majority of its people lived outside the centre's fortified walls where law and order rather than banditry and rebellion prevailed. The Kingdom was a stable and peaceful place, where only two crises were recorded over four and a half centuries prior to the Mongol attacks of the late thirteenth century.

Since the kingdom's wealth – essentially irrigated padi land and labour – was dispersed over a wide area rather than concentrated in the capital, even if the latter were conquered its economy would not have collapsed. Pagan did not have a central vault filled with precious stones and metals; it consisted of rice fields dispersed throughout the kingdom. The bulk of the grain produced in the country (its 'GDP' as it were) largely remained where it was produced, and need not (indeed did not) physically move to the capital, except perhaps for a portion for security against siege.

What really 'moved' were the *rights* to that wealth, and in the opposite direction: from the king to his provincial governors as part of their responsibilities and payment. Hence there was little need for good roads and the kinds of infrastructure for physically moving large amounts of heavy goods from the provinces to the centre. And if one of the centres of agrarian wealth (such as Kyaukse) was taken – and that never happened in Pagan's history – there were still the Minbu and Mu Valleys left untouched. Similarly with labour, the kingdom's other source of wealth; it was also dispersed over the land. If an enemy raided the Pagan kingdom for people it would have to settle for the number taken only from the place it conquered; just a portion of the entire population. Thus even a direct conquest of the capital did not mean the kingdom would have collapsed.

That configuration of state and society was precisely what allowed the kingdom and dynasty of Pagan to survive for four and a half centuries. And when central authority did *disintegrate* in the late thirteenth and early fourteenth centuries, it was this same configuration (of dispersed wealth and power) that saved Burmese state and society from disappearing into oblivion.

THE DECLINE OF PAGAN

The 'decline' of the Kingdom of Pagan, then, meant its inability to any longer maintain its integrated character. It does not mean the towns and cities, the cultivated fields and their farmers, the soldiers and their stockades, the artisans and craftsmen, the monks and their monasteries, the temples and their devotees, the communities of occupational and social groups, or even the royalty and elite, all disappeared.

So also the less tangible components of state and society – the conceptual system (beliefs about man and his world, the supernatural, the cosmos); notions of power, legitimacy, authority, acquiescence; and sentiments about social hierarchy, patron–client relations, and the Dry Zone did not disappear. Both the physical and ideological components of Pagan remained to do what they had always done; only they were no longer *integrated* under one centre.

Decline, therefore, was not so much 'decay' or disappearance of the institutions and ideologies of state and society in absolute terms, but the fact that they were no longer held together by one authority. That inability to hold the state together, the *dis*-integration, was caused by 'remote' long-term structural factors as well as 'immediate' short-term historical events. The most important of the former was the 'structural contradiction' that had developed between church and state; while the latter mainly refers to the activities of the Mongols and the chain of domestic events they generated.

Panorama of Pagan, 1980s.

'REMOTE' STRUCTURAL CAUSES

More specifically, by the last three (or so) decades of the thirteenth century, the monumental temple construction programme and general patronage of the Sangha, which had initially enhanced the growth and development of the Pagan kingdom, had become a liability. Since most religious donations were given and kept in perpetuity, once that wealth became church property it could no longer be used for state purposes. And after 400 years of wealth continuously flowing to the tax-exempt sector, by the late thirteenth century nearly 63 per cent of the then cultivated land and a large proportion of hereditary labour, along with much silver and gold, had become tax-exempt religious property. This is demonstrated by the chart provided whose data reflects all the currently known, original stone inscriptions of Pagan.

The state could not confiscate this wealth without violating the belief system on which its own legitimacy lay, nor would it destroy the Sangha militarily, as was the case in Japan where the religious sector was also armed, and therefore met in kind. In Myanmar monks are not even allowed to physically touch money, while their monasteries were not armed stockades guarded by military retainers. Because the use of force against the Sangha could not be condoned the state dealt with the problem *ritually*.

And the most effective ritual, sanctified by religious law itself, was *sasana* reform that would return the religion to its original 'purity'. This was done by purging the scriptures of 'false doctrine' and the Sangha of corrupt elements, especially princes who had taken sanctuary in monasteries just waiting for the opportunity to rebel. It was easy to prove unorthodoxy and corruption of the Sangha, for the wealth held by the Sangha obviously violated its own vows of poverty and asceticism. *Sasana* reform also addressed the needs of genuinely reform-minded segments of the Sangha who continued to live by the tenets of orthodoxy, so that the state had the support not only of the most orthodox members of the Order, but of like-minded lay devotees.

The complicated procedures and scale of *sasana* reform required the prestige and might of the state behind it if it were to be successful, as well as a strong king, for there would be fierce opposition to it from groups whose economic interests would be deleteriously affected. *Sasana* reform allowed the king to declare problematic segments of the Sangha 'impure', defrock them and legally confiscate their property, returning both to secular jurisdictions. Successful *sasana* reform also effectively transformed the entrenched Sangha hierarchy in favour of a more orthodox group headed by the king's favourites.

In other words *sasana* reform not only purified the doctrine and the Sangha it recouped some of the state's economic resources, pared down

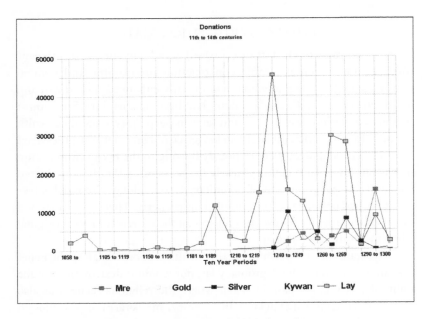

Religious donations to the Sangha, 11th–13th centuries.

the size of the Sangha, overturned the previous hierarchy in favour of the state and removed a dangerous political sanctuary, all without undermining the king's role as chief patron of the Religion or society's as a community of devout Buddhists. It was as much a political and economic counterbalancing mechanism to limit or inhibit the runaway growth of an already entrenched, wealthy, powerful, large and established church as it was a genuine religious reform.

Yet *sasana* reform was only a temporary measure for the state's economic and political problems, for as the re-ordained Sangha was considered more orthodox and 'pure' and since the quality of merit accrued from patronizing pure monks was superior to that obtained from patronizing 'impure' ones, donations to the Sangha tended to increase rather than decrease after purification. Indeed the successors of reformer kings, benefiting from their fuller coffers and fewer tax-exempt lands, would donate even more to the new Order to prove their own greater legitimacy.

In time, then, the 'purified' Sangha would become much like its predecessor that had been reformed: wealthy and powerful. The whole process of wealth flow to the church and tax-exempt sector, along with the problems for the state associated with it, would begin again. For as long as the legitimation of state and society was dependent on the patronage and promotion of the Sangha in *economic* ways, and the material and demographic resources of the inland agrarian state more or less remained stable, the problem of wealth devolution to the tax-exempt sector would recur.

On the one hand, then, state and Sangha had a symbiotic ideological relationship; on the other, they were competing for the same finite material resources. This 'structural contradiction' between state and Sangha continued well into the twentieth century and persists today, albeit on a smaller scale.[12]

IMMEDIATE EVENTS

Towards the end of the thirteenth century the drain of state resources to the tax-exempt sector had weakened central authority, making it more vulnerable to 'incidents of the moment'; that is, events. In this case it was the Mongol attacks, which also provided opportunities for domestic centres of power to strike out for autonomy. During the last several decades of the thirteenth and beginning of the fourteenth centuries the Mongols made three forays into the upper reaches of the Pagan kingdom, while Muttama, one of Pagan's most important governorships in Lower Myanmar, declared its independence.

Yet the Mongols were *not* successful in destroying the Kingdom of Pagan in any of their three attacks; in fact, they never reached the capital city itself, as the current convention has it.[13] But they did *accelerate* the long-term trends and patterns already in progress, exacerbating them further. The resources and energy spent in the defence of the kingdom also exacted a heavy toll on state and society, which when combined with the already depleted treasury was a burden from which the dynasty could not recover intact.

In short the Kingdom of Pagan declined because the factors that had nurtured it in the first place became, in time, forces that contradicted and destroyed it. The seeds that sowed the destruction of Pagan are what earlier made its success possible, and the institutions that led to prosperity and power eventually involuted and impoverished the state. What had been a blessing had become a curse. But because Pagan society was unable (and unwilling) to change what were once constructive forces when they became destructive ones – creating an 'inexorable dialectic' – the political power of the dynasty collapsed.[14]

Henceforth, with one short exception, every capital after Pagan until the colonial period would be located in the dry central plains of the country, dependent upon surrounding oases of intensively irrigated tracts of land. Inland and agrarian, with trade playing a subordinate role in the acquisition of wealth, and the swamps of Lower Myanmar not yet drained and filled to be a factor in the economy, the wealth (hence, power) of the Burmese state would continue to rely on agriculture for another six centuries. Whereas trade was 'only' *important*, agriculture was *vital*; the principle upon which nearly every dynasty and kingdom in pre-colonial Myanmar's history was based.[15] It was here in this demanding and limiting material environment that the first kingdom of Myanmar emerged, and it was also here that the last ended.

5

Ava and Pegu:
A Tale of Two Kingdoms

When the great Kingdom of Pagan declined politically in the late thirteenth and early fourteenth centuries, Upper Myanmar separated into three main centres of power, each led by a member of the ex-royal family. Meanwhile, Lower Myanmar, now independent of Upper Myanmar's hegemony, began the process of state-formation for the first time. During the next half-century this 'transitional' situation continued until two kingdoms emerged: the First Inwa (Ava) Kingdom founded in 1364, and the First Pegu Kingdom of 1385. Both began in the late thirteenth century, reached their pinnacles in the fifteenth and declined before the first half of the sixteenth century had ended.

The history of the state in Myanmar during those centuries is about the relationship between these two kingdoms: one inland, agrarian and old, the other coastal, commercial and new. Although both kingdoms had relations with other places, the most dominant, sustained and important one in fifteenth-century Myanmar was that between Ava and Pegu. It was a classic Southeast Asian 'upstream–downstream' *geo-political dualism* – rather than a *binary ethnic* struggle as convention has it – epitomizing one of the most important patterns in the history of early Myanmar and Southeast Asia.[1] What that relationship did (among other things in Myanmar's history) was to open up a new option for subsequent dynasties to consider: a balanced polity of agriculture and trade that challenged the long-held tradition of agrarian domination by the interior, an idea that had an impact on the behaviour of future leaders and their dynasties. Before discussing that dualism between Ava and Pegu in greater detail, however, their individual histories need to be summarized.

ORIGINS AND DEVELOPMENT OF AVA

The Ava period, commonly dated between 1364 and 1527, represents a significant gap in Myanmar's historiography, yet to see a single book-length monograph in English. What little has been written characterizes these years as 'a period of fragmentation'; a 'dark age' of 'civil war'; a 'bedlam of snarling Shan states'; and a 'welter of barbarism'. It has also been depicted as 'a century of unrest' and 'the most troubled period of Burmese history'.[2] Perhaps most important to the historiography of Myanmar, the Ava kingdom has long been regarded as a *new* Shan polity that had replaced the Burmese kingdom of Pagan, thereby creating a historical niche for the Shan (T'ai) speakers in the making of modern Myanmar.

Although there are slivers of historicity in this perspective, it is neither sound analytically nor accurate historically, the most recent research suggesting an entirely different picture.[3] The fourteenth and fifteenth centuries in Upper Myanmar were actually an era of important religious, administrative, military and especially literary accomplishments, when 'barbarism', fragmentation, unrest and disintegration were far less prominent than integration, sophistication in culture, peace and stability – the latter representing nearly a century and a half of history, the former only a few intermittent decades. Most evident, Ava was an old Burmese kingdom (Pagan) resurrected, not a new and decadent Shan kingdom recently created.

Indeed, the very notion that Ava had lapsed into a 'dark, medieval' era, representing a distinct break from the cultural and political achievements of its predecessor, Pagan, and the military and economic accomplishments of its successor, Toungoo, is ultimately based on the conceptualization and organization of *Western* history into classical, medieval and modern periods, a colonial construct that simply does not fit Myanmar's history.[4]

It is true that the initial years following Pagan's 'decline' in Upper Myanmar were characterized by a certain amount of political and economic instability. At the same time, however, three powerful governorships that had been under Pagan – Sagaing, Pinya and Myin Saing – assumed central authority shortly after the Kingdom's decline to provide some regional stability and peace. These three centres were held by the famous 'Three Brothers' – Yazathingyan, Athinkhaya and Thihathu – ministers of the Pagan court who, with their descendants, re-established and reformulated the structural principles of the Pagan kingdom over the next several decades. Instead of competing for supremacy the Three Brothers cooperated, turning that region into the dominant political centre of Upper Myanmar for several centuries.

The shift of the centre of gravity northeast from Pagan to these three centres addressed an important concern of every Upper Myanmar kingdom: invasion from the north down the Irrawaddy valley. The 'P'iao' were invaded in the ninth century from the north by Nanchao, Pagan fought unnamed 'enemies' from the north in the early twelfth century, and in the late thirteenth century it was again invaded from the north by the Mongols, all of these attacks moving along the same general routes. Pagan's leadership had realized this problem early on, and it was the reason Aniruddha built the line of 43 forts on that route of invasion down the valley of the Irrawaddy. But after Pagan declined Upper Myanmar's leaders had little choice but to move even closer to the north, for they had to be right next to the two main economic resources of the land – Kyaukse and the Mu Valley – in order to maintain their hold over them.

The Pagan system which the Three Brothers resurrected eventually crystallized mid-century with the Kingdom of Ava, which became part of the 'national' standard for Burmese society thenceforth. The organization of king and court; the administration of provinces and villages; the arrangement of society into attached and unattached groups; the agrarian, redistributive nature of the economy; the principles of jurisprudence and structure of the justice system; the role and place of the Sangha and religious affairs in state and society; the ideologies of the conceptual system were all virtual replicas of Pagan's. At the same time the demographic and material environment of Ava society remained essentially the same. Thus the First Ava Kingdom was *not* a new 'Shan kingdom' but a new-old Burmese one.[5]

Not a single inscription recovered so far erected by royalty or commoner; not a single stanza of verse (of many) composed and not a single sentence in any royal edict proclaimed, administrative and provincial record submitted, legal code compiled, cadastral survey taken, political or religious treatise produced or religious donation made during the Ava period was written in the Shan (or T'ai) language. All genres of writing at all levels of society throughout the entire kingdom during its life (and beyond) were written in Old Burmese. It was Ava's *lingua franca* and the written language of state and society; hence the majority of the population of Ava was composed of Burmese speakers, whose culture was also prevailing, accounting (in part) for Ava's obvious achievements in Burmese literature.[6]

The crucial difference between Pagan and Ava, then, was *quantitative* not *qualitative*: in size and scale, wealth and power, influence and image. In short, Ava was Pagan writ small.[7] There were few other options available for the new leaders of Upper Myanmar in any case. Since they chose to remain in the 'heartland' they inherited the same material environment and demographic base, along with the same agrarian economy, social and political organization, religion and cosmology, language and alphabet; in other words, the same system. Obviously there was new leadership but it too was drawn largely from the old royal families. And as they knew no other structure by which to guide state and society they simply resurrected and reformulated old principles and institutions.

In the late 1350s and early 1360s Syam (Shan) raids on Sagaing and its environs (held by Yazathingyan's family, the eldest of the Three Brothers) upset the status quo, threatening disintegration of the inchoate kingdom. But the Shan only raided, looted and left, leaving the area in chaos and its leadership in doubt. So, in 1364, Thadominbya, the governor of Tagaung (a provincial centre farther north), claiming descent from Yazathingyan's family, marched downriver to re-establish order and the 'royal' line. And at a site across the river from Sagaing he founded the city of Ava, which became the capital of the First Ava Kingdom and Dynasty.

Inwa, as it was known in Old Burmese, lay right at the confluence of the Irrawaddy and Myitnge Rivers. This location gave it close and direct control of the richest rice growing region in the land – Kyaukse – crucial to anyone with visions of unifying all of Myanmar. At the same time Thadominbya realized that Ava had to have better defences than Sagaing did. So he deliberately turned the urban area of Ava into a makeshift island. On the city's north and west lay the Irrawaddy, while on its east was the Myitnge River which flowed north into the Irrawaddy, so that Ava was naturally surrounded on three sides by water. On the fourth (and south) side the king dug a canal between the Myintge and a stream already present that ran west into the Irrawaddy. That surrounded the larger metropolitan area of Ava on all four sides with a formidable natural-cum-man-made moat. Within this was built the walled palace-city itself with another moat around it that manipulated the river systems, as seen in the satellite image.

Satellite image of the capital city of Ava, 15th century.

Although Thadominbya (*reg.* 1364–8) died (of smallpox) within four years of establishing the First Ava Dynasty, fortunately he was followed by a succession of able rulers. Minkyiswa Sawke (1368–1401), the governor of an important town in the Dry Zone, who succeeded him, relentlessly pursued the consolidation of Ava. He focused on creating alliances with the Shan Sawbwas, building and repairing the irrigation works in the Kyaukse Valley and establishing good relations with Pegu's Binnya U. However, it did not last, for Yazadarit (1385–1423) came to the throne in Lower Myanmar and asserted Pegu's growing might, which challenged Ava's for several more decades to come.

Mingyiswa Sawke died at the ripe old age of 70. After the usual struggles for the throne, it was won by one of his sons, known as Mingaung the First (1401–22). He continued the consolidation begun by his predecessors, particularly that of his father, who had saved Ava from premature collapse after Thadominbya's untimely death. Mingaung re-established relations with Pegu, to the extent that his relations with Yazadarit became legendary. Indeed, when Mingaung died, Yazadarit followed him within the year, allowing the chronicles to embellish their story as a case of two 'soul mates' on opposite sides.

The 'founding fathers' of Ava were followed by other extraordinary and able kings – with brief intermittent exceptions – who took the kingdom to greater heights. Nearly all the data for this period comes from over 300 Old Burmese inscriptions erected at Ava and other literary sources of the period, along with a short narrative of the travels of Niccolò de Conti, a merchant of Venice who visited the city in the 1430s.

Of Ava's early kings, the reign of 'Narapati the Great' (1443–69), remembered as the 'donor of the Htupayon Pagoda' by the chronicles, best represents the efflorescence and zenith of the Kingdom of Ava. Politically, militarily, culturally and religiously, Ava during the fifteenth century was, relatively speaking, exemplary. Apart from the 'birth' of Burmese vernacular literature (which began prior to Narapati's reign), his economic relations with others (especially in porcelain and rubies) and diplomatic contacts with China were important, while his religious contacts with Sri Lanka were also noteworthy. Narapati's domestic achievements include building a bridge (possibly a pontoon bridge) across the Irrawaddy between Ava and Sagaing, on which, he declared in an original inscription, the four-fold army could cross abreast.

He was followed by Mingaung the Second (1481–1502), another capable leader. His reign began to show some signs of political and military effeteness in the provinces, as Toungoo, one of Ava's governorships, grew stronger by the decade and in time came to challenge Ava's authority. In 1486 Ava's *myosa* appointed there was assassinated by his nephew, Minkyinyo, who was to become the founder of what subsequently became the great Toungoo Dynasty that would attain military achievements hitherto unmatched in the history of Myanmar and mainland Southeast Asia. Mingaung had little choice but to 'reappoint' Minkyinyo as Ava's governor to Toungoo. But such incidents emboldened other princes and governors to do the same.

Yet the political and military problems appear to be out of character with the outstanding literary figures and literature produced during that time, suggesting peace and stability (at least) at the centre. The names of Shin Uttamagyaw, Shin Thilawuntha, Shin Maharattathara (all monks or ex-monks) and (during Mingyiswa Sawke's reign) Wunzinminyaza, a learned minister to three successive kings, are exemplars in the history of Burmese literature. Some of the (mainly) religious works of the former three are considered unmatched to this day, while the latter's most well-known treatise is a unique historical–cum–political work that became a model for future scholars. There were also several women writers in the male-dominated court of Ava who excelled in poetry. Two of them are celebrated for their poems on religious subjects, while one maid of honour, Yaweshinhtwe, wrote an *angyin* poem on the 55 hairstyles used by Ava's maids of honour. (These hairstyles have been reproduced and are currently displayed in the Pagan archaeological museum.)

By most measures the zenith of the Kingdom of Ava was approximately the fifteenth century (including the first two decades of the sixteenth). It was a time when Ava was politically and militarily dominant in Upper Myanmar, and although not nearly as large as the Pagan kingdom had been – for it did not have Lower Myanmar and its maritime regions – it nonetheless exercised considerable influence over Lower and Western Myanmar as well as the northern highlands. It was a time when the court was resplendent and Ava considered a model Buddhist kingdom by its peers, when its military force was strong enough to (twice) repel invasions by Chinese forces and hold at bay the 'Syam' and other domestic competitors such as Pegu. In the cultural sphere, as noted above, not only did Ava produce brilliant Burmese poetry and other forms of literature, it also built hundreds of temples and monasteries and produced fine works in the arts and crafts. Then in approximately two decades, Ava lost it all. How and why did that happen?

DECLINE OF AVA

The causes for Ava's decline are varied but, as with Pagan's, they were a combination of 'remote' and 'immediate' factors. The first are structural and institutional in nature that had been ongoing for a considerable period of time, while the second are 'incidents of the moment' – crises that can occur any time. It is their 'conjuncture' – when they come together at a particular time – that triggers the 'critical mass' needed to generate substantive change.

Of the 'remote' factors, the devolution of wealth in the form of cash, labour and productive land from the state to the Sangha was still the problem it was during the Pagan period. As long as the merit-path to salvation remained the primary social and political ideology of Ava state and society wealth continued to flow to the religious sector, creating the kinds of problems already discussed. Although the absolute amount of wealth that moved to the tax-exempt sector was less than it was during the Pagan Dynasty, relatively speaking, Ava's percentage was equally as high.

Another 'remote' factor in Ava's decline was the perpetual factionalism at court, created by a plethora of legitimate claimants to the throne especially when succession became an issue. The primary contenders around which these factions coalesced were (usually) the eldest sons and younger brothers of the king: the invariable uncle–nephew struggle. And when coupled with the dwindling of material resources the situation was only exacerbated.

At the heart of this factionalism lay the patron–client system based on the personal loyalty of individuals less than the authority of institutions. Yet this same patron–client principle was the administrative and political basis for the structure of the *myosa* ('to eat') system used to govern and provide stability to the kingdom and its provinces. In times of crisis and during occasions when, at maximum, approximately twenty miles a day could be covered by a large contingent of troops if moving by land (although in a fraction of that time by water), it made perfectly good sense to assign royal favourites and supporters certain strategic towns and cities that were more or less evenly distributed over the kingdom. From any one of these centres crown troops assigned to each *myosa* could reach any other *myosa*-ship (invariably the nucleus of any rebellion) very quickly, taking no more than one day from each of the 50-odd *myosa*-ships known to have existed during the kingdom.

Thus while the *myosa* system helped stabilize and integrate the polity at its inception when human and material resources were fragmented and conditions unstable, the same structure also provided the wherewithal for instability once the kingdom had expanded and grown. In fact every domestic rebellion during the Ava period (indeed during *all* of pre-colonial Burmese history) was an elite (usually princely) affair, not a genuine peasant rebellion for and led by peasants.

In these essentially elite contests the throne was the ultimate prize. They were not conducted on behalf of presumed downtrodden masses nor were they revolts for independence by the periphery against the centre. Rather, they were contests between and amongst elites, where centres

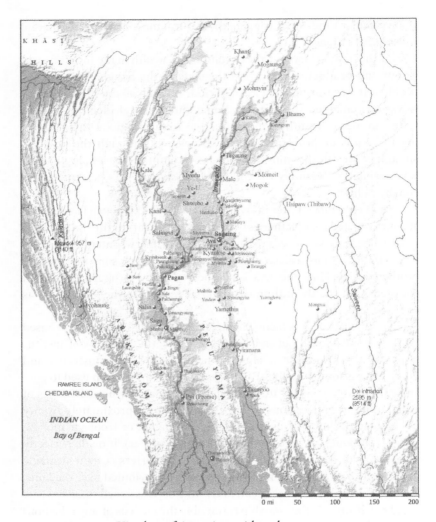

Kingdom of Ava at its zenith, 15th century.

vied with centres. In each case the leader of the rebellion was usually royalty who either wanted the throne for himself (or herself), for someone else he (or she) supported, or to deny it to the holder and/or formal heir to the throne. Thus the *myosa* system provided as much opportunity for strengthening the state as for weakening it.

The 'immediate' causes for Ava's decline are clearer and less complex, having more to do with 'incidents of the moment', far more unpredictable than the long-term 'remote' factors also at play. When Mingaung the Second died he was succeeded by his son Shwenankyawshin (1502–27) whose reign, though long, was nonetheless troubled, marking the beginning of the end. The relentless rebellions by claimants who had been denied the throne only strengthened the rising centre, Toungoo, with which the disgruntled allied. Most, if not all, of them were motivated by narrow and personal self-interests, with no thought to the viability and/or rejuvenation of the kingdom as a whole. Toungoo's 'chipping away' at Ava's strength also emboldened those Shan Sawbwas who were not its allies, while other centres such as Prome adopted a 'wait-and-see' attitude. Then there were the serendipitous events, such as the untimely death of the brilliant Crown Prince just when things were turning around for Ava, the errant arrow that killed another most talented prince and major crises instigated by some jealous queen over some triviality.

Such activity continued to weaken Ava until in 1527 the Sawbwa of Mohnyin, whose governorship lay at the head of the Mu Valley and its vast irrigated rice fields, finally took the capital. He gave the city to his son Thohanbwa, whom Harvey called 'a full-blooded savage'.[8] He was the first of Ava's tributary Shan chiefs to take the throne in Myanmar. But he was young and inexperienced and had no vision larger than maintaining his own power, demonstrated by his hostile behaviour towards Burmese culture and Buddhism and by his cruelty in general. Thohanbwa was killed by a member of the old Ava court, Minkyiyanaung, who had remained at the capital to serve the new leaders. He refused the throne offered him, preferring instead to enter the monastery. After two more Sawbwas sat on the Ava throne, it was finally retaken by a member of the old Ava court in or about 1553, who held it until King Bayinnaung of Pegu, in 1555, reunified the country, the story of the next chapter.

Thus the so-called 'Shan Period' in the history of Myanmar did not begin until 1527, and ended after a mere 24 years, so that its historical impact on Ava (and the country as a whole) was fleeting and insignificant. However, its impact on the historiography of Ava and Myanmar is quite a different issue. Because historians considered Ava to have been a major shift in the history of the state from Burmese to Shan rule – labelling the era the 'Shan period' in Myanmar's history – it was given a historical significance it never had. That, in turn, had enormous implications for the country's modern history in the politics of post-Independence Myanmar whereby the (alleged) role of the Shan in the country's history was used to gain special concessions in the Constitution of 1947, which in turn had serious repercussions in the subsequent decades that resulted in one of the immediate causes of the coup of 1962, a topic to be discussed in chapter Twelve.

What is actually more interesting historiographically about this short Shan rule is that the Burmese chroniclers included these three Shan Sawbwas in the formal list of Ava kings at all, acknowledging their legitimate membership in what was in essence a Burmese dynasty. What this suggests is that the ultimate criterion for determining a legitimate dynasty was not ethnicity (as so often claimed) or even genealogy but *sacred place*. Ava was sacred because it had received a Buddha prophecy, and whoever ruled from there, Shan or Burmese, was considered legitimate. It was Ava that gave its rulers legitimacy.[9]

When the city fell in 1527 many people fled to other important governorships, not to the 'hills' or the 'periphery' as alleged by some. The largest number was reported to have sought haven in Toungoo further south, swelling its population thereafter with the most prized possession in early Southeast Asia: labour. Not only had these refugees lost their king and royal family – the sustainer of their culture, the patron of their religion and economic livelihood, the model for their social and political beliefs – but also their path to nirvana, as many of the Sangha had also fled. The exodus included the best writers, philosophers, religious virtuosos, musicians and artists, as well as the most experienced administrators of the kingdom – ministers and advisers – and, of course, the most militarily talented. It was a huge 'brain-drain' from Ava to other centres, especially Toungoo.

With these human resources Toungoo soon became the premier centre in Upper Myanmar. Minkyinyo established his own dynasty there, tracing its genealogy back to Pagan and Ava as legitimation. Ava's loss, then, was Toungoo's gain; had Ava not been taken by the Shan Sawbwas, the great Toungoo Dynasty that conquered much of Southeast Asia in the sixteenth century, including (ironically) nearly all the Sawbwaships, might never have materialized.

But at the time, in the first half of the sixteenth century, Toungoo remained hemmed in, with Ava to its north and Pegu to its south. None of the three centres of power seems to have had the desire or the wherewithal to unify the country at the time. Subsequently the burgeoning of trade and commerce in the maritime regions of Southeast Asia, including Lower Myanmar, would change all that. Meanwhile, Ava, once the exemplary centre in the country, had become just another centre.

THE AVA LEGACY

Apart from the literary accomplishments mentioned above, the First Ava Kingdom was significant in the history of Myanmar in at least two other ways. First, by preventing Pagan's total dismemberment Ava was able not only to retain intact the latter's human and material resources but its traditions and institutions that provided the wherewithal to subsequently reunify Myanmar by the peoples and cultures belonging (or who believed they belonged to) the Pagan Burmese tradition. The First Ava Dynasty and period was thus the bridge between 'Classical' and 'Early Modern' Myanmar.

Second, had the Kingdom of Ava not become the centre in 1364 of a formidable and distinct military, political and cultural barrier at that particular time and place it might not have been able to prevent and divert the massive migration of T'ai speakers during their 200-year *drang nach suden* down the river valleys of western and central mainland Southeast Asia to the coasts of Lower Myanmar. Had that not happened, the Burmese speakers would have been either absorbed to become a large minority group, integrated into an even larger nation-state whose national language and culture would be Shan/T'ai or would have been pushed farther south, in turn pushing the Mon and Karen speakers into what is now southern Thailand and the northern parts of Malaysia, possibly altering the geo-political and ethno-demographic composition of the Upper Malay archipelago and Thailand (hence, their histories) forever.

In short, had Ava not been where it was when it was Thailand today might be the largest country in mainland Southeast Asia, stretching from the borders of India to Cambodia. And since that did not happen, why it did not is a reasonable question that should have been asked had the Ava kingdom been a 'Shan' polity since the end of the Pagan dynasty as convention has it.

THE ORIGINS AND DEVELOPMENT OF PEGU

Recent historical research suggests that Lower Myanmar prior to the eleventh century was the 'frontier' for Upper Myanmar, a 'backwater', inhospitable for the most part, consisting largely of marshes and swamps.[10] The only known settlements that existed at the time were the small port-towns that had emerged during the Urban Period of the first millennium AD whose ethno-linguistic make-up is not known.

But by the mid-eleventh century Aniruddha's conquest and Kyanzit-tha's pacification of the south had established new urban settlements there. Linguistic and historical evidence suggests that the Burmese speakers were responsible for this second wave of settlements in Lower Myanmar. Some of the most important of these were located in areas with commercial promise: coastal towns with direct access to the Gulf of Muttama and the Bay of Bengal, as well as to points southward and the rest of maritime Southeast Asia. As the twelfth and thirteenth century progressed the region came more and more under Pagan's control.

One of the most important of these towns was Muttama, located where the Thanlyin (Salween) River empties into the Gulf of Muttama. It was founded by King Narapatisithu of Pagan in the late twelfth century, one of whose inscriptions also mentions Pagan's control of the region south of Muttama, the Tenasserim Peninsula. Muttama's main regional competitor in Lower Myanmar was Pegu, a nearby governorship first mentioned in Old Burmese epigraphy (as Payku) only in the 1260s, with no dated original evidence to prove that it was any older. Pegu was thus a relatively new settlement and an extension of the interior, not an old polity going back to the Buddha's time, as convention would have it in the myth of Ramannadesa.

Its governors were likely appointees of the Pagan court who were sometimes members of the royal family. They administered the kingdom's affairs and supplied the revenue and manpower needs of Upper Myanmar by taking advantage of this earlier 'Age of Commerce' between the eleventh and thirteenth centuries, stimulated by south India, Sri Lanka and several maritime regions of Southeast Asia that had been part of the old Empire of Sri Vijaya.

When, in the late thirteenth century, Pagan lost its hold over Lower Myanmar because of the Mongol incursions on the northern border, Muttama struck out for independence. Pegu chose to rebel at the same time. Both then contested for regional supremacy which Muttama won, led by one Wagaru (also known as Wareru, *reg.* 1287–96), said to be of either Shan or Mon background and descended from a she-demon. Towards the last decade of the thirteenth century Muttama became the dominant power in Lower Myanmar under the new Wagaru Dynasty. Shortly thereafter it sought (and received) recognition from China as an independent kingdom. In short the coasts of Lower Myanmar evolved from an undeveloped and sparsely populated swampy region to one that would later contest power with an established Upper Myanmar. Unlike Ava, therefore, Muttama's rise was not a matter of resurrecting something old but beginning something relatively new.

Of whatever ethnic (or supernatural) background, this was the first time in the history of Lower Myanmar that a polity ruled by a 'dynasty' and independent of Upper Myanmar had emerged. Much of Muttama's historical (and legendary) relations lay with T'ai centres located east of it, especially Sukhotai and Chiang Mai. Indeed, Wagaru's claims to royalty had nothing to do with Lower Myanmar (as there was no tradition there at the time to which he could be linked) but with Sukhotai, one of the first 'kingdoms' founded by T'ai speakers. He was said to have eloped with the daughter of the King of Sukhotai, which (by marriage) gave him the royal credentials he needed, along with a white elephant given him subsequently. Unlike Ava, which had 400 years of Pagan tradition to which it could tie its genealogy (real or imagined), Lower Myanmar had none, so sought it amongst demons and T'ai traditions.

Finally, by the second quarter of the fourteenth century, in 1385, within two decades of Ava's rise as a new kingdom, the centre of authority in Lower

Myanmar shifted from Muttama to Pegu. Although the reasons given in the Mon chronicles for this shift were metaphorical, geo-politically, however, Pegu had better natural defences than Muttama, which was more vulnerable to attacks (or control) from the T'ai speaking areas that were rapidly developing on its East with Ayuthaya's rise, as well as the Malay-speaking areas south of it since the decline of Sri Vijaya and the rise of Melaka. Pegu was farther inland so that an invader from coastal Southeast Asia would have to negotiate difficult terrain just to reach it, whereas Muttama was right on the Gulf and could be attacked (in the back) from Ayuthaya through the Three Pagodas Pass via land, as well as from the open sea from any direction.

But this shift to Pegu was important domestically as well, for once again it came under the orbit of Upper Myanmar and its political and economic interests, now within easy physical reach of Toungoo and Prome via the Irrawaddy and Sittaung river valleys. Had Muttama's leadership not moved to Pegu (thereby returning it to the politics of Upper Myanmar), the Tenasserim Peninsula today might well be part of modern Thailand rather than Myanmar.

Pegu's leaders made certain, however, that its genealogical ties with Muttama and its 'royal' line from Wagaru were preserved. Binnya U (*reg.* 1353–85), although considered to be the founder of a new Pegu Dynasty, nevertheless considered himself to be the last of the Wagaru

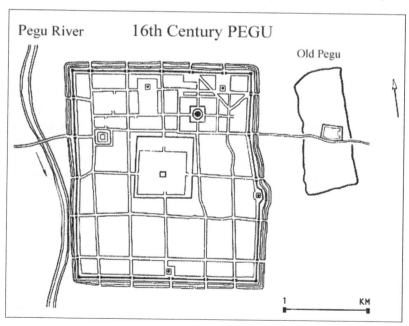

Old and new city of Pegu, mid-13th to 16th century.

line. Beginning as a small provincial centre, Pegu subsequently expanded into a strong kingdom under a militarily endowed and talented king, the famous Rajadarit (Yazadarit, 1385–1423), who succeeded Binnya U to become a serious contender for the control of Myanmar.

Thereafter the Kingdom of Pegu grew to religious and cultural heights hitherto unknown in Lower Myanmar, particularly under two of Yazadarit's successors, Shin Saw Bu (c. 1453–72), the only documented woman sovereign in the country's history and her 'son-in-law', King Dhammazedi (1472–92). Shin Saw Bu was known for her piety and patronage of the Religion and Dhammazedi for his reform of the Sangha. (It was he who in the late fifteenth century began the myth of Ramannadesa, claiming that this 'Camelot' of the Mon speakers went back to the time of King Asoka, the quintessential period and king in Buddhism's history.)

There is not much recorded in original sources about the monarchs who followed Shin Saw Bu and Dhammazedi, although enough is known to suggest that after a period of cavalierly reaping the harvest sowed by the latter two rather than using these resources to strengthen the kingdom, Pegu began its downward spiral. Then when the Portuguese arrived with their superior firearms and scientific technology – disrupting the balance of power in the region – and Toungoo began to challenge Pegu's place as premier port on the coasts of Lower Myanmar under the militarily brilliant Tabinshwehti, the First Pegu Dynasty could not hold itself together any longer.

DECLINE OF PEGU

Much like Pagan and Ava, Pegu's decline echoed some of the patterns and trends evident earlier: the flow of state wealth to the tax-exempt Sangha and the patron–client system at its worst. At Pegu the former was less in the form of land than cash and other liquid assets, garnered from the growth in trade and commerce that the maritime world of Southeast Asia was enjoying. Nonetheless, whether cash or land, the economic effects were just as deleterious. As for the patron–client system, the loss of revenues to the Sangha only exacerbated the omnipresent factionalism, as loyalty to individuals continued to pre-empt institutional authority. Not surprisingly, succession struggles at the Pegu court were also mainly between uncles and nephews, suggesting that the political institutions underlying kingship there were quite similar to those of Ava.

In terms of the 'immediate causes' for Pegu's decline, simply put, it had become too important to be left independent. To reiterate, the growing Toungoo Dynasty located at the edge of the Dry Zone on the Sittaung River (strategically poised just a few days' march north of Pegu) had benefited from Ava's demise in 1527 when large numbers of its population fled to it for safety and patronage. Its leaders, in their efforts to unify the country, had decided to take the commercial coasts first rather than the agrarian interior, reversing what had been the established pattern of taking the agrarian interior before unifying the rest of the country. Pegu's strategic location, at a time in coastal Southeast Asia when trade and commerce was expanding tremendously, simply could not be ignored.

Thus, in 1539, one of the most militarily talented and successful kings of Myanmar, Tabinshwehti (*reg.* 1531–50) of the Toungoo royal family,

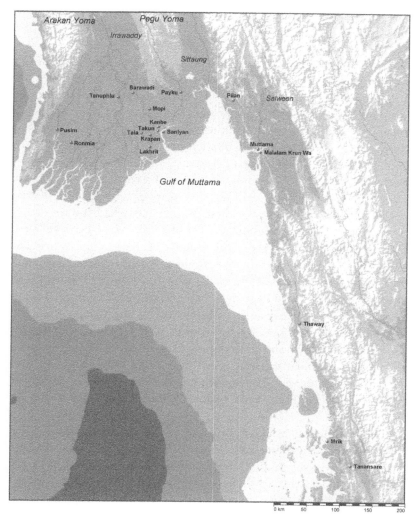

Kingdom of Pegu at its zenith, 15th century.

took the city of Pegu and politically and administratively incorporated it into his own kingdom. The event was not a case of destruction but one of assimilation, whereby the institutions, people, culture and society of a maritime commercial society were absorbed by a Dry Zone agrarian one. Subsequently the city of Pegu became de facto capital as Tabinshwehti moved his operations there from Toungoo, for the growth of trade and commerce in Lower Myanmar had grown too important to be managed from Upper Myanmar. Although known as the Toungoo Dynasty (and kingdom) in the English-language historiography of Myanmar, we here call it the Second Pegu/Toungoo Dynasty (and kingdom) for obvious reasons.

PEGU'S LEGACY

Pegu was the first capital of a bona fide Lower Myanmar kingdom. It was also the first time that the region economically and militarily challenged Upper Myanmar domination, even if temporarily. Further, the maritime values steeped in trade and commerce of Lower Myanmar opened the eyes of agrarian Myanmar, introduced Westerners and their culture and offered trade and commerce as a viable supplement (even option) for maintaining the state. And in Shin Saw Bu, as noted above, Pegu could also claim the only documented woman sovereign in the country's history.

Perhaps as important, the First Pegu Dynasty had laid the structural foundations for the establishment of the Second Pegu/Toungoo Dynasty. Most notably the achievements of the militarily brilliant Yazadirit, his strategies and tactics, diplomatic skill and single-minded focus were unparalleled in the early history of Lower Myanmar. The military legacy he left at Pegu must have inspired leaders of the Second Pegu/Toungoo Dynasty such as Tabinshwehti and Bayinnaung (*reg.* 1551–81) who later went on to make Pegu the capital of the most expansive kingdom in the history of mainland Southeast Asia, conquering both its western and central parts, leaving only Cambodia and Vietnam unconquered. The empire was the largest ever in Myanmar and mainland Southeast Asian history, a phenomenon that was never again repeated.

In the sphere of religion, especially under Dhammazedi but also Shin Saw Bu, Pegu attained a stature in Theravada Buddhist orthodoxy of the Sinhalese school that theretofore had been unknown in Lower Myanmar. It was during their reigns that the region's most sacred shrines, the Shwedagon at Yangon and Shwemadaw at Pegu, assumed national stature; they previously had enjoyed only a regional and local reputation. And that national stature continued to sustain the entire country for several centuries well into the twenty-first, until today the situation is once again ambiguous; for when the new political and administrative centre of the country (Naypyidaw) was moved back to the Dry Zone in 2005/6, a new palladium of state was also established in the Uppatatheinti Pagoda ('protection from calamity').[11]

And finally, to reiterate, King Dhammazedi unknowingly created a modern historiographic legacy when he linked his kingdom and Sangha to a mythical Ramannadesa, a myth that remains not only a most important academic but also a highly emotional political issue.[12]

AN UPSTREAM−DOWNSTREAM DUALISM

The individual histories of Ava and Pegu, interesting and valuable in themselves, must also be told in tandem, for Myanmar in the fifteenth century is really a tale of *two* kingdoms. This is particularly true in terms of the contrasting but mutually beneficial geo-political contexts of Upper and Lower Myanmar. It is also true in terms of their economic and military relationship and, in some respects, their culture and identity. In fact the tremendous dynamism of fifteenth-century Myanmar was derived as much from the vitality of each individual environment as from the relationship and interaction between the two.

The fifteenth century was also the first time in the country's documented history that two distinct dynasties ruled two discrete kingdoms that were coterminous, nearly equal in strength, each dominating opposite ends of the main political, economic and demographic artery of the country – the Irrawaddy River valley. That situation had not existed theretofore, so that its consequences on the history of the country were also new. The phenomenon seems to have created as much centrifugal as centripetal energy, providing an equilibrium that defined the period.

Equilibrium, of course, need not imply harmony, but however contentious Ava and Pegu's relationship may seem at times they invariably sought to maintain the status quo. The main reason is that the relationship was based on economic and political necessity, a *modus vivendi* that was in both their interests. In fact Ava attempted to resurrect the old Pagan hegemony over Pegu several times, and there were occasions when the latter responded in kind. Yet neither coveted each other's space particularly, so made no serious attempts to conquer or destroy the other. In other words the history of their political and military relationship does not suggest any genuine desire to eliminate the other.

Besides, unless Pegu were willing and able to conquer the Dry Zone, keep it and maintain its agricultural economy along with its infrastructure – and it was not – it had little choice but to preserve the status quo.

Similarly with Ava: despite political and military behaviour that suggested designs to control Lower Myanmar, in fact it could not, so ended up preserving the status quo as well. Their relationship, therefore, was less an irreconcilable *binary* antithesis of two antagonistic ethnicities, regions and cultures, than it was a workable synthesis in a *dualism* of differences.

In fact, and in general, the true competitors of ('upstream') agrarian states in Myanmar as well as other parts of Southeast Asia were usually not their ('downstream') maritime counterparts but other agrarian states like them, such as Pagan and Angkor. Similarly the maritime states; they rarely, if ever, destroyed their agrarian counterparts but went after one another instead. The Cholas conquered Sri Vijaya, Arakan took Pegu and Dai Viet, Champa. Dissimilar states needed each other's resources in the most important ways, while similar states did not.[13]

One of the more cordial, cooperative and non-violent areas of this dualism was in the sphere of religion. Although Ava's claim to preeminence in Theravada Buddhism outstripped any Pegu could muster, King Dhammazedi's famous fifteenth-century reforms at Pegu were reason enough for respect and perhaps even envy at Ava. And while Dhammazedi publicly invoked exemplary Upper Myanmar kings (such as Aniruddha and Narapatisithu) as models of Buddhist kings, Ava also invited learned monks from Lower Myanmar to grace the capital with their presence.

This was not ideologically difficult for either kingdom, as both believed they had received their Theravada Buddhism from Sri Lanka. Thus when two famous monks in the fifteenth century returned from Sri Lanka, even during a period of antagonism between the two kingdoms, their decision to accept Ava's invitation to reside there rather than in Lower Myanmar was nevertheless honoured by Pegu, which, with great pomp and ceremony, escorted them to Prome, the accepted border between the two kingdoms. In the sphere of religion the 'upstream–downstream' relationship was more than dualistic: it was singular.

Maintaining the political and military status quo and sharing the same belief system does not mean, however, that they were not competitive, that their daily lives were the same or that their views of and dependence on the outside world in all aspects were shared. In terms of the latter Ava and Pegu were importantly *dissimilar*, the result mainly of their respective material environments and the priorities they engendered.

More specifically, Ava appears to have been more provincial, homogeneous and conservative, for its primary concerns were focused on its domestic environment: the maintenance of irrigation works, cultivated fields, agricultural production, control over its precious stones and interior products and the retention of its valuable population of cultivators.

As a result Ava was far more cognizant of rainfall patterns in nearby regions that fed its rivers, and that members of its population, especially the cultivator class, remain in their socio-legal categories, than it was (say) of Muslim invasions of North India or the rise of the Ming in China, which did not directly affect the daily lives of its people.

In contrast Pegu seems to have been more cosmopolitan, heterogeneous and less conservative. Since its economy was dependent upon international and regional commerce it had to be acutely aware of what was happening in the outside world and so was concerned with political and economic trends and patterns in India, China and the rest of Southeast Asia. After all its survival often depended on rebellions in China and invasions of India by external enemies. As a result Pegu was more flexible, adaptable, willing to change, with an outward looking view.

To this 'upstream–downstream' dualism must be added a third complicating component; namely, the hills, adding a 'tripartite' element to the 'dualism'. These hill regions were the real 'interstices' of the Ava–Pegu dualism. But that does not mean they were a non-entity; they comprised an important, distinct, geo-economic, political and demographic component of the whole with a discrete cultural and ethno–linguistic space. In fact, for Ava, especially during the fifteenth century, these hill regions of the north were nearly as important as the maritime coasts and, at particular times, even more so.

Economically these 'interstices' provided the gems, teak, earth-oil, perhaps some of the precious metals, certainly new technology from China (such as firearms) in exchange for lowland rice, foodstuffs of the plains, certain manufactured materials and (to reiterate) 'high culture'.[14] The hills also replenished the labour pool of the plains, particularly in the agricultural and military sectors. When politically allied with Ava they supplied valuable reinforcements in times of war, while during peacetime they were a permanent buffer that blocked the traditional (northern) paths of invasion. Their elite intermarried with Ava royalty to forge some of the more lasting political alliances, whose offspring in time came to be regarded as members of the Burmese court.

Thus although the 'upstream–downstream' relationship in the fifteenth century between Ava and Pegu was more important overall, in select *political* and *military* ways, the relationship between Upper Myanmar and the hills may actually have been more important. And for Ava that relationship turned out to be both a blessing and a curse. For, on the one hand, some of the Shan Sawbwas became reliable allies of the Ava court and helped in numerous ways, including repulsing the 'Chinese' twice in the fifteenth century, and thereafter becoming more or less a permanent buffer in the north against future incursions, as noted above. On the other hand, others of the Sawbwas became strong enough to challenge Ava; indeed, to eventually take the centre in 1527, as Ava always had to always worry about the coasts and was therefore constantly looking over its shoulder at Pegu.

For Pegu these northern hills areas were of little (or no) concern, while the dualism between Upper and Lower Myanmar itself had a different impact on it. Lower Myanmar enjoyed being an independent power for the first time, in contrast to being dominated by Upper Myanmar in the more usual and long-standing single-kingdom situation. As a result one of the most important long-term historical patterns in Myanmar's history since the Pyu period – Dry Zone Paramountcy – was successfully challenged for the first time in the fifteenth century and postponed for nearly two centuries.

And although ultimately both Dry Zone Paramountcy and its con- comitant, Burmese rule, returned and prevailed in the long run, because Pegu was able to successfully prevent Ava's conquest of Lower Myanmar during the fifteenth century the memory of an independent homeland of the Mon was expressed in the idea of an ancient Ramannadesa, with historical, historiographic and political consequences that went far beyond the fifteenth century. It remained thereafter a cause célèbre for aspirations to autonomy by Lower Myanmar in succeeding centuries, and for those who, although living elsewhere in Thailand today, nonetheless identify themselves with the early Mon of Myanmar.

Then, just before the middle of the sixteenth century, within a decade of each other, both Ava and Pegu were taken by two different domestic powers, ending the fifteenth-century 'upstream–downstream' dualism. Whereas Ava remained a fragmented polity for nearly a quarter of a century thereafter – returning to the same old components whence it came although with a new/old power at the helm – Pegu, in contrast, was rejuvenated by a new leadership and dynasty that originated from an old place, Toungoo.

What is important to realize about both these conquests is that neither Ava nor Pegu society was actually destroyed, discarded or eliminated. Rather, their human and material resources were retained, reformulated and reconfigured as much to create something 'new' as to preserve some- thing old.

The history of Ava and Pegu between the mid-fourteenth and first quarter of the sixteenth centuries is thus much more complicated than a simple ethnic rivalry between Burmese, Shan and Mon since time imme- morial, as convention has it. For nearly two centuries that notion has framed the analysis of Myanmar's pre-colonial history. By so doing it turned the relationship between Upper and Lower Myanmar into a *binary and adver- sarial* relationship when it was really *dualistic and symbiotic*.

That, in turn, skewed the chronological contexts in which Ava and Pegu existed by *reversing them* – making Ava new rather than old and Pegu old rather than new. Such historiography had serious consequences, leading to erroneous conclusions about the country's history and misunderstandings about the way in which the nation of Myanmar came into being, still a political bone of contention today.

6

The 'Early Modern' Experiment

After only 24 years the rule of Ava by the Three Shan Sawbwas ended. But Ava did not immediately regain its stature as capital for another half-century, becoming just one of several important centres of Upper Myanmar. Pegu, on the other hand, emerged as the dominant power in the country, absorbed and reinvigorated by the Toungoo Dynasty; hence our name for it – the Second Pegu/Toungoo Dynasty. It proceeded to unite the land once again, regaining both the inland agrarian region (including Ava) and the coasts, looking much like the old Pagan Dynasty in terms of size and power. As a result, both 'Dry Zone Paramountcy' and the 'upstream–downstream dualism' ended temporarily, while for the first (and last) time in the pre-colonial history of the country the capital was in Lower Myanmar.

At its zenith, to reiterate, the Second Pegu/Toungoo Dynasty would conquer all of western and nearly all of central mainland Southeast Asia. Although the kingdom was the largest in terms of territory in the history of Myanmar and mainland Southeast Asia, it was also the shortest lived, for its capital, Pegu, was burned to the ground in 1599. Lower Myanmar thereafter turned into a desolate place while Upper Myanmar revived once again to remain the seat of authority until the end of the monarchy in 1886.

Following Pegu's demise 'Dry Zone Paramountcy' reappeared with the Second Ava and Konbaung Dynasties of Upper Myanmar for the next three centuries, while the 'upstream–downstream dualism' of the sixteenth century ended. However, in the post-colonial history of Myanmar, and as a *binary* relationship, this dualism reappeared one more time. That was when the British conquered the country and shifted the centre of political and economic gravity back to the coasts, making Rangoon de facto capital, reversing a long-term indigenous historical pattern.

But it was temporary. For, in a matter of about 60 years, uncannily similar to the 61 years when Pegu was capital of the country, the political centre in 2005/6 once more moved back to the 'heartland' and the Dry

Zone to Pyinmana, an old governorship north of Toungoo adjacent to which the new capital of Naypyidaw was recently built.[1] That means, of approximately 2,300 years of Myanmar's history, the seat of authority in the country has remained in the Dry Zone for all but 217. Dry Zone Paramountcy, which began during the Urban Period in the early second millennium BC, is once again the prevailing historical pattern in Myanmar today.

THE SECOND PEGU/TOUNGOO DYNASTY: 1539–99

The sixteenth century is often considered the height of the 'Early Modern Period' in Southeast Asian history, particularly for historians who give 'agency' to trade and commerce.[2] The history of especially maritime Southeast Asia during this era is regarded as one of vibrant seaborne commercial activity, in part due to Ming expeditions during the previous two centuries into the region's waters and beyond to the Red Sea and, some would say, North America as well. The Portuguese also played an important role when they entered Southeast Asian waters during the fifteenth century, as did the Spanish who had opened up a pipeline of gold from the New World to the Philippines.

Of course the South Asians, Middle-Easterners and Southeast Asians had never ceased commercial and other seaborne activity in Southeast Asia since the previous millennium. The great seaborne empire of Sri Vijaya, thought to have been centred in southeast Sumatra, had already declined, replaced by its 'heir', Melaka, still Malay although no longer Buddhist but Muslim, equally adept at trade and located on the east side of the Straits of Malacca through which the bulk of all the seaborne goods to and from East Asia passed.[3]

Geo-economically and politically, Pegu and Lower Myanmar as a region in the 'early modern' period was very much an integral component of that maritime world, a crescent-shaped swath that hugged the coasts and encircled mainland Southeast Asia on the West, south and east, stretching from Arakan to north Vietnam and points farther north and east in China and Southeast Asia. It was a zone that was physically, economically and conceptually connected, the habitat of similar coastal settlements involved in common commercial and cultural activities and well known to each other.

At the time Pegu was the most important commercial and political centre in Lower Myanmar and the 'most-favoured port' there for international trade during the sixteenth century. Pathein (anglicized as Bassein), another port-city on the western part of the Lower Myanmar Irrawaddy Delta had been the favourite earlier during the eleventh and twelfth centuries. Now it was considerably farther inland, as parts of the delta had grown considerably, becoming less convenient for seafarers. Pegu was beginning to experience the same phenomenon, but was still reasonably accessible and remained the most important entry to Lower Myanmar.

The Toungoo rulers, whose capital was near the southern edge of the Dry Zone on the Sittaung River, realizing that at this particular time in history Lower not Upper Myanmar was key to unifying the rest of the country – it was usually the other way around – and with the food supplies in the irrigated regions of Upper Myanmar in the hands of various un-wieldy and fissiparous powers, decided to take Pegu first before reunifying the rest of the country. It was a brilliant move. Within a decade or so (by 1539) they had taken Pegu, led by their famous King Tabinshwehti, after which most of the rest of Lower Myanmar also fell under his sway.

Tabinshwehti (*reg.* 1531–50) had thus benefited from Ava's plight and the flight of population to Toungoo (the 'brain-drain' mentioned in the previous chapter) as well as from the surge in trade and commerce of the maritime regions just when he assumed the throne. He was young (only fifteen) and brash but both he and his future brother-in-law, Bayin-naung (who was to become Myanmar's greatest general) were counselled by a host of more experienced ministers, so that youth and experience were both responsible for Pegu's energy and subsequent success. The story most remembered by historians of Tabinshwehti's brashness was having his ears pierced at the Shwemawdaw Pagoda at Pegu, the palladium of state of the First Pegu Dynasty, whose leaders could do nothing about this studied insult but sit and fume.

Before taking Pegu Tabinshwehti made certain that its flanks were also pacified and under his control, particularly Pathein and Myaungmya

Aerial photograph of the city of Toungoo, mid-15th century.

on the west, important centres in their own right, with the potential to become foci of resistance unless subdued first. Although Pegu was well defended Tabinshwehti manipulated the inherently suspicious nature of the court by having it eliminate two of its own commanders, resulting in wholesale desertion of Pegu's troops. At this Pegu's king fled to Prome, allowing Tabinshwehti to enter the city in 1539 without, as the chronicles are wont to say, 'breaking a single sword or lance'.

That was only the first step, since the Toungoo rulers knew that wealth from commerce alone was not sufficient to control all of Myanmar; the interior's population and its irrigated regions had to be reintegrated and rejuvenated as well. But that was not to happen until after Bayinnaung had assumed the throne in 1551. In the meantime Tabinshwehti decided to reintegrate all of Lower Myanmar, first by taking Muttama, Pegu's biggest competitor and a most important prize.[4] It was one of the richest cities on the coasts with probably the largest and wealthiest foreign population trading and living there. It included Portuguese (of course) but also Greeks, Venetians, Moors, Jews, Armenians, Persians, Abyssinians, Malabari and Sumatrans. As usual the Portuguese were the favourite mercenaries, and here as well had been hired to defend Muttama, led by an adventurer named Paulo Seixas. Tabinshwehti employed Portuguese soldiers on his side too, his favourite being one Diogo Soarez de Mello.

In 1541 Muttama was taken after much fighting and destruction, so that Lower Myanmar was beginning to look as it had under Rajadarit's First Pegu Dynasty, with the exception of the region south of Thaway (Tavoy) which was under Siamese hegemony.[5] After Muttama was taken much of the commercial revenues of the coasts fell under Pegu's control. Only then did Tabinshwehti begin to make a move to take Upper Myanmar.

In 1542 he took Prome, the 'gateway' to the Dry Zone and Arakan (thence to the Bay of Bengal). Arakan's centre, Mrohaung, was invaded in 1546–7, but Tabinshwehti could not take it, as it was well defended by one of its most celebrated kings, Minbin (*reg.* 1531–53). Moreover Ayuthaya, seeing that Tabinshwehti was away in Arakan, took advantage of the situation and raided Thaway. So Tabinshwehti quickly reached a modus vivendi with Arakan and after exchanging pleasantries returned to the maritime world to deal with the Siamese.

Tabinshwehti must have realized then that unless Ayuthaya was neutralized or weakened he could never take Upper Myanmar and the 'heartland', so decided to move on the Siamese capital first. And although he was at Ayuthaya's walls for a whole month, he could not take the city whose defences included Portuguese mercenaries led by one Diogo Pereira. Knowing he had to retreat before the rains came and do so unmolested, Tabinshwehti managed to capture some Siamese princes whose release was then used as bargaining chips for his safe passage out. The story of this campaign is much embellished with acts of bravado recorded in both the Burmese and T'ai chronicles.

But Tabinshwehti would not live to see the fruits of his labours. Those would be enjoyed by his successor, the great Bayinnaung. Portrayals of Tabinshwehti after his Siamese campaign and during his final years had him falling to drink and debauchery in the company of a young (and mysterious) Portuguese adventurer, which modern popular Thai movies embellished by presenting him (Tabinshwehti) as effeminate, and there-fore unworthy of his reputation as a famous general. As his behaviour grew less and less kingly, Bayinnaung pleaded with him to reform. Tabinsh-wehti was said to have retorted: 'I have made friends with drink. Brother, do thou manage the affairs of state. Bring me no petitions. Leave me to my jollity.'[6]

Although egged on by Tabinshwehti's own ministers to take the throne, Bayinnaung refused, and instead protected his brother-in-law at a safe haven away from the palace. But the king was subsequently assassi-nated by his own bodyguards, alleged descendants of the First Pegu Dynasty, who then retook the city of Pegu. Bayinnaung was elsewhere suppressing a rebellion, led by an ex-monk, also an alleged descendant of the First Pegu Dynasty, who had flung off his saffron robe to justify his political activities.[7] The assassins of Tabinshwehti then placed one of their leaders on the throne at Pegu, one Smim Sawhtut.

Bayinnaung was now, as one colonial historian noted, 'a king without a kingdom'.[8] His own 'brothers' holding fiefs at Prome and even Toungoo (the very home of his dynasty) would not support him but simply looked on, perhaps gloating about his commoner heritage. After all, he was the son of Tabinshwehti's wet-nurse and a toddy-palm climber while his 'broth-ers' were of royal blood. Made *Einshemin* (heir apparent) by the ex-king despite his low birth surely incurred jealousies that now played out.

But they forgot one thing: he still had enough battle-hardened, loyal soldiers and experienced ministers in strategic fiefs just waiting for the right moment to come over to his side, as well as enough money to renew the loyalty of Tabinshwehti's Portuguese captain who had served both well: Deogo Soarez de Mello. Although out of the country at the time (perhaps residing at Goa in Western India, a Portuguese enclave), de Mello returned when Bayinnaung called upon his services. With a small but cohesive unit of fighting men, they decided to first take the original home of the Toungoo dynasty, Zeyawadi, the city of Minkyinyo, founder of that dynasty.

Once there, many of the ministers and soldiers of Tabinshwehti's old court fled Pegu and Muttama to join Bayinnaung. That they belonged to different ethnic groups, many of whom were Mon speakers, demon-strates once again that vertical patron–client structures often pre-empted horizontal ones, even those as strong as ethnic identity and culture. This turn of events persuaded the governor of Toungoo to throw in his support for Bayinnaung, a highly important victory for the king, symbolically as well as materially.

Since in Myanmar (as elsewhere) nothing succeeds like success (although expressed as the law of karma), the gaining of Toungoo was the beginning of the end of resistance to his rule, as city after city came over to his side. Finally, Pegu was retaken within the year (1551), an outcome said (by the chronicles) to have been decided by a battle of champions on elephants, between Bayinnaung and Smim Hhtaw (the Xemindoo of the Portuguese writers and successor of Smim Sawhtut). Bayinnaung's victory, embellished in a dramatic battle, ended the campaign for Pegu.

But during the grab for spoils his friend and supporter de Mello also met his end. He was alleged (by Portuguese sources no less) to have attempted to carry off a beautiful woman during her wedding ceremony, killing the bridegroom in the process.[9] Here ended the fascinating life of this man who had spent much of his life outside of Portugal, about whom we know very little in the history of Myanmar. After Bayinnaung regained his throne at Pegu all centres of resistance collapsed except one: Ava.

The latter had access to most of the population in the country and all of the most important agricultural regions in the land, hence also its food supplies. Bayinnaung bided his time, allowing his men to recuperate, recruiting additional soldiers, acquiring more armaments and instilling discipline in his troops during this time of respite and preparation. After three years he was ready to pursue his vision to reunify the country under his suzerainty. He marched on Ava in 1555 in a two-pronged attack, one up the Sittaung valley and the other up the Irrawaddy. He led the latter in his magnificent royal barge, over 200 feet long and shaped like a *hamsa*, a mythical bird and symbol of Pegu whose formal name is Hamsavati.

Ava was taken without much effort, after which Bayinnaung secured the Mu Valley on its northwest and its vast irrigated rice lands all the way up to Myedu (its northern entrance). He did the same with the Kyaukse valley, at the time the granary of the country. It lay on Ava's east and south, at the head of the Sittaung River valley, up which had marched his second column. He now controlled both the Irrawaddy and Sittaung river valleys, the corridors to and from the 'heartland' where most of the food of the country was produced and its population lived. He then spent the next several years securing allegiance from all of the Shan states, including Manipur (now in India) along with Chiang Mai in Thailand and Viengchang in Laos.

Chiang Mai, especially, gave him the northern path he needed for a two-pronged attack of Ayuthaya, his most serious commercial (hence political) rival at the time in mainland Southeast Asia. By the mid-sixteenth century he had taken that centre of the T'ai people twice: in 1564 and 1569, making Pegu the most powerful kingdom in western and central mainland Southeast Asia.

Bayinnaung had expanded his kingdom to an extent never before (and never again) experienced in the history of the country and mainland Southeast Asia. It fulfilled the image he had of himself, a *cakravartin* ('world conqueror') that even some of his conquered peoples, the T'ai, shared.[10] And all this had been accomplished in a matter of approximately 40 years. Such ambitious and risky activities had never before been attempted, even by Pagan kings, and must have been motivated by goals more pertinent to larger economic and political forces in the region than by domestic, inland, agrarian concerns as was usually the case. More specifically, the 'Age of Commerce' in Southeast Asia was an important factor in Toungoo's initial decision for moving to Lower Myanmar, establishing Pegu as its capital and controlling its eastern neighbours in ways theretofore not done.

Bayinnaung celebrated his success by building a new palace-city at Pegu adjacent to (and to the west of) the old one. When the founder of the First Pegu Dynasty, Bannya-U, moved his capital there from Muttama in the thirteenth century it was a small provincial governorship under the Pagan dynasty, not the seat of a royal dynasty, and approximately a third the size of the new one Bayinnaung built. Bannya-U's Pegu also appears to have been devoid of Buddhist symbolism, its oblong shape said to have represented the egg of the Hamsa (Brahma's vehicle), hence its name Hamsavati, although it is likely an *ex post facto* projection by a later on an earlier age.

In contrast, as we have seen, the majority of the capital cities of Myanmar symbolized the Buddhist universe on earth, with their twelve-gate symbolism of time and space, part of the Dry Zone tradition that goes back at least to the Urban Period where it is found in second century AD Beikthano and several of its contemporaries and 'successors', particularly seventh-century Sri Ksetra and ninth-century Pagan.[11] Although there are some differences in the shape of the cities themselves – some were perfect squares, others were circular and still others more or less rectangular – they still symbolized the larger Buddhist universe.[12]

The new city of Pegu that Bayinnaung built was also a near-perfect square like his family seat of Toungoo, within which was another fortified square at whose centre was the *Myenan* ('Earth Palace'), its buildings placed on an elevated plinth in the traditional manner of Myanmar palaces. When the new palace-city was completed in 1567 Bayinnaung performed the traditional 'ritual of possession' (*nan thein pwe*) symbolically taking possession of the city and throne by circling it on the moat three times on his royal barge, followed by the whole court on their ceremonial boats.

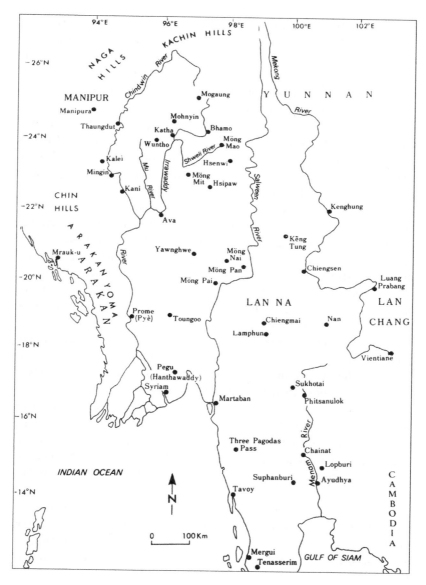

Bayinnaung's Empire, mid-16th century.

And when he entered the city gates not only did he take physical possession of the exemplary centre, but also what it represented – the kingdom – along with the power, rights and privileges appertaining thereto.

In stark contrast to the cosmic symbolism of Upper Myanmar's capital cities, Bayinnaung's Pegu was importantly different in several ways. First, the original *Myenan* and its main (Lion) throne most likely faced west rather than east while the many buildings adjacent to, and

135

behind the *Myenan* were located on the east rather than on the west side where they should have been. We know this from archaeological excavations during the early 1990s on the foundation plinth on which the palace stood, as well as from a copy of an old drawing of the palace–city and palace made by Letwe Nawyahta, a minister of a succeeding dynasty who participated in the later siege of Pegu.[13]

Second, Bayinnaung's new city had twenty gates, not the traditional and cosmologically symbolic twelve. This is confirmed not only by Letwe's manuscript but by a foreign visitor, Cesar Frederick, another merchant of Venice who was in Pegu during Bayinnaung's time.[14] More important, those twenty gates had nothing to do with Buddhist cosmology since each was named after the political centres Bayinnaung had conquered or that were at the time under his hegemony. Thus gates named Nyaung Shwe, Mone, Theini, Kale, all important centres in the Shan states, also Ayuthaya, Zinmme and Linzin, named after major centres in Thailand and Laos. Muttama and Pusim (Bassein) were also included, the major political centres in Lower Myanmar. Of course, Ava, Prome and Toungoo, the three most important Dry Zone centres, were under Bayinnaung's sway as well and therefore had gates named after them.

Third, each of the 222 teak pillars used to build the *Myenan* (175 of them have been recovered in the above-mentioned excavations and now housed at the site) has inscriptions on their bases recording the names of the towns and/or cities (and sometimes of their *myosas*) in the kingdom under Bayinnaung's suzerainty. Each governor had to submit a palace post as demonstration of allegiance and subordination. These teak pillars, therefore, were not only the foundations that physically supported the main palace of the king and his court but also represented the political and administrative infrastructure upon which the entire kingdom lay.

However, there are several unresolved problems. As Bayinnaung's palace was burned to the ground in 1599 by the Arakanese and another palace built in its place, Letwe's drawing probably represents the latter, *not* Bayinnaung's. And as Alaungpaya was said to have burned *this* later palace also, in 1757 when he took Pegu, where did Letwe get his information if both palaces had been destroyed?

Even if he had obtained the plans from a surviving manuscript, the new palace that was standing at the time Alaungpaya took Pegu should also have been built at dead-centre of the city whose space had been previously occupied by the old (Bayinnaung's) palace (and its posts). If so, the latter had to have been removed to make room for the new posts, especially since palace posts stood on stone bases at the bottom of deep pits lined with stone or brick that largely survive fires. That means the posts recently excavated and displayed in the museum today alleged to belong to Bayinnaung's palace may actually belong to the subsequent palace. Either that, or the new palace was not built at dead-centre, so that *its* posts were the ones discovered, not Bayinnaung's. If so, the latter posts have yet to be found. Of course, it is also possible (although not probable) that neither the Arakanese in 1599 nor Alaungpaya in 1757 set fire to Bayinnaung's original *Myenan* as reported.

Be that as it may, Cesare Frederick's description of Bayinnaung's palace, particularly the twenty gates, is sufficient to suggest that his palace-city did not represent the infinite time and space of the Buddhist universe but the political realities of the 'here and now'. It was a statement, a 'text', about the military and political status quo of western and central mainland Southeast Asia during his reign. Bayinnaung was of *this* world and wanted to celebrate his illustrious career as a military-king *in the present.*

That may be one of the reasons it did not bother him that the *Myenan* faced west rather than east, regardless of how inauspicious it might have been in the context of Buddhist tradition. Indeed, it may have been even more personal than that; he may have wanted his palace to face the direction that was true to his horoscope and birthday, for he is reported to have been born on Wednesday, perhaps the 'dark side' of it representing inauspiciousness (*amingala*), the sunset, west and the direction of death.[15]

In short, Bayinnaung, a product of the 'early modern' period behaved as one, rejecting the past and embracing the present, focusing not on abstractions but on reality. The son of a toddy palm climber and wet-nurse, a man of this world with an early personal past that was not particularly exemplary, Bayinnaung's palace was an endorsement of the present, the maritime world and the 'early modern' values which had made him what he was.

His most distinguished advisor was Bannya Dala, said to have been of Mon ethnic background with fluency in both his mother tongue and Burmese. He is known not only for his down-to-earth personality but also for military and administrative abilities and literary talents, particularly the writing of the *Razadarit Ayedawpon*, the earliest extant 'history' of the Myanmar Mon. It describes the origins of their first dynasty and 'kingdom' in the country beginning with Wagaru and Muttama, ending with Razadarit at Pegu. However, towards the end of Bayinnaung's reign, Bannya Dala was said to have fallen out of favour with the king and despite his long-time loyalty was exiled to a remote village where he died.

When Bayinnaung died at 66 in 1581, he was said to have left 97 children, one of whom, Nandabayin, designated crown prince, became king (*reg.* 1581–99). But every time an effective leader dies, his successor invariably had to prove himself. Apart from the usual uncle–nephew rivalry – in this case, his uncle held Ava – there were others who would adopt a wait-and-see attitude not only to test the newcomer's mettle but to join the winning side, amongst whom was famous T'ai prince, Pra Naret, left as governor of Ayuthaya after Bayinnaung's conquest. He was ordered by Nandabayin to bring troops to put down the Ava rebellion. He complied, but came late (perhaps deliberately), and finding the king already gone to do battle, ravaged the Pegu area and deported thousands of prisoners-of-war to Ayuthaya.

To avenge such cheek Nandabayin attempted several times to retake Ayuthaya but was not successful, as his father had been. From that time onwards (mid-1590s) until 1767 Ayuthaya remained either on the offensive or enjoyed no threat from its western competitor. Nandabayin's inability to subdue Ayuthaya eroded his power at home further and instead of going to his aid most of the governors of the major centres such as Toungoo, Prome and Ava (who were either siblings or cousins) behaved in ways that weakened rather than strengthened central authority. Again they acted more as 'spoilers' in pursuit of their own interests than leaders and visionaries acting in the interests of the larger entity, the kingdom.

In 1599 mighty Pegu was burned to the ground by little Mrauk-U, a newly arisen and heretofore nondescript maritime centre located in Arakan. It was aided by a jealous Toungoo and (belatedly) by a vindictive Ayuthaya. After a mere 61 years, then, this most expansive kingdom ever known to Myanmar and mainland Southeast Asia had been brought to its knees relatively easily. The Second Pegu/Toungoo Dynasty was the most adventurous and militarily successful in the country's history but it was also the shortest lived.[16]

There are several reasons the powerful Second Pegu/Toungoo dynasty collapsed, and rather rapidly.[17] First, the kingdom was simply overextended. Although its conquests provided additional labour that was used to settle on cultivated or cultivable land in Upper Myanmar, the kingdom had neither the kind of population to sustain a territory that size, nor any experience in administering far-flung peoples who spoke different languages, had different values, recognized different laws, ate different foods and often behaved in unfamiliar ways. This was Myanmar's first conquest of genuinely foreign territory that lay outside the country's cultural orbit; not even Pagan attempted to do that.

Second, the 'merit-path to salvation' that legitimated Myanmar state and society continued to shift taxable wealth into the tax-exempt Sangha, creating the all too familiar economic (and political) problems for the state. Even though the Second Pegu/Toungoo Dynasty was not an agrarian kingdom (so that relatively less land was donated than with Pagan or Ava), much of the new wealth obtained from its military conquests and commercial enterprises, mostly in 'liquid assets', still managed to go to the promotion of the religion and legitimation of the state. Such depletion of state resources to the Sangha, in turn, would have exacerbated long-standing court factionalism whose parties were dependent on those resources. The decline of the 'Age of Commerce' by the end of the sixteenth century may also have worsened Pegu's dwindling resources, which as a rule brings to a head underlying and dormant structural tensions.

And, finally, Pegu was simply too exhausted militarily from its far-flung campaigns to seriously resist the attacks by Mrauk-U and Toungoo. Militarily brilliant leaders such as Bayinnaung and Tabinshwehti were long gone by then, with no equals to take their place. In such a situation garrisons deserted en masse, knowing that as fighting men in labour-scarce Southeast Asia, their chances for acquiring gainful employment after the fracas was over while still preserving life and limb were very good.

After looting Pegu both Mrauk-U and Toungoo returned to their respective centres, the Arakanese reportedly setting fire to the city before leaving and taking back with them 3,000 households from Pegu. When the Siamese finally arrived the city was said to be a charred ruin, so they went after the nearest 'Burmese' centre, Toungoo, suggesting motives that were not just geo-political and economic but also inchoately 'national' and perhaps even personal. They were badly defeated and returned to Ayuthaya to lick their wounds. Even had they won, the Ayuthaya forces belonged to a different culture whose home was elsewhere, and so probably had no desire to actually rule Myanmar. Mrauk-U on the other hand, although part of the Burmese political and cultural orbit, neither had the strategic location, historical experience, demographic wherewithal, political will nor desire to unite Myanmar, even under its own aegis.

After Pegu was destroyed in 1599 the surrounding area became desolate and Lower Myanmar lapsed into anarchy for decades, ruled by war-lords, including a Portuguese adventurer named Filipe de Brito y Nicote, who symbolized the heterogeneity of the place and the decentralized conditions of the time. Although some of Pegu's population was reportedly taken captive to Ayuthaya and Arakan, many Burmese speakers must have also migrated to Upper Myanmar to a familiar culture where the bulk of the country's Burmese-speaking population was ensconced. Others may have chosen to remain in Lower Myanmar in the same remote villages where they lived and worked, since centre activities, even a collapse, did not necessarily affect their daily lives much.

A Jesuit report recorded the aftermath of the destruction of Pegu of this once populated and thriving region. The people 'have been brought to such misery and want, that they did eat man's flesh . . . parents abstained not from their children, and children devoured their parents. The stronger by force preyed on the weaker, and if any were but skin and bone, yet did they open their entrails to fill their own and sucked out their brains.'[18] (Such anarchy is not new, and occurs regularly in Myanmar history, to the extent that anarchy is feared far more than is tyranny in the country.[19])

Both the conquest of Pegu and its aftermath once again illustrate the recurring theme that those who destroyed centres of leadership and authority were often not genuinely interested in replacing them with viable alternative options, even under their own rule. They were mere 'spoilers', without visions larger than themselves and their own self-interests, who contested not to build a viable alternative but simply to destroy what was established; in other words, to disallow the presence of *any* overarching authority. (This pattern was to repeat in modern times.)

And because both Toungoo and Arakan, for whatever reason, did not resurrect the Kingdom of Pegu but left it in ruins, that inaction turned out to be disastrous for them 200 years later, for it was precisely what gave agrarian Upper Myanmar another opportunity to realize its vision of re-unification and reassert its dominance once again over the whole country.

CONCLUSION

The story of the Second Pegu/Toungoo Dynasty was atypical in several ways: the territory it acquired outside Myanmar's cultural orbit, the location of the seat of authority, the focus on the 'here and now' as symbolized by the capital city, the temporary change in policy towards trade and commerce, and the heterogeneous character of its population and atmosphere. But it was typical in other ways. Apart from the conceptual system that was shared by the country's major centres, one component that stands out is the nature of the political struggles in Myanmar: to reiterate, they were nearly all (if not all) elite affairs, whereby princes – most often uncles and nephews – vied for the throne. These were not landed nobility of the kind one finds in medieval Europe or Japan with independent sources of wealth that created a balance of power. Rather, their wealth stemmed from the crown and was held while 'in favour', or as the Burmese phrase has it, 'at the royal compassion'. The ultimate power, therefore, lay in the throne and at the centre.

In these struggles, moreover, most of the fighting was done by a particular class of people – crown troops – allotted to *myosa* to govern their fiefs, which were usually major towns with strategic and economic value. And because these battles were limited to crown troops they did not create massive depopulations; cholera and other diseases probably kept the population levels down more effectively than any war ever did. Also, since fighting men were more valuable alive than dead, when the situation warranted most would desert en masse in favour of the impending winner. Thus much of the blood-letting in Myanmar's history occurred amongst the elite: contesting princes and their heirs, and less amongst their troops. The common masses, usually comprised of cultivators, were rarely involved in these struggles.

This elite most often acted out of self-interest and would cooperate for the benefit of the larger entity (state, kingdom) only (or usually) when it was clear they had few other options; that is, when there emerged strong leadership at the top with the military wherewithal and political will to unify the country and ultimately bring stability to the kingdom. Such 'loyalty' based on self-interest, of course, was not the only motivation; kinship, personal and broader visions of state and society must have been involved as well. But when the chips were down most did not operate on the basis of the latter but the former.

At the same time, when such unity and stability were achieved – regardless of the reasons for it – a kingdom often experienced genuine social, cultural and economic development, manifest in areas such as religion, the fine arts, literature and law. And even if after the passing of unifying leaders such as Bayinnaung society once again reverted to its parts, what was accomplished during times of stability was not lost but remained to affect the next cycle of stability and unity.

7

Return to the 'Heartland'

Pegu's leadership was already looking towards Upper Myanmar to make a fresh start even before the capital was burned to the ground by the Arakanese in 1599. They neither dwelled on that defeat very long nor wallowed in self-pity to create an image of themselves as victims. Instead they went back 'home' to the 'heartland'. Since they had originally come from the interior (Toungoo) and were, after all, *anyatha* ('offspring of the upstream region') not *akyitha* ('offspring of the downstream region'), the latter's lifestyle and overall system (particularly the unsettling and unstable nature of commerce and trade) never really became deeply embedded in their psyches or institutions. Life in Upper Myanmar was also far less complicated than life in Lower Myanmar, with its constant flux and unpredictability, varieties of cultures and peoples some of whom spoke languages mostly unintelligible to those in Upper Myanmar and had 'peculiar' customs and manners.

It appears that the country's leadership, with the exception of Bayinnaung, was never genuinely committed to Lower Myanmar for the long term and never stopped yearning for, therefore kept looking back at, the agrarian heartland, to a more familiar, hence more comfortable way of life. That was evident in the resettlement of prisoners-of-war in Upper not Lower Myanmar, and assigning some of the most talented princes in the choicest Upper Myanmar fiefs, revealing where their priorities lay and their ultimate intent to move back into the interior.

Thus the initial move from Toungoo and the Dry Zone down to coastal Pegu during the first half of the sixteenth century by Tabinshwehti did not appear to have been considered a permanent one. Nonetheless, and although ad hoc, it was a rational decision, created by the fall of Ava and the rise of commerce in the maritime regions of Southeast Asia and Lower Myanmar. It would have been extremely short-sighted not to have taken advantage of what the coasts were offering at the time.

All of this goes a long way to explain why the next dynasty to rule the country, the Second Ava Dynasty (the topic of this chapter) was not on the coast, but back in the 'heartland'.[1] Whereas even twice-conquered Ayuthaya chose to remain on the coasts, the successors of Pegu did not. The agrarian interior was always beckoning for, after all, that was the home of Myanmar's ancestors, where Pagan, the exemplary centre of the country's first integrated kingdom in all its ruined glory, lay and where some of the most sacred temples enshrined with the holiest of the Buddha's bodily relics made the landscape hallowed. Thus after a mere 61 years in Lower Myanmar the capital of the country returned to the Dry Zone whence it came and remained there for nearly another three centuries until the end of the monarchy.

NYAUNGYAN MIN AND THE SECOND AVA DYNASTY

As noted above, well before Pegu fell several sons of Bayinnaung were already holding important Dry Zone fiefs. One of these was the important *myosa*-ship of Nyaungyan, located right in the heart of Meiktila district south of Ava, and a prime agricultural area in Upper Myanmar at the time. It was held by Nyaungyan Min, 'the Lord of Nyaungyan' (*reg.* 1600–1605), a favourite son of King Bayinnaung by a minor queen. Anticipating Pegu's impending doom he had moved on the city of Ava a few years earlier in 1597 (when its governor had gone downstream), took it and subsequently made it his capital.

In 1600, after Pegu had fallen, he crowned himself king of the Second Inwa (Ava) Dynasty, also called the 'Later Toungoo' and 'Restored Toungoo' Dynasty by Western historians.[2] Thus, by the beginning of the seventeenth century, the Burmese monarchy had been resurrected once again. And as usual it was centred in the Dry Zone, whose agrarian environment and way of life neither the leadership nor the majority of the people would abandon.

Once secured, Nyaungyan proceeded to reunify the country as the Kingdom of Pagan had done nearly 600 years before. He reorganized people into their traditional units of attachment and non-attachment: *ahmudan* (crown-service groups, the old *kyun-taw*), *paya kyun* (Sangha subjects) and ordinary *kyun* (private, usually household retainers) and those not attached (*athi*) to anyone. He also repaired and rebuilt irrigation works and, of course, monasteries and temples as well.

Since neither Pegu nor Toungoo on Ava's south was a serious threat for the time being, Nyaungyan looked north to subdue the Shan areas. If one wanted the whole country, that region had to be secured first before the coasts could be retaken. During Pagan times the great empire of Nanchao had been that buffer in the north, but had been taken in the mid-thirteenth century by the Mongols. Now Nyaungyan had to secure that frontier all over again, for central control ceased with the death of Bayinnaung.

But Nyaungyan died after only pacifying the region and before he could take Lower Myanmar and reunify the country. That was left to his son Anaukphetlun (*reg.* 1605–28) whose name means 'one who died on the west'. He had already proved himself a capable military leader and so did not hesitate in seizing the palace and assuming the throne before his brothers had even learned of their father's death. In fact he was said to have administered the oath of allegiance to his kinsmen even before the cremation fires of the king had died.

Then, step by step, using the foundations built by his predecessor, he proceeded to reunify the country. This meant pacifying the three main centres of power at the time: Toungoo, Prome and Syriam, and only subsequently the southernmost coastal areas on the Tenasserim Peninsula. After taking Toungoo and Prome he placed garrisons there, removing much of their population to Ava, the modus operandi for addressing the perennial labour shortage problem of early Southeast Asia.

But Syriam, virtually on the coasts, presented an interesting problem and a new twist to the story. It had replaced Pegu as the most favoured port after the latter's conflagration in 1599 and the devastation of the area. Not only did the Pegu River continue to silt up, rendering it less and less effective, but Syriam lay right at the confluence of the Pegu and Yangon rivers, both on the edge of the Gulf of Martaban (Muttama). It effectively controlled the entrance to both Yangon and Pegu, thence points inland. Syriam's ruler was the Portuguese adventurer Filipe de Brito, mentioned in chapter Six, one of the 'warlords' who had carved out a domain for himself after Pegu's fall, an invariable pattern of decentralism in the country's history whenever central authority collapses.

Like those of other Portuguese adventurers in the region, his is also an interesting story. Most of them were without pedigrees but were able to establish links with local elites by marrying into their families. De Brito rose from cabin boy to de facto Lord of Syriam. His wife, whose mother was Javanese, was the niece of the Viceroy of Goa in southwest India, a Portuguese enclave until 1963, and his son received in marriage a daughter of the Lord of Martaban. He built a church in Syriam led by two Jesuits, while his men consisted of a mixture of Eurasians, local 'Negroes' and others from the Malabar coasts of South India.

His economic base lay in the tolls he collected from vessels forced to dock at Syriam. This meant the cost of foreign goods in the interior rose along with de Brito's profits, felt mostly by the inland agrarian powers. He had no regard for Buddhism; temples were despoiled for their treasures (as the Shan Sawbwa Thohanbwa had done at Ava during his short reign). Precious stones were removed from their finials, gold was melted down for resale, and bronze bells for cannons.

However, the final straw came when he interfered in the politics of the country: de Brito and his brother-in-law, the Lord of Martaban, attacked and took Toungoo which was considered an Ava *myosa*-ship, held by Anaukhpetlun's cousin, Nat Shin Naung. At that Anaukphetlun marched down and took Syriam after laying siege to it for 34 days, and put de Brito to a cruel death by impaling him on an iron stake placed high above the fort walls where his fate could be better seen. There de Brito agonized for two days before dying. As for Nat Shin Naung, who aided de Brito, his chest was cut open.

Nat Shin Naung was also an interesting character, mainly remembered by foreign scholars for aiding de Brito against his own king and having converted to Christianity. To the Burmese people, however, he is best known for his poems, one of which survives as a model of unrequited love. Since the princess he secretly loved was already married to another, he longed for her in silence for many years, during which time he wrote the following poem. Finally her husband died and Nat Shin Naung was able to marry her, only to be killed that same year. The poem, as translated by John Okell, in part reads:

I ached with longing, I knew not good from evil in my anguish. From that day I beheld her, allowing my eyes to rest where they would, I cannot forget. Stricken with an immense and uncontainable tenfold misery, I only wish to make her mistress of my life. Should even Sakka, King of the Gods, seeking her match in the Second Heaven, set beside her one chosen to compete, then would people say that my mistress shines like the bright moon beside a little star. In trying to tell of her glowing brown smooth beauty, her fresh tender grace, her pure nature, he who sees her becomes bewildered and dizzy, he gropes for words, and tries to speak but cannot describe her. Again and again I gaze on her loveliness, far surpassing all rivals, and wherever I look I only have eyes for her face.[3]

After Syriam was conquered and Toungoo retaken, the 'entrance' to the Dry Zone via the Sittaung valley on the country's east was finally secured. (Prome had the same role on the west via the Irrawaddy River valley secured by Dagon, known later as Yangon, thence Rangoon.) Both entrances to the interior were once more in the fold of Upper Myanmar. Anaukpetlun spared the lives of many of de Brito's followers who were experts in European firearms and resettled them in Ava. Some of their descendants were still there when the British annexed Myanmar over 250 years later.

After Toungoo and Syriam fell under Ava's hegemony it was only a matter of time before the major centres further south on the Tenasserim

Peninsula fell, for Anaukpetlun not only had the human and material resources of the Dry Zone now but also much of maritime Myanmar's revenues. Martaban, which had been allied with Syriam and Siam, quickly came over to Anukpetlun's side. With this important alliance Anukpetlun's forces proceeded towards Tavoy and Mergui to recapture the 'tail' of Myanmar. He took Tavoy but Mergui, located in the far south across the strip of land from the Gulf of Siam, put up a stiff resistance with Siamese and Portuguese help.

So he left Mergui alone and instead decided to subdue Chiang Mai on his eastern flank. In 1614–15, he attacked that city and by 1617 had it. He even made feints on Ayuthaya and attacked some border towns, but had no intention of over-extending himself, having learned the lessons of history taught by Bayinnaung, his grandfather. With Anaukhpetlun, then, the domestic territories of the Pagan and Second Pegu/Toungoo dynasties had been more or less restored. And had he taken Mergui, the Second Ava kingdom would have been approximately the size of the Pagan kingdom.

The fall of Syriam in 1613 may well mark the end of serious Portuguese influence in Myanmar. Soon thereafter, if not already, the Dutch and English, rising commercial powers in the maritime regions of Southeast Asia, had begun to put pressure on the Portuguese. This was happening well before 1641 when the Portuguese were finally ousted from Melaka by the Dutch. The English and Dutch set up 'factories' at several important centres in Myanmar: Syriam, Mergui, Ava, Pegu and even Bhamo in the far north near the China border.[4] The French had a small foothold in Syriam, off and on, that remained well into the late seventeenth century.

With the Dutch and English inroads, Pegu and the commercial coasts of Lower Myanmar once again began to look as attractive as it had under Tabinshwehti and Bayinnaung with the Portuguese. Indeed, since Anaukhpetlun had already moved most of the royal family from Ava to Pegu, he may have even contemplated returning the capital to Lower Myanmar or at least to make it a 'second' capital in a reformulation of the old 'upstream–downstream' paradigm. Only this time, as under Bayinnaung, both regions would be controlled by one centre located in Lower Myanmar.

In 1628, while Anaukhpetlun slept in the women's quarters located on the west side of the palace at Pegu, he was beaten to death by one of his sons whom he had threatened to roast alive for having an affair with a woman of the harem, the daughter of a Shan Sawbwa given to the king as part of the usual marriage alliances between the centre and its peripheries.[5] This son, Minyedeippa, was young and inexperienced and no match for the king's more mature and militarily experienced brothers who had equal rights to the throne.

As the brothers were out in the field at the time, the ministers placed the patricide prince on the throne. His uncles, however, would have none of it. That triggered several governors of important towns to revolt, not necessarily in support of either the uncles or the prince, but in their own self-interests. It allowed them to play a waiting game to see who would win, then join that side to enhance their position subsequently. The uncles had to prove their military abilities all over again, but with each success previously undecided *myosa* came over to their side. Realizing how the situation was going to turn out, the ministers who had originally supported Minyedeippa sent a deputation to ask Thalun, the most prominent uncle, to take the throne. He accepted and upon arrival at Pegu where Minyedeippa was holed up, put him to death, despite the standard plea by the condemned to allow him to enter the monastery. But Thalun knew that 'becoming' a monk was often a ruse from which one could launch future rebellions. In 1629 Thalun was crowned king at Pegu.

At each royal coronation the path to the throne for certain royal lines was invariably cut off. No sooner was Thalun crowned than rebellion erupted at Moulmein, farther south. He quelled that, along with one more potential rival, Chiang Mai, which he took without much trouble. With both the southern coasts and their eastern flank now secured by mid-century, much of the country was once more militarily under his hegemony.

Although it is true that Thalun had to fight his way to the throne, much of the kingdom's territories had already been recouped by the time Anaukhpetlun was assassinated, so the task Thalun had was more of a 'mopping up' operation, institutionalizing the groundwork laid by his predecessor, than reunification from scratch. But unlike his brother Anaukhpetlun, who had showed signs of moving to Pegu and making it the capital once again, Thalun returned to Ava. And to highlight that decision he conducted a formal coronation in 1635 in his newly constructed palace. This was a major and deliberate statement about his sentiment and policy to change his predecessor's plans. Perhaps had Anaukhpetlun lived and made Pegu the capital, seventeenth-century Myanmar would have been more like its next-door rival, Ayuthaya, and today more like Thailand with its capital on the coasts rather than in the interior, agrarian Dry Zone.

Instead, the seemingly simple act of returning to the 'heartland' to be crowned in a newly built palace demonstrated that Thalun intended to resurrect agrarian institutions and values and reformulate previous Dry Zone models rather than continue the 'new' commercial model of Bayinnaung's Pegu. Even though Thalun's dynasty was originally founded by Nyaungyan, who genealogically belonged to the Second Pegu/Toungoo Dynasty of Bayinnaung, both the actions of that prince and those of his successors were in essence statements about the importance the Dry Zone and its agrarian way of life had on their psyches, while at the same time it was a repudiation of the commercial coasts. Not that they did not need or want to *control* the coasts; they just did not want to *live* there.

In substance as well as style, then, Thalun's kingdom was in numerous ways a return to conservatism and traditionalism. And in order to implement this policy more effectively, he conducted the traditional decennial cadastral survey in 1638, basically a revenue inquest and population census that allowed the state to more accurately assess its wealth, particularly distinguishing it from that of the Sangha and other ancestral claims.

He also re-established the old ways of agrarian Upper Myanmar, both in terms of apparatus and content, starting with the local and moving to the 'national'. First, he continued Nyaungyan's policies of reorganizing society into its traditional hereditary categories of *ahmu-dan*, *paya kyun*, *kyun* and *athi*, which had been disrupted by the wars of reunification. His efforts focused on the organization of crown-service groups (*ahmudan*), the demographic mainstay of the monarchy, particularly of infantry restructured into disciplined units based on rank and numbers. He also distributed cavalry throughout the kingdom, whose names revealed to which *myosa*-ships they were assigned (such as the 'Pagan Horse') while others retained their ethnic designation (such as the '*Syam* Horse').

Second, Thalun could not, of course, neglect the economic foundations on which the state was based, so he repaired, rebuilt and reconstructed the agrarian infrastructure as well, especially making sure that the irrigation works were fully operational and new ones built when necessary, thereby allowing the rice fields to once again produce at their optimum capacity.

Third, his administrative reforms went beyond the village and township levels to include central and provincial ones, using the age-old system centred on the *myosa*. He also continued and/or reinstated the traditional judicial system (of judges, attorneys, plaintiffs, defendants, appellate courts and so on) whose legal principles, understandably, favoured the agrarian classes and agrarian social customs and mores. In that endeavour earlier codified legal texts of Pagan, Ava and the Second Pegu/Toungoo dynasties were recopied, adjusted and rewritten to serve as ultimate precedent or, in some cases, written anew.

Fourth, the state's relationship with the Sangha was reinstituted. Thalun issued an edict early in his reign prohibiting cavalier ordinations into the monkhood although obviously he could not prohibit ordinations indefinitely, for becoming a monk (or nun) was an integral part of Burmese society. He also 'purified' the Sangha in the tradition of earlier kings, conducting investigations to weed out bogus and lazy monks who attempted to use the Sangha as cover for evading taxes, corvée, the law, secular activities and gainful employment. He scrutinized old stone inscriptions to distinguish state from glebe property and was powerful and confident enough to confiscate what proved to be fraudulently exempted.

These actions allowed some control over the never-ending flow of human and material resources to the tax-exempt sector, while a 'purified' Sangha was not only smaller (hence, less expensive to maintain) but better served the state in its legitimation scheme as an orthodox Buddhist kingdom. The Sangha also continued its role as an intimate and integral part of the agrarian economy, both in its capacity as a major redistributor of land and resources (being one of the two biggest land-owners) and in its ability to cultivate virgin land or restore old plots that had become fallow.

Yet state patronage of the religion could not be avoided altogether, neither could the construction anew of royal works of merit that out-shone those of his predecessors, for legitimation of state and society continued to be based on the ideologies and rituals of earlier times. In fact the king's edicts showed that his policies were less to truly reform and change the structure of society than to reformulate older institutions to make them more efficient and effective.

This desire to return to 'ancient' (and hence 'purer') forms is best revealed in the temple style he chose in building his great work of merit. The imposing Kaunghmudaw ('Royal Good Deed', officially called the Rajaculamani) completed in 1635 was modelled after Sri Lanka's Maha-cetiya to symbolize the orthodoxy of the past, in contrast to the less orthodox 'new styles' represented by the Shwemawdaw and Shwedagon pagodas developed at Pegu and Yangon. The Kaunghmudaw of King Thalun was a statement about honouring the 'purity' of the interior's (agrarian) past, while rejecting the 'decadence' of the maritime world's (commercial) present.

Thalun's death in 1648 began a slow process that unravelled what he and his predecessors had laboriously built, ultimately bringing the kingdom to its end. Such state disintegration at the death of strong leaders suggests not so much an absence of viable institutions but that institutions simply functioned more effectively with strong leaders. They were the glue that held institutions together and enhanced their auth-ority. When a strong 'head' of state was removed the 'body' went into convulsions. Another strong leader could salvage the situation but none materialized at this time. At root was the patron–client structure which permeated society from top to bottom, so that cleavages, to reiterate, were nearly always vertical not horizontal.

Indeed, the rise, development and decline of the Second Ava Dynasty followed a pattern very similar to nearly every dynasty in Myanmar. In

The Kaunghmudaw Pagoda of King Thalun, Sagaing, built in the 17th century.

this case, after the first three kings had reunified, reconsolidated and rebuilt the kingdom by the middle of the seventeenth century, their successors could not sustain the momentum. Rather than strengthening the state further they reaped the fruits sown by the founders instead, often untroubled and carelessly, inevitably shrinking resources and compromising the viability of the kingdom. Dwindling resources, in turn, triggered or exacerbated challenges to established authority, erupting at 'crisis laden' occasions such as succession and other instances of disorder. And these challenges invariably came from within the legitimate pool of royal contenders not from outside it.

The state would subsequently begin to fragment into its parts once again, creating a situation that often invited external invasion as well. In this case it was the overthrown remnants of the Ming taking refuge in Yunnan that disrupted the balance of power amongst the Shan Sawbwas, which, in turn, had an impact on Ava. But almost always, as central weakness grew, an internal rather than external enemy would bring the kingdom to its end. Decentralization and anarchy would follow for a time until a new leader once again rose from the ashes to create a new dynasty and more or less repeat the process all over again. All six dynasties of Myanmar went through a similar process: each rose rapidly, established their rule over much of what is now Myanmar and nearly as quickly declined. And all, except Pagan, lasted no longer than two centuries each.[6]

Several less able kings inherited these disintegrated conditions after Thalun died: Pindale (*reg.* 1648–61), Pye (1661–72), Narawara (1672–3), Minyekyawdin (1673–98) and Sane (1698–1714). Yet not everything was bleak during these reigns. The *Jatatawbon*, one of the most reliable treatises on the horoscopes (therefore dates) of Myanmar's earliest kings, is attributed to Minyekywadin's reign. Even more important, the most comprehensive chronicle of the state produced in Myanmar, the *Mahayazawingyi* by U Kala, on which virtually all other 'national' chronicles of Myanmar are based, was written during the reign of King Taninganwe (1714–33). Admittedly, and although that is a major achievement, it had little or nothing to do with state viability, for U Kala was a private individual with independent means to support his passion.

Indeed, long-term patterns, such as the drain of crown-service groups (*ahmudan*) and other forms of taxable wealth into the tax-exempt religious sector went unchecked during these decades when no strong leaders emerged to arrest the trend. King Pye reportedly stated that only if military *ahmudan* were content would the king be secure. So he lavished favours on them perhaps at the expense of other groups. Despite this favouritism, crown labour continued to flow to the Sangha anyway, for as economic or social conditions deteriorated, crown-service groups disproportionately bore the burden, so their recourse was to enter the ubiquitous 'safe haven' of society, the Sangha. It offered protection, economic security and ease of life. In 1728 Taninganwe issued an edict to arrest this trend, forbidding *ahmudan* from changing status to become either *paya kyun* or monk. (Although such statements have been construed as evidence of 'flight' to the periphery and 'leakage' from the centres by some, it is really a case of *ahmudan* attempting to change their status *while remaining within* the centre.)

And as in earlier times the Sangha itself had problems of sectarianism, particularly disputes over the degree of imagined orthodoxy, such as that between the austere and ascetic forest monks and the more 'worldly' village dwelling ones. Amongst the latter as well there would be minor disputes, such as whether one should cover one shoulder or both shoulders with the saffron robe, a controversy that continued into the nineteenth century. Much worse, there were incidents of bogus monks such as the Hein Pongyi who had become a bandit leader whose men terrorized rural areas.

The Second Ava Dynasty continued its downward spiral, attested by signs of disintegration: effete leadership, court intrigue and factionalism, and the appearance of external enemies on the kingdom's borders, an invariable consequence of internal weakness. In 1736 there were executions at court of ministers attempting to overthrow the king; raids from Manipur (northeastern India) began the same year; while wealth continued to flow to an increasingly wealthy, uncontrolled and heterodox Sangha, in part as an attempt to arrest these disintegrating factors by invoking religion but which only exacerbated the problem. As noted there were also raids by Ch'ing armies pursuing military leaders of the Ming dynasty who had fled to Yunnan and northeast Myanmar with their troops.

Taninganwe's son, known by his regnal title of Mahadhamayazadi-pati ('Chief of the Great Dhammarajas'), succeeded his father in 1733 and ruled until 1752, a relatively long reign of nearly 20 years. And although in the broader scheme of things it too was part of the period of decline, it was known for at least one famous literary scholar, Padethayaza. Considered by scholars of Burmese literature to be an outstanding figure in the field, he continued to write *pyo* (a kind of verse that goes back to the Pagan period).

His 'Maniket Zattawgyi', a *Jataka* play about a horse with a ruby eye, is considered to have been a new form in Burmese literature which some scholars think may have been borrowed from Siam. He wrote classical songs, concerned mainly with praises of his king, but also a quite different genre called *tyabwe*. These are short songs written not for the king and court but for ordinary folk. Four such songs survive in one form or another, in which the simple joys of village peasant life through the changing seasons are described. One called the 'Tari-palm climber' *tyabwe*, is as follows:

In the beginning of the hot weather, when the haze rises,
With his ladder and inseparable pot,
His sharp knife stuck in his waist,
To the tari buds and tari branches luxuriantly sprouting,
With his seat slung from his shoulder he climbs.
Tari stalks and spreading tari leaves
He cuts and notches a main to win the first fresh tari juice.
His loving wife collects the tari juice.
He shouts and cries to his sons and grandsons and calls to the
dogs and pigs.
And behold! a hare-net corded with tari-fibre.

The noise of calling resounds; men are clamorous;
Dogs yelp; men yell; they strike and beat.
Chamaeleon, hare, partridge – all that are in the bushes –
Quail, fowl, iguana, snake,
Wolves too straightway come out.
With joyous zest the wife
Gets a mixed load of curry-leaves good and indifferent.

The husband's concern is the hares and such other
Creatures of the wild as he encounters;
He takes and puts them in his sack.

And so returning and having rested a little,
They do their roasting at the jaggery fire on sharp spits.
When the curry-pot boils they put in the roast.
And stir the pot, and cook it in water.
They have too Mo-hmyaw [sky-gazing] chillies.
When all is set on the large wicker tray,
Daughters and sons, so many there is scarce room,
Push and thrust with only one knee – there's not space for both –
Vying with each other and determined to eat.
They fall to in fine style plying the coconut dipper.
Each with bent head takes handfuls and gobbles.
When they have finished there's no washing up –
They leave what remains to the dogs.[7]

Writing of this kind disappears for about 100 years after Padetha-yaza went into captivity with his king in 1752 when Ava was taken by Pegu and the whole court moved to Lower Burma. Curiously, however (or perhaps not surprisingly) Pegu of this period does not produce anything noteworthy, at least not known to have survived, even with virtually the whole Ava court intact, including Padethayaza. The subsequent battle for Pegu may have destroyed much of the data.

THE END OF THE SECOND AVA DYNASTY

The conquest of Ava has been depicted in the historiography of Myanmar in the standard framework of analysis: an ethnic war whereby the Mon speaking masses of Pegu had arisen in rebellion against an oppressive Burmese-speaking monarchy at Ava. In terms of both analysis and evidence that simple perspective cannot hold, for the immediate causes of the conquest of Ava were not only far more complicated, they had little or nothing to do with reified ethnicity.

The spark that lit the kindling had to do with the revolt by the governor of Pegu, an appointee of Ava no less, who wanted to strike out for himself when the Manipuris (from eastern India) began raiding Ava in 1740, preoccupying it in the north. It was, once again, an elite contest, triggering other discontents to also revolt, exacerbating the situation. In times of such crises the concepts surrounding the idea of a *minlaung* ('incipient king') who will bring order to the chaos come to the fore. Of course, every group vying for the throne would claim its leader was the *minlaung*.

In this particular case the most celebrated one was an ex-monk who had sought monastic sanctuary earlier, waiting for the right moment to fling off his saffron robe. He eventually took the throne of Pegu, adopting a Mon title, Smim Htaw Buddhaketi, even though he was a member of the Ava elite. Chiang Mai, also waiting for the right moment to throw off Ava's yoke, immediately recognized the usurper's legitimacy by presenting him with a royal daughter and a 'white' elephant.[8] He and his chief assistant, Binnya Dala, subsequently spread their authority until by 1743 they had taken Syriam, Tavoy and Martaban, at the time under Ava's hegemony. Their governors fled to Ayuthaya where they and their troops were well received, resulting in some détente between Ava and Ayuthaya, as gifts and diplomatic envoys were exchanged. (Padethayaza even wrote a poem on these Siamese envoys.)

Eventually Smim Htaw Buddhaketi was deposed and Binnya Dala ascended the throne of Pegu, where he vowed that the glory days of Bayinnaung would be restored. At the end of 1751 he moved upon Ava in exactly the same way Bayinnaung had done 200 years earlier: a two-pronged attack, one up the Sittaung River valley taking Kyaukse (thereby denying Ava the most important granary of Upper Myanmar), the other moving up the Irrawaddy River towards Ava, taking it in April of 1752 and burning it to the ground. Thus the conquest and elimination of the Second Ava Dynasty had little or nothing to do with ethnicity, as so often contended. Rather, long-term geo-political and economic factors, along with unique 'incidents of the moment', were ultimately responsible.

Leaving only a third of his forces garrisoned at Ava, Binnya Dala took the king (Mahadhamayazadipati) and his entire court, including the royal family, all the court records that survived and transported them back to Lower Myamar. This was not an act of compassion: he needed the 'high culture' of Ava, for after the destruction of 1599 the maritime region no longer had vestiges of an exemplary 'tradition' to emulate. Yet by leaving Ava and the Dry Zone, where the bulk of the population and the country's history lay, Pegu's leaders were in effect admitting that they had no intention of reuniting the country or forging a new 'national' dynasty that represented the majority of the people in the land.

Had Pegu been genuinely interested in creating a political entity larger than itself it would not have abandoned the interior. That it did suggests that they were mere 'spoilers', who although given the opportunity had neither the vision, courage, confidence nor experience to assume that leadership. At the same time they did not want anyone else to take the helm. They certainly showed no interest in ruling an agrarian population; preferring instead the excitement of a bustling commercial region with its many different peoples, languages and ways of doing things.

Thus, like the Syam raids of the mid-fourteenth century, and those by the Arakanese and T'ais in 1599, this time as well Pegu returned home without committing to and certainly not securing the Dry Zone. And, by leaving, Lower Myanmar once again left the door open for Upper Myanmar to reassert its paramountcy, the story of the next chapter.

8

The Last Myanmar Dynasty

Upon taking Ava in 1752, Pegu had sent out contingents of troops to important *myosa*-ships in Upper Myanmar demanding oaths of loyalty. Across the Irrawaddy River from Ava lay one of the richest irrigated regions of the Dry Zone, the Mu Valley. There, in an ancient provincial centre, Moksobo ('chief of the hunters'), whose origins go back to the Pagan period, was a charismatic headman named U Aung Zeya. He had watched the whole process unfold before him. Anticipating the inevitable demand for his loyalty, and intending not to comply, he began repairing and preparing his defences. When Pegu's contingent of troops finally arrived, he soundly defeated them and did so twice more, seizing their arms, especially their muskets, the most valuable prize of war at the time. When word spread of his victories many fighting men flocked to his side. He encouraged more people to join his resistance by providing land to all those who agreed to become his *ahmudan* (literally, 'bear [his] burden'), supplying them with rice, clothing and arms.[1]

Since Aung Zeya was not of royal blood he had to devise a genealogy that traced his lineage back to Pyusawhti, the legendary founder of Pagan. This was in part assured, for as de facto lord of the Mu Valley he already fulfilled one of the criteria of legitimate Burmese kings: a *kammaraja*, whose karma rather than his genealogy made him what he was. Still, he needed more, so ensured that all the proper prophecies and omens 'foretold' his reign, while invoking *Gavampati*, the tutelary deity of capital cities in Myanmar, to be guardian of Moksobo, renamed Shwebo.[2] His regnal title, Alaungmintayagyi ('Great Imminent King of Righteousness') is approximately the Burmese equivalent of the Pali that integrates two other notions of Burmese kingship – a future bodhisattva who will 'save' all humans and a current *dhammaraja* ('lord of morality') who will rule righteously – echoing the royal titles and conceptions used by Pagan kings. He was later (and more popularly) known as Alaungpaya.

At the auspicious time, on 21 June 1753, he constructed a proper capital with the seven requisites, giving it the formal title of *Yadana*

Theinga Konbaung Pyi ('The Konbaung Capital of the Jewelled Lion'), simply known as Shwebo. He had enticed former court officials of Ava who had escaped the conquest and were familiar with state ritual and other procedures of the old court to his new capital. He would need them later when the time came to actually administer the state. Also in the traditional manner and to legitimate his authority he appointed the monk who was his former teacher as chief adviser of religious affairs. As the latter belonged to one of the main orders (who covered only one shoulder with their robes, hence called the 'one shoulder' sect), his choice invariably reduced the influence of the other ('two shoulder' sect) which had gained in prominence during the previous dynasty.

Such preliminary steps were necessary before retaking Lower Myanmar, his main goal. He would begin in the Dry Zone, consolidating its economic and military resources there first, only after which he would move downstream. The primary objective in Upper Myanmar, of course, would be Ava, defended by a Pegu garrison, with its valuable human and material resources, fortifications, strategic location, symbolism and sacred genealogy. On 3 January 1754 he marched on Ava and took it. Upon hearing the news Pegu assembled its forces and marched on Ava. The naval forces sent up-river were smashed by Alaungpaya's fleet, panicking the land forces that accompanied them. As this news spread back to Pegu, fighting men flocked to the winning side, swelling his forces even more. The time was now ripe to take Lower Myanmar and put it back into the fold.

Modern reconstruction of Alaungpaya's Palace, Shwebo, built in the 1990s; the original was built in the 18th century.

Methodically and patiently, step by step, he took the most important fortified cities on the Irrawaddy critical to holding that most crucial north–south artery. First, Prome was taken in February of 1755. Then, in April of the same year, Dagon, en route to Pegu, fell to his forces and was renamed Yangon, 'End of Enmity'. A year later, in July, he took Syriam, a well-fortified port across the river from Yangon and defended with French guns. Thereafter only Pegu was left as the main obstacle to his vision of a united kingdom.

On the night of 6 May 1757, before the rains arrived and forced him to return to Upper Myanmar, commandos scaled the walls of Pegu, opened the gates and set parts of the city afire as signal. Although the conquest of Pegu has been called, by some colonial historians, a 'holocaust' and an alleged 'extermination' of the Mon 'race' by the Burmese, it was neither. Alaungpaya's policy was not a matter of 'race' but a matter of loyalty within the context of the traditional patron–client structure. Those who identified themselves as Mon but acknowledged his suzerainty survived, while those identifying themselves as Burmese who did not, were killed.[3] Even this (latter) action was likely very limited and required some circumspection, for in a region where labour was scarce and fighting men were prized, killing a soldier was a great waste. On the part of the soldier, survival preempted 'ethnic' (or ideological) loyalties – had there been any to begin with – so that acknowledging the winner's suzerainty was an issue of little (or no) importance.

It is true, however, that unlike other unifiers for whom this 'race card' was not available during their reigns, Alaungpaya did in fact exploit it by appealing to the large population of Burmese speakers in Upper Myanmar. But that does not mean the *reasons* for his actions against Pegu were racially motivated. They were not any different from Pegu's earlier (geo-political and economic) reasons for taking Ava or, for that matter, any number of such examples in Myanmar's history. Rather, Alaungpaya used 'imagined ethnicity' as a rallying cry for political and military purposes, as some of his most trusted followers were both Burmese and Mon speakers.[4] Reified ethnicity, therefore, was *not* a causal factor in the making of history in pre-colonial Myanmar, as colonial historiography has it.

Alaungpaya returned to Upper Myanmar after taking Pegu, leaving it in charge of a governor loyal to him. Thus within a mere five years he had retaken all the important governorships in the country, subdued the main contender, Pegu, and had unified Upper and Lower Myanmar in one kingdom. And it was all accomplished in a manner and speed repeated by nearly all of Myanmar's dynasties.

To reiterate, next to Kyaukse, the Mu Valley where Alaungpaya began his quest for reunification was the most important region of rice production in all of Upper Myanmar. Whoever controlled the strategic towns in those two valleys controlled nearly all of the human and material resources of Upper Myanmar. The modus operandi of his operation, then – even down to the specific military strategy used – was much like those of the ancient kings of Pagan. Aniruddha, Kyanzittha and Narapatisithu and the founders of virtually every other Upper Myanmar dynasty began their conquests by taking one of the main irrigated valleys, then the other two, only after which they would proceed to the coasts. (The exception, of course, was the Second Pegu/Toungoo Dynasty of Tabinshwehti and Bayinnaung which was already on the coasts, so had reversed the process by accumulating wealth from trade and commerce first, only after which the Dry Zone was taken.)

Within the next ten years Alaungpaya was at the doorsteps of Ayuthaya. From the inception of the Konbaung Dynasty to this point numbered less than fifteen years, nearly the same amount of time Pagan king Aniruddha took – thirteen years – to establish himself in Upper Myanmar before conquering all or most of the country back in the mid-eleventh century. Although it is easy to understand the reason Lower Myanmar was important to Upper Myanmar, it may be less clear why Ayuthaya was. Conventional interpretations have normally attributed motives and consequences that are either trivial and/or disparaging of Myanmar's monarchy: that is, the act of simple-minded and barbaric kings laden with superstitious beliefs, particularly the burning desire to obtain a 'white' elephant (actually an albino). The latter is invariably cited as the most important reason for attacking Ayuthaya.[5] Other reasons implied an almost innate militarily aggressive nature of Burmese kings. Such interpretations were very much part of the demonization process of the 'Other' by the colonial powers for justifying their own conquests *ex post facto*.

The quest for a 'white' elephant (or for that matter, the Holy Grail, or in today's context, to establish 'democracy'), true or not, is often a rationalization nonetheless for political and/or economic hegemony, not unique to Burmese culture and found in many societies with some history of expansion. Indeed, there exist far better examples of such behaviour than Myanmar. The critique here is not so much the particular object (white elephant or the Holy Grail) used for legitimating military and political designs, but their rationalization in religious and ideological terms.

The answer to 'why Ayuthaya', lies in the geo–political relationship between Lower Myanmar and Lower Thailand. The two regions had been intimately connected in numerous ways since at least the late thirteenth century. When the Second Pegu/Toungoo Dynasty was located in Lower Myanmar the concern over Ayuthaya was obvious: it was a direct competitor demographically, militarily, economically and politically. And although there was no appreciable competition between Dry Zone agrarian Ava and largely maritime Ayuthaya, as long as Lower Myanmar itself was part of Ava's total vision, Ayuthaya was invariably a factor. In the long-term interests of Upper Myanmar, that included Lower Myanmar, the latter could not remain secure or viable unless its direct competitor, Ayuthaya, was subdued or at least weakened.

There were other more immediate factors before and during Alaungpaya's reign that affected these more or less long-term principles. During the conquest of Pegu in 1599, the wars of reunification by the Second Ava Dynasty and, most recently, when Alaungpaya subdued Dagon, Syriam and Pegu one by one, much of the population reportedly was either deported or fled to the border areas of the T'ai kingdom, seriously depopulating Lower Myanmar. In order for the coasts to be economically viable and useful to Ava, they had to be repopulated, and for that a nearby, high-density urban area was needed: that was Ayuthaya. Conquest of such a place was far more cost-effective than taking non-urban, especially sparsely populated, hill areas. And there was always the incentive of the spoils of war for the victors, not only in terms of the acquisition of much needed labour for the state, but immediate rewards in cash and other valuables for individuals who participated.

But conquering an exemplary centre such as Ayuthaya also had to do with domestic and regional political concerns. It confirmed the king's image of a *cakravartin* ('world conqueror') not only to neighbouring states that shared the same ideology but to his own population and ruling elite. Such successful conquests were often more than enough to persuade uncommitted 'fence-sitters' as well as other semi-autonomous centres of power in the region to throw in their lot with the winner. Domestically it legitimated (with the ideology of karma) one's position as king *ex post facto*. Even for the vanquished, the fact of losing itself provided the kind of crisis needed to justify changing the political status quo in one's own interests.

Alaungpaya died in 'friendly fire' in 1760 from wounds incurred when one of his own cannons exploded while laying siege to Ayuthaya. His body was taken back to Shwebo and his remains interred there, now marked with a modest tomb over which is a small building with traditional layered 'towers' (*pyathat*) on whose walls are painted a map of the routes taken for his military conquests. There is also a realistic statue of him at the Shwebo palace site representing his full 5'11" height and muscular frame as described by one British envoy who met him personally.

After the brief reign of Naundawgyi (1760–3), Alaungpaya's son and crown prince who died peacefully, his brother Hsinbyushin ('Lord of the White Elephant') succeeded. He reinstated Ava as capital and moved

Statue of King Alaungpaya, Shwebo, made in the 1990s.

there in 1765. Two years later, on 28 March 1767, he finally accomplished what had long escaped his father: the conquest of Ayuthaya. The campaign was led by two single-minded and dedicated Burmese generals who spent three years on the conquest, including a year and a half on the siege itself.

At the time Ayuthaya was the most powerful kingdom in central mainland Southeast Asia and did not give up without a long hard battle. In the end they succumbed to the Ava forces (in which were Burmese, Shan and Lao levies). The conquerors found the body of the Siamese king, who was identified by his brother, a prisoner under the deceased king, suggesting a scenario of court factionalism at Ayuthaya similar to the one at Ava. There is some discrepancy in original and contemporary sources as to whether Ayuthaya was totally burned to the ground or remained mainly intact, and placed in the charge of a member of the royal family who swore allegiance to Ava. That much booty and people (although not a 'white elephant') were brought back to Ava, however, seems clear enough.[6]

Part of the reason Ayuthaya was a tempting target is that being largely a maritime commercial centre much of its wealth lay in the form of liquid assets that were kept at the palace itself, so that conquering it meant immediate acquisition of that wealth. In contrast the bulk of the wealth of the Burmese state lay in the rice fields distributed throughout the kingdom – and even that was seasonal – while much of its liquid assets was usually earmarked for or already spent on the Religion. Taking Ava was not about to make any enemy much richer, whereas taking Ayuthaya was.

Only a year after the campaign for Ayuthaya had begun (1764) there was a series of four Chinese invasions of the kingdom of Ava from the north that lasted for several years between 1765 and 1769. It seems the Ch'ing wanted to maintain their hegemony and balance of power in mainland Southeast Asia by preventing any single power dominating it, and so created another 'front' in the north to force an end to the Ayuthaya campaign.

But the generals on the Ayuthaya campaign were not recalled by Hsinphyushin, while the northern army of Ava managed to hold off the Chinese, utilizing the series of stockades that had been built in the mid-eleventh century by Aniruddha and maintained throughout the centuries. By 1769, with Ayuthaya conquered and the Burmese armies back at Ava, the Chinese decided they could no longer sustain any more losses (reported by their own sources to be around 20,000 men, along with a sizeable amount of arms and ammunition) and therefore sued for peace.[7]

Although concerned about the wrath of their king if they were too conciliatory towards the Chinese, the Burmese generals nevertheless accepted honourable terms, in part, noted the Burmese chronicle, to give the Emperor a face-saving device that was in the future interests of the Burmese kingdom. The peace terms that were signed at Kaungton, one of the strongest northern stockades of the Burmese kingdom since Pagan times, allowed safe passage to the Chinese withdrawal. The treaty also allowed for the restoration of trade relations and reinstated the sending of diplomatic missions between the two states at given intervals. The where-withal to successfully fight on two fronts against formidable foes, one of them the superpower of Asia, says much about the military capabilities of the state in Myanmar during the early Konbaung Dynasty.

After such victories Burmese kings normally patronized the Religion in a very public way, not only to demonstrate their good karma but to fulfil their role as legitimate Buddhist kings who, among other things, propagated the Religion, as the quintessential Buddhist king Asoka had done. They built monasteries and pagodas, gilded them with gold leaf, endowed them with tax-exempt lands and people and heaped other forms of largesse on the Religion and its guardians, the Sangha. (Such practices and their underlying ideology continue into modern times.)[8] The consequences of such profligate spending by Hsinphyushin and his immediate successor, Singu (*reg.* 1776–82), however, fell on the Badon Prince, another son of Alaungpaya who became known as King Bodawpaya (1782–1819). It was left to him to 'balance the budget', which he did in part by conducting two full-scale revenue inquests towards the last quarter of his reign.[9]

When he first ascended the throne Bodawpaya wisely reappointed the former ministers under Hsinphyushin to their old positions. Others who aided in his acquisition of the throne were rewarded, while those who attempted to oust him were handled in the usual fashion. After a year he moved his capital north from Ava across the Irrawaddy River to Amarapura ('City of Immortals').

The shifting of capitals in Myanmar has been interpreted as acts of superstition and/or irrationality determined by astrology and paranoia. Although astrology is indeed very important in Burmese society, it is not necessarily the *reason* for this particular action. Rather, auspicious dates are considered seriously in order to determine the best time to undertake such important activities, whose decisions have *already been made* for other, usually strategic reasons.[10] As Ava had recently been taken at least twice by forces from the south, Bodawpaya may have regarded Amarapura as a more defensible site, protected on its south and southeast by large bodies of water: the Irrawaddy, Myitnge and large lakes. It is true that Ava was also protected on all sides by water but Amarapura was more difficult to attack from Lower Myanmar, which had become the direction of concern after the Chinese had been repelled in the north.

Bodawpaya may have also deemed Amarapura to be healthier and more open on the north as Mandalay had not yet been built. It was certainly less congested and therefore less vulnerable to disease and fires.

At the same time there is no doubt that the building of a new capital had to do with Ava's increasing inauspiciousness, especially after the many centuries of blood-letting that had occurred in the palace and its grounds. This reason is particularly important in light of having secured a most sacred image of the Buddha, the Mahamuni, from Arakan after its conquest in 1784, which was enshrined at the new capital. (It remains one of the most sacred images in the country today.) The Arakan conquest was justified with the standard ideology for expansion in most Buddhist kingdoms, *dhammavijaya* ('righteous victory'). Such an act was considered one of the most important activities a Buddhist king could possibly perform to prove his worth.[11]

As with nearly all other previous dynasties Amarapura's 'front door' faced north towards China, not south to the Gulf of Martaban, the 'back door' where the West would soon enter in great force. The diplomatic relations begun at the Treaty of Kaungton in 1769 with China were maintained throughout Bodawpaya's reign (and beyond) as China sent missions to Myanmar regularly: in 1787, 1790, 1795, 1796 and 1822, while Myanmar sent missions to China in 1782, 1787, 1792 and 1823. No equivalent official diplomatic exchanges occurred with Western powers in the country's pre-colonial history, even after they had appeared on the scene by the fifteenth century at the 'back door' of Myanmar.

Western-trained historians consider King Bodawpaya's administrative achievements his most important, notably his two revenue inquests mentioned above, one in 1784–6 and another in 1803. They were based on the written depositions of village headmen in the kingdom who reported on their personal genealogies, the boundaries of their jurisdictions, the type of produce their villages yielded, the amount of revenue collected and submitted, the amount of exempt religious lands in their domains and the number of males and females in their charge.[12]

In part these censuses were meant to record and assess the resources of the state, as King Thalun had done during the Second Ava Dynasty and others before him, but were also intended to distinguish religious from state property more clearly in order to determine the extent of tax-exempt religious lands in the kingdom, thereby giving the state a better idea of what was taxable and what was not. The strategy also included collecting stone inscriptions, the ultimate legal records of religious property (in effect, title deeds) or copying those that could not be removed from their original place. Both originals and copies were placed at a central location at Amarapura, most of which are still there today. Like other kings before him, Bodawpaya had to control the flow of wealth to the Sangha, an organization with which he was also said to have some problems.[13]

But he did not conduct a full-scale *sasana* reform as King Dhammazedi had done in the late fifteenth century. Instead Bodawpaya directed the process by issuing royal edicts, one of which ordered the people to stop using the term *hpon gyi* ('great glory') for monks, as 'he thought them too numerous . . . lazy and ignorant, and issued orders that stricter examination should be made into the attainments of heads of monasteries.'[14] To further counterbalance the influence of the Sangha he publicly patronized the Mahagiri Nats, the recognized guardian spirits of the Burmese kingdom (according to some, representing the 'competing' ideology to Theravada Buddhism), making two new heads for them in 1785 on Mount Popa, their national abode, and subsequently replacing them with larger ones in 1812.

His strategy also included using 'orthodox' methods that challenged the interpretation of certain crucial Buddhist doctrines, based not only on his personal knowledge of the scriptures but ensuring that the kingdom's Primate supported him (usually the king's teacher when he was still a prince and his appointee as head of the Sangha when he became king). Notwithstanding Bodawpaya's problematic situation with the Sangha, the relationship between state and church in Myanmar's history was generally more cosy than adversarial, a situation that continued well into the twenty-first century, periodic contestations notwithstanding.[15]

The inquest of 1784 must have been effective, for it reportedly filled Bodawpaya's treasury and, as a result, in 1785–6 the king began preparations for the conquest of Siam, perhaps less for the reasons noted above than to enhance his own stature as *cakravartin*.[16] What Bodawpaya did not realize was that the Siam of his time was no longer the Siam of Hsinbyushin's time, so that the Burmese armies were repelled at virtually every step once inside its borders, although he continued to send them until he ran out of money.

At court he attempted to stabilize the succession, a curse in the history of the Myanmar monarchy. Although many princes were legally eligible for the throne, there had been an established and well-understood law of succession since the Pagan period. Not only was the eldest son of the king and chief queen customarily designated crown prince (*Einshemin* 'Lord of the Front [East] Palace'), his formal position was also materially supported by his control of the Tatmadaw (lit. 'main royal armed forces') as *ex officio* commander-in-chief.[17]

Nevertheless, that rule of succession automatically creates a rift between uncles and nephews, for the king's brother (as a son of the previous king and chief queen) is as eligible for the throne as the king's eldest son. And if the present eldest son of the king were to become king, then the entire line of the king's younger brother would be forever removed from the path to the throne. That tension was played out regularly in coups and counter-coups throughout Burmese history beginning with the Pagan period, largely *elite* contests for the throne. As noted above they were not struggles between peasants and elite but between elites left out of the power structure and those in the establishment, and were not *revolutions* to change society but *revolts* to take control of the governing apparatus.[18]

Wishing to follow the orders of Alaungpaya (that succession move from 'son to grandson'), Bodawpaya's son was designated crown prince. That effectively cut off Bodawpaya's two brothers the Pahkan and Pindale princes from the throne, who, predictably, rebelled. They failed; one was executed, the former retired into obscurity. In this particular case the king and crown prince were in firm control even if the situation were ripe for many intrigues. Bodawpaya left the affairs of state to the crown prince more and more as he became older. The crown prince and another son of Bodawpaya, the prince of Prome, in effect ran the Government. Indeed, so effective was the set up that the king often talked of stepping down in favour of his son. But that was difficult, for Bodawpaya had six sons altogether, all with good fiefs and well supplied with crown troops.

And as typical of successful rulers, as the king got along in years he began to devote more of his life to religious affairs. In 1790 he planned to surpass all the kings of Pagan by building the largest temple in the land, the Mingun Pagoda. It was located across the Irrawaddy River from Amarapura north of Sagaing, where he spent much of his time, even establishing a temporary palace there to personally supervise his work of merit. The huge brick and mortar lions guarding it still stand, and are 95 ft high, their eyeballs 13 ft in circumference, while the great bell (that is normally part of each temple) is the largest ringing bell in the world, weighing 80 tonnes. The temple itself would have been 500 ft high had it been completed. But an earthquake struck before that happened, creating the usual *ex post facto* prophecies and omens about the impending demise of the kingdom.

Around 1800, for reasons that had to do with the ministerial power at court, Bodawpaya deposed his four *wungyis* (chief ministers) without replacing them. With the ministers removed and all the princes given fiefs of some worth, the kingdom was ripe for a power struggle if anything happened to the crown prince or the king. Something did happen to the crown prince: he died. So Bodawpaya immediately replaced him with the Sagaing prince, son of the crown prince. And to ensure his security, in addition to the usual treasures, arms, fiefs and portfolio of commander-in-chief reserved for that office, the new crown prince was given over 25,000 houses as part of his fief, along with 3,620 musketeers.

And when the Toungoo prince, half-brother of the crown prince, showed signs of fortifying Toungoo, Bodawpaya personally led a force of 50,000 to dismantle it and returned him to the capital. The king thus resumed a personal role in the running of the kingdom after the original and competent crown prince, whom he trusted, died. This pattern of *personal* governance, of trusting *people over institutions*, is still very much a part of the political fabric today. That means once a strong leader dies, unless another strong leader steps in to replace him, the state is vulnerable to the usual centrifugal forces that lead to disintegration.

DECLINE OF THE KONBAUNG DYNASTY AND DEMISE OF THE BURMESE MONARCHY

The last years of Bodawpaya's reign may have been the beginning of a decline of the dynasty and kingdom from which the monarchy would not recover. The king died on 5 June 1819, at the age of 75. After a funeral reserved for *cakravartins*, the crown prince, later known as Bagyidaw ('Royal Uncle'), ascended the throne (*reg.* 1819–37). The standard attempted coups, counter-purges and executions were said to have followed. With hardly any opposition thereafter, he reigned supreme. For unclear reasons he also decided to move the capital back to Ava.

He must have been an enigmatic figure in other ways, for the accounts of him are contradictory. The conventional one paints him as an irresponsible tyrant with fits of insanity who cared mainly about gambling, cockfighting and drinking.[19] It is clear this image of the king was carefully crafted by the British merchant community of Lower Myanmar, in league with some missionary groups, to demonize the monarchy not only as an 'outmoded' impediment to 'free trade' but to Christian salvation, all the while clamouring for military action by the British Government of India to colonize the country.

However, there are accounts of him that are just the opposite. One (colonial) historian wrote that he was 'graceful and dignified in public; in private he had charming manners and was most approachable. He took exercise daily, riding an elephant . . . and he delighted in the magnificent regattas which were such a feature under the kings.' Bagyidaw was said to be so kind and beloved that there were no rebellions during his long reign.[20] Religion was said to have been resplendent during his reign as well. One of the treasures of this period is the brick monastery, the Maha Aung Mye Bonzan, built by his chief queen, still a favourite tourist attraction today.

From the variety and nature of the accounts we have of him it appears that the second assessment of the king is more accurate, although ironically, that kind of personality was precisely what made him even more

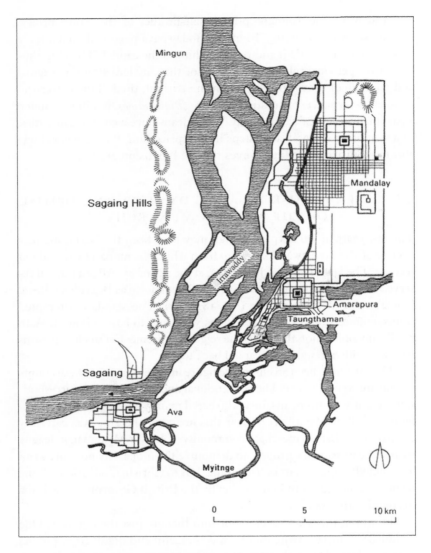

Ava, Amarapura and Mandalay, mid-18th to late 19th century.

vulnerable to external foes. The First Anglo–Burmese War (1824–6), which began during Bagyidaw's 'watch', was the first of three blows that would eliminate the Burmese monarchy before the century was over. The Second occurred in 1852 and the third and last in 1885–6, which turned Myanmar into a British colony.[21]

As a consequence of the first war the Kingdom lost Arakan and Tenasserim, its most important maritime revenue-bearing regions and their populations, seriously weakening the state. At the end of the second it lost all of the Lower Myanmar Delta including Pegu and its adjacent teak forests. By then the Kingdom was completely landlocked, a situation not experienced before, so that the last decade or so prior to the last war and final annexation was the country's weakest hour.

Thus, as fate would have it, at the precise time when Britain was one of the most powerful countries on earth, Myanmar was at one of its weakest stages. The kingdom was not the same during the first half of the nineteenth century as it was in the second half; for by that time the Burmese state was at the 'bottom of the barrel', not the pinnacle of integration as conventionally portrayed. In terms of political and military power, wealth and territory, Ava and Amarapura under Alaungpaya, Hsinphyshin and Bodawpaya were simply not the same as Mandalay under Mindon (*reg.* 1853–78) and Thibaw (1878–85), final successors of Bagyidaw.

The last two kings, Mindon and Thibaw, stand out in English-language historiography as a paradigm of good and evil. The first was applauded for his even-tempered, principled and almost obsequious nature (when dealing with the British), while the second was said to be weak, with delusions of persecution and grandeur. Yet it is clear that both these images have been crafted to be commensurate with certain desired consequences.

Mandalay citadel and moat, built in the 19th century.

Western writers invariably paint Mindon in a 'positive' manner, as a 'reformer' who introduced some Western ways: salaries to replace *myosa* allotments, the telegraph, the Burmese Morse Code. However, if Mindon were asked what *he* considered his most important achievements, he surely would have pointed to the convening of the Fifth Buddhist Synod in 1871 in the tradition of the most exemplary of Buddhist kings, Asoka of India. This great religious event culminated with the completion of the Kuthodawgyi ('Great Royal Work of Merit'), a large pagoda that sits at the foot of Mandalay Hill in whose precincts the entire Theravada Buddhist scriptures, 'purified' in that Synod, were inscribed on 729 marble slabs. That, along with his patronage of the Religion in general, would have been his own criteria for evaluating his reign, not developing a Burmese Morse Code.

In contrast Thibaw has been demonized by both Western and indigenous historians; the first, in order to justify the Third Anglo–Burmese War and annexation of his kingdom, and the second, for having lost it. But in fact, he was said to have been a mild-mannered, playful, studious type, who never wanted to be king in the first place, 'hen-pecked' by his queens and bullied by his ministers.[22] He also had no chance against the mightiest industrialized power in the world at the time. (Indeed, none of the kings of the Konbaung Dynasty would have been able to withstand Britain's military might.) Thibaw happened to be the wrong king, in the wrong place, at the wrong time. However, that does not justify the way he has been depicted in (especially) the English-language historiography of Myanmar: a nineteenth-century 'axis of evil' whose toppling was allegedly applauded by most.[23]

Neither king received much praise from their most famous minister either, Kinwun Mingyi. He regarded both as relatively weak, although certainly not evil.[24] At the same time, the criteria for his judgement were not based on Burmese political values, but those acquired recently from the Western world. The minister had travelled abroad and visited at least three of Europe's most important capitals at the time: Rome, London and Paris. As a result he had become less concerned with the standard litmus test of good Burmese kings – maintaining a powerful military, ensuring agricultural productivity, promoting the religion and Sangha, performing important rituals of state and society (such as the erecting of finials on famous temples), preserving the social hierarchy, upholding law and order – than he was with their ability to demonstrate strength in times of crises and address matters of *realpolitik* vis à vis the new modern invaders, the British.[25] Besides, ministers had a certain amount of natural disdain for royalty, convinced that it was they, not royalty, who were the true unselfish guardians of the kingdom and state; hence Kinwun Mingyi's 'lukewarm' assessment of the two kings.

Indigenous or exogenous, written from inside the court or outside it, the historiography of Mindon and Thibaw (and the dynasty itself during its waning years) is in need of serious reassessment and good scholarship, particularly with research that uses primary indigenous evidence and interpreted from an 'angle of vision' that is not shaped by a current political agenda. Imagine the history of Cuba written only (or mainly) by American observers, using as primary source material only (or mainly) the testimony of the Cuban American community in Miami and State Department files.

Indeed, most English-language histories of Myanmar have character-ized the Burmese monarchy in general and this dynasty in particular as ignorant of the outside world, naive, arrogant and superstitious; a demonization process that rationalized its conquest subsequently. Quite regularly too, we read that Myanmar's kings were insane; not unlike the kinds of assessments made of the present Government by those in the Western world who do not understand it. (In fact some of the same vocab-ulary and phrases used in the nineteenth century for the Konbaung kings have reappeared in the English-language press today in depicting the recently dissolved military leadership.)

The British took Mandalay with relative ease in the Third Anglo–Burmese War of 1885, ending the 1,200-year-old monarchy. Three days of burning and looting by the conquerors followed, in which the Dynasty's palm-leaf records were piled up and burned as trash.[26] When it was finally stopped, the *remainder* filled 32 cart-loads which were sub-sequently transported to Yangon and earmarked for preservation. By the New Year the country was formally annexed and presented as a 'pre-sent' to Her Majesty the Queen of England by the Governor General of India. Myanmar was now part of the British Indian Empire, its mon-archy summarily dissolved when its last king, mild-mannered Thibaw, was exiled to India.

As he and his queen, along with a small entourage of attendants, were being led to the docks for the ship to India within a narrow gaunt-let of imposing British Indian Army soldiers in khaki uniforms with long sabres at their sides, throngs of Burmese (mainly women) lined the street, old and young, most on their knees, sobbing and wailing. The king and queen, symbolic 'father and mother' of the kingdom were being forcibly removed from their house and home by big terrifying-looking strangers, in front of their bewildered and distraught 'children'.

There had been other invaders before, of course, but Myanmar had never met such an external foe as the British. The Chinese had been the most powerful the country previously encountered, but even they were more often than not successfully withstood. This time Myanmar faced the most industrialized, technologically superior and most politically

Saya Chone, *The Exile of King Thibaw and Queen Supayalat*, painting, late 19th century.

unified nation-state in the world at the time. Its military enjoyed the most modern weapons, machines and tactics, not to mention the latest scientific knowledge, all financed by one of the world's largest economies with an endless supply of wealth derived from its many colonies around the globe. And it came through the 'back door' unexpectedly, for the bulk of the kingdom's defences were located in Upper Myanmar facing its 'front door', north towards the traditional routes of invasion.

This time too, the conquerors were not from the region, and did not understand the indigenous conceptual system, know the physical environment, share a common history or look like its people. The invaders' 'ethnic' background, homeland, history and culture could not have been more different. The intentions of the new invaders were also different; they were going to remain in and rule Myanmar for as long as they could. The Mongols, the Chinese, the T'ai, not to mention the Arakanese, the Mon and the Shan had attacked and, when victorious, taken the loot and returned home. Not this one, not this time.

Since the conquerors intended to stay for an indefinite amount of time they implemented changes of a substantive (structural) nature, in principle as well as in practice. The colonial market economy, egalitarian ideals, modern bureaucratic administration, elements of representative government and the ideologies that rationalized all of them came from civilizations and world views that could not have been more different. Their implementation insured that Myanmar would never entirely be the same again. At the same time religion, language, patron–client structures and values, socio-political and religious hierarchy, kinship patterns, notions of legitimacy and authority remained largely intact. It is that struggle between old and new, the past and the present – as stated in the Prologue – that still confounds and confronts Myanmar today.

9

Disintegration of the Burmese
Kingdom, 1824–1886

PRELUDE TO WAR, ON THE EDGES OF EMPIRES

Although the entry of the British into the history of Myanmar overlaps with the longer story of other European traders, adventurers, soldiers of fortune and priests who had been part of the region's dynamism for centuries, the British were actually latecomers to the country. In 1617 Henry Forest and John Staveley, perhaps the first Englishmen in Myanmar, were sent to Yangon to collect goods left by an agent of the (English) East India Company (EIC), who had died in Syriam, an important port city at the time, across from Yangon. Just 30 years later the company's efforts to establish a British presence bore some fruit with the arrival of the ship *Endeavour* and the securing of permission from the Burmese court to build a house and dock in Syriam.

The Dutch were already trading in Myanmar, while the Portuguese had been in Southeast Asia since the sixteenth century, having also established bases and factories along the coasts of East Africa, India, Goa, Sri Lanka, Malacca and Macao, and (as shown in previous chapters) had long been visible in the politics and history of the country. They had also played an important part in introducing new food products, ideas and technology into ports such as Pegu, Syriam and Yangon. Firearms, cannon and men trained in European military tactics were key resources which the Burmese throne immediately recognized and lured into royal service. We have seen how the successes of King Bayinnaung in his mid-sixteenth-century campaigns that unified the kingdom and extended Burmese territory briefly over Siam and Laos were, in part, the result of having incorporated Portuguese adventurers, their firearms and their tactics.

In addition to the Portuguese and Dutch were Armenians who provided the Burmese court with further European visions of the world. But all these necessarily took a 'back seat' to influences from India, China and neighbouring Buddhist kingdoms that had been in circulation for centuries throughout the kingdom. Moreover, Europeans had less influence on communities in the interior and hill areas than on those living on the coasts where they first established themselves.

By the end of the seventeenth century the East India Company sent a mission to Ava to establish closer relations with the court but, all the while, their gaze was more focused on other parts of Asia. Towards the middle of the eighteenth century strategic factors compelled the Company to establish a settlement in the island of Negrais (off the coast of southwest Myanmar), which was believed by then Governor Saunders to provide access to 'all parts of the King of Ava's dominions' and to be a good port from which to counter French influence in the region. Having a representative at the Burmese court was also a key priority for the Company, an issue pursued by future British missions seeking to regularize relations with the Burmese throne.

Despite these activities British influence in Myanmar would remain limited throughout the eighteenth century, as they were merely one of several communities (Asian, European, Middle-Eastern) that intermingled in the kingdom's coastal ports. The Burmese court was interested in English trade but only to a certain point, for there were already significant and fruitful commercial relations with the Portuguese, the Dutch and the Armenians. More important were Asian trading partners such as China and India, which remained a priority.

For the British, their most valuable colony remained India, and as late as the early nineteenth century they were still focused on developing their presence there. However, India's eastern boundaries at Bengal were contiguous to the Kingdom of Ava (as Myanmar was known to them) and that would soon become a bone of contention. Thus, although the British were relative latecomers to the region and to the peoples of Myanmar, their impact on the country in the nineteenth century was to be out of proportion to that tardiness.

The larger force behind it, ultimately, was the Industrial Revolution, which released socio-economic, ideological and political forces that were far larger than either the Burmese or the British, and very much factors in the 'remote origins' of the Anglo-Burmese wars that led to the annexation of the country. That growth of industrial power was, of course, rationalized by certain popular ideologies of the time that persuaded Britain it was the moral 'watchdog' of the world, its conscience so to speak, with a God-given (and natural) right to impose Western civilization (its religion, secular ideology, culture, economic and political systems) on 'less civilized' people.

This *mission civilisatrice* had the 'scientific' support of several new disciplines, especially in Darwin's work, and when applied to British society by the Social Darwinists, further 'explained' certain realities assumed to be 'universal'. Such ideas were further popularized by the 'adventure literature' of the time by writers like G. A. Henty, H. Rider Haggard, Rudyard Kipling, and sensationalized by the new journalism. In the forefront were the missionaries who went to all corners of the world, including Myanmar, proselytizing the divine plan. All of this was 'proved' by Empire itself, whose process, 'imperialism', historians would later attribute (in alliteration) to 'gold, god and glory' – that is, the economic, ideological and political factors.

By the last two decades of the nineteenth century Britain was the most powerful nation on earth, having conquered parts of Africa, the Middle East and nearly all of India, while its navy roamed the oceans with impunity. It reached as far as China, obtaining numerous concessions from it after the Opium Wars of the 1840s. By then however, it had competition in Southeast Asia. The French were to take Vietnam by mid-century, and soon thereafter Laos and Cambodia as well, advancing towards the British (or so they claimed) from 'the other side'. The geo-political competition between Britain and France on the European continent had continued in Southeast Asia, as the two European powers jockeyed for position there also, drawing indigenous actors into their ongoing commercial and political rivalries. The acquisition of spices, teak, cotton, coffee, tea and supplying China's potential market through 'the back door' (via Myanmar and Vietnam) were incentives for these two nations who pursued the 'colonial enterprise' either through trading companies or direct government initiatives.

For the Burmese kingdom it was the Chinese, not the British, who were regarded as the dominant power in Asia, notwithstanding the former's ability to hold the Chinese off several times in previous centuries, while the Siamese were their closest competitors. Myanmar was, after all, Jambudipa, the Southern Island, where *cakravartins* ('world conquerors') were born and where the future Buddha Maitreya would descend. But the growth of British India over the next 100 years and a weakened monarchy in Myanmar by the beginning of the nineteenth century would change both these long-held perceptions and the realities on which they were based. So when secular, capitalist, industrialized Britain – the real 'world conqueror' at the time – clashed with religious, agrarian and 'medieval' Myanmar, the outcome was predictable.

The long-term economic, social and political 'kindling' was (so to speak) subsequently lit by the 'immediate origins': the particular local geo-political circumstances, the personalities and egos, the cultural misunderstandings and simple accidents of history. And once the First Anglo–Burmese War had begun, the eruption of the next two was only a matter of time, given the global position of Britain and its growing might. To reiterate, although each of the wars had its own peculiar, 'immediate' causal factors, at bottom lay the worldwide phenomenon of Imperialism.

THE 'IMMEDIATE' ORIGINS OF THE THREE ANGLO–BURMESE WARS

The First Anglo–Burmese War of 1824–6 had to do with a border dispute in western Myanmar where the 'inviolable' and scientifically defined boundaries of British India collided with the 'porous' and 'casually' defined ones of the Kingdom of Ava. These differences were essentially cultural, based on dissimilar systems, environments, histories, world views, values and beliefs, but also a matter of power. Myanmar lost that war, and had to pay an indemnity of a million pounds sterling, much more than it had in its treasury at any one time. The reader might remember the nature of the Burmese economy whereby only about 10 per cent of production was taxed in silver while the other 90 per cent remained on the land as padi to pay for the rest of the state's expenses at harvest time. The British also demanded and took the provinces of Tenasserim, Arakan and Assam, the first two of which could have provided the monarchy with the trade revenues needed to pay the indemnity. But because the coastal areas surrounding the kingdom were now blocked (or controlled) by the British, the king had no choice but to levy a surcharge on the people to pay the indemnity, an extraordinary burden, especially for the ordinary cultivator.

The immediate origins of the Second War of 1852–3 had more to do with personalities and displays of power and less with different world views and cultural misunderstandings. All but the staunchest pro-British historian would blame British Commodore George R. Lambert for starting the war.[1] Not surprisingly, the Burmese lost this war as well and, once again, Britain took another large piece of territory, this time all the way up to Prome, the entrance to the Dry Zone and the 'heartland' of Myanmar. The new British map now included a British 'Lower Burma'.

By the end of the Second Anglo–Burmese War, then, Britain had completely landlocked the kingdom of Myanmar, leaving it with only its 'heartland', the Dry Zone. Its territory was reduced to where it was during the First Ava Kingdom of the fifteenth century. Lower Burma's traditional role – as window to the outside world through which came many intellectual and commercial influences – was now gone or filtered through a British 'sieve'.

The kingdom of Myanmar survived in this manner until 1885 when the last Anglo–Burmese War ended and Britain took the capital, Mandalay. It was sacked, most of its records were burned in a bonfire that lasted three days, and its treasures looted. This last war also had nearly everything to do with economic and political concerns. The British wanted access to the mythical 'back door' of China that led to an imagined large Chinese market, to exploit the country's rich natural resources along the way – the ruby mines district north of Mandalay produced the best rubies in the world – and harness the bulk of Myanmar's cultivator population to meet Britain's export designs concerning rice and other agricultural products. Politically, the British claimed that all of Myanmar had to be secured to prevent France from securing a foothold in a potentially hostile country right next door to British India and its important province of Bengal.

THE FIRST ANGLO–BURMESE WAR OF 1824–6

British troops were sent to northeast India during the last decades of the eighteenth century to confront Burmese troops that were chasing Arakanese rebels into Chittagong, the easternmost British province adjacent to Burmese controlled Arakan. Although the issue was temporarily settled, by 1811 groups of Arakanese, taking advantage of the limited presence of both British and Burmese authority along the border, renewed attacks on Burmese strongholds located there. The British were further alarmed when Burmese troops in 1816 entered Bengal, Assam, Chahar and Manipur to chase the rebels, and even more unsettled by the suggestion by the resident Burmese governor that taxes from there be directed to Amarapura, the Burmese capital at the time.

Bengal was too important to the British to have what they claimed was a potential security threat on its east, so that moving troops to secure it and the eastern edge of the Bay of Bengal at the same time was very much a strategic decision. To the Burmese throne, on the other hand, insubordination by local leaders was unacceptable and allowing them to seek protection under a foreign power was even more intolerable. This ambiguous nature of the shared frontier and the assertiveness of rebels were to bring the British and the Burmese court into direct conflict.

The Arakanese rebel leader Chin Byan and his followers used hit-and-run tactics, retreating to the safety of British territory. Eventually he successfully took the entire province and offered his allegiance to the British. From the perspective of King Bodawpaya's court the British had not only neglected to secure their own border, but harboured and armed a fugitive who made war against the throne and had taken the centre of one its provinces. And, as if to dare the Burmese to do something about it, the British had refused to hand over Arakanese rebels to Burmese troops.

The Burmese court therefore ordered its forces into Chittagong to capture fleeing rebels, which raised the level of conflict between the two powers. Arrogance, suspicion, ignorance and over-confidence on both sides compounded matters, exacerbated by a local dispute over a worthless nearby island and a later confrontation in January 1824 at a place called Cachar. This led to more minor skirmishes between British and Burmese troops, finally resulting in British declaration of war on 5 March 1824.

On the surface the immediate issues surrounding the movement of Arakanese resistance fighters between the boundaries was what brought the British and the Burmese into open conflict. From a broader perspective and within the context of the eighteenth and nineteenth-century domestic priorities of the Burmese kingdom, the same series of events can be interpreted as attempts to reintegrate separatist regional centres of authority that had been historically, linguistically, culturally and politically within the patronage network of the Burmese kingdom.

These campaigns in Arakan were also conducted to secure new sources of labour to replace royal servicemen who had slowly moved towards non-crown, secular and religious sectors of society. As in other Southeast Asian kingdoms power lay in the number of people a king/state commanded – less in territory per se – and as early as 1820 the Burmese monarchy was said to have already lost nearly 25 per cent of its manpower. From such a domestic perspective these events at the beginning of the nineteenth century were no different to the Burmese throne from earlier attempts to secure labour, strengthen control over rival commercial centres or weaken the authority of provincial polities and competitors. To the population living in the 'heartland' the rising tensions that were festering in Arakan had little effect on their daily lives. Restoring order to a peripheral territory and disciplining insubordinate provincial leaders gave no reason to suspect that the future of the kingdom was at stake.

In addition there were symbolic and ideological reasons, mentioned in earlier chapters. When King Bodawpaya took Arakan, he not only brought back a sacred Buddha image to his capital to prove his *cakravartin* status and his stature as an exemplary Buddhist king, he also brought back the Arakanese king along with 20,000 captives, just as earlier Burmese kings were wont to do when densely populated territories were conquered. Yet these essentially domestic affairs in the early nineteenth century were being conducted in a new and different context. Whereas earlier patterns of integration were local or regional affairs which everyone understood, the current one involved one of the strongest powers in the world which had totally different views of politics and the world.

When the British declared war on the Kingdom of Ava, Thado Maha Bandula, a highly decorated Burmese commander, was sent to the western front to settle the matter once and for all. He and the Burmese army had recently tasted victory against the Chinese in Yunnan and were confident that they would win against the British. After all, the royal army was facing the security forces of a mere trading company. Given the lack of intelligence on the capabilities of the East India Company's

Sepoys (local Indian troops) it is understandable why Burmese military officers were not the least worried at the time.

Upon crossing the river Naaf in Arakan, the 'border' between British India and Burmese Arakan, Bandula received word that a sizeable British force from the Andaman Islands in the Gulf of Muttama had landed at Yangon, outflanking the majority of the Burmese forces that had marched to Arakan. In an effort to save Yangon and prevent a possible attack on the capital up the Irrawaddy Bandula redeployed his troops south over the Arakan hills towards Lower Burma and requested additional forces to be sent southward from the capital. With little resistance, however, Yangon fell quickly to the British. They then set up a garrison atop one of the holiest shrines in the country, the Shwedagon Pagoda – of course, without taking off their boots. It was the area's 'high ground' to be sure, but also the 'palladium' of the kingdom and therefore a symbolic slap in the face.

But poor preparation and a lack of local knowledge nearly defeated the occupiers. Lack of supplies, bad sanitary conditions and disease racked the expeditionary force and reduced their numbers from 11,000 to 4,000. When Bandula's 60,000-strong army arrived to retake Yangon that same year, the much smaller British force managed to fend off the numerically superior Burmese forces until reinforcements arrived from India. These defeated the Burmese assault and proceeded to advance northward towards Prome and the Dry Zone. Along the way, the Burmese suffered another devastating setback: in 1825 Bandula was killed at Danubyu trying to halt the British advance.

Modern technology and tactics gave the British a distinct advantage and enabled them to move all the way to Pagan, resulting in negotiations with the Burmese court. On 24 February 1826 King Bagyidaw signed a peace treaty at a place called Yandabo. The terms of the treaty included an indemnity of £1 million in silver; the secession to Britain of the provinces of Tenasserim, Arakan, Manipur and Assam; the acceptance of a British resident at the Burmese court; a pledge not to wage war on Siam and a commitment to an expansive commercial treaty. In 'return' the British agreed to withdraw to Yangon, which would now be under their authority. Arakan was eventually absorbed into the Presidency of Bengal while Tenasserim was governed from Penang (in Malaya) until 1834. Although few anticipated it, the Burmese kingdom was coming to an end.

The British withdrew to Yangon (renamed Rangoon), leaving the briefly occupied territories in anarchy. Order had to be restored by the returning Burmese authorities who also sought to punish collaborators who had aided the British. Fearing reprisals for their role in the invasion, some Karens fled the scene while others formed resistance groups, unwilling to give up their newly acquired autonomy. Lower Myanmar subsequently erupted into civil war as minority communities, former officials and other local groups competed with returning royal elites to take control of the territory, its revenue and its resources. Crops failed, villages were burned and commerce suffered as the throne attempted to restore stability. Meanwhile the increasingly factionalized Burmese court struggled to maintain unity while dealing with the enormous indemnity it was obliged to pay the British.

CONSEQUENCES OF THE FIRST ANGLO–BURMESE WAR AND THE BEGINNING OF BRITISH BURMA: 1826–52

In the midst of the social turmoil following the end of the First Anglo–Burmese War the East India Company set out to administer its newly acquired territories. In 1826 the Company's first resident commissioner, N. D. Maingy, arrived in Tennaserim (the 'tail' section of Myanmar in the far south), marking the beginning of official British rule in Burma. Maingy hailed from Penang, one of the more important ports that the British had established in the Malay world. The changes that he and his colleagues would initiate in Tennaserim were not part of a single master plan devised in Calcutta or London, but a collection of policies and priorities that balanced the needs of the Company (its merchants, its stockholders and its London controllers) with those of Burmese society 'on the ground', but as they understood it.

More often than not, many of these interests were in conflict with each other, resulting in a wide range of rules and approaches to governance with the appearance of each new commissioner. Consequently, colonial governance tended to differ from province to province, and commissioner to commissioner. Arakan, being closer to India, was governed as an appendage of Bengal and treated as if its social structures, economic relationships and cultural orientation were Indian. Tennaserim was placed under the jurisdiction of Penang, whose interests were more closely linked to the Company's broader interests in maritime Southeast Asia than those of the actual province it governed.

The ways in which Burmese communities interacted with these early Company officials may have also differed from place to place, affecting the way in which British influences were regarded and remembered. Abolishing the hereditary status of *myo-thu-gyi* (township headman) and other traditional officials appeared to have severed the connections between society and state, as traditional criteria that legitimated local leaders had been based on personal relationships developed over generations. In other cases the roles of these leaders were adjusted to fit the administrative demands of the Company, directly affecting how the state interacted with the population. Later, variances between the governing of lowland areas and hill tracts also affected the relationship between those communities and central Government.

As topography often determined how well governments could implement rules, communities in mountainous places or in areas that had little immediate economic potential were simply left alone – limiting not only their exposure to colonial forms of rule but also mitigating the formation of a collective identity with those who were under more direct governance. For the British, as with the Burmese monarchy, the central Irrawaddy River valley and the forests adjacent to it, along with the growing Irrawaddy Delta region would demand the keenest attention of the colonial state.

These variances in the intensity and scope of colonial rule – later called 'indirect' and 'direct' rule – had implications not only in terms of the way the British interacted with people in particular areas, but also affected post-colonial relationships among the colonized themselves. The seeds of twentieth- and twenty-first-century separatist movements by various Kachin, Chin, Shan, Mon and Karen communities can be traced to this period.

While British policy in Arakan reflected little continuity with traditional structures of administration, Commissioner Maingy established magistrate courts, basic laws and a judicial process in Tennaserim that attempted to reflect Burmese society as he *imagined* it to be. The new commissioner demonstrated what he thought was a laissez-faire approach to governance, using Burmese customary law as the basis for a British legal code that combined local administrative practices with British structures. Local leaders were also incorporated into his service for policing, municipal, judicial and revenue duties. At first glance it would appear that Burmese social structure, laws and customs had been preserved under the new authority.

In fact, however, Maingy and other colonial officials were transforming traditional patterns of administration in ways that redefined relationships between state and society. Much of Burmese society, history and culture was being interpreted through the lens of the Company's experiences in India, for officials thought that Burmese society could be transformed in much the same way that it was being done in India. Although some local Burmese officials were reinstated to their posts, their actual functions were intentionally redefined so as to conform to the administrative needs of the Company.

As a result relationships that were once based on patron–client ties became impersonal, bureaucratic ones. Links between towns and villages, thought to be just like their Indian counterparts, were therefore created via these (mis)understandings, not realizing (or ignoring) the vast differences between the two countries. Settlements were redrawn on maps and assigned to salaried headmen who were now representatives of the Government. The new local official could be assigned to any village as required by Government, without the personal bonds that had linked the former hereditary *myo-thu-gyi* and his township. All this redefined the criteria that were once associated with legitimate village leadership.

In short, new relationships were being formed at the grass-roots level, new conceptions of leadership were being introduced and new spaces were being managed in a manner consistent with the administrative vision of the colonial authority. Due to the erosion of the patron–client system of leadership, levels of disorder rose as these new local leaders commanded little respect from and had little authority in the eyes of the people. As a result many communities living under the British in Tenasserim continued to maintain allegiances and economic relations with their former local headmen and patrons, while others chose to remain personally connected to families, business partners and monks that defined their sense of community.

At the same time, other people from within the Irrawaddy River valley 'heartland' took advantage of the new-found mobility, migrating to British areas in search of opportunities. The British also began to bring in Chinese labour from Malaya to enhance the rice, timber and shipbuilding industries. When they began to flourish, more people migrated into British territory. Between 1835 and 1845 the population of Lower Burma is said to have increased by 50 per cent, and by 1852, another 50 per cent. Yet for those communities living in the lower parts of the Irrawaddy River valley, Maingy's administrative transformations far in the south had little effect on their lives. This would soon change with the Second Anglo–Burmese War.

THE SECOND ANGLO–BURMESE WAR OF 1852

The Treaty of Yandabo of 1826 that formalized the end of the First Anglo–Burmese War in part required the Burmese Government to pay an impossible indemnity of £1 million and provide for an exchange of diplomatic representatives. The Burmese court had hoped that the territories ceded as part of the Treaty provisions might be returned once the payment was complete. But it soon realized that, to the British, the terms of the Treaty were final and binding and quite distinct from the indemnity itself. The war also had domestic repercussions, as the loss of territories, resources and labour was exploited by claimants to the throne as a direct reflection of the king's diminished merit and ability to rule.

British perceptions that the court was not as conciliatory towards the Calcutta Government, then the seat of authority in British India, also lingered, and were exacerbated by Burmese port officials in Yangon who reportedly enforced regulations in a consistently unbending manner, antagonizing members of the powerful foreign business community. Thus when two British ships were fined by the governor of Yangon for evading customs duties in December 1851, the British Governor-General of India, Lord Dalhousie, ordered two Royal Navy vessels to the port with the ultimatum that the fines be dropped and the governor replaced.

Fully aware that this could lead to a new war, the Burmese court reluctantly accepted the terms. But Commodore Lambert (called the 'combustible Commodore' by secret British dispatches at the time) who was in charge of these battleships, went well beyond his orders, stole the king's ship and blockaded the harbour. Faced with the fait accompli Lord Dalhousie issued an ultimatum for a payment of 1 million rupees. At the same time, deciding that war was inevitable regardless of the Burmese response, the British Government of India conducted a 'pre-emptive strike', taking Yangon, Bassein and Martaban, the three major gateways of Lower Myanmar and its windows to the outside world.

Though the Burmese attempted to defend their territories, it was for naught, and at the end of hostilities, Pegu was also seized – along with a large area of adjacent teak forests that, wrote Dalhousie to Arthur Phayre who conducted the negotiations, were to be included when redrawing the map of the new Province of Burma.[2] The latter comprised nearly all of Lower Myanmar south of Prome, including Myede and Toungoo, turning the Burmese kingdom into a land-locked state for the first time in its history.

CONSEQUENCES OF THE SECOND ANGLO–BURMESE WAR AND THE BIRTH OF LOWER BURMA: 1852–85

The expansion of British authority into the heart of the Burmese realm convinced the court that it was facing a crisis like no other. The overthrow of King Pagan by a rival faction and King Mindon's ascent to the throne suggested to the British that relations between the two 'Burmas' might proceed more smoothly with the new monarch, who seemed more amenable to British demands. Yet the social disorder and instability caused by the Second War made it difficult for both Burmese and British officials to re-establish authority in their respective spheres of influence.

Many Burmese who had participated in the governance of the newly occupied territories on behalf of the British simply withdrew, leaving the latter without local assets with which to administer their newly acquired territories. When the British approached their Mon and Karen allies to help govern, the latter were unable to exert any authority over the population, as they had no claims to legitimacy over these communities that

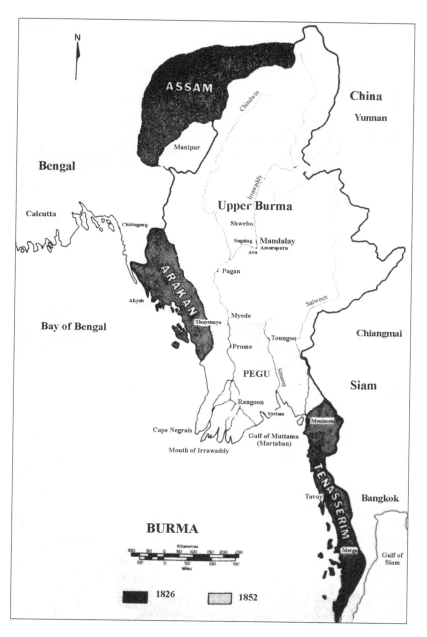

Myanmar after the second Anglo–Burmese War, mid-19th century.

had retained strong personal ties to their traditional headmen who had not collaborated with the British.

Other township and village leaders formed resistance groups that impeded the establishment of a new order. The social fabric of society began to unravel further, especially in the newly conquered territories, as traditional elites retreated from the groups with which they had nurtured strong personal ties of clientage. Back at the capital, King Mindon initiated several reforms that would not only provide a better understanding of the British and enable the court to anticipate the behaviour of the foreign occupiers, but attempted to demonstrate to the British (in vain as it turns out), that he, like his counterparts in Thailand, was more cosmopolitan and 'modern'. Although this conciliatory approach won him praise and a favourable historical record in the English-language histories of Burma, he antagonized the more conservative and 'hawkish' members of his court, especially his own chief minister, in whose view the king was a weakling.

The coexistence of a separate Lower and Upper Burma was nothing new; for it resurrected the 'upstream–downstream' dualism of earlier times, only this time the 'downstream' was more powerful than the 'upstream' and held by a foreign power.[3] Yet, the economic and political meaning conveyed by these two different regions had changed, for they were no longer just a dualism of differences within one kingdom and culture, but an actual separation of powers, finances and ways of life. Until Myanmar regained independence and the whole country once more became one, the former scenario would remain.

For many local communities exposure to British administration was an impersonal experience. The 'face' of colonial rule was often that of a local intermediary who was now a salaried official, an Indian Sepoy or a member of a minority group who held his position of authority only 'at the pleasure' of the colonizer. They were virtually all strangers to the people and the locale. 'Invisible policies' also articulated the new order in a foreign language.

Villages were now grouped together into artificial 'circles' under an official that often had little, if any, past connection to their lives. Familiar titles (such as *myo-thu-gyi* and *taik-thu-gyi*) were still being used by these new officials, but their socio-cultural and administrative functions were only a shadow of their predecessors'. As a result villagers did not engage them in the way previous villagers had done. These new officials conducted their business in unfamiliar ways, appearing on time to collect taxes but rarely attending the local *pwe* (outdoor theatre) or the *shinbyu* and *nadwin* (ordination and ear-boring ceremonies for boys and girls), seldom conferring their blessings on or contributing to the costs of village weddings or participating in festivals that bound local leaders to their communities.

Even former headmen who managed to retain their offices and titles were required to play entirely different roles. Since much of their authority and connection to their home villages had been removed, they no longer held the same honoured position as genuine representatives of the people vis à vis the central authorities. Their mediation functions were also removed, so they were no longer the 'peacemakers' of the village, representing its 'wisdom' in local disputes. By 1867 they would have to pass exams and learn how to survey land (with unfamiliar sextants and other modern gadgets) if their posts were to be retained. Most importantly, these headmen had to answer to a foreign authority, abide by its rules and try to speak in an entirely different language to its superiors.

In time new postings for the job of headmen came to be based on the ability to understand and administer new colonial procedures. Knowing how to survey, as noted, but also understanding simple financial concepts of the market system, and familiarity with British Indian law set one candidate apart from another. Soon a new official was created, the *myo-ok*, to handle communication between the headmen and the British District Officers, which further eroded the status of local headmen while providing the *myo-ok* with opportunities in a system which the headmen had little or no chance. And since the office of *myo-ok* was not hereditary like the traditional headman's position, his promotion was based on how well the state, rather than the village, was being served. Thus village headmen who once enjoyed status and influence were now little more than revenue collectors for the state. They had lost their power and status respect and their function as intermediaries between the village and central Government was no longer viable.

Other rules were also changed that affected commoners. What was once free access to forest products was suddenly forbidden in British Lower Burma when timber resources and forests came under the management of a new Forestry Department and were leased to British timber firms. Rice acreage also increased in Lower Burma with the reclamation of delta land and establishment of new mills and other mechanisms geared for the export market. Steamboat technology, shipping schedules and overseas demand contributed to the emergence of a new industry along the Irrawaddy, while new social relationships between suppliers and sellers and different notions of time (with the industrial workday) began to intrude upon the lives of the Burmese. Private enterprises such as the Irrawaddy Flotilla Company soon exerted a dominating presence on the main artery of the country, affecting the livelihoods of the more modest riverine communities as their activities could not compete.

Transport development brought railways to certain areas of the country, changing the landscape it touched by bringing new vitality to towns and villages along the tracks. However, these towns that rose with the railways had little or no sacred or religious importance to local inhabitants. Rather, their locations were determined by military and economic concerns, important mainly to the interests of the colonial state and its burgeoning rice, timber or mineral industries. Where once the presence of a pagoda that housed a sacred relic or *pongyi kyaung* (monastery) in which lived a famous monk determined the importance of a village, now it was whether or not the village or town was designated an official stop, undermining the way local communities once viewed their habitats.

Finally, the benchmark for the establishment of a colonial government was the introduction of British Indian law, even if these rules, regulations, procedures and institutions were incomprehensible to the majority of people now subject to them. Legal institutions and their officers were given authority and legitimacy that was disconnected from traditional notions of authority and legitimacy. Not only did secular law now justify the state's existence, it was the means to enforce that justification with the police might of the state. The majority of agriculturalists living in villages were now exposed to the agents and laws of the colonial state which they neither liked nor understood.

THE THIRD ANGLO–BURMESE WAR AND THE ANNEXATION OF MYANMAR: 1885–6

The rise of a strong commercial lobby in Lower Burma influenced policy-makers in Rangoon, Calcutta and London. These interests were perceived to overlap closely with security concerns for India, as imagined 'instability' in Mandalay was also regarded as bad for the booming rice industry in Lower Burma. Beyond the 'inefficiencies' attributed to King Thibaw (who had succeeded Mindon), relentless pressure for direct control of Upper Burma was mounted by the Rangoon commercial lobby, which presumed to give foreign companies unfettered and unlimited access to the interior's natural resources, along with the imagined markets of southwestern China.

Aware of the possibilities of complete annexation, and the kingdom's inability to withstand the military technology of the industrialized west, the Burmese court attempted to secure foreign support by signing a treaty of friendship with the French in early 1885. France had emerged as a major power in Southeast Asia and the Burmese hoped that such an agreement might at least mitigate British inclinations for total control. Plans to develop the transportation sector, establish a new bank and manage the ruby industry attracted the French to Mandalay. But 'hawks' in the British administration were able to use these French investments in Upper Burma as adequate reason for invoking the 'catch-all' security threat to eastern India.

The immediate cause for the declaration of war in 1885 stemmed, not surprisingly, from a commercial dispute. The Burmese Government had fined the Bombay Trading Company for logging in areas beyond their agreed contract. The case went to Mandalay where it was discussed at the highest levels of the Council of Ministers. While the case was being deliberated, an ultimatum from Calcutta was issued demanding that the original fine be overturned and that all decisions regarding foreign relations be ceded to Calcutta's control. The court sent a reply that acquiesced to all of the demands except surrendering the kingdom's sovereignty. As Burmese ambassadors consulted other European partners for advice, the British prepared for war.

Unlike colonial territories elsewhere, conservative elements within India did not support 'indirect rule' and felt that complete annexation was necessary for a variety of economic and political reasons. One of these was the 'inability' of finding an 'appropriate' replacement for King Thibaw (to British India's liking). He was regarded in official circles – a sentiment that was then projected in the press – as a 'tyrant' and 'oppressor' of the Burmese people. None of them knew anything about Thibaw except what they heard from the merchant community in Rangoon, while a few were concerned that total annexation would be costly, difficult and administratively near-impossible since armed resistance would surely follow.

At the head of nearly 10,000 troops, Major-General Sir Harry Prendergast was directed by London to occupy Mandalay as quickly as possible. His Burmese counterpart, the Hlethin Atwinwun, commander of operations in the northwest, was given the task of organizing the Burmese forces and final defence of the kingdom. Employing an armed flotilla, Prendergast captured the strategic Minhla Fort on 17 November and a few days later defeated the forces under the Hlethin Atwinwun. This was followed by a demand for unconditional surrender, implemented on 29 November 1885. Upon entering Mandalay Colonel Edward Sladen informed King Thibaw that he would be exiled to India – this was carried out that very same evening. And on 1 January 1886 the British Government formally announced the annexation of the kingdom.

CONSEQUENCES OF ANNEXATION

The three wars that erupted in sequence over a 60-year period reduced the Burmese kingdom incrementally. The elimination of the monarchy resulted in the disintegration of the kingdom, returning it to its individual parts, just as when the Pagan, Ava, Pegu/Toungoo and the Second Ava Dynasties declined, so that the socio-economic, religious and cultural components that had been held together by the king and court were now isolated.

The announcement of annexation in January 1886 had an immediate impact on the capital in Mandalay and surrounding areas. The whole of Upper Burma revolted, especially when it was heard that King Thibaw, Queen Supayalat and other members of the court had been exiled to India, for amongst other things, it had created a crisis for both the mundane and the psycho-spiritual worlds. In terms of the former, the elaborate network of relations that depended on the king's patronage were in disarray as royal ministers (*wungyi*), princes (*mintha*), minor court officials (*wundauk*), the Sangha Council, the royal army and headmen (*thugyi*) were left without an effective pivot upon which their system operated. With their future on the line, they took to open resistance between 1886 and 1890. They collected men and weapons to resist the occupation of the upper country, much of their appeal and support coming from loyal clients and followers who relied on them for patronage and saw in them the potential to restore the monarchy and the socio-economic relationships it entailed.

In terms of the latter – that is, from a religious, cultural and psychological perspective – the elimination of the king had even more far-reaching consequences. As discussed in previous chapters, the Burmese regarded the king as protector, provider and promoter of the Buddhist religion. His responsibility was to maintain the purity of the doctrine and the Sangha to ensure that donations and other acts of merit and forms of piety by the people retained their spiritual value. Removing the Burmese king was as fundamentally disruptive for Buddhists and Buddhism as removing the Pope for the Catholic world.

Without a king there was no authority left to appoint a new Thathana-baing, the supreme head of the 'church', when he died in 1895. His was the single most important office that maintained the viability and integrity of the Religion and discipline in the monkhood for ten centuries. When the British refused to appoint a new Primate – claiming they did not wish to interfere in religious affairs – the most prominent sects within the Burmese Sangha nominated their own abbots as Primate, none, however, recognized by the others. And without a supreme head of the 'church' to keep the religion unified, even if only symbolically, the Sangha became factionalized, cracks and divisions immediately appeared. This deterioration of religious discipline and behaviour continued for three quarters of a century until 1954–6 when U Nu convened the Sixth Great Buddhist Council in an attempt to reform and reunify the Sangha. Thus the elimination of the king effectively 'decapitated' the Burmese state, and the two pillars that had held up the 'Burmese house' for a thousand years – the monarchy and the Sangha – came crashing down. On this psycho-social 'rubble' was built the British colonial state, the topic of the next chapter.

The loss of central control meant that regional and provincial leaders had to fend for themselves, bringing to a halt the larger functions of state that had kept society together. Royal service corps, soldiers and other keepers of the peace struggled to maintain stability in their different charges without the personal oversight and support of the monarchy. As a result local concerns and agendas became much more of an immediate priority, exacerbating the disintegration of the old state even more. For the majority of the communities living in the core areas of Upper Burma Mandalay was still the centre to which they looked, but everyday practicalities meant that local leaders and local affairs would now play a more prominent place in their lives.

This disintegration of the kingdom to its local parts can be seen in the resistance itself. Because many revolts relied on personal ties and lacked the means to communicate beyond the range of their immediate locale, they were limited in duration, extent and support. Even if led by higher members of the old court there was no central command. Realizing that their world had collapsed with the monarchy while their local leaders had been weakened, many villagers joined various groups of rebels, bandits and questionable claimants to the throne, spreading the resistance throughout most of Upper and parts of Lower Burma. Most important, they lacked the capabilities of defeating a unified, modern, well-equipped and well-trained occupational force.[4]

The rebellion created disorder for both the British and local communities as everyday commerce, transportation of goods, the flow of currency, the harvesting of agricultural products and the movement of people were hampered by roving bandits and British Indian troops. British military officers found themselves in the midst of a widespread and full-blown rebellion without an identifiable and centralized opposition that could be 'taken out', for the highest leaders who had represented the Burmese order were banished or detained. To complicate matters, acts of resistance mirrored the hierarchical social structure of Burmese society, whereby men of status, prestige and influence led the 'masses' against British forces. Resistance was also variable in composition, scope and scale, and difficult to predict, so required large amounts of resources, men and time to subdue.

As a result British tactics were particularly harsh in dealing with the rural population; the option to burn villages, publicly execute suspected rebels and shooting anyone armed on sight was approved by commanders between 1886 and 1887. Military installations were established throughout Upper Burma, beginning with ten in 1886 and increasing eventually to 25, providing a network of security posts patrolled by their soldiers.

Some Karen communities aided the pacification programme of the British, as they saw opportunities to improve their situation by aligning themselves with the new masters. Many Karens had been receptive to earlier overtures by Christian missionaries, and by 1881 the Karen National Association was formed to facilitate cooperation amongst that ethno-linguistic group and to promote political interaction with the British.[5]

The opportunity to align oneself with the British was enhanced by British policy of 'divide and rule', commercial opportunities and American missionary activities, but such allegiances also stemmed from the previous social, religious and economic status of these communities. For many Karen-language speakers, aligning themselves with the British appeared to be in their interests for they considered themselves low on the 'totem pole' anyway. Such decisions, however, would have serious political consequences nearly a half a century later.

For the British this period of resistance was just another phase in the annexation process that they called 'pacification'. For the ordinary Burmese the resistance was an attempt to restore their traditional ways of life by getting rid of these foreigners who had disrupted it. For the Burmese elite it was to regain their sovereignty, privilege and political freedom.

By the turn of the nineteenth century the rebellion was all but stamped out. By 1890 many of the districts began to report that order had been restored, allowing the reduction of occupation troops. Although 'pacification' in terms of suppressing overt military resistance may have ended, Myanmar was never really 'pacified' in a broader sense of the term until Independence in 1948. And the 'order' that the British re-established did not have much meaning to most Burmese, for not only did the British create much of the disorder in the first place, what replaced it was totally foreign and a threat to their very being.

A glance at the traditional territories of the pre-colonial state suggests that much of what we associate with contemporary Myanmar's geo-political shape was already present in the past. With the exception of the farthest and most mountainous areas on the northeastern and north-western regions of the country, the vast swathe that constituted the flood plains of the three most important river valleys – the Irrawaddy, Chindwin and Sittaung – along with much of the hill areas immediately surrounding them, resemble, to a great degree, the core of the pre-colonial state. This core represents not only the physical habitat of the majority of the people of the country but also their thought-world, comprised of Theravada Buddhism-cum-spirit worship; their material world of agriculture and overland commerce and their socio-political world of patron–client relations. In short, the Burmese state during the past millennium where it 'made' its history was the same core area under the British and the nation of Myanmar today.

At the same time the contemporary Myanmar state is also the heir of a new state in terms of certain institutions that were created by the British only in the nineteenth century. With it came new ways of living, working, interacting, resisting and interpreting the world for a large minority of the population. Mountainous regions considered on the periphery by both Burmese and British administration were thenceforth connected, even if tenuously, to new lines of communication, transport, ideas and borders. Burmese worlds that might have once been largely separated were now connected, at least by ink lines on a map if not by road and rail on terra firma. Cultures, peoples, languages and pasts were united (even if by coercion) under a single rubric called 'British Burma', which was itself artificially attached to an equally artificial 'British India'.

Old state or new state, it cannot be disputed that the collapse of the monarchy in 1885–6 stands as a significant juncture in the history of Myanmar, marking the passage from a particular type of political entity (the Buddhist monarchy) to another (colonial 'British Burma'). Yet when 'British Burma' is placed in the broad sweep of Myanmar's history and its rhythms of state disintegration and reintegration it becomes just one of several political entities that succumbed to these oscillating forces. The state was reintegrated as 'British Burma' after the fall of the monarchy in 1886, only to disintegrate in 1942 with the arrival of the Japanese, to once again be reintegrated in an Independent Myanmar in 1948, a process of reintegration still going on today.

That raises the question of how *extensive* and *permanent* was the transformation to 'British Burma'. Did it penetrate much beyond the state, its supporters and its institutions? Did it last beyond colonial Burma itself? As the following chapters will demonstrate, although the change was mainly of the *state* – in principle as well as in practice, and primarily of the urban and *elite* sectors – *society* as a whole, particularly rural society and its religio-cultural values, remained basically unaltered, so that the process, once again, has been an imperfect and perhaps uneasy integration between old and new.

10

Reintegration and British Burma, 1886–1942

THE DEVELOPMENT OF NEW COLONIAL COMMUNITIES

The pacification of the Burmese kingdom and the extension of colonial authority into Upper Burma occupied the British for the next 40 to 50 years, resulting in a single entity called British Burma. As power shifted from the Burmese monarchy to the British, many of the conquered people (beginning with those in Lower Burma) who were quite familiar with the nuances of patron–client relations began to align themselves with the new patron, while others saw the whole process as a threat to their political influence, economic interests and identity as Burmese, therefore resisted the process. Nonetheless, both found themselves in a new 'Burma' they did not understand or barely understood.

For those segments of minority groups amongst the Karen and Mon speakers who were not yet well assimilated into Burmese society – although most had long been – the British seemed to offer new opportunities to raise their socio–economic status. Empowered by colonial patronage, the elites of select traditional minority groups suddenly rose in economic, social and political stature. Their new identities would now be closely linked to their affinity with British and Western culture in general. (Even new messianic myths were created in the late nineteenth and twentieth century, particularly amongst the Karen, that 'prophesied' the 'coming of the white man' who would 'save' them.) Such processes would have important consequences on the inevitable contest for the state in Myanmar subsequently.

With Rangoon serving as the new centre of authority, communities in Lower Burma had a longer and more direct exposure to the colonial system and its culture, language, architecture, laws, economics and technologies than the territories in Central and Upper Burma which were taken more recently. Conquered almost 60 years later – representing an entire generation – transformations there had not only begun later but were more superficial. As for the hill tribes and other relatively inaccessible frontier areas, they had even less contact with the British until the early 1890s. This mixed and uneven process of conquest and 'pacification' had important effects on the politics of identity in the twentieth and twenty-first centuries.

Groups that had once interacted through kinship, religious, social, cultural and commercial ties were now being separated by new, more rigid and different categories of classification, such as reified ethnicity, occupation, class, dress, language, food, religious beliefs and knowledge. New ideas of how cities should look, operate and connect to hinterlands were introduced, affecting both city dwellers and rural communities that realigned or resisted these new processes. New definitions of well-being, order, health, discipline, sanitation and education challenged existing understandings.

In short, while the encounter with British colonialism brought new ways of defining, expressing and contesting what it meant to be 'Burmese', this was true mainly for the urbanized elite. For the majority of the population which was non-urban, however, 'Burmeseness' was hardly ambiguous and was seldom a political issue. But that very difference in self-image between elite and the vast majority of the people was to become central to the direction the nation was to take in the twentieth and twenty-first centuries.

Between 1885 and 1942, then, British ways of living, working and seeing the world were exposed to more people in Burma than ever before, particularly the Westernized elites. A new language of state, religious beliefs, ways of doing business, conceptions of time, aesthetics, clothing, food, entertainment, architecture and landscapes would begin to enter the consciousness of some of those communities living close to or within the orbit of colonial centres, particularly Rangoon, the colonial capital.

But this exposure to British Indian culture, administration and violent police action was uneven because of the different circumstances and settings that characterized life in the new province. Most communities never saw 'more than a glimpse' of a British official (as one contemporary commentator put it), so limited was the contact with the interior and most of the common people. A few 'became' British, if not in their dress and habits, then certainly in their minds. Burmese experiences with colonialism were either intrusive, disruptive and deadly (in most cases) or beneficial, uplifting and opportune (in a few cases). These encounters were affected by one's social status, occupation, class, geographical location and personal connection to various institutions and individuals in society.

Generally, how important a particular area was to British commercial and political interests determined British administrative priorities and the intensity of their rule. River valleys and lowland agricultural areas were key zones of control for the British (called areas of 'direct rule'), while hill tracts, swamps and inaccessible sections of the forests of lower priority (called areas of 'indirect rule'), were less exposed to these influences, except for the extraction of prized teak. Falling within the newly demarcated borders of British Burma, many upland communities that were equally a part of the histories of China/Yunnan, India and Siam were now, officially and at least on the new maps drawn by the colonial powers, connected to the new history and culture of British Burma.

Moreover, invisible borders cut across landscapes and communities that were once connected by history, language, kinship, beliefs and material life. While some of these people recognized the authority of the British, many others continued to live semi-autonomous lives as before, never really undergoing the fundamental changes to their everyday experience felt by those living in the core zones. The areas of 'indirect rule' that the British called 'excluded areas' were those territories in the hills that surrounded the main river valleys of the country where distance from the colonial centre was the greatest and British influence the weakest.

As a result the boundaries, policies and actions of the colonial state produced a mixture of reactions from Burmese communities. A small minority defined themselves as subjects or citizens of the colonial community using the new terms, symbols and ideas that were associated with the British, while the majority chose more familiar traits connected to their traditonal beliefs and languages in order to express their identity. The history of colonial and post-colonial Burma might therefore be seen, in part, as a story of how different communities came to define themselves, their past and the possible future that lay ahead.

One reason for these different experiences was the importance placed on particular resources, products and labour by the British authorities. Much of the early British business interests lay in developing the rice, timber and mineral industries. As a result areas that were rich in natural resources or those newly opened for cultivation (such as the Lower Burma Delta) experienced more sustained colonial interaction, creating new centres and new peripheries. As we have seen, people were drawn to these economic enterprises even before annexation, with many migrating from Upper to Lower Burma, where opportunities for wage workers and agriculturalists had grown tremendously, weakening the monarchy even further by depleting manpower resources. The rice industry especially was labour-intensive and required enormous amounts of human energy.

New immigrant communities from outside the colony – mainly from India, Malaya and China – were also attracted to these same opportunities that were being advertised by British officials, private companies and regional middlemen. Many sought employment working for the teak mills and rice companies newly founded in various parts of Lower Burma.

Following the opening of the Suez Canal in late 1869 shipping costs for companies decreased and new notions of the 'workday' now competed with traditional patterns of daily life based on the rising and setting of the sun, the rains, the 'cold' season, religious holidays, harvest festivals and so on. The global effects of the opening of the Suez Canal resulted in an invigorated amount of economic activity in Lower Burma, as Europeans began to expand their interests from the rice industry into mining, oil and other mineral enterprises.

These new business projects with their new labour requirements brought different local and immigrant populations into contact with each other. Relations amongst local and foreign workers remained stable so long as there was land that needed to be cleared and goods that needed shipping. However, social relationships based on profit margins, expediency and market shares began to intersect with, and sometimes replace, patron–client notions of reciprocity and support, changing the way people viewed and interacted with their neighbours and associates. And in the 1920s these relationships would turn violent as economic opportunities began to diminish,

Those who had access to English language training and could operate within the private/public sectors of the colonial economy had an advantage over those who did not. Elites (and select minority groups such as the Karen) were among the first to learn English in the few new schools while some went abroad for further education, returning to British Burma to work for the Government or foreign companies. Some had learned their English in the missionary schools already in the country.

These people became a new middle class, equipped with the tools needed for political and social reform that were also to come later. Although new technology was introduced into Burmese communities as well, this was an uneven process as they were connected to jobs and occupations concentrated in urban areas and their suburbs. Much of the rice industry, for example, did not utilize new technology, and remained heavily dependent on manual labour.[1]

As Lower Burma was annexed earlier, it was several decades ahead of Upper Burma in its exposure to and understanding of these changes. Overall, however, the vast majority of the population did not have access to the education, the machines, or were subject to the industrialized schedules especially in the cities, resulting in different attitudes towards the new authorities and the changes occurring around them.

At the same time different ideas about what it meant to be 'Burmese' began to be introduced by the British at the turn of the century. Colonial surveyors – often with local guides and interpreters – demarcated the space that constituted British Burma and the communities that belonged to it. Political officers, ethnographers and local interpreters began to study, categorize and organize Burmese society and culture into 'inviolable' documents and reports. Languages were studied, organized and collected into dictionaries by officials who would become some of the colony's earliest scholar-administrators.

Terms of classification would freeze identities and create new ones while preconceived definitions of 'religion', 'crime', 'inheritance', 'law', 'race', 'native', 'traditional' and 'politics' helped produce notions of difference in the way some people regarded themselves and their neighbours, with important ramifications in the future.[2] Place-names were changed to fit the sensibilities, orientations and language abilities of foreigners, as English words entered the Burmese language and new meanings and phrases were created.

Thus, for example, phrases to connote concepts such as 'thank you' or 'good morning', not found in indigenous Burmese, would be created to accommodate the new social milieu by mixing up certain indigenous words. 'Myanma' (or 'Bama'), used as an adjective (in Burmese) was transformed (in English) into a noun (such as 'Burma') to characterize the new province and its 'components'. The location of the capital (and therefore the psychological epicentre of Burmese society) was changed from Mandalay in Upper Burma to the colonial port city of 'Rangoon' on the coast. None of the important symbols, rituals or architectural styles that represented an 'exemplary centre' was used in 'Rangoon'. For the British had different conceptions of what an 'Imperial' city should look like and what its functions were. Their notions of authority, legitimacy and power were expressed in the form and function of the capital, so that Rangoon came to 'resemble' Delhi, Singapore and other important colonial cities in particular ways.[3]

Finally, British administrators, military men, archaeologists and political officers compiled and wrote histories of 'Burma' that reflected what in reality were their own perspectives and understandings of their own past. Categories relating to ethnicity and culture were also identified, interpreted and recorded by ethnographers for administrative purposes, shaping the way Burmese minorities were understood, and in turn influencing how these groups came to see themselves.[4] The past was also recorded for groups who were perceived by the British or by themselves to have been disadvantaged or disenfranchised by the traditional Burmese state. For these communities, old customs, languages and beliefs were revived, recreated or sometimes erased to bolster new and different claims of belonging that aligned themselves with the interests of colonial authorities.

Thus much of what constituted this new community called 'Burma' emerged out of a need by colonial administrators, local elites and eager opportunists to organize the territory into something understandable.

Policies that appear to represent a laissez-faire approach to the management of local society were, however, often not regarded as such by those who were directly affected by them.

Burmese communities interpreted the changes around them in different ways, as policies initiated from Rangoon and Calcutta often had different results when applied 'on the ground' by local officials. The encounter with colonialism was thus a mixed experience, with some communities being exposed to severe changes while others carried on life pretty much as they had under the kings.

When British administrators began to regard the population as a potential source of tax revenue, comprehensive surveys were initiated to help facilitate the process. Locals were used to do some of these things, as well as to serve as security escorts, aid in translations and participate in rural administration. Yet the majority of Burmese villagers, cultivators, monks, women and even elites, did not necessarily share in, comprehend or accept this new conception of the community that was being created. Convincing the local population to adopt this imagining would take decades of persuasion, coercion and repression – and was, in the end, largely unsuccessful.

THE MAKING OF BRITISH BURMA

New Authorities, Uneven Change

With the former Mandalay Palace made into the headquarters of newly appointed Chief Commissioner Charles Crosthwaite, by the last decades of the nineteenth century the symbolic and formal incorporation of British Burma into the province of British India began. Much of this transition involved extending administrative patterns of Lower Burma to Upper Burma, while addressing certain administrative problems that had troubled government thus far. Most communities at the township and village level had already seen their traditional headmen lose much of their authority and privileges with the appointment of new officials, most of whom had little (or no) connection to the communities they ruled. Traditional social life was almost completely uprooted as the bonds that held village society together were severed, not only with the introduction of new officials but with new rules and procedures.

In 1887 Crosthwaite had already introduced the Village Act that effectively broke down traditional township configurations (*myo*) into individual 'village' units that limited the ability of local leaders (*myo-thu-gyi*) to govern or develop personal ties with the people under their charge. These acts were conceived in the context of military strategy and meant to be a counter-measure to resistance by severing the ties between hereditary leaders and their communities. But that only eroded the social, cultural and historical bonds that had shaped these communities. Villagers very quickly saw the families and individuals they had traditionally looked up to for mediation, support or guidance lose their authority to strangers who only came around periodically to collect taxes. This administrative village structure was created to suit the commercial and administrative needs of the new colonial state.

Through such policies some Burmese lives were brought together while others were separated. For many communities these initiatives brought the colonial authorities, their local representatives and their policies much closer into the everyday lives of the colonized, but rarely did villagers see an 'English' official from the central Government.

The expansion of colonial administration into interior towns and villages with staff from the new colonial state filled a power vacuum created by the collapse of the Konbaung Dynasty. And like colonies elsewhere in the region the creation of the 'Province of Burma' produced a space where the everyday lives of Burmese were now affected by the decisions and expectations of foreigners whose world views were totally different from their own.

One of the affected areas was the collection of taxes. Traditionally, local elites were able to collect revenue on behalf of the state by managing the amounts turned over to the central authorities. They were allowed to keep some for themselves as their 'salary', give away some as religious donations and/or patronage and also had the discretionary power to relieve tax burdens in times of famine and drought. The introduction of salaried tax-collectors by the British aimed at better efficiency, however, undermined the above 'cultural cushions' provided villagers.

The British did this by eliminating the personal and discretionary role local headmen had in the compilation and reporting of statistical data required by the centre. Now the British themsleves collected the statistics, especially the population figures on which the capitation (head) tax was imposed, so that the revenue required was not contingent upon the headman's own figures which could be 'fudged' to help his village out. The resulting gains by the colonial state, especially after the 1870 survey, demonstrated that British Burma could survive modern financial management and independently of British India's economic support.

For traditional headmen these changes were interpreted as a direct challenge to their authority and privileges associated with the hereditary post. Not only was the state encroaching into local sources of revenue but it was undermining the network of personal relationships that were at the heart of village stability and security. Villagers were now led by new officials who may have looked local but did not behave in the old familiar ways. The practices that had been associated with patron–clientism were now reclassified as 'bribery' and 'corruption' in the world view, language and laws of the colonial state.

Communities could now be punished by Indian soldiers and military police who accompanied these officials if they continued to seek patronage through traditional means. Regular and unyielding tax-cycles also became part of everyday life. While this kind of scheduled annual collection represented a boon for the financial security of the colony and redefined the relationship between state and subject, for many Burmese communities these expectations were irreconcilable with traditional agricultural cycles of collection with which were linked religious festivals and other social celebrations.

With the annnexation of the kingdom the British were now also compelled to rethink how to manage all of Burmese society, for with Upper Burma now a part of British Burma there was a sudden increase in population, territory and commercial opportunities. Some adjustments had already been implemented prior to 1885 in Lower Burma, such as the creation of new judicial officers and courts to relieve the growing duties of the then chief commissioner, although most of the main business of central Government was run by commissioners, deputy commissioners, sub-division officers and township officers.

By 1897 the post of chief commissioner was upgraded to the office of lieutenant-governor, accompanied by a new legislative council of nine nominated members that was soon increased to fifteen in 1909 and thirty in 1930. For a very few local elites, businessmen and lawyers, these changes provided them with opportunities to participate in the new instruments of power. Other more senior posts were also created to run jails and hospitals, land revenue, the new courts and judicial services, which up to 1906 had been run by local district officers. A fully functioning secretariat along with other administrative bodies was also created to manage forests, agriculture, fisheries, welfare, education, sanitation and public health. The appearance of these new state bodies had the effect of integrating government and society in a way that relieved and reduced the local autonomy of district officers and subordinates in favour of a more centrally managed and theoretically efficient administrative system.

Secularization of Burmese Society

The conceptual glue that held the administration together was a secularized, impersonal and rigid set of rules and procedures that had evolved out of the legal experience in British India. For village elders, traditional headmen, healers, monks and other individuals with some sort of cultural authority, British colonial law lacked the flexibility of customary law that arbitrated behaviour at the local level. Worse, the Code of Civil Procedure was developed in India, exported to Burma and managed by deputy commissioners and district magistrates.

For those Burmese who encountered the system of courts, the law and its application would have been entirely foreign to the type of personal mediation and jurisdiction that occurred at the local level under local leaders. New procedures involving 'evidence', 'witnesses', 'testimony' – although thirteenth-century Pagan's court procedures had such requirements – confounded most Burmese, for it was not based on Burmese but Indian customary law whose foundation was the caste system.

The nature of the British Indian legal system also alienated most Burmese who regarded its courts and procedures to be completely impersonal and 'cold' while its modes of arbitration and mediation were totally different from those of pre-colonial village Myanmar. In most cases the judge, the wig, the courtroom, the robes, the oaths, the Indian bailiff and the ritualized language had little to do with village custom of achieving 'harmony' rather than 'retribution' normally practised at that level. Moral and religious principles on which criminal and (particularly) civil law was based, as well as conceptions of justice itself, were totally different.

Courts, prisons and police stations became real and symbolic centres of authority of the colonial state, visible nagging reminders of the new principles that now governed the state and its power. In time indigenous elites would realize that a command of the new language and a mastery of these procedures were ways to engage and eventually resist the colonial state.[5]

Prior to 1870 many of the changes implemented by the colonial Government coexisted with local patterns of governance. Village notables held on to positions of status and prestige as best as they could despite the implementation of new village-level procedures. Disputes were still managed to some extent by the local *myo-thu-gyi* (township headman) while local patterns of commerce continued despite the ever growing presence and saturation of the British Indian colonial export economy. Eventually a situation emerged whereby a 'traditional economy' and a 'colonial export economy' existed and functioned side-by-side, generating further economic and racial divisions between those who worked in the former (usually Burmese) and those who worked in the latter (usually Indian or Chinese immigrants).

In subsequent years local communities experienced the effect of rules governing everyday life in ways that could never have been imagined. The challenge for many directly exposed to the law was the 'disconnect' between its principles and the expectations the colonized subjects had of those implementing that law. The deliberate separation between the sacred and the profane in the colonizer's laws and their administration was especially troubling (often traumatic) for many Burmese Buddhists. The secularization of Burmese society had begun in the early nineteenth century as part of the larger process of the 'rationalization of the state' (as one astute scholar of the country has phrased it).[6] But it was the removal of the monarchy in 1885 and the subsequent refusal to appoint a new Thathanabaing (head of the Buddhist 'church') following his death that aggravated that separation between the sacred and the profane.

From a Burmese Buddhist perspective the attempt by colonial authorities to remain 'neutral' in religious affairs was simply not the way one governed. The state was *supposed* to be involved in 'church' affairs. As explained in earlier chapters, the throne was intricately connected to the purity and maintenance of Sangha institutions and it was the state's responsibility to ensure the peoples' ability to make merit. Religion and the state were, and were meant to be, intricately embedded in one another. Thus, as noted above, British refusal to replace the Primate when he died in 1896 ultimately led to religious decay of the Sangha caused by the extreme factionalism which ensued amongst its many sects.[7] Without a Primate to enforce ecclesiastical law, it became less and less meaningful, losing its ability to control the behaviour of monks. They became considerably more relaxed with their religious vows and another source of embarrassment and humiliation for a public already insecure about the socio-political situation. Some of these monks even collaborated with former court elites to rise in rebellion.

Members of the Sangha who belonged to less well established and 'unorthodox' monasteries increasingly ventured into the secular realm, becoming involved in political disputes, forbidden social issues, violent crime, sedition and even uprisings. But they were now subject to British secular law, especially if they committed criminal offences, further confounding the notions devotees had of their moral exemplars. Although religion and the state would be legally separated only in the twentieth century, the state nevertheless asserted its authority on religious matters through civil courts in a consistent manner, effectively utilizing secular law to define what constituted 'religion'.

As the strength and vibrancy of the Religion declined with the monks many communities whose economic livelihood depended on their robust presence and financial support of religious festivals, arts and crafts, dramatic performances (normally with religious themes) and other related industries, were deleteriously affected. Pagoda festivals and temple-markets were reduced in frequency and number.

Thus, for example, when the rents previously collected by the Shwe-mawdaw Pagoda at Prome were appropriated by the British Government in 1882, the temple almost immediately fell into ruin and disrepair. Worse, the social and economic life of the area surrounding it, which had depended on these religious endowments, decayed. People moved away to find jobs and start their businesses anew, industry and commercial activity declined significantly and the area became desolate, exacerbated by reducing the temple as a pilgrimage site.

The decline in the number of monastic schools (discussed below) was also an indication of how Buddhism was slowly being disconnected from notions of social service and cultural authority in favour of secular education. British conceptions of the state's role in religion and society were totally different from those of the Burmese.

Whereas the monarchy's legitimacy was connected to the mainten-ance of the kingdom's spiritual and ritual life, colonial authorities created an unequivocal distinction between the public and private sectors, whose policies were designed to regularize, standardize and streamline the functions of these 'different' sectors and their separation. Efforts towards administrative integration per se were not fundamentally different *in purpose* from initiatives by the pre-colonial state but the principles and philosophy behind them were. The more impersonal, secular and function-ally bureaucratic the state appeared, the more legitimate and modern the British regarded it to be.

Just as former provincial officials and their followers asserted local autonomy at the collapse of the monarchy, hierarchy – the social stabilizer – also unravelled along doctrinal, regional and personal networks, reveal-ing the extent to which the fabric of the kingdom depended on vertical links at whose apex were the king and primate. Festivals, *zat pwe* (dramatic theatre) architectural projects, literature, music and other forms of Burmese cultural expression began to wane in quantity and quality, for they had invariably been connected to religious celebrations, patronage and schedules.

At the same time, while secular processes were part and parcel of the colonial administration, people living in rural communities near sacred sites continued to make religion a part of their daily lives. Lay stewards continued to help manage pagoda affairs, families continued to send sons to monasteries and the general public continued to give alms every morning to monks. Secularism clearly had its limits, dependent on the extent to which the colonial state and its various agents penetrated soci-ety. But many of the new ideas, concepts and values connected to the secular world view of colonial administration would soon be translated, assessed and internalized through Buddhism by some reformers who emerged from the new educational system. Buddhism, for some, *had* a place in a secular world and was used as a lens through which that world was made relevant.

Social commentators began to apply notions of political identity and organization to Buddhist principles, eventually forming social reform groups that attempted to think about secular topics using Buddhist idioms and terms. Students debated the place of Buddhism in the modern world and asked whether traditions associated with particular forms of Burmese identity could coexist within a secular state. Ideas of the nation as a form of community also penetrated the religious realm, providing terms through which particular values were articulated. In decades to come nationalists and nation-builders who equated secular principals with notions of modernity continued where colonial authorities left off, creating government institutions, policies, universities and programs that regulated and regularized the religious domain.

A Smaller World: Communication and Transport

Changes in the social and administrative landscape were accompanied by changes in the physical landscape. Addressing transport priorities had begun after the Second Anglo–Burmese war with the establishment of a railway line to Prome, which at the time was the accepted 'border' between 'the Kingdom of Ava' and 'Lower Burma'. The Burmese saw new Chinese immigrants from Malaya enter into their worlds to help build the railways, as many locals were not attracted to the type of work that such projects entailed.

The railways brought mechanized transport into the lives of many Burmese working in the interior. Soldiers, officials and new immigrants with different cultural and social expectations also made their way into Burmese worlds through the railway. Towns that had train stations became centres for their particular area, often housing a deputy commissioner or junior administrator. Goods deemed luxuries for most Burmese flowed through these rural stations, which only a few urban elites could afford. Local cultivators found that their products and delivery schedules changed according to the railway lines and train schedules. New distribution centres, new jobs and new labourers sometimes caused the decline of older networks of economic distribution, affecting the social lives of many communities.

By 1889 the rail line was extended to Mandalay and later to Myitkyina, approximately 50 miles from the Chinese border. Burmese goods, people and correspondence could travel much quicker between Mandalay and Rangoon, a development which slowly changed the perception regarding distance and connectivity between communities in Upper and

Lower Burma. Travel and communication via water had also improved with the advent of the steamship, so that by 1900 the Irrawaddy Flotilla Company was the dominant presence on the main artery of Burma. While many Burmese were not initially affected by these new transport measures, in time a few wealthy landowners, rice brokers and mill managers were able to take advantage of these innovations and indirectly connect their clients, workers, villages and relatives to the rhythms of the colonial economy.

Distances between communities were shortened, affecting those whose lives were connected to the steamship and railway industries. At the same time traditional modes of transport via secondary rivers and pathways continued for the vast majority of cultivators, producers, weavers and potters whose lives did not overlap directly with the growing economy. While annual pagoda markets continued to draw local traders, novel mass-produced foreign products began to appear on the rattan mats used to display wares, whose possession often reflected a person's standing in society and exposed other potential buyers to the material world that was developing around them.

The Formation of a 'New Frontier'

Rural world views, especially in Lower Burma, were affected by the transformation of the rice industry, which directly exposed cultivators to the rhythms and cycles of the global market. Initially local economies were concentrated on trade with British India as its primary partner. The Province of Burma would supplement British India's position as a global supplier of raw materials, food products, timber, minerals, cotton and tea. The wide range of administrative policies that governed and organized society were largely implemented to enable commercial enterprises to operate more efficiently between the two colonial administrations and at the same time attract outside investment in order to spur on economic development of Burma's rice, transport, oil, mining and rubber industries. But it was in the enormous expansion of rice production in the Burma Delta where most Burmese would begin to experience the changes implemented by the colonial state.

From the perspective of most local communities the development of the Irrawaddy Delta was an odd choice as it had always been a frontier, a vast territory of swamps and marshlands that was not an area of settlement. Centres of religious and royal authority were inland where annual festivals, celebrations and ceremonies were regularly held. Population movements in Lower Burma in preceding centuries had concentrated on places such as Bago, Bassein, Martaban and Moulmein, not in the areas now being targeted by British surveyors and private companies. However, global market demand for rice would soon trigger heavy investment in the area, compelling potential foreign patrons to look for new labour among existing communities and foreign ones.

Some Burmese would begin to reorient themselves to the new centre of authority in Lower Burma, mainly due to the economic opportunities that were being created. Internal migration from Upper Burma and other provinces contributed to expansion, making up nearly 12 per cent of the population in 1881 and 10 per cent of the four million inhabitants in 1901.[8] Between 1855 and 1905 the rice industry in Burma would expand from 162,000 tonnes of exported rice and padi to nearly 2 million tonnes by the turn of the century. During this period the total area under cultivation would increase from about 800,000 acres to nearly 6 million acres.[9]

The infusion of capital into British Burma meant there were more jobs available than there were people able to fill them, more virgin land to be developed than existing labour could handle and more opportunities for creditors in the growing needs of new landowners. As a result of this investment communities along the Irrawaddy river delta saw their environment becoming one of the most important economic zones in the region, as well as one of the most populated, with the immigration of labour from British India, Malaya and Upper Burma. Newcomers hoped to lease or obtain land, grow the requisite amount of crops required by their landlords and then use the surplus to buy goods. Others came with more modest goals in mind, simply to find work, earn a wage and eat.

Lower Burma residents began to encounter more outsiders in their day to day lives as demands for labour increased. Most of these new peoples spoke Burmese since they were born in Upper Burma. But over the last twenty years of the nineteenth century more and more Indian immigrants (up to 297,000 by 1901) became part of the socio–economic landscape. A total of 70 per cent of the Indians lived in Rangoon in the early 1870s and, by 1901, 50 per cent of the city's inhabitants were Indian. Between 1852 and 1937 some scholars suggest that nearly 2,600,000 Indians migrated to Burma. Much of the expansion in the rice economy of Burma stemmed from the settlement of Indian communities in Lower Burma.

By the 1880s local and foreign credit operators had already entered the scene and begun to influence the industry as the price of land (and the amount of loans required to develop it) increased for first time farmers. Local moneylenders began to see their businesses decline as urban creditors, Indian Chettiars (a community of money lenders and bankers) and large landowners began to exert their dominance on the rice economy. For the majority of small-scale Burmese cultivators profit was difficult to make as the circumstances surrounding the boom of the rice economy required financial and economic tools that were not readily available to them. Still, scholars estimate that total land cultivation rose from around 1 million acres in 1870 to 8 million acres by 1930.

The Development of a Middle Class

These socio-economic changes in the Delta contributed to opportunities for enterprising individuals who began to fill the slot between the colonial state and Burmese society. A small but prosperous class of Burmese landowners, mill owners, moneylenders and traders emerged in the 1880s with the increasing investments that poured into the agricultural sector. Some members of this generation became the first to think about political identity, community and social reform using terms and concepts learned from their new English-language education. As future journalists, publishers, members of book clubs, cultural societies and student organizations, some sought to implement change through channels sanctioned by the colonial Government. But these remained a very small group in Burmese society.

Many members of this community had their roots in villages but some were able to respond to the state's demand for local talent. They were among the first, along with traditional elites, to fill the very limited spots in secondary level English-language schools, giving them the advantage of being able to work more closely with the administrative and commercial authorities of the colony. These predominantly male students were also the first to get a university education in Rangoon, British India and, in rare circumstances, in Europe.

Part of a growing class of intellectuals, technocrats and administrators that stemmed from colonized communities throughout the Indian Ocean region, this group was among the first to internalize, absorb and disseminate world views derived from Europe and colonial Burma. They were often the first to be selected for white-collar administrative jobs in the colonial administration and the financial sector. Some, understandably, chose to align themselves culturally, personally, spiritually and politically with the colonial authorities, while others continued to operate according to the particular situation, acting as cultural brokers and political interlocutors only in certain contexts.

Socially, many in this group began to express their identity in new ways, sometimes through the clothing they wore, by the language they spoke at home, the houses they lived in, the books they read, the music they listened to or even the food they preferred to eat. Values in health, decorum, work, leisure and other aspects of daily life were also open to modification as exposure to European world views was often equated with being current, up-to-date and modern. Sons and daughters hoping to differentiate themselves from their parents' generation found refuge in these new ways of living, immersing themselves in the attitudes, fashions and issues of the day.

For some Burmese adopting new ways to express one's identity was not a simple matter. Young women drew criticism from older women and men for their decision to demonstrate their modernity through new types of particular hairstyles, cosmetics and clothing. Nationalists writing in newspapers criticized women as unpatriotic if they wore a particular style of (sheer) blouse which was associated with the British.[10]

Thus the middle-class experience for Burmese was more a common than a disparate one, as priorities surrounding material interests, consumerism and being modern were merged with issues of political reform, nationalism and heritage preservation. The ways in which different segments of urban middle-class society dealt with these choices and pressures contributed to the way the Burmese saw themselves and their immediate neighbours. Notions of generational, gender, class and ethnic differences emerged from these experiences, sometimes reinforcing pre-existing social divisions while at other times causing new ones to rise to the surface. Yet there were others who remained more or less cautious about the way they approached change, preferring to demonstrate their identity through more familiar symbols, clothing and behaviour. Much of this cultural 'debate' took place in an urban environment.

A New World View

While pre-colonial education had made Burma one of the most literate societies in the world, it was colonial education that provided the language and concepts through which a small Burmese minority would be able to engage the colonial state more directly. Following an early attempt to use the monasteries as centres for education, the British established a Department of Education in 1866, which soon took a leading role in the establishment of secular Government schools. By the early 1890s nearly 900 of these schools were in operation, managed either by the Government or missionaries. By the first two decades of the twentieth century 4,650 secular schools were open, since Burmese parents hoped their children could graduate and obtain a lucrative Government position.[11] Monastic schools were still the only option for the vast majority of the population but for a select few a colonial school education provided a better chance for benefiting from the rapidly expanding economy and ever-growing bureaucracy of the colonial state.

As a result of the colonial educational system many of this new class began to articulate the problems facing society through the words and ideas associated with the rhetoric of empire. Many began to believe that Burmese culture was indeed inferior to Western civilization and as a result embraced the ideas associated with the colonial ideology of the Burmese being 'rescued' from the burden of their own traditions. Some saw the potential of localizing political ideologies from the west through Buddhist idioms and other cultural forms. Others saw the need to embrace new forms of organization commensurate with issues important to their interests.

The creation of membership lists, volunteerism, committees and elected officers contributed to the viability of 'associations' as useful forms of mobilization. While more passive than those that emerged by the 1930s, these groups used print technologies, a shared understanding of social activism and a willingness to work within the boundaries set by the colonial state to realize their goals. The difficulty for many of these future reformers was in deciding how to make sense of the technology and new ideas associated with the British, how to translate these notions to the larger population and how to negotiate with the colonial authorities to aid them in improving the social conditions of their fellow 'country-men'. A generation later students entering universities and colleges in the 1920s would see themselves, their parents, the British and the colonial situation in a different light and would choose far more radical methods to implement their world views and growing opinions.

The Young Men's Buddhist Association (YMBA) was one of the first organizations to enrol a large following in the first two decades of the twentieth century. Founded in 1906 by U May Oung (a Cambridge graduate) and U Kin, the organization actually emerged from a movement to preserve and propagate Burmese cultural traditions being challenged and believed to be in decline since the 1890s. Groups concerned with heritage, language preservation and culture began to sponsor the development of schools such as the Sam Buddha Gosha Anglo-vernacular High School (1897) and the Buddha Thana Noggaha School.

These secular Buddhist schools utilized a Western curriculum and administrative structure to provide young Burmese with an alternative to both the traditional monastic schools that were declining and the Christian missionary schools that were too expensive and difficult to attend. Graduates from these schools who were able to attend college or university continued their efforts, forming social improvement clubs, debate groups and college associations that began to use new forms of print media to share their concerns. One such group, the Rangoon College Literary and Debating Club, discussed issues such as the relationship between poverty and crime, the importance of hosting pagoda festivals and the place of indigenous sport in society. Clearly, most Burmese did not have the luxury to think about such topics, but those who did take part in these discussions were among the first to use these concerns as a new way of thinking about Burmese identity.

This experience created the first generation of reformers, many of them sons (and and a few daughters) of former ministers and men of influence. As students they were the first cohorts to learn about the priorities of empire as the colonial educational system was seen as a means to produce law-abiding civil servants who could take part in the daily management of the province. Lieutenant Governor Spencer Harcourt Butler's 1916–17 Committee on the Imperial Idea planned to make education in general and universities in particular the front line for inculcating the idea of empire (British, of course) in its Burmese subjects. They learned English, British mannerisms and shifted their perspective of the world from Mandalay and the past to London and the future.

Sport, theatre, debating groups and other social clubs were encouraged as a means to instil an emotive connection to the 'colonial project'. Through state-run celebrations, English holidays and other events, it was hoped Burmese might be drawn to the idea of empire. Many in fact saw themselves as being firmly a part of the British Empire and sought to uplift their own society from within the colonial system. Unlike their forefathers, the notion of community was not based on principles of kinship but on values associated with British legal systems, procedures and attending institutions. Many in this growing class were familiar with and eager to debate recent politics and ideas coming from Europe, but rarely attempted to challenge the authority and legitimacy of the colonial state.

While some of its guiding principles were originally tied to matters of preserving Burmese culture, education and the use of indigenous products, generational differences within the YMBA led to the apolitical nature of the group. One issue that merged culture with politics was the issue of Europeans wearing shoes within Buddhist monuments. This kind of behaviour was a public affront to and showed a total disregard and disrespect for one of the most common practices and cherished customs of Burmese Buddhist society. By identifying what might be considered common 'Burmese' traits, values and symbols, these early reformers planted the seeds for more aggressive uses of culture as a means of demonstrating a 'national' consciousness. Passionate editorials in newspapers and rallies throughout the country urged the Government to find a solution. In 1918 the Government ruled that each local head of a pagoda could ultimately determine his own shoe policy, perhaps an attempt to separate any bonds of allegiance that could develop between the YMBA and the monkhood or simply an attempt at 'divide and rule'. While Government did not capitulate, for many middle-class Burmese the issue became an important topic through which the nature of the colonial situation could be discussed, debated and lobbied.

Whereas the YMBA was only marginally political, its successor, the General Council of Burmese Associations (GCBA), was virtually created for political activity in 1920. Differences in class, political strategy, policy and commitment to the colonial state eventually caused the YMBA to split along generational lines, with the youthful members pursuing more direct means of reform, particularly over political issues. One arose in late 1920 when a group of students held a protest against plans to make Rangoon University more of an elite institution by modifying its entrance requirements. The University Act of 1920 was designed to raise admission standards by changing high school final exam entrance levels and requiring all incoming students to attend a probationary residence for one year. The legislation in effect reduced the number of students entering university but also provided, inadvertently, a link between educational issues and the political agendas of nationalists. Since 1919 the issue of whether constitutional reforms for India should also apply to Burma had been under discussion. Some officials, notably Sir Reginald Craddock, felt that the Burmese were not yet ready, ostensibly because of the lack of both university-educated people in the Burmese community and political experience in self-government. The University Act unintentionally provided the opportunity for the more aggressive elements within the GCBA to combine what was essentially a local educational issue with a broader message of political reform.

The call for a University strike began at the Shwedagon Pagoda with the support of urban reformers, concerned parents, monks and even a handful of Indian nationalists who were eager to promote the boycott of all authority. In the early months of 1921 students from neighbouring institutions began to boycott their classes, while groups of editors and monks began campaigning for a 'national' school system. The importance of this event highlighted the role of education as a political issue. In years to come the GCBA would make education and the formation of non-Governmental schools a platform to attract the attention of urban and rural parents concerned about their children's future.

Dyarchy

The issue of political reform became much more public in the 1920s and 1930s. While the University Strike of 1920 galvanized young students and activists, the broader question of the day on the minds of seasoned politicans was whether constitutional changes promised in the India Act of 1919 would be extended to Burma, since it was technically still a province of British India. Many felt that if the political system was being liberalized on the Indian subcontinent then surely Burma should enjoy the same changes. At the heart of this issue was Burma's political relationship to India, a topic that changed the political landscape a decade later, leading to the separation of Burma from India.

For the moment, however, most Burmese politicans in 1921 were concerned with articulating their desire for an extension of political opportunties, although they often disagreed on how best to achieve these common goals. Some groups, such as the GCBA, felt that boycotting the sessions of the visiting Burma Reforms Committee in August 1921 conveyed more accurately the disatisfaction of the general population with regard to the dyarchy plan, which in their opinion had fallen short of their demands for home rule. Other more moderate voices testified before the committee on issues of forestry administration, communal representation in the legislative council and education. After the findings of investigative committees were submitted to London the formal structures of dyarchy were officially recommended for Burma in 1921.

On 1 January 1923 Burma was officially established as a governor's province under a new dyarchy constitution. A governor, high court and legislative council would manage affairs at the top while a system of district councils elected by circle boards was created to manage local Government. In 1922 and 1923 considerable political energy was spent on implementing the measures approved by London that included holding elections, establishing the 103-member legislative council and incorporating new local ministers into the formal structures of the administration.

Sharing government responsibilities, the real intent of the dyarchy system, was interpreted differently by concerned parties. Moderates who accepted the dyarchy reform programme saw the transfer of administrative subjects concerning agriculture, excise, health and public works as sharing duties and a step in the right direction. Although a small space had been created for Burmese to have a say in their future, therefore an improvement, it was not complete. Other politicians, notably members of the GCBA and the monk-led GCSS (General Council of Sangha Sammeggi), regarded the entire enterprise as too big a compromise that gave up home rule, sovereignty and remission of taxes. Furthermore, the 'reserved' subjects of general administration, law and order, land revenue, labour and finance – the most important areas in the Government's portfolio – remained in British hands. As a result of this a massive boycott of the 1922 elections saw only a few participating.

That meant many of the grass-root elements in the growing middle-class political movement were not represented in the first incarnation of Dyarchy Government. At the same time those who were elected were often independent candidates rather than members of a broad coalition,

British governor's mansion at Maymyo, built in the early 20th century.

either unable or unwilling to unite with other candidates through issues that crossed patron–client relations. Candidates in the first and subsequent councils were too fractured by individual interests, political priorities, ethnicity and patronage to form any viable coalition.

One nationalist group that did contest seats was in fact a splinter group within the GCBA, seeing the dyarchy system as a way of voicing the concerns of their constituencies. On the surface, dyarchy would appear to be a move by the colonial Government to broaden the spectrum of political participation in Burma. In actuality the world views of the Council's members represented only a small portion of Burmese society and masked the deeper political divisions within the legislative body and in the broader political landscape.[12]

Separation from India

One particular issue that crossed religious, ethnic and class distinctions was a proposed plan to separate India from Burma administratively, a plan that was supported by British authorities in Rangoon. The Indian Statutory Commission (also called the Simon Commission after its chairman, John Simon) visited India and Burma between 1927 and 1929 to assess the standard of constitutional development, a task that became noticeably difficult once it arrived in Burma in 1929.

The majority in the GCBA felt that constitutional progress in Burma was predicated on advancements made in India, resulting in an 'anti-separation' platform that would be aggressively maintained by its members. More extreme factions within the GCBA, however, wanted to boycott the process altogether, seeking home-rule rather than recognizing the purpose of the Simon Commission.

Other educated elites, businessmen, legislative council members and editors agreed with the British position that separation and engagement through the process offered by the commission was the better option. One such coalition, calling itself the 'Separation League', was made up of representatives from the Karen National Association (representing about ten branch groups), the British Burman Association, the People's Party (a conglomeration of three nationalist parties) and other more moderate political voices that supported separation but were concerned with securing a fair and representative constitution. The issue brought to the surface the fundamental question for Burmese politicians: whether they could achieve reform through the system or by non-cooperation.

Ethnic minority groups were more concerned with securing communal representation in the central Government and seats in the district councils while the interests of Burmese-Indians opposed separation on the basis that their interests and well-being would be lost in the hands of a more independent administration. Communities of mixed heritage (Eurasians, Anglo-Burmese, Anglo-Indians) lobbied for separation, since their experiences, education and occupation lay closer to British policy and they were at the top of the socio-political pile in Burma. The challenge facing the Simon Committee was not limited to assessing the capacity for constitutional Government in Burma. In actuality the committee was being asked to establish a single perspective of a country that in fact represented a diverse population with a wide range of political and social experiences often at odds with each other. It would be no easy task.

After a series of official meetings involving a delegation of pro-separation politicians the Simon Commission determined in June 1930 that official ties to British India were not in the interests of the Burmese and that a quick separation which included the establishment of a Burmese constitution with several political guarantees would improve the climate and atmosphere in which Burmese political reform functioned. The Commission felt that financial and political factors favoured separation and that the majority of Burmese would benefit from such an arrangement. The committee's report did not state how deep the divisions were over the issue of separation nor did it take into account the opposing views of the majority of Burmese. For many nationalists the picture was clear: reform through officially sanctioned channels would only go so far, therefore new strategies and positions needed to be adopted.

Monks and Politics

While the involvement of secular middle-class activists was important in mobilizing communities around what might be called early forms of collective 'nationalism', the monkhood also played a decisive role in the years leading up to the Second World War. Mirroring in some ways the generational differences amongst the middle class, younger monks in the countryside began reacting to the manner in which the new colonial state had marginalized the role of the Buddhist faith in society. With the advent of secular schools, civil courts and a secular Government, monks were no longer the sole source for education, arbitrators in disputes or the recipients of state donations for temple and monastic upkeep.

Reacting to these and other developments, the GCSS, although initially concerned with improvement of lay standards of Buddhist practice and discipline amongst the various sects of monks, became more passionately involved in issues that directly questioned the role and place of the colonial state. Monks like U Ottoma and U Wisara toured the countryside in the 1920s, raising awareness of issues that affected the Buddhist faithful while organizing an infrastructure that could continue the means of communication between rural and urban centres.

The GCSS soon began training and educating a corps of political monks called *dhammakatika* who would further expose rural communities to these new political ideals and acted as advisors to the new 'defence' organizations (*wunthanus athin*) that were formed at the village level. Officially these groups were meant to protect villagers from the abuse of tax collectors and provide a link with urban politicians who could articulate village concerns. At the same time, they provided an alternative network that rivalled the official structure mandated by the dyarchy plan, giving peasants alternative patrons to whom they could pledge their loyalty.

Thus the development of these political organizations reflected the socio-economic transformations occurring throughout society brought on by the colonial state. At the same time these organizations reveal the highly complex and often contested range of visions that made up the 'nationalist' movement. Many were drawn from different generational, occupational, geographic, class and educational backgrounds that affected not only the way in which they perceived the policies of the British but how they would react to them in articulating reform.

While some, such as the older middle-class elites of the civil service, might advocate cooperation within the parameters alloted to them, the younger generation chose to take a more confrontational approach using methods borrowed from the Indian Nationalist movement. Whereas one group might be satisfied by seeking reform through the Burmese Legislative Council, others saw change coming only by boycotts, strikes and non-cooperation. Still others took their frustrations out on some of the more recent immigrant communities such as the Indian dockworkers, resulting in an escalation of tensions amongst the varied colonized communities.

All these strategies were, in many ways, still operating within the parameters of urban politics. But with the onset of the Depression and the disastrous affect on rural cultivators, a more direct form of protest rose from that sector, particularly the Lower Burma rice delta. These experiences may not have been the same for everyone as this growing community of 'nationalists' came from a variety of backgrounds, but everyone felt the Depression.[13]

Educational, religious, occupational and geographical differences also shaped the way members of this class regarded themselves in relation to a colonial society already divided by ethnicity, status, talent, capital and genealogy. Competition amongst these groups – especially between local members of the middle class and newly immigrant Indian communities – became especially intense, as opportunities in British Burma attracted clerks, civil servants, lawyers and accountants from British India for jobs in the colonial administration.

Commercial traders from India enjoyed dominance of Burma's external trade due to their strategic partnerships with European industrial mining and timber owners. Anglo-Indian lawyers who earned their wigs working in the vast legal structure of British India set up practices in Burma, dominating both the field of law and future political seats in the soon-to-be-established Burma Legislative Council. Their command of English was key to practising British law, giving them an advantage over many local learners of the colonial lingua franca.

As members of the Indian middle class were also more involved in daily economic affairs than other groups, Indians came to represent the face of the foreign economy that was displacing opportunities for Burmese at both the lower to middle-class levels. In later years such frustrations would come to a boil against the Burmese-Indian community. Europeans may have reserved most of the highest positions in state and finance for themselves but other foreign communities dominated the most lucrative positions in society. It was with these, not those at the top, that the ordinary Burmese came face to face on a daily basis. Nonetheless, to most Burmese, their economy, education and administration were being dominated by foreigners at all levels.

By the 1930s very few Burmese moneylenders could finance their own operations, leaving the Chettiars and other urban-based loan institutions unchallenged in the delta region. More to the point, peasant cultivators were now seeking loans exclusively from these new sources of credit, whose ties to Indian banks and joint-stock companies connected the rural villager to quick and accessible capital but also to demands that were often beyond the grasp of the ordinary local farmer. Of growing concern was the increasing alienation of cultivators from their lands as dips in the price of rice during the 1920s affected their ability to pay their mortgages.

Whereas the burst of activity from the rice industry in the Irrawaddy Delta initially saw the growth of local landowners/cultivators, by the late 1920s and 1930s many of these lands began to come under the ownership of non-agriculturalists, whose interests were towards renting the padi fields to cultivators for a profit. Official census figures reveal that in 1921 there were 33,000 landowners who were not involved directly in the cultivation of rice. By 1931 this group had increased to 39,000 while the number of cultivator-owners fell by over 50 per cent.

These new landlords, consisting of moneylenders and other urban commercial interests, owned over half of the most important agricultural lands in the Burma Delta and represent a rise in the wealth of a small number of landlords who were often identified as Indian; stoking an already existing fire of discontent amongst local cultivators. Lacking direct ownership of the lands one worked had disastrous results for farmers as the value of their rice began to decline when the world-wide depression hit the colonial economy. Local cultivators were left with little surplus to pay rent and other monthly instalments, resulting in foreclosure on their lands. At best the Burmese cultivator had become a tenant on 'his' own land.

At the same time rapid price increases in consumer goods and other basic commodities exacerbated an already precarious existence for rural cultivators who were hovering just above subsistence levels. While many of these developments had been occurring since before the First World War, it was not until the drastic fluctuations in rice prices of the 1930s, coupled with the growing presence of Indian competitors for land and the ill-timed regularity of the capitation (head) and land tax, that the delta region was turned into a potential hotspot of communal tension and political unrest. In the cities the Depression created a rise in anti-foreign feelings as Burmese labourers vented their frustration on Indian coolies and Chinese businessmen. Violent racial riots brought arson, murder and intimidation to the streets in 1930 and 1931, highlighting the fragile links that kept colonial society in equilibrium.

The first incident occurred in Rangoon in May 1930 when a group of Indian coolies struck for better wages, with Burmese workers taking their places. When the Indian coolies agreed to come back, the Burmese replacements were dismissed, and were allegedly taunted as they left the docks. Enraged, Burmese labourers went on a rampage, targeting any member of the Indian community, resulting in nearly 100 casualties and 1,000 wounded. Riots occurred later in the Rangoon Central Jail in June

1930 when inmates decided they would rather attack the superintendent than escape. Indian troops were brought in to quell the jailbreak, which did little to warm relations between the two communities

Violence towards Chinese was reported in early January 1931 at the hands of frustrated Burmese who blamed their economic plight on foreign communities. In March and April of 1931 Indian cultivators were also attacked in neighbouring districts of the Irrawaddy Delta, compounding the sense of confusion and social instability that was connected to a growing peasant rebellion at the same time.

In the villages the regular collection of the capitation tax (*thathameda*) by the colonial administration contributed to the difficulties of rural communities and added to the fodder of activists. The tax was actually a source of revenue for the pre-colonial state also, but when put into application by the colonial administration it affected the lives of farmers more directly and more systematically due to the efficiency of the tax collection system enforced by armed regiments.

Other taxes that drew criticism were the land tax and indirect tax on rice production. The former called for 10 per cent of the cultivator's gross return while the latter was an export duty on the country's rice. Such demands could total 25 to 50 per cent of a farmer's net production and in severe times reduce his surplus to almost nothing. While the local colonial officer assigned to manage these villages could have granted a reprieve from these taxes, most did not, further antagonizing cultivators and compounding the financial strain they already carried.[14] As previously discussed, during the monarchy such taxes were managed by local headmen who would be sensitive to the needs of their village. But an independent revenue collector who was paid by the Rangoon authorities was normally not interested in the problems of villagers. The erosion of personal relationships by the creation of an impersonal civil administration had a direct effect on the way in which rural communities now viewed the state and its moral responsibilities. Where headmen were once seen to represent the interests of the village, now headmen and district commissioners were agents of the state. Although calls to temporarily waive the collection of taxes eventually reached the Legislative Council through sympathetic members, such appeals usually fell on deaf ears when it reached the desk of the executive, providing yet another issue that would draw more closely the needs of farmers with the ambitions of urban reformists.

A CONSEQUENCE OF BRITISH BURMA:
THE REBELLIONS OF 1930–32

As a result of the growing connections between urban reformists, Buddhist political associations and village leaders, rural communities became more closely linked to wider questions of colonial rule than ever before. Not only were rice cultivators more aware of the political issues in the cities, many had begun to adopt organizational strategies that allowed them to come together and voice their concerns to both colonial officials and urban reformists who began to call themselves 'nationalists'. Through associations like the *wunthanu athins*, village communities became more aggressive in conveying their concerns over taxes, rising rents and, by 1930, the decline in rice prices, which were allegedly being controlled by a group of rice companies called the Bullinger Pool.

Village groups began to link themselves with neighbouring ones, increasing the likelihood of a shared political agenda, although local and often personal priorities still existed. Colonial authorities were wary of these developments and began monitoring the movements of urban-based nationalists as well as the interaction between village headmen and the *dhammakatikas*, resulting in the arrests of these monks and, in some cases, the closure of the associations they helped found. But some slipped through the net, so that villagers' complaints over tax collection abuses, the prohibition of using forest materials and strain of daily life due to the fluctuations of the market economy were heard by the urban-based nationalists.

Village reformers were also trained in political mobilization, given information about regional networks and kept up-to-date on issues brewing in the legislature, such as the question over the separation of British Burma from India. Saya San, a sub-committee member of the GCBA, was one of these travelling reformers, and in December 1930 he allegedly began what would become one of the largest peasant insurrections in Burmese history.[15]

While the extent of Saya San's role is uncertain, it is clear that several acts of armed resistance spread throughout the Lower Burma Delta districts in the early months of 1931, with several others occurring in Upper Burma and even the Shan States. Burmese cultivators, deeply affected by the drop in rice prices, began attacking and destroying symbols of the colonial state. They attacked railways, district officers, rural buildings and headmen who were deemed collaborators with the British. Official statements claimed the rebellion to be a 'typical' movement that desired the restoration of the monarchy by ridding the country of all foreigners.

Saya San was accused of having tricked superstitious peasants into believing that he was the 'returned' King of Burma, endowed with special powers to protect them from the bullets they would no doubt face. When Saya San and several rebellion 'leaders' were eventually caught and put on trial before a special tribunal, it came out that rural cultivators were often fighting for different reasons, following different leaders and often were not even aware that the rebellion had anything to do with the restoration of the monarchy.

Considerable debate ensued regarding the causes and character of the rebellion. Officials claimed that many of the rebels had been connected to the *wunthanu athin* movement, the network of nationalist, grass-root organizations that sought to become a channel through which village concerns and priorities could be articulated and protected. From this official perspective the series of uprisings represented a political movement that was bent on restoring the monarchy.

Sympathetic members of the legislative council and nationalist leaders pointed to economic hardships caused by the Depression and the role of immigrant communities in causing cultivators to take up arms. At stake here was the image of 'Burma' and whether the general population was capable of self-governance as in India. Thus debate over the rebellion was very much connected to the larger question over Burma's ability in modern self-governance.

Later assessments would suggest that the rebellion was possibly a product of a shared Buddhist world view that equated the decline of religious standards, the Depression and the breakdown of society as signs of the end of the world. From this perspective peasants were thought to have regarded Saya San as a future Buddha who would usher in a golden era following the end of the world. By supporting Saya San's movement cultivators were said to have used Buddhist motifs to understand and make sense of the enormous changes that were occurring around them under the British.

Whatever the explanation, the rebellion, like society in general, was characterized by multiple experiences, motivations and interests. In the end counter-insurgency forces, which included a few thousand troops from India, overwhelmed the various rebel groups and eventually restored order. Saya San was caught and placed before a special tribunal. He was hanged in November 1931.

For many students involved in youth politics the peasant rebellions of the 1930s seemed to confirm their perspective that despite different world views, class and experiences, Burmese from rural and urban settings seemed to share a sense of nationalist spirit stitched together by anti-colonialism, anti-foreigner and anti-tax sentiments. The economic hardship of the Depression, though experienced in different ways, was one issue that loosely connected urban and rural constituencies in their criticism of the Government. Even urban-based politicians saw the various peasant uprisings as symptomatic of economic frustration and an indictment of the colonial Government's tax policies.

Anti-colonial politics – which loosely described a multitude of specific social-economic issues – became the link that brought young students, peasants, political monks and a range of middle-class/elite politicians together. Middle-class youths joined or formed their own volunteer corps, clubs and unions while political leaders such Dr Ba Maw and the outspoken Legislative Council member, U Saw, actively engaged youths in developing their constituencies. Street parades and youth rallies were popular with these budding activists, but by the end of the 1930s the All Burma Students' Union and the Dobama Asiayon ('Our Burmese Party' or 'the Party of us Burmese') were just two of many that were formed to bring these various interests together. For many of its members the methods of past political reformers had failed to produce any tangible results. The elites who worked within the Government were seen to be not only of a different generation, but a kind of politician who envisioned a completely different future for Burma than that sought by the Dobama Asiayon.

Less moderate in its political stances, the Dobama Asiayon was aggressive in establishing a public image of itself that directly challenged the British Government and other 'foreign' communities within Burma. Members were younger, more ambitious and more willing to differentiate themselves from established political elites and existing political institutions in which older politicians worked. Many came from lower-middle-class families who could afford English education and university – but just barely. They had little interest in the coveted positions offered by the civil service nor did they see allegiance to the earlier generation of politicians. They were perceived by more conservative politicians as confrontational, by other immigrant groups as racist and by British authorities as threats that disrupted law and order.

Many attached the term 'Thakin' to their names, a deferential title meaning 'master', normally used when addressing European (or other) superiors. But used for each other, it became a parody of the 'white master' while suggesting that they were the captains of their fate who would control the country's future. For these Thakin, nothing short of self-determination and independence would be satisfactory. Many were attracted to Marxist ideas of the period that helped articulate their sentiments. Important communist leaders who later fought the Japanese and formed the core of the AFPFL (Anti Fascist People's Freedom League) such as Thakins Than Tun, Soe and Thein Pe were early members of the party.

These younger Burmese politicians would find themselves challenged by the myriad differences amongst fellow opposition groups, who might have shared a common goal in securing more political autonomy from the British but differed on the means to achieve it. Many of the issues that fragmented political parties stemmed from differing ideas about how the current Government should be structured, what powers should be handed over to the Burmese and how extensive British authority should be. In time members would concentrate on organizing connections with industrial workers in the oil, mining and mill industries, forming bonds across class, occupational and generational lines. The student strikes of 1936 and the 1938 strike against the Burma Oil Company were attributed to their mobilization tactics and are indicative of the generational differences they had with older politicians.

In the late 1930s the Dobama Asiayon would split along ideological and generational lines but also over more fundamental questions of whether to pursue reform by engaging in existing political processes being offered by the British or by a completely different route that did not involve the British at all. Members such as Aung San, Ne Win and Than Tun did not align themselves with British-educated Dr Ba Maw and his new Government that emerged in 1937, which was itself challenged by internal factionalism, interest groups and personality-based allegiances. Instead several of the Thakins looked elsewhere for inspiration and support as current politicians in Burma and the British colonial Government continued to hold all the keys. That support and inspiration came from an Asian country: Japan.

In the reintegration of the state that produced British Burma several questions remain. We are compelled to ask *how* new and *how* different was British Burma, and for whom? In other words, what saw fundamental, structural change and what did not, and who was affected by those changes and who was not? Essentially, the answer depends on the entity to which 'agency' is given.

If religion, language, patron–client structures, notions of leadership and legitimacy, the writing system, literature, civil law, food, dress and such socio-cultural ingredients are given 'agency', British Burma had not changed much for the majority of the population living in most of Burma, or indeed, even for select groups of urban elites living at the capital and other centres. A visitor from eleventh-century Pagan would have been quite familiar with the religion and could even have worshipped in some of the same temples he/she worshipped in back then. He/she would have been able to speak with present day Burmese-speakers, read written Burmese after some orientation, would have known what many of the foods tasted like, his/her attire would have been no cause for surprise or laughter and he/she would have recognized most cultural rituals and festivals.

If, however, 'agency' is given to urban society – its social classes, its party politics, its market economy, its modern way of life, its architecture, its technology especially – and to certain features of the colony as a whole – its military, provincial administration, revenue structure, justice system, physical infrastructure – then someone visiting even from the last dynasty might not recognize many of these transformations. In other words, in British Burma, as today, both the old and the new can be found.

II

Fragmentation and the Union of
Myanmar, 1942–1962

Between 1942 and 1962 the Burmese endured some of the most difficult circumstances since the collapse of the monarchy in 1885. Competition between imperial powers turned the country into a battlefield as the armed forces of Britain, Japan, China and the United States fought for supremacy in the Second World War. Burmese of various backgrounds joined in this contest, as local competition for power overlapped with more global contests concerning co-prosperity spheres and national self-determination. Entire populations were displaced, families separated, neighbours estranged and agreements broken with the departure of the colonial authorities.

The differences among and between key political parties, business interests, monks, politicians, students and colonial administrators of the pre-war era continued in wartime Burma. The entry of Imperial Japan into Burma amplified these differences as various groups with a wide array of interests, loyalties and concerns sought to take advantage of, or merely survive in, the political vacuum created by the retreating colonial administration. Just as the collapse of the monarchy in 1885 created opportunities and calamities for a wide range of people, so too did the collapse of the British administration when the Japanese invaded.

The appearance of the Japanese on the Burmese horizon affected the internal dynamics of the country as wartime disorder brought people together to create inseparable bonds while other groups were torn apart. With a new power in charge, those (mainly older, Anglophile leaders) who had connected themselves with the previous colonial order were marginalized and replaced by politicians, students and youth leaders who were anti-British and savvy about the changed political conditions. Beliefs about European superiority was questioned, while indigenous languages, symbols and traditions were resurrected in a new pan-Asian identity.

In this context of war and transition an old-new institution – the army – re-entered the political arena in a dominant position, not only because in wartime militaries are invariably paramount, but because after

Independence Monument, Yangon.

this war they were considered heroes who had won independence from Britain. It was not illogical at the time to have perceived the army (which had vowed never to let the country be conquered again) as guardians and protectors of the Burmese state after independence was achieved. However, its rise to power created tensions with other elites, especially returning civil servants who had served the British, along with minority ethnic and other personal militias in the rural areas.

Certain seminal developments highlight this period of 1942 to 1962. These include the rise of the Burma Independence Army (BIA), the creation of a 'national' political party, the Anti-Fascist People's Freedom League (AFPFL), the securing of independence (mainly by leaders of the military), the introduction of parliamentary democracy, the beginning of a devastating half-century of civil war (the brunt of which was borne by the military), the military 'Caretaker Government' of 1958 and the *coup d'état* of 1962. They all can be viewed as part of the process in the development of the Union of Myanmar. Of these events, perhaps the half-century of civil war best characterizes the period, its 'winner' ultimately reintegrating the state and implementing its version of the new nation.

That competition for the nation-state became most intense and divisive after Independence in 1948, for the common enemy, the British, who had united disparate groups together in a common goal – their own ouster – was gone. Now came the true test of national unity as different groups, many of whose leaders were once friends and comrades, fought each other over who best could implement this new political entity called the Union of Burma.

Central authority waned considerably in the post-Independence period as the new Burmese Government was barely able to control territory much beyond the major urban centres, including areas just 50 miles from the capital. Finding ways to tame the periphery and unite the nation was the single most important goal of the state, an effort that was eerily similar to those made during the twelfth, sixteenth and eighteenth centuries. Much like competition for an empty or weakened throne, twentieth-century politicians competed for supporters and resources in order to secure the power of government.

At the heart of this twenty-year period between 1942 and 1962, then, was a thousand-year-old issue: which group of Burmese had the most able leaders, the political will, the demographic and material wherewithal and the most appealing notion of Myanmar to reintegrate it. Not surprisingly, especially in such a period of disorder, it turned out to be the army.

Yangon City Hall.

And the story of this period is essentially the story of that institution in its various incarnations, sporadically 'interrupted' by short-lived civilian alternatives.

NEW PATRONS AND THE FORMATION OF THE BURMA ARMY

One of the fundamental challenges facing middle-class reformers, political elites and grass-roots nationalists during the late 1930s was uniting their socio-economic, educational, geographic and particularly generational differences. The members of the Dobama Asiayon were convinced that the older generation of politicians had become so much a part of the colonial establishment that they could not be trusted. They were thought to have traded their principles concerning self-rule for a government salary, status and a comfortable material life.

In addition many of the more moderate members of the colonial administration and Legislative Council stemmed from minority communities that had enjoyed a privileged missionary education and other such advantages. Although urban minorities spoke Burmese, dressed in the traditional Burmese *eingyi* and *longyi* (blouse and skirt) and carried on their daily lives without a hint of ethnic distinction, identity politics (imagined and otherwise) emphasized differences rather than similarities. To create a movement that was strongly anti-colonial leaders of the Dobama Asiayon had to smooth over these differences and disputes between those considered culturally 'Burmese' and those who were not, which had fractured earlier political parties.

The Thakin leadership was also divided by nuances in ideology, having learned their politics from different sources and educational institutions. Even then, as most of them came from similar middle-class backgrounds, their views were more cohesive than those of their parents' generation, whose perceptions of the monarchy, India, the British and modernity in general were significantly different. And, of course, there were always the personality differences that were often at the heart of what appeared to be ideological or class differences.

All these differences would affect the way the members of the Dobama Asiayon saw the world, themselves and the future of Burma. But one thing that united them was their approach: cooperation through established political channels and representatives selected by the colonial state was not an option. Rather, 'mass struggle' was considered necessary to facilitate their vision of 'Burma'. But as long as the colonial security forces were in place such a move was highly unlikely.

Nonetheless, the Dobama Asiayon's more confrontational approach against the colonial Government, their frequent use of the boycott as a

St Mary's Cathedral, Yangon, built in the early 20th century.

form of protest and their growing popularity with peasants and oil field labourers made both the authorities and establishment politicians wary of this party.

Support for the Thakins arrived from an improbable external source: the Japanese. When Japan failed to secure fuel arrangements with the

Dutch in 1941 they set into motion contingency plans that involved Burma. They had begun to make overtures towards the Burmese as early as the 1930s by setting up an international student's institute and purchasing newspaper companies. U Saw's *The Sun* and Dr Thein Maung's *New Burma* both began to publish pro-Japanese stories and editorials in the late 1930s, likely with support from Japanese funds.

In 1939 Japanese secret agents made contact with a handful of young Burmese activists in an effort to enhance their anti-colonial sentiments. Under the guise of a dentist, masseur and journalist, Japanese intelligence assessed the political climate in British Burma to ascertain whether local nationalists would be useful in the event military operations were launched there.

However, parties such as the Dobama Asiayon were more attuned to the possibility of Chinese sponsorship at the time. And when British police closed in on its leader, Aung San, for his political activities, he slipped out of Rangoon in 1940 to seek Chinese support. Armed with a letter written by his Communist colleagues within the Dobama Asiayon, Aung San was however intercepted by Japanese agents and would have been imprisoned had not pro-Japanese colleagues back in Rangoon intervened on his behalf. Convincing his Japanese captors that he was in fact reaching out to them, Aung San set in motion a plan to collaborate with his new Japanese patrons in exchange for training and financial support.[1]

In 1941 a small group of Thakins joined Aung San at Hainan Island for training in espionage, sabotage, military tactics, demolition and organizational strategy that would enable them to form their own resistance force. Under the tutelage of Colonel Keiji Suzuki the 'Thirty Comrades', as they came to be known in Burmese history (and mythology), were sent to Bangkok where they began to recruit for what would become the Burma Independence Army (BIA).

For the first time since the fall of the monarchy, the possibility of raising a standing army in British Burma composed of Burmese became a reality, so the Thakins used this opportunity to instil in their recruits many of the ideas central to the Dobama Asiayon, with an added dose of Japanese imperial propaganda for good measure. Ideas about security priorities, notions of citizenship and conceptions of a national community were shaped during this wartime experience. In this way they began to establish foundations for associating army membership with patriotism, that is, those who struggled for the nation.

To the wide range of recruits including nationalists, Communists, Socialists and 'bad hats' who joined the BIA, the range of ideas was made more cohesive with the focused notion of 'Burma for the Burmese'. That plus their wartime experience together established close bonds of loyalty with their immediate leaders. Colonel Suzuki (also known as Bo

Mogyo or 'Captain' Thunderbolt), Aung San, Let Ya, Zeya and Ne Win, moreover, were seen as not just commanders within a wing of the Japanese army, but as Burma's 'own' (indigenous) military heroes. They were also future social and political patrons who could protect their clients.

While some national histories and commemorative museums portray the BIA as a coherent, unified and ideologically driven group of patriots from the start, the story 'on the ground' indicates a more complicated picture.[2] Officially the BIA would be in charge of supporting Japan's Fifteenth Army and recruitment within the country once the invasion started. BIA officers would be assigned to particular districts, many in rural areas along the invasion route of Japanese regulars. That was meant to raise a force that could provide support as well as guidance through local terrain. But tensions within the Japanese army over the role of the BIA surfaced once they became operational.

Colonel Suzuki regarded the BIA as his own little liberation army, part of the 'Asia for the Asians' message central to Japan's public relations machine. He was even mythologized as having belonged to Burmese royalty, destined to return and free the Burmese. But some of his Japanese colleagues viewed the BIA as a necessary evil since it was really not in a position to offer the Imperial forces much in terms of their overall strategic plans in Myanmar while it took up scarce resources.

To Aung San and his troops, however, the BIA was perceived as the country's only viable vehicle for Independence (hence its name), an army of 'freedom fighters' whose goal was to rid their country of the colonial oppressors. Yet some within the group of Thakins were uneasy about the alliance with the Japanese, as the latter's Fascist doctrines and principles conflicted with their own leftist (Socialist and Communist) politics.

When the Japanese forces entered the country in late December 1941, local colonial administrators considered the BIA and its leadership as treacherous rabble who had turned on their colonial partners. Middle-class Burmese working in the civil service, certain ethnic minorities and others 'collaborating' with the British also did not regard the BIA as heroes. The Thakins made little effort to recruit ethnic minorities such as the Karens or Mons either, for they were perceived to be favourites of the British and not to be trusted. Such sentiments sowed the seeds for ethnic tensions subsequently when Independence came.

Matters were not helped when BIA officers were left behind to administer territories on behalf of the Japanese. Placed in charge of rural administrative committees some abused their power to the point where even the Japanese authorities were unable (or reluctant) to resolve the difficulties created. When violence broke out between BIA troops and Karen communities in the village of Myaungmya, for example, the Japanese had to step in to quell the mini war within the larger war.

Eventually the Japanese disbanded the BIA after eight months of operations and trimmed it down to a few thousand soldiers, renaming it the Burma Defence Army (BDA). This 'downsizing' worried Aung San and other Thakin leaders, for their authority and influcence depended directly on it. Tensions with their Japanese patrons and dissatisfaction with the extent of their representation in the new provisional Government of 1943 allowed by the Japanese, eventually led to secret negotiations between the Allied forces and the BDA, in which the latter revealed their intention to switch sides and turned against the Japanese at an opportune time during the Allies' counter-attack. (Incidentally, the first strike for the country's independence by the Burma Defence Army as a unit occurred at Pyinmana, where the new capital Naypyidaw is now located.)

Of course, the army's role in the national history of Myanmar is remembered in different ways depending on whether or not one benefited from their activities and also when such assessments were made. If made during the twenty years after Independence, the army were heroes; if more recently, they were not. Legitimacy is often a matter of dates. It also depended on the ethnic group with which one identified. Certain minorities, villagers (who had direct contact with the BIA) and indigenous civil servants would remember it in ways that were not shared by the Thakins and most nationalist histories.

In hindsight the formation of the BIA is, *historically* speaking, considered very important by all Burma historians. Not only was it the first time that an indigenous Burmese army representing the majority of the people had been created in British Burma – heretofore the domain of the British Indian army – but many of its leaders at Independence and its troubled aftermath continued to be the country's leaders for the next several decades.[3] The present army is the direct heir of the BIA: its history, its structure, its mythology and much of its *raison d'être*.

THE DECLINE OF BRITISH BURMA

As the BIA marched northward from Moulmein and other sections of Lower Myanmar British authorities were uncertain and unprepared for the turn of events that had suddenly come upon them. When the British bastion in Southeast Asia, 'impregnable Singapore', fell to the Japanese relatively quickly and easily, considerable shock waves reverberated throughout the colonial administration, so sure had the British been that their position in Asia was secure. Decisions by then-Governor (of Burma) Dorman-Smith's office were slower than what was required given Rangoon's large population and inadequate infrastructure. The small British community eventually evacuated their capital city, at first moving northward into Upper Myanmar but eventually to India, where an exile government was established in Simla, one of the 'hill-stations' with a temperate climate.

With the retreat of the civil administration social order quickly turned to anarchy. Hospitals and schools were closed, prisons and mental asylum doors were flung open and even zoo animals shot. The docks on the Rangoon River became deserted as many Indian workers, coolies and labourers fled, exacerbating the shortage of supplies. Disease spread amongst the populations as public water supplies, power, transport and sanitation infrastructure broke down. Thousands of Rangoon and Lower Burma residents from various Indian communities, along with American missionaries, fled northwards on a trek which saw 400,000 perish in their attempt to reach India.

Some well-to-do Burmese families relocated outside city limits, as Japanese bombing runs became a daily part of urban life. Higher-ranking members of the civil service would commute into Rangoon from neighbouring townships as they were able to afford the ferries that served the colonial capital on the Irrawaddy's tributaries. Memoirs from the period tell us that many held on to their posts as long as they could, carrying on their official duties, collecting pay from the local post-office and even applying for leave and moving expenses due to the war.[4] When the official decision to leave Rangoon was made by colonial authorities, this group had the means to arrange transport for themselves, their families and their servants. Their views of the Japanese and the BIA troops that supported them were likely unfavourable even though some were asked to and did join the 'provisional Government' of Burma created by the Japanese and headed by Dr Ba Maw in 1943.

Other members of the Burmese middle-class elites did not retreat with the colonial administration, since the arrival of the Japanese was not at first considered detrimental to their interests. In fact many were excited by news of Japanese victories over the British, the first modern Asian nation to beat a Western one, that also happened to be Buddhist. When news reached Mandalay that the Japanese were rapidly approaching, reports of old songs being revived to celebrate such victories were heard – as memories of the Konbaung monarchy still ran fresh.

Young writers, publishers, activists, students and politicians who had not aligned themselves with the British initially regarded the new order under the Japanese with enthusiasm, an opportunity to strike out against the colonial power. Psychologically they were very much attracted by the idea of 'Asia for the Asians' that pro-Japanese presses were celebrating. The prospect of determining their own future was alluring for many who were born into the world as colonial subjects.

While many were supportive of these events, subsequent abusive treatment of local Burmese by Japanese soldiers made intellectuals like

'Journal Kyaw' U Chit Maung realize that one day they would have to drive the Japanese out as well, for one colonial power had simply replaced another.[5] Some Burmese were recruited to work for the *Kempeitai*, the Japanese Military Intelligence Office, while others were drawn to the new provisional Government led by Burmese Dr Ba Maw. Certain minorities had a harder time as many were arrested and imprisoned for their allegiance to the British. But others chose to cooperate with the Japanese in hope that their interests would be protected.

The Japanese did try to alter their public image through publicity campaigns that focused on common links to Buddhism. This programme involved hosting a Greater East Asia Buddhist Conference in Tokyo that found holy relics to donate to newly built pagodas in war-torn Rangoon. Other programmes directed towards Karens and youth were more successful, such as the creation and support of the East Asia Youth League, which mobilized youths to improve education, libraries and sanitation works throughout the country. Drawing youth from a wide range of ethnic and immigrant communities, the organization was well appreciated by the public. However, it later joined the Anti-Fascist People's Freedom League (AFPFL) in 1944.

Despite the success of the East Asia Youth League, the new Japanese-backed administration enjoyed limited support and controlled only Rangoon and its immediately adjacent areas. Personal rivalries re-emerged amongst politicans who were excluded from Dr Ba Maw's cabinet. Some, especially those with ties to Communist and Socialist networks, began to plan for eventual resistance against the Japanese, while others felt they had not been properly compensated by their new patrons for their efforts against the British and, as clients, were simply looking for alternative patrons to attain their goals. Of course, there were those who considered Ba Maw's a puppet government of the Japanese and would neither participate in nor cooperate with it.

These internal fissures at the centre, a pattern seen before, weakened Ba Maw's Government and affected its ability to establish serious administrative control outside the capital. Local autonomy returned to rural areas, as ex-BIA members, Thakins and traditional headmen filled the political vacuum left by the British. Upland territories that had been designated 'Frontier Areas' that were ruled 'indirectly' by the British were maintained as such by the Japanese, essentially preserving the status quo and therefore autonomy. Lowland cultivators had suffered greatly from the shortages of war along with abuses from BIA administrative committees, rogue Chinese forces and Japanese troops.

In short, although the Burmese war experience was a mixed one and socio-economically difficult for all, some nonetheless rose in prominence because they had established patron–client relations with their new patrons.

THE RISE OF THE UNION OF MYANMAR

When the Japanese authorities decided to disband the BIA and replace it with the Burma Defence Army (BDA) at least two initiatives were set in place for more effective control. First, the existing members of the BIA were assessed for their military abilities and professional commitment, thereby weeding out the 'undesirable elements' that had slipped through. Second, the now streamlined force, numbering only a few thousand, was put through a new regimen that included officer training. Perhaps most important, the combined experience of fighting, training and learning together, more than any single event or idea, created a deep sense of cama-raderie amongst the cadets, a bond that would prove to be invaluable in subsequent decades.[6]

Despite the short-lived existence of the Burma Independence Army it left an important mark on the future history of state-formation in Myanmar. One reason is that the BIA and its successor, the BDA, created an extensive network of fighting men who were thenceforth bound by personal ties, wartime experiences, ethnicity and corporate identity to key nationalist figures in the army command structure. In effect the BIA/BDA provided a new framework for the organization of civilians in the absence of a state apparatus during these war years, thereby indelibly immersing military with civilian components. Although personal *tats* (militias) had been created and employed in limited amounts by politicians, activists and other leaders since the 1930s, the BIA/BDA was a much larger unit that operated an extensive 'national' web of personal relationships infused into a military-style chain of command.

Another way in which the army helped in creating a nation-state was the compatibility of its structure with traditional Burmese socio-political ones. Moreover, the military's clear command structure provided real potential for advancement, and its members, an *esprit de corps* that cut across different backgrounds and reified ethnicities and offered a sense of cohesion, stability and order in a time of chaos and anarchy. (In that sense, the army was much like the Sangha, a stable and disciplined environment during times of instability and chaos.) These attributes enabled wartime and future leaders such as Aung San and Ne Win to successfully recruit many able people, not only into the army, but also into its political wing that was quietly being formed to resist the returning British in the political arena after the war.

The establishment of a formal war office allowed Aung San and other members of the Thakins to begin working 'in the field' and independently of the Japanese command structure, as they were now relieved of administrative duties. This enabled Aung San to renew his contacts with the Communists and Socialists, who were not only beginning to make overtures towards collaboration with the British High Command upon its return to Burma, but also to form a secret Anti-Fascist Organization (AFO). Eventually the AFO would secretly work with Lord Mountbatten, chief of the Southeast Asia Command (SEAC), with the hope that independence would be granted the Burmese when the time came. This loose alliance of ex-BIA/BDA (and later) BNA (Burma National Army) soldiers, the Communist and Socialist parties, guerilla fighters and ethnic resistance groups became the foundations of the leadership of the Union of Burma.

The AFO soon changed its name to the Anti-Fascist People's Freedom League (AFPFL), extending its membership to include a wider range of political parties and nationalist groups whose ultimate goal was independence. Broad-based and outwardly inclusive, like its Indian counterpart the Congress Party, the AFPFL recruited representatives from nearly all sectors of the political landscape and provided a framework that united the short-term interests and priorities of a wide range of communities in wartime Myanmar.

But not surprisingly these alliances that had been forged to defeat the Japanese quickly dissolved when victory was at hand in 1945. Members turned on each other in anticipation of that outcome, trying to pre-empt their rivals in securing power. Old grudges, personal rivalries and strong ideological differences once again rose amongst the AFPFL, former civilian authorities, SEAC forces and certain minority groups. Parties took irreconcilable positions with regard to the future of the country, as leaders worried about losing their position to rivals within their own ranks if they did not take a hard line.

The returning civil administration under Governor Sir Reginald Dorman-Smith attempted to reclaim what it considered its rightful authority after having been chased out by the Japanese and Aung San's BIA, whom they considered traitors. Some elements of the returning civil service even wanted Aung San placed on trial and hanged for treason. To make matters worse London was slow in deciding whether to help promote Burmese self-government or try to re-establish economic foundations for British commercial interests first.

Aung San, now de facto head of both the dominant political party and the military (AFPFL and BNA), wanted to keep the military component intact to ensure the British honoured their agreement to allow the country to be run by indigenous leaders. But members in both groups tended to distrust each other. The Communists, allied with Aung San through the new AFPFL, wanted assurances from the British (and also from Aung San) that they would be given a key role in deciding the shape of whatever new state apparatus was formed. Minorities, especially the Karen National Union, were also concerned about the future power structure of the country and wanted their interests and concerns recognized.

But the British White Paper of 1945 which contained a blueprint for the rebuilding of the country fell short of the AFPFL's expectations, suggesting that economic recovery and infrastructural development would have to occur first before self-government could be considered. A stalemate thus arose between Governor Dorman-Smith and Aung San over details regarding AFPFL representation in government, leading to mass demonstrations at the Shwedagon Pagoda in 1946. Yet factionalism within the AFPFL, especially with the Communists (led by Aung San's brother-in-law), threatened to weaken the League. While the country's future continued to be dictated by former colonial authorities, factionalism amongst its own political leaders added little to the solution.

Following the appointment of Sir Hubert Rance in August 1946 to replace Dorman-Smith as Governor, a general strike by the police and an ultimatum by Aung San that London grant independence to Burma, an agreement was signed with British Prime Minister Clement Attlee on 27 January 1947. It promised Burmese independence within the following year.[7] Aung San immediately made plans to reach out to minority communities in the Frontier Areas, which were uneasy about joining a nation dominated by Burmese speakers without guarantees of representation, financial aid and some local autonomy. Different ethnic groups had varying concerns about their relationship with the purported new nation, complicated by differences of opinion within their own ranks.

Earlier in 1946 Aung San had travelled to Panglong to meet representatives of the Shan, Kachin and Chin communities at a conference to discuss terms and conditions of inclusion into the Union. That conference exposed genuine concerns that some of them had in terms of sharing a future in Aung San's Burma. Nonetheless, he offered assurances to the groups that they could have a place within the nation with their autonomy intact, a promise that would later become a curse. After Constituent Assembly elections in April 1947 seated a large majority of AFPFL candidates, ties with the British Empire were symbolically severed when, on 10 June 1947, a resolution was adopted not to remain within the Commonwealth.[8]

With Independence almost upon them, a most devastating blow nearly unravelled the process of reintegration. On 19 July 1947, on a Saturday morning around 10:30 am, as Aung San was presiding over his Executive Council at the Secretariat, he and several colleagues were gunned down by assassins dressed in military uniform using British sten guns. It was, and is still, believed that the assassins were in the pay of rival politician U Saw, with material support from two British officers who had supplied the arms and ammunition. Aung San was only 32 when he was assassinated, in the prime of youth, with much accomplished in so short a time against incredible odds, and so much to look forward to.[9]

Deputy Prime Minister, U Nu ('Mr Tender'), was sworn in to lead the new nation. London and Myanmar formalized their separation through a series of parlimentary and constitutional procedures that led, finally, to the declaration of Burma's independence in the early morning hours of 4 January 1948.

CIVIL WAR AND THE CONTEST FOR THE NATION

Almost immediately after Independence was secured the country erupted in civil war. Three groups – the Communists, the People's Volunteer Organization and the Karen National Union – decided to fight the Government of U Nu for a wide range of ideological, personal and political reasons. Around the same time members of the army who were associated with these groups also deserted (sometimes in whole regiments), illustrating strong personal, ethnic and patron–client affinity that superceded both ideology and the corporate identity of the armed forcies.

U Nu's Government faced an enormous crisis; the Government exercised little control over areas much beyond Rangoon as many rural areas were controlled by local leaders and insurgent groups. At the heart of the rebellions lay fundamental differences about the shape, form of governance and content that this new 'Burma' was to take. But it was not all ideological; there were historical, personal, socio-economic and cultural concerns as well. In its very first year of existence the young Burmese Government nearly collapsed.

The Communists had some legitimate grievances to warrant dissent. They had done poorly in the Constituent Assembly elections and seated only a few representatives. Policy differences with U Nu's Government and the eventual expulsion from the AFPFL were the final straws. To make matters worse the Communists split along personal and ideological lines amongst themselves, some following Thakin Than Tun's faction and others following Thakin Soe's more radical and militant one. When the Government ordered their arrest the movement went underground and began armed resistance.

The People's Volunteer Organization, which served as an unofficial armed force connected to the AFPFL, was also dissatisfied with its exclusion from the new coalition Government. It too decided that rebellion was the only way its interests could be preserved. Roads, bridges and other arteries of transport were held hostage by these forces, consisting of local leaders and their 'pocket armies'. Disruption to social and cultural life spurred migrations of refugees into neighbouring districts.

Karen grievances stemmed from a mistrust of Burmese authority likely beginning with the Japanese invasion but also from specific terms in the new constitution regarding territory as well as uncertainties over their place in the new national army. Under the British the Karen rose to the top ranks in the British Burma Army while 'Burmans' (by which the British meant the abstract and reified ethno-linguistic group) were not even allowed to join the military or police. After Independence the situation reversed, since the Karen's patron, the British, were no longer there.

The Karen therefore opted to form their own Karen-Mon State, demanding territories in Tennasserim, certain Irrawaddy districts and parts of Lower Myanmar where many Burmese speakers also lived. Finally, the KNDO (Karen National Defence Organization) broke out in armed rebellion against the Government in 1949 and almost took Rangoon as their forces had overrun Insein, just west of the city, close to where today's airport is located. Had it not been for the national army led by General Ne Win, along with Socialist party forces and other irregular troops, the Government most likely would have collapsed and the capital taken.

In addition to military threats there were massive general strikes during this immediate post-Independence period, including one by civil servants which compounded the fragmentation and disorder in the political arena. Achieving order and stability had become as much a political objective as anything else, a foremost priority of the Government for many decades yet to come.

Thus under the anarchic conditions of post-Second World War the most able – that is, the strongest of these groups – rose to the occasion to dominate the scene and 'save' the Union from disintegration. And that was the army.

U Nu's Government managed to continue despite the problems it faced, especially the eruption of civil war. Although the countryside surrounding the capital and major urban areas were eventually (and incrementally) retaken and secured by the armed forces during the next decade or so, much of the mountainous and jungle areas remained in the hands of the Communists, the KNDO and numerous other insurgent groups for several more decades, some until the late 1990s. U Nu had this burden to bear throughout his tenure.

Although U Nu attempted to connect with the outside world by joining the group of non-aligned nations, much of his focus was on domestic affairs where most of the problems of the nation lay. The bombing of the country in the Second World War had devastated the infrastructure, which had not been repaired, as the AFPFL opted for an immediate transfer of political power and the ensuing civil war left no opportunity to begin recovery. When U Nu approached the United Kingdom for aid and arms, the response was conditional: if the Government of Burma resolved its issues with the Karens through Commonwealth mediation, funds would be offered. U Nu refused the terms as they allowed foreign powers to interfere in domestic politics.

Yet Myanmar's timber, rice, oil and mining industries were in desperate need of foreign capital that was not forthcoming in the post-war years. Internal commerce was also hindered by infrastructural damage, insurgencies and civil war. By 1950, however, considerable warming between the Government and Commonwealth nations resulted in interest-free loans from the United Kingdom, India, Australia, Pakistan and Ceylon.

Increasing stability in the countryside as a result of the army's pacification campaigns enabled the Government to pursue other programmes that were also important to nation-building. Most administrative structures were inherited from the British, with willing and able English-language trained civil servants still available to fill the posts vacated during the war. Promising scholars and students were sponsored by the Government and sent around the world for technical training at universities in North America, Britain, Australia and India.

U Nu's Government even had the wherewithal for the creation of the Burma Historical Commission, established in 1955, which was sanctioned to oversee the founding of a national archive and the publishing of a national textbook. British scholars, former officials and missionaries were invited back to work as consultants for the Government, an offer that was taken up by some. A national stadium, a national zoo and a national library were also planned, suggesting that secular notions of what makes a nation-state were being recognized and seriously adopted.

At the same time U Nu made overtures to traditional ideas of Burmese kingship, authority and legitimacy by his patronage of Buddhism. Convinced that it was compatible with Socialist principles, he began to explore ways in which the Burmese past might be reconnected to the nation's present. In 1949 he introduced the Ecclesiastical Courts Act which allowed the state to officially support Buddhism by establishing a lay Buddhist Sasana Council, along with a Ministry of Religious Affairs, a Society for the Propagation of Buddhism, a Pali University, while hosting the Sixth Great Buddhist Council in the tradition of exemplary Buddhist king, Asoka of India.[10] Although U Nu's religious programmes received overwhelming support from the public, these measures alienated certain minority religious and ethnic communities that did not consider Buddhism, its cultural symbols, ideals and propagation necessarily representing them or their beliefs and cultures.

Christians, Muslims and, of course, the Communists felt threatened by these moves to 'officially' connect the state to a particular Buddhist past. While such links appealed to the majority of Burmese Buddhists, the potential threat of making Buddhism the state religion exacerbated a tense situation in which minority groups were already threatening to secede from the Union for political reasons. Besides, in a land that was already nearly 90 per cent Buddhist, there was really no reason to make Buddhism the state religion. Such 'irrational' decisions by the Prime Minister did not go unnoticed by army commanders who were growing more and more confident in their abilities, and less and less in those of civilian authorities to establish order and run the country effectively.

On 26 September 1958 U Nu invited General Ne Win and his army to form a government for a specified length of time, 'clean up the mess' and return authority to civilian Government thereafter. (This period was later extended so that the army could complete a particular military campaign it was on.) For the extension to be constitutionally legal General Ne Win insisted on Parliament's formal passing of such an act.[11]

In the emotional context of the past twenty years of military rule, however, this 'Caretaker Government' of 1958 has come to be called a 'coup', a revisionism commensurate with one's view of recent Myanmar history.[12] U Nu himself also called it a 'coup' but only after his ousting in 1962, for at the time all his public announcements show that he requested the army to step in. Coup or not, it is clear that the civilian Government was losing control not only of the countryside, where banditry was rife, but also in urban areas where crime was at an all time high. And the Shan may have been putting pressure on U Nu for concessions, as it was now ten years from Independence, when their right to secede from the Union could be invoked as called for by the 1948 Constitution.

Thus when tension arose between the Home Minister (in charge of the Union Police) and the Defence Minister (in charge of the army) it threatened to create even more disorder and become a national issue. U Nu asked the only person able to command the respect and loyalty of the army and the people, General Ne Win, to establish the 'Caretaker Government'.[13] And at the time the army was the only institution capable of restoring order. Thus it was less a simple military versus civilian contest for power than a desire by *both* sides to prevent anarchy; a deep-rooted fear found throughout the long history of Myanmar.

During these eighteen months of the 'Caretaker Government' the army's influence spread, permeating non-military sectors of society as well. The Defence Services Institute, which began as an army canteen/supply store, in time became a business conglomerate, buying banks, shipping lines, department stores, construction firms and transport companies on behalf of the military. In later years it would provide all kinds of perks for military officers, attracting more and more men into the armed services as it offered better security and benefits than the civil service or the private sector.

Beyond economic interests, youth idolized famous military heroes while the institution itself became a desirable career goal. Literature during the 1950s celebrated the military career as a noble one which everyone should honour and respect.[14] Finally, in 1960, when the extension granted by Parliament to the army expired and the latter had quelled the troubles which had prompted the request for the extension, the army returned power to the civilian Government, not only ensuring that the scheduled elections proceed as planned but actually managing and arranging their implementation.

But almost as soon as U Nu and his party won the 1960 elections and returned to power, the political bickering and factionalism, insurgency and banditry in the countryside and lawlessness in urban areas also returned. This state of affairs continued for two more years, until on 2 March 1962, General Ne Win staged a *coup d'état* (explained in greater detail in the next chapter). In that coup the army arrested 50 leading Government ministers including the Prime Minister, the President and the Chief Justice, and with only one (reported) casualty, civilian Government was ended, ushering in military rule for the next several decades.

Because the country was once more in the hands of its owners and finally independent of foreign rule, the period was meaningful to most; hence our phrase to characterize this period – 'disorder with meaning'. But, as the phrase suggests, it was a mixed blessing, as Independence also plunged the country into civil war. With the common enemy (the British) gone, the fissures that had divided Burmese society for years once more reappeared, so that one now had only onself with whom to fight.

In that difficult political milieu a totally foreign and mainly untried system of governance was installed: parliamentary democracy. It was not well understood, its most basic principles (such as egalitarianism and sovereignty in the people) were political concepts completely foreign to most of the population (who were cultivators). There were neither conceptual nor structural foundations for it in most of the country's history, and it certainly was not a priority for most people at the time. Not surprisingly, this untried system and the people chosen to implement it could not restore social order and curb anarchy, the most pressing concern of Burmese society. The only organization left in the country with the physical and structural wherewithal to restore that order was the army.

And although it did restore order and prevent the Union from disintegrating, curb banditry and lawlessness in the countryside and reduce violent crime in the cities, it could not, as the old Chinese saying goes, 'rule from horseback'. After all, it was comprised of soldiers, not economists, philosophers, intellectuals or administrators. Certainly such individuals were recruited to help run the state but they were few and far between and, in any case, had to operate within a 'traditional', vertical patron–client structure. The result was often a mix of contradictory

Former building of the Supreme Court of Burma, Yangon, completed in 1911.

243

ideas, methods and goals. That heritage continued to plague the nation for the next several decades until the November elections of 2010. But whether or not the previous pattern has completely ended still remains to be seen.

12

Reconstruction and Nation-Building, 1962–2013

Until 2 March 1962 the army had acknowledged the authority and legitimacy of an elected government not only by arranging and managing the elections of 1960, but also by handing power back to its winners as promised. The army did this at a time when public sentiment regarding it was extremely favourable, appreciating its discipline and no-nonsense competence to quell social disorder: the highest priority of Burmese society.

Such public sentiment was in stark contrast to the then prevailing perception of the civilian Government as corrupt, weak and undisciplined and hardly able to control its own members, let alone the lawlessness in society, exemplified by the behaviour of rogue monks, who throughout the mid-1950s committed acts of violent crime, including rape, murder, internecine violence and drug smuggling, in general abusing their honoured status in society and becoming a law unto themselves.

In other words the civilian Government's general ineptness at re-establishing law and order was an issue the army could have capitalized on to justify retention of power after 1960. But it did not; instead, it gave authority back to the civilians. In hindsight that may have been a bit too soon, for only two years later the army staged a coup (this time uninvited) and ruled as the Revolutionary Council. Twelve years later it created what it stated had always been its ultimate goal – the establishment of a civilian Government, this one led by a single party called (in English) the Burma Socialist Programme Party or BSPP.

Government, however, was neither entirely civilian (in terms of personnel distribution and control) nor military (in terms of principle and structure). It remained in that hybrid mode until the anarchy and disorder of 1988 erupted and, when it did not dissipate but spread throughout the country, the army once again took over the governance of the country, this time keeping it for 23 years.

Finally, in January 2011, the legal authority of government was once more returned to an elected 'parliament' (Hlutdaw) composed officially of civilians. In the following two months elected members to the Hlutdaw were seated and on 30 March 2011 the previous military government known (in English) as the State Peace and Development Council (or SPDC) that had managed and arranged this transition of authority (as had the 'Caretaker Government' of 1958) was officially and legally dissolved. What happened between March 1962 and early 2013 is the focus of this chapter.

THE COUP OF 1962

Mainly domestic but some external factors contributed to the coup of 1962. The reason given by the army was the need to preserve the integrity of the Union, which was being threatened by two minority groups, the Shan and the Kayah. They were invoking their right to secede from the Union after ten years, granted by the Constitution of 1947. In exchange for joining the Union in 1948 Aung San had personally crafted and carried out the deal. At the time it seemed the practical thing to do but it was clear by 1962 that the issue was never really resolved, just postponed, and now the same threat was being used again. General Ne Win, as one of the country's leaders in his own right as well as Aung San's torchbearer, was not about to see the Union he helped create simply unravel, and so staged the coup.

Official press releases by the army following the early-morning event explained to the people that the previous Government's policies had failed to protect the Union, a genuine and ever-present concern for the military whose responsibility it was to actually implement it. In this regard the army considered ex-premier U Nu's actions towards the Shan and Kayah to be appeasement. From the perspective of the army's regional commanders, Yangon was being 'soft' on its Frontier Areas by giving these groups too much autonomy that weakened central power.

The army was also concerned that if those territories became more independent they would attract the patronage of and interference by foreign powers, which in turn would affect domestic affairs. That had been the case during the First Anglo–Burmese War and also more recently with the Kuomintang (KMT) forces, which had fled to the remoter border regions of Myanmar from where they waged a war of rebellion against the People's Republic of China, supported by the CIA.

America's involvement in Korea, and in Laos and Vietnam, made clear that the new world powers were taking an interest in nations bordering any Communist country, particularly China and North Korea. To the battle-weary soldiers of Myanmar who had been fighting a civil war against their own countrymen for over fourteen years, however, it seemed as if the civilian Government did not have the strategic foresight, the political will or the ability to protect the country from both internal and external threats.

Particularly annoying to the army were U Nu's efforts to make Buddhism the state religion, for it needlessly created a non-issue, as close to 90 per cent of the population was already Buddhist. It galvanized ethnic (Christian) minorities on the border and others already in rebellion by providing them with additional ammunition for their cause of autonomy and secession. Although U Nu's proposal was ultimately rejected by parliament, he had nonetheless exacerbated the situation.

Similarly, his 'solution' to ward off calamities by building 80,000 sand pagodas and the World Peace Pagoda, along with hosting the Sixth World Buddhist Synod, might have garnered much merit for him and the country, but were not going to do much to solve problems of national unity, banditry in the countryside and the high crime rates in the urban areas – all getting more and more intolerable for society at large.

Finally, it was clear to army strategists that the problem was not just the civilian Government, its personnel or its policies – it was the system itself. From the army's perspective, parliamentary-style government (and federal systems in general) had inherent structural weaknesses for they tended to reduce the power of the centre and encourage local autonomy. In Myanmar's case it was precisely at a time when such activities needed to be curbed with a strong central government.

In addition, special interest groups, personal rivalries and partisan party politics had further weakened an intrinsically weak system, allowing politicians to serve their own interests in a way detrimental to the larger community. To the military, then, civilian ministers 'playing' parliamentary games at the capital, detached from what it considered to be the real world outside Yangon, showed how unaware the latter were of the tenuous links binding parts of the country.

Whatever the reasons given for, or attributed to, the staging of the coup, in the final analysis it is indisputable that the disorder of society after the Second World War and Independence had put the military in power and 'raised its stock' as *the* indispensable component in Burmese society. And because of the general reputation and trust in the army by the public in the 1950s and early 1960s, its success in 'cleaning up the mess', its professionalism (in handing power back to civilians as promised once its legally allotted time was up) and the general social order their rule reestablished, the coup of 1962 saw very little (if any) opposition from any significant quarter.

There were no riots or demonstrations against it; no country broke diplomatic relations or recalled their ambassadors, no heads of state summoned Myanmar's ambassadors to reprimand them and certainly no economic sanctions were imposed on the country. Indeed, some of the regional press – in India, Thailand and other Southeast Asian countries – applauded the event at the time, while none condemned the coup.

Anti-communists also regarded the coup as favourable to checking the growth of Communism both in Myanmar and neighbouring Indochina. Most realized that the army was probably the best and only solution to the country's foremost concern: the personal and collective safety of the public and the integrity of the nation.

After the coup General Ne Win and his commanders replaced the AFPFL-dominated civilian government with a 'Revolutionary Council' of army officers which had a clear chain of command. Then on 4 July 1962 it announced that a single party (the BSPP) was to be created to function as the channel through which all participatory politics must take place. All other political parties were banned by the 1964 Law to Protect National Solidarity.[1]

The new power holders had many ties to their former civilian colleagues although their actual experiences may have been quite different. The former were battle-hardened soldiers who had not only fought the Communists, Karen rebels and insurgents of various colours, but whose senior members had been part of the BIA and therefore directly involved in the original struggle against the British for Independence. The post-war army's reputation was much like that of George Washington's after the American Revolutionary War or, closer to home, the Viet Minh and their role in the defeat of the French in Vietnam.

Perhaps as important, the troops knew General Ne Win had the credentials to lead: he had fought for the nation, saved the capital from being taken by Karen rebels in 1949 and had been the trusted lieutenant and torchbearer of the country's 'father', Aung San, keeping the army together after his assassination. In their view he was 'saving' the nation from disintegration once again. He was the Burmese equivalent of Vietnam's General Giap. In other words, this particular group of military leaders and the coup of 1962 had political legitimacy as defined by Burmese culture and history.

For the first three months of the new Government the lives of most people did not change much. Little by little, however, it became apparent to citizens that men in green fatigues would be the new political elites. Military values, behaviour and protocol, already familiar to the public in these post-Second World War years, entered the consciousness of Burmese people even more fully, as prestige, status and power became associated with an army career.

Elites from a wide range of backgrounds would have to decide whether to fall in line or face the socio-economic and political consequences of opposing the new Government. This was not too difficult for some, as Ne Win invited many former civil servants and other seasoned politicians to join his new party, much as kings in the past had done by retaining experienced ministers even if they had served previous monarchs who had been opponents. Especially those who had been marginalized under the U Nu regime decided to climb on board, while those who had been in charge under the previous administration opted not to participate. Intelligentsia would migrate overseas as the army dismantled most of the government institutions in which they had played a primary role.

U Nu himself would eventually leave the country with his close associates, hopeful that the military Government would have a quick demise. Establishing a Government-in-exile in Thailand, he recruited people who had been negatively affected by the coup. He even went to the United States to raise funds for his cause. On one occasion at the University of Illinois, Urbana, he declared in a public lecture that 'with a rifle in one hand and democracy in the other' he would return to overthrow the military Government.

The judicial sector, the legislature and the regional councils that were meant to provide 'ethnic states' with a channel of communication set up by the 1947 Constitution were all eliminated, leaving very few openings for experienced bureaucrats. The power emanating from these core institutions was transferred to the Chairman (Ne Win) and the Revolutionary Council. The eventual nationalization of heavy industry, business, banking and other sectors between 1962 and 1970 prompted a mass exodus of Myanmar-born Indians, Chinese and minority groups involved in those economic enterprises to seek a living elsewhere.

Those from the Karen community, but others as well, who could prove to Australian Immigration that they had 'Western blood' flowing in their veins to some degree (and could afford it) migrated there. Others went to India and even London, convinced that their concerns and priorities would not be well served under military rule.

But the vast majority of the country's population who were cultivators (or tied to the land in some way), comprising nearly 80 per cent of the population at the time, stayed, as life under the military did not immediately affect them all that much, and actually got much better for them as time went on, as the Government focused its priorities on rural Myanmar and the peasantry and less on the urban areas and their inhabitants. Indeed, overall the coup probably did not alter the lives of most Burmese immediately, although in subsequent years important changes took place as the Revolutionary Council attempted to transform Burmese society more thoroughly.

Its first objective was to more effectively seize control of the state to protect its position. The second was to identify key weaknesses in society and eliminate them, particularly the socio-economic instability that the nation faced, handcuffed by crime in the urban areas and lawlessness and banditry in the countryside. Another concern was the political landscape itself, which was corrupt and far too decentralized to be effective.

In the span of the next several years politicians and activists found the political space shrinking as new laws made it illegal to politically oppose the Government.

Importantly, the army banned official Government links to the (lay) Buddha Sasana Council, reversing U Nu's attempt to continue the traditional cosy relationship between 'church' and state. Educational and cultural institutions also came under the authority of the Revolutionary Council in order to better manage and monitor them, particularly since they were the foci of political agitation.

A fourth policy distanced the country from external (especially Western) values, culture and politics. Burmese became the official language in Government and education, although in practice this had always been the case. Only a relatively small number of the population was English-educated and participated in Government anyway, so that much of the negativity surrounding anti-Western policies was actually targeted at the conspicuous lifestyles and attitudes of English-speaking middle-class elites who enjoyed privileged status before and immediately after Independence.

Even bus numbers were changed back to Burmese script, and street names honouring British officials – such as Phayre Street, named after Sir Arthur Phayre, prominent colonial historian, and Dalhousie Street, named after Lord Dalhousie, Governor General of British India – were changed and given names of famous figures in Burmese history instead. Windsor Road became Shin Saw Bu Lan, for example, named after the only woman sovereign in Burmese history.

Another effort at resurrecting Burmese culture was the National Literacy Council, which encouraged the use of Burmese. The National Language Commission also attempted to promote Burmese literary proficiency, translations and instruction. (Indeed, the country received the UN prize for literacy in 1971.) It was also commissioned to produce a national dictionary. But because English was dropped as a kindergarten subject, it affected the education and world views of the next generation of students whose consequences we still see today: very little English is spoken in the country even though the language has been a compulsory subject in lower education now for many years.

All these policies were attempts to resurrect the 'purity' and glory of Burmese culture and tradition and to reject (perhaps forget) the humiliating colonial past. The elite during U Nu's tenure was also associated with the colonized class of 'collaborators' whose values, world views and consciousness were mainly British, epitomized by the main antagonist, U Saw Han, in Ma Ma Lay's extremely popular novel at the time, *Mon Ywei Ma Hu* (Not out of Hate).[2]

The Revolutionary Council's vision of a true patriot was one whose ordinary experiences did not partake of what it felt was 'corrupt' Western culture but things Burmese. Many young adults might have been disappointed when Western-style beauty pageants (including one for 'Miss Burma'), music/dance competitions, dress and other 'indelicate' public performances were banned (as was horse racing and gambling). In a final move to remove all possible vestiges and conduits of external Western influence, the Burmese Government cancelled external funding sources such as the Asia Foundation and the Fulbright scholarship programmes.

Yet at the same time that it rejected things foreign, the Government also wanted to forge a 'modern' and 'revolutionary' state, which it felt could be done without foreign aid or influence, perhaps a notion influenced by China attempting to do the same around that time. Thus internal as well as external, military as well as cultural, threats (real and imagined) were removed. From its own perspective the army had been fighting for 'real' independence since 1942, and twenty years later it was still doing it.[3]

THE BSPP AND THE BURMESE WAY TO SOCIALISM

On 2 March 1974, the twelfth anniversary of the 1962 coup, a new formal apparatus for the institutionalization of a 'civilian' Government was established. It was based on a new constitution that effectively eliminated the 'decentralized federalism' of the earlier one written in 1947 that had provisions seriously weakening the integrity of the Union. The 1974 Constitution effectively returned power to the centre – in fiscal, administrative and political ways – dominated by a single, mass organization called (in English) the Burma Socialist Programme Party (BSPP).

Its structure and principles were based upon Eastern European/Chinese models of socialist states but with an ideology called the Burmese Way to Socialism. As noted in the Introduction, this ideology was Marxist in inspiration, Leninist in implementation and Buddhist in its goals. It was an ideology that sought to benefit both the material and spiritual well-being of the people. These actions and the ideas that rationalized them were meant to address larger anxieties plaguing the country at the time, particularly the search for a national identity which every newly independent country in Southeast Asia that had experienced the trauma of colonialism was going through. And although the Revolutionary Council and the BSPP governments handled the psychological (social, cultural, religious) needs of the people fairly well, in the end both failed to adequately provide for their material ones. And that would turn out to be most important.

Initially the BSPP attracted politicians, activists and intellectuals who were formerly connected to the Dobama Asiayon, as the new party's vision and methods reminded these new recruits of the pre-war socialist values that had originally inspired them to take part in political activities. Although there were certain ideological links with the Dobama Asiayon of old, the BSPP also wanted to be more precise in its political orientation, for the Government wanted to avoid being labelled Communist by foreign governments and anti-religious by its citizens. While most Burmese might not have been aware of such nuances, party members felt it was important to engage society according to certain socio-economic principles and take into account the cultural landscape in which they lived. In this regard the BSPP wanted a national revolution where all communities – not just a particular class – could participate in and benefit from the nation-state.

For party leaders the only way the entire nation could benefit from the efforts of the Government was to make sure all its citizens were included in the process. And since the rural population made up the bulk of the country, and was ultimately considered the true 'guardians of tradition', the Government began to create programmes that focused on the peasantry, whom they believed had been given a lower priority by the colonial and immediate post-colonial governments.

That changed the focus from industry and manufacturing (and external modern forces) to the peasantry and agriculture (and internal historical ones). The Government designed a series of initiatives that directed economic investment, resources and infrastructure development towards the agricultural sector. Along with that, Ne Win (but also U Nu earlier) had resurrected aspects of pre-colonial leadership, authority and spirituality that redefined this link with the peasantry and Burmese history, pre-empting contemporary notions of legitimacy that had been introduced by parliamentary democracy. Twenty-six years of acting upon these values that favoured agrarian rural society while marginalizing the commercial urban one had important political and economic repercussions for the country in subsequent years.

The focus on the peasantry was part of a much larger programme to unite a society that was believed to be weak at the seams. While the U Nu Government had tried to adopt a conciliatory policy of equality that recognized the claims of minority groups as distinct ethnic communities, that position nonetheless reinforced the idea of difference measured by one's ethno-linguistic orientation, which was counter-productive to the type of nationalism being pursued by the BSPP. It wanted to neutralize ethnicity as a political discussion in its mission to seek a different kind of community, defined not by one's ethnic identity but by equal status, health care and education.

The Government worked hard to develop this different notion of community by attempting to engineer a more culturally sensitive citizen. Burmese attending the new Academy for the Development of National Groups learned about the wide range of symbols, performances and arts that were included as a part of the Burmese cultural experience, after which they were sent out into the peripheral areas to propagate these ideas. Symbols such as the rice stalk, sickle and machine gears (put on the national flag) were used to represent a new conception of the nation that was *not* ethnic. At the heart of these initiatives to promote a national identity was one that transcended the many national groups of *Myanmar Pyi* (The 'nation', 'country' of Myanmar).

Public events that facilitated national integration were also sponsored by the Government, making connections to the country's Buddhist heritage and cultural traditions. When the Revolutionary Council originally took power, it officially ended state sponsorship of Buddhism and dissolved the Buddha Sasana Council. It may have sensed the economic consequences of state patronage of religion that for so long had plagued the monarchy. But more likely – since the monarchy was no longer a factor – it probably wanted to genuinely separate 'church' from state, in part so that the legitimacy of the state would no longer depend entirely on the 'endorsement' of the church. It also knew that such policies only worsened the position of the state in the eyes of certain ethnic communities that were not Buddhist, even though these were a very small minority.

Government's attempts to control the Sangha resulted in confrontations with it in 1965, 1969 and 1974 when monks (contrary to their vows) interfered in what were clearly secular political issues. Yet, to have the Sangha as ally rather than as 'opposition party' was a far more realistic and smart stance for the Government to take. Thus by 1980 its public position began to change. It started by sponsoring the 'First Congregation of the Sangha of All Orders for the Purification, Perpetuation and Propagation of the Sasana'.

On that occasion the Sangha crafted a new constitution for itself, with rules and procedures meant to maintain its integrity. It also created a new structure for itself based on the secular administration of the state, linking the smallest village monasteries and their monks to those in the high council. Following these sessions Ne Win (in the tradition of ancient monarchs) ordered the release of nearly 14,000 prisoners and invited former political prisoners – such as the exiled U Nu – to return. (The latter accepted the invitation as his 'Government-in-exile' and fundraising activities to overthrow the military had fizzled out. He returned to begin translating the enormous volumes of the *Tipitakas* – the Theravada Buddhist Scriptures – into English.)

The new National Sangha Mahanayaka Council was founded to regulate the affairs of officially recognized sects, register their members and maintain certain standards in terms of monastic education, training and proper conduct. In later years a Buddhist Missionary University was created – complete with a PhD programme – to train monks from overseas to promote the religion in other countries. Many of these initiatives created

the impression that there would be a continuing commitment to preserve Buddhism as national culture. Some scholars also suggest that
these acts by General Ne Win (and previously U Nu) were made to invoke
traditional ideas of legitimacy and authority associated with Burmese
Buddhist kingship.

The Government also promulgated a cultural campaign that other
countries in the region (and elsewhere) had been doing for some time:
fostering public history. Meant to engage the citizens of the country, it
was part of the larger nation-building project that was meant to instil
a sense of belonging to a shared place and past. In Myanmar that was a
Buddhist past, simplified to cater to the majority of the population.
But, as with other nations, particular narratives and experiences that
did not fit into the national story or certain minorities and religious
communities that did not find as prominent a place in this public history
project as the major group did (the peasantry) were either left out or
glossed over.

Focusing on this class in terms of public history became almost as
important to the BSPP as patronage of the Buddhist Sangha had been to
the monarchy. Both 'clients' were core components of state ideology: the
king was considered legitimate as protector, promoter and purifier of
the monkhood while the socialist Government was legitimate so long
as it also protected and supported the peasant class. The Burmese Way to
Socialism was the ideology behind it. It is interesting to note that the
continuous financial relief from the state of the pre-colonial Sangha and
twentieth-century peasant/agricultural sector also contributed to the
eventual weakening of the state.

Making peasants a priority in domestic policy had a practical side to
it as well. Focusing on local villages and the agricultural sector enabled the
state to better administer them economically, while integrating distant
rural communities into state administration more directly and effectively.
During the 1974 elections peasants were visited by representatives of the
Government who set up village Security and Administrative Committees (SAC) that established direct links to state, regional and centre administrations. SACs at the village level were headed by army personnel who
in time developed relations that personalized the bureaucratic structure
to a certain degree. There were also Peoples' Councils (for legislation)
and Peoples' Courts (for justice), village-level innovations into which
peasants and cultivators were drawn whenever they conducted official
business with the state. In short, rural communities were being introduced to procedures and concepts that heretofore had been the purview
only of higher-level bureaucracy.

Thus after 1962 Burmese farmers found themselves involved in state
programmes more than they had ever been. They met more dignitaries

from the central Government, had a voice in how the country was run and participated in local councils, courts and elections. They were given land to till whose produce was not heavily taxed. Peasants could keep the same plot of state land year after year with the approval of village Land Committees. And although they could not sell, mortgage or rent out that land to others, they could control their produce and sell what they wanted.

Many peasants who could not pay their rents were protected by the Government's Peasants' Rights Protection Act that prohibited the seizure of their land. This may have been the direct consequence of what happened to the Burmese peasantry during colonial times when it lost most of its land to Indian moneylenders. Eventually peasants were asked to sell a part of their produce to the state. But while the BSPP kept to its basic principle of protecting the peasant from economic ruin, the rest of the national economy foundered.

By the second half of the 1980s Ne Win and his cabinet began to realize that their policies were not managing all sectors of the nation's economy equitably. Although the Government had been generally frugal in terms of spending, the state had little capacity to generate new sources of income for the maintenance of even basic services. The BSPP's policy to protect and insulate peasants from over-taxation (for ideological and security reasons) eventually hurt the state's ability to raise revenue. By the mid-1980s the Government ran out of money to even buy fertilizer normally allocated to the peasants at hugely discounted rates.

The resulting decision to demonetize the currency in 1985 severely hurt many people, as there was inadequate compensation and the Government had little credibility in managing the economy to begin with. Moreover, between 1981 and 1987 the price of rice and timber had dropped by 51 per cent, again affecting the peasantry and others in rural sectors the most. When the Government decided to more effectively curb the black market that had developed soon after 1962, it affected urban residents, for the crackdown eliminated their main (if not only) access to certain 'essential' commercial goods.

Realizing too late that the country's economy was now in trouble, Ne Win called for a special meeting of the Central Committee of the BSPP, asking for a plan to help reform it. It was a little too little and a little too late. Not much came out of this meeting, and the next morning lines began to form at banks as people were worried that there might be another demonetization of the currency. A newspaper immediately denied the rumour but the following day the Government demonetized the currency again, sending urbanites into the street in protest. Matters only got worse when Myanmar could not meet the deadline to pay foreign creditors and was given Least Developed Country (LDC) status by the UN, a severe blow to its collective pride.

1988 AND THE UNIVERSALIZATION OF DOMESTIC MYANMAR ISSUES

Myanmar's 'Year of Living Dangerously'

The historiography of the events of 1988 and their consequences still awaits an objective hand. For the present work, the following synopsis – more concerned with the way these events shaped the trajectory of Myanmar's history in a general way – must suffice.[4]

It all started on 12 March 1988 at a local tea shop when a fight broke out between a group of university students and local youths over whether modern rock or traditional Burmese music was to be played on a radio. The tea shop was located near the Yangon Institute of Technology where tensions already existed between 'town and gown' communities. In this incident a student was injured. The police arrested the alleged culprit but he was released, because of his alleged personal connection to a Government official. When word began to circulate the next day that the arrested youth had been released a group of students took to the streets to protest the police's handling of the matter. The police responded by shooting at the demonstrators, killing one student and seriously escalating the incident.

Students from other parts of the city began to join the demonstrations for a variety of related and unrelated grievances that took on an anti-police and anti-government character. Police reports indicated that acts of arson, vandalism and looting also took place, prompting riot police to surround and enter the campus of the Yangon Institute of Technology. Meanwhile the army was dispatched to numerous parts of the city, including the main campus of Yangon Arts and Sciences University, where unconfirmed reports stated that nearly 283 persons had been killed.

Different renditions of the above events appeared in the international press, but mainly from a perspective that favoured the protesters. A Government report stated that 41 students died by suffocating in a locked police van while other accounts from students, demonstrators, political exiles, journalists and activists claimed considerably higher casualties. Different versions of the same event and varying 'first-hand' accounts captured by the press only complicated the picture and raised the country's visibility internationally.

What had been clearly a local incident that began as a brawl amongst local youths now took on a life of its own. Domestic and external activist groups joined in to connect this event to unrelated movements abroad. Because of the 'global' framework in which it was placed, a simple tea shop incident became a 23-year international crusade for 'regime change' in Myanmar. The violence in Yangon spread to other urban areas of the country that had been affected by similar economic factors. Adding to the growing instability was the perception that the country's leadership was also divided on a course of action. U Ne Win's announcement on 23 July 1988 that he and senior members of the BSPP would be resigning left the impression that changing the entire political system – as opposed to just addressing student grievances and socio-economic policies – became a viable option for 'the opposition'.

Ne Win's call on the BSPP Congress to find a way to resolve the domestic situation and his proposal to hold a public referendum to determine whether the country should return to a multi-party political system changed the terms and expectations of those debating the future of the country. Predictably, the BSPP membership did not want to concede power, but the open question of a structural change galvanized other elites, students, labour unions, underground communists, exiled politicians, overseas dissidents, private foundations and eventually foreign governments into thinking that political change was not only possible but necessary and desirable.

By the first week of August 1988 Burmese began to hear on their radios that a general strike would commence that week. The newly established Government led by U Sein Lwin tried to re-establish order through force. Met by force in return, the situation became more violent and anarchic, a situation which spread to other urban areas, allowing ethnic grievances and class animosities to surface amongst the demonstrators.

In a pattern reminiscent of the disorder that followed the retreat of the British in 1942 and the civil war that ensued after Independence in 1948, anarchy spread and became the norm. Ordinary policemen were beheaded in Okalapa (a suburb of Yangon), their heads wrapped in newspapers and given to their wives or hung from trees, while their bodies were roasted on spits and eaten.[5]

The underlying causes of these riots were economic 'bread and butter' issues which can be attributed to the previous 30 years of the Burmese Way to Socialism. Its stagnant economic policies saw earlier eruptions, but by 1988 they had crystallized in more recent events such as the demonetization of the currency and the stigma of LDC status.

To these largely long-term economic factors must be added socio-cultural and administrative ones, particularly the general arbitrariness of Government and its unsympathetic bureaucracy. Not surprisingly – and against their own vows – monks joined these demonstrations, in some places even acting as local governments when local authorities either fled or were intimidated to resign. And whenever disorder got out of hand the police were nowhere to be found, having 'melted away'. Rioters could act with near complete impunity and under such conditions personal vendettas emerged among disgruntled street people, thugs and hooligans who joined the disorder.

As noted in earlier chapters, in Myanmar anarchy is feared far more than is tyranny, so that Government's inability to maintain law and order between March and September 1988 resurrected that deeply rooted fear. The situation was so horrible that families moved in with relatives who had houses with walls and gates, hiring Gurkha guards for protection. Many in the civil service linked to the Government were bullied or intimidated to join the demonstrators (or give lip service to their cause), while their offices were targeted by looters, gangs, thugs and protesters. Factories and government stores were stripped to their foundations (including the brickwork and metal frames) since there were no police to mitigate such behaviour.

University laboratories were looted or destroyed while in the city's main cemetery buildings, tombstones and fences were stripped, its iron bars and bricks sold on the streets. Swords, spears, dart-throwing *jinglees* (slings) were openly sold in the bazaars. In one sad and well-known case, an innocent boy at the wrong place at the wrong time was beheaded by a mob when someone in it accused him of being a Government spy who had poisoned the water supply. It was anarchy of the worst kind.[6]

Yet nearly all Western media, anti-government members of the Burmese public, some overseas communities and certain foreign governments not only attributed the cause of the riots to *political* reasons – a populous movement for 'democracy' and a strike for 'freedom' against the 'tyranny' of government – but to a specific *ideology*: democracy. Thus most English-language media reports at the time characterized the riots as a 'pro-democracy' movement, an oft-repeated mantra at the time for virtually any protest against government in the non-Western world.

It is clear that the 1988 riots were anything but that, or that they were even ideological in nature. As a specific political issue by a specific political group 'democracy' as an issue did not appear until much later when the Government was already on its heels. In other words it was not the *cause* of the 1988 riots, but a *consequence* – the riots were far more complicated, their underlying socio-economic origins went back at least 30 years (to the Burmese Way to Socialism) while their immediate cause was a tea-shop brawl.

Part of the problem with Western media interpretations was that they were shaped by the international context of the 1980s, whereby the events in Myanmar were being placed within the perspective of post-Cold War politics. When the rivalry between the United States and the Soviet Union had thawed after perestroika and glasnost and the USSR dissolved eventually, the priorities for the remaining superpower also shifted from security and anti-Communism to human rights and democracy. Certain highly publicized events of that decade (and beyond) seemed to fit well into the paradigm: the Philippines with Corazon

Aquino, Pakistan with Benazir Bhutto, China with Tiananmen Square and South Africa with Nelson Mandela.

This post-Cold War interpretation of the above events was regarded as 'evidence' of a world-wide victory of capitalism and democracy over Communism and command economies. Such a view presumed that all countries and peoples were ultimately the same – ignoring important social, historical and cultural differences amongst them. One of these differences was (and is) the nature and 'culture of protests'.

Whereas in Western democracies protests are mainly expressions against specific issues (such as civil rights, the Vietnam War, abortion), in countries such as Myanmar (and more recently, Libya, Syria, Egypt and Yemen), the objective of such protests is the overthrow of the current regime or entire government. That makes the contest a 'zero sum game', an all-or-nothing situation, hence the extreme violence generated. In Myanmar both sides knew this – but not the foreign media.

After almost three decades of relative 'isolation', suddenly Myanmar's main players on both sides found their domestic situation to be the topic of discussion internationally. Heretofore, certainly before 1988, news about Myanmar rarely made even the back pages of remote English-language newspapers and, as noted above, neither the coup of 1962 nor the 1974 Constitution and the creation of the BSPP had drawn much foreign attention. Then all of a sudden what had been considered part of the domestic political scene since the 1920s – general strikes, violent protests, crackdowns – not only became major news items outside the country but also everyone else's business. And virtually everything that annoyed ordinary people on a daily basis – the slowness of 'city hall', the price of rice and gasoline, long lines at the post office – was interpreted within a framework of freedom versus tyranny.

Government officials, politicians, soldiers and activists began to realize that their struggle to shape the national community – a process that had been going on since the colonial period and part of the domestic 'conversation' – was now being watched, judged and interpreted by their neighbours, the United Nations, human rights organizations and other influential nations in Asia and in the West. The various contenders also realized that publicly using terms such as 'democracy', 'human rights', 'elections', 'regime change', 'transparency' and 'the Burmese people', evoked certain responses (sometimes knee-jerk reactions) by many Western governments, international development institutions, aid organizations and the international press, which could be manipulated for one's public image.

Groups within and without Myanmar responded to this new configuration and internationalizing of domestic affairs in various ways; some contributed to its dissemination while others ignored it, both continuing to articulate *their* version of events and of the future of Myanmar. That new external picture painted of Myanmar's internal political situation assumed the universalism of particular, parochial Western ideas regarding notions of legitimacy and authority and the principles on which they rest. And by engaging in that essentially domestic debate, external commentators, governments, aid agencies, lobbyists and media had actually entered a discussion that had been ongoing within Myanmar itself since 1942. It was nothing new to the Burmese although it was to outsiders. And this time, with their money and power, these new voices and their framework of analysis dominated the conversation in a global way for the next 23 years.

To many of these new voices it was as if Myanmar's modern history began only in 1988, since most knew almost nothing about the previous four or five decades. The unsophisticated way in which the Government responded to both that external image and the situation itself did not help matters either, reflecting not only its inexperience with modern public relations but its concern mainly with internal affairs.

Dissolution of the BSPP, the rise of the SLORC/SPDC and the NLD

When the Government in September of 1988 replaced U Sein Lwin and his hard-line tactics with the more moderate and Yale educated ex-Chief Justice Dr Maung Maung as head of the civilian Government – perhaps to assuage international criticism and pressure – his more accommodating manner was seen (especially in domestic circles) as weakness, so it did little to convince the now emboldened leaders of the various groups of demonstrators to come to the negotiating table.

Instead they demanded even more: the formation of a new interim Government. Protest leaders felt they were in a position of strength, especially as they were now supported by many powerful Western countries and their media, and so made demands for a transfer of power that the Government simply could not and would not accept. Meanwhile, the military which was watching from the sidelines was near the end of its patience with the civilian Government's inability to control continued violence and disorder.

With the Government internally divided and the demonstrators lacking unity and a coherent vision (other than a vague mantra called 'democracy' which they often also disparaged), it was clear that negotiating a peaceful and achievable solution was nearly impossible. All this convinced the army that only they had the means to restore order – and they were right. On 18 September 1988 the BSPP and its civilian Government were dissolved. The new military Government was officially named the State Law and Order Restoration Council (SLORC). In a sense Myanmar had returned to 1962 to address a similar issue of anarchy and disintegration, although it was not exactly the same situation.

Ironically, the power vacuum that was filled by the army also created political 'space' for a variety of contesting groups with different experiences, agendas and ideologies, each asserting its right to define its version of what Myanmar is and what it means to be a Burmese citizen. Former ministers, retired army generals and other moderately high-level officials who had their power curbed under the BSPP now began to make plans to re-establish their status. Unfortunately, however, only *their* experiences, perspectives and agendas were considered legitimate and only *they* were said to represent the interests and welfare of the 'Burmese people'.

As a result the key players in the post-1988 period – including the SLORC, governments-in-exile, domestic political parties, students and ethnic nationalists – adopted irreconcilable positions that made it impossible to compromise when genuine opportunities appeared. Each group interpreted its position in Burmese history and society as being totally different from that of its competitors, ignoring the fact that the past from which they all claimed legitimacy was more often shared than not.

Indeed, many had experienced the same history, invoked the same genealogy and worked in the service of the same country which the SLORC now also claimed for itself. Some were ex-Thakins, while others, especially those who had worked alongside people now in power, saw themselves as equally good nationalists.

The army was the key stakeholder as it was by far the most well-organized and strongest of the contestants vying for the state. The military's entrenched administrative presence (from BSPP days), its widespread influence in key commercial, transport and industrial sectors and its near monopoly on arms provided it with an almost incontestable hold on the country's institutional channels of governance once it had formally severed ties with the BSPP. The army, as before, saw itself as the protector of the nation, the only group that could prevent the Union from disintegration, and remain above politics. (They were probably right on the first two of these three counts.)

Much of this self-image was inherited from a tradition in the military that linked its legitimacy and roots to the anti-colonial nationalist movements, the Dobama Asiayon, the Thakins, the Thirty Comrades, the Burmese Independence Army, the post-1948 counter-insurgency campaigns, the defeat of invading KMT forces in the 1950s and, most important, its role in rescuing the Union from disintegration in 1949 and 1962. Indeed, many members on both sides had been part of the same history and had been shaped by the same experiences.

Urban Burmese were more frequently exposed to these perspectives of the nation through the vernacular press, billboards, public announcements and educational textbooks. Through national holidays such as Armed Forces Day, Martyrs Day and to a lesser extent Peasants Day, urban people were reminded publicly of the military's role in nation-building. In contrast rural and hill communities were less acquainted with such images, as their encounters with the new leadership were connected mainly to infrastructural development projects such as the building of bridges, schools, roads and irrigation works.

Some of these self-perceptions are captured in the Defence Services Museum, probably the only one in the country that publicly displays the official political history of the nation. Not on the normal tourist circuit, the museum is very interesting nonetheless, containing the military history of the different branches of the armed services and regional commands. The main exhibit traces the place of the military from the earliest (pre-colonial) times to its role in contemporary development programmes and projects. Viewers are presented with a chronological account of the military, projected as always having been a part of the 'national struggle', even if in nascent form. A special memorial for generals Aung San and Ne Win, represented by two massive portraits side by side, links the memory of the two former Thakins, establishing a continuous, though problematic, narrative of unity in the history of the armed forces.

Such claims are not unusual or unexpected considering that most of the nation's history is seen by the military as being threatened by disunity, separatism and civil war. Interestingly, political opponents would make similar claims of legitimacy and authority using some of the very same figures, histories and events. In other words, both sides saw themselves as champions in a struggle, but for different ends using different means.

When the army retook the streets of Yangon in mid-September 1988 a number of protest leaders, activists and criminals were killed or detained in the process. Fearing further arrests, the mixture of students, ex-civil servants, politicians, artists, writers and intellectuals that took part in the demonstrations quickly dispersed, some fleeing overseas while others joined insurgent groups that had been waging their own protests since the late 1940s.

Although the Communists and ethnic separatists had been resisting incorporation into the national community for decades, the events of 1988 and the recruitment of some of the student protesters into their ranks brought their decades-long armed insurgency into the public gaze of international observers for the first time. Suddenly the 40-year-old insurgencies that few outside the country had known (or cared) about had become a cause célèbre. Observers read these events in the same post-Cold War context as they had read the urban events: 'freedom fighters' rebelling against an authoritarian Government for democracy and autonomy.

In reality, however, there were many generational, geographical, class, linguistic and religious differences between the urban-based political dissidents and the borderland insurgents, even more than the former had with members of the Government they opposed. Nonetheless, foreign commentators, media and political activists conflated the motives and agendas of the urban demonstrations with the issues and concerns of those in the border areas, creating an image of a unified and coherent opposition to the SLORC.

As noted above, one of the results of the dissolution of the BSPP in 1988 and the SLORC's purge of certain political elites, civil servants, teachers, as well as army officers with alleged socialist leanings or questionable loyalties, was the re-emergence of political parties that had been curbed under the BSPP's one-party system. The most well known and best organized of these was the National League for Democracy (NLD), which was formed after August 1988.

The NLD rose to become – especially in the eyes of external observers – the *only* legitimate 'opposition' party in the country, said to represent the 'Burmese people' and their democratic aspirations. Led by long-time members of Government, former General Aung Gyi and former General Tin U, along with the new (and now famous) Daw Aung San Suu Kyi (daughter of General Aung San, 'father' of modern Myanmar), the NLD epitomized the political changes occurring in the late 1980s. But it also contained some 'baggage': past political and personal rivalries that would rear their ugly heads when the opportunity presented itself.

Many former military officers, ex-bureaucrats, lawyers, journalists, activists and students who had been disenfranchised by the BSPP's single-party system joined the NLD. SLORC's rise to power and its purge of the BSPP had also given them some political space needed, although some had been marginalized by the turn of events after 1988 or frustrated by the socio-economic challenges that had preceded them.

Each of the prominent members of the NLD, however, brought different experiences, motivations and agendas to the new party that initially provided it with a diversity of opinion. Those who joined the NLD's rank and file also brought with them built-in factionalism, as each had his/her own supporters, expectations and visions for the future. It was anything but a party united in ideology, methods, agendas, generation or social class. Nonetheless, this diversity was strength in times of unity against a common and highly visible opponent, although weakness when difficulties arose. The NLD hardly represented the 'Burmese people', who were mostly rural cultivators; rather it was composed mainly of urban, educated groups vying for 'the throne', as it were, led by new and old elites.

Like earlier political parties in the 1930s and 1940s the NLD adopted a structure that put much of its decision-making power in an Executive Committee, in which (initially) Aung Gyi was Chairman, Tin U Vice-Chairman, and Suu Kyi General Secretary. (They were collectively known as Aung-Suu-Tin.) Aung Gyi would eventually break with the NLD for personal and political reasons – when former Communists joined the party – leaving Suu Kyi and Tin U at the top. Soon Suu Kyi would assume the mantle of de facto leader of the NLD, particularly when her public speaking, charisma and 'correct' genealogy propelled her to greater domestic and international stature after receiving the Nobel Peace Prize in 1991.

For many Burmese who were tired of the previous Government's lethargic economic policies, pseudo-socialist priorities and 'geriatric' generation of leaders, Suu Kyi as a political figure was refreshing, if not mesmerizing. Although she had little experience in governance at any level – in part revealed by the absence of a specific national platform that differed from the establishment (other than the general reference to 'democracy') – she looked like her father Aung San, an identity she publicly embraced by having earlier added her father's name to hers (hence Aung San Suu Kyi), a practice not customary in Burmese culture. She also had a 'stage presence' demonstrated in passionate public speeches about freedom, democracy and non-violence (made in Burmese) while drawing Western journalists towards her rather than other leaders in the NLD with her command of English. Many young student activists were attracted by the way she directly criticized Government and its policies, although older listeners were often turned off by her confrontational manner. That was not the way the young were supposed to treat their elders in Myanmar, still an important cultural norm even in the vociferous political arena.

Aung San Suu Kyi was most attractive to those from a Western liberal-democratic experience, particularly since she spoke fluent English – in a crisp British accent at that – using symbols and metaphors meaningful to Western history and culture. She appeared to embody the best of both worlds: Asia and the West. On the one hand she was Western-educated and had lived much of her life overseas, so knew Western society well. On the other she was fluent in Burmese, had an 'impeccable' genealogy, dressed in Burmese clothes and seemed well attuned to things Burmese. Some of her writings even attempted to link modern democratic ideas with Burmese Buddhism, arguing that the seeds for the former can be found deep within Burmese culture.

She also made allusions to Myanmar's recent history by attempting to associate the NLD's political agenda as a 'second' struggle for independence, implying that the 'first' 'unfinished revolution' against the British begun by her father was now being conducted by the NLD's campaign against the military Government. Yet that argument was tricky, for it was her father who had 'created' the present army, which means she was invoking and distancing herself from that particular legacy *at the same time*. Nonetheless, her message struck a hopeful chord amongst those who had suffered under BSPP socio-economic policies and envisioned a change from those conditions. Her writings appealed most to Western audiences, exiled political communities and a wide range of urban-based followers within Myanmar.[7]

Despite her public persona as presented in the West – a Joan of Arc who could do no wrong – she was inexperienced, stubborn, steadfastly uncompromising, idealistic and playing a 'zero-sum game' in a field where most of the cards (and keys to the tanks) were held by the other side. Holding the 'moral high-ground' worked for Gandhi and Mandela (her models) but whereas the political and social context was favourable for them, for her, it was not. Besides, her own party was not of one mind, so that attempting to quell the factionalism within it – most notably between those who were realistic and wanted to compromise and those who held out for 'principles' – must have been a time-consuming and unenviable task.

Ironically, 'correct' genealogical links (to Aung San), resistance to colonialism and patronage of Buddhism were also employed by the SLORC to convey their message of legitimacy, demonstrating that very different groups within the country articulated their country's past and future in strikingly similar ways but for different political ends. Although both the military Government and political parties such as the NLD attempted to speak on behalf of 'the Burmese people', it was difficult to ascertain who that might be in such a diverse, personalized and hierarchical social-political landscape. In other words a shared past to Aung San, Buddhism and anti-colonial struggles was not exclusive to either the SLORC or the NLD.

Even certain insurgent groups, particularly the Communists, could legitimately claim to have been part of these same histories. And although their loyalties to particular leaders and ideas (therefore visions of Myanmar's future) may have been at odds with those in Government, many had belonged to the original Burma Independence Army and fought against the British and later the Japanese. Many had been members of the AFPFL as well. In fact, the most prominent leader of the Communists, Thakin Than Tun, as noted in an earlier chapter, was Aung San's brother-in-law – making him Suu Kyi's uncle – so he could claim a similar historical and genealogical legitimacy as the foremost leader of the NLD.

In contrast, although some ethnic minority groups such as the Karen, the Shan and the Kachin could claim some of the same pasts as the majority Burmese speakers, theirs were quite different from the one pre-scribed for them in the name of the nation by both the Government and the National League for Democracy. Indeed, their struggle was as much against the inheritors of the state – the AFPFL, the BSPP, the SLORC – as it was for the British, since many had worked closely with them, so they did not share the same past or vision of the future with the majority. Not only did minority ethnic politics not conform to a 'national narrative', it was a major obstacle to it.

The separatist movements of these minority groups proved to be the single biggest threat to the unity of the state, making the ending of the civil war and the insurgencies one of the highest domestic priorities for Government. But the terrible fighting over many decades was very difficult to forget when negotiations with the state were once again launched in the post-1988 period, particularly when there was relentless interference by dissidents and external powers for their failure.

Oversimplifying the complexities of the domestic situation into a polarized scenario was a useful tactic that the army, domestic political parties, ethnic insurgents and exile groups used in order to solidify their own positions amongst their supporters. While some groups were able to successfully absorb and adapt these new ideological values, terms, symbols and strategies to fit their local agendas, other groups were able to do so less effectively and were subsequently drowned out by images and representations that began to appear in the new global media.

The Constituent Assembly Elections of 1990

Perhaps the most important of these events, that (mis)represented the country's domestic situation most deeply in the consciousness of inter-national observers, was the May 1990 Constituent Assembly elections that U Ne Win and Dr Maung Maung had promised to convene. These were meant to elect representatives to a Constituent Assembly charged with the writing of a new Constitution. Yet for more than twenty years, this has been erroneously presented in the Western media as *national elections* with the purpose of transferring power, whose results the Government was said to have ignored.

Even with its most conspicuous leader (Suu Kyi) under house arrest, the NLD had received about 80 per cent of the constituencies (seats) con-tested, winning approximately 60 per cent of the votes cast for sending representatives to the Constitutional Assembly. It was a clear victory for the NLD and a statement that the old political elites and patrons, such as U Nu (whose party did not win a single seat), were no longer relevant to or effective in this new generation. How these Constituent Assembly elections were interpreted internally and externally reflected the varied interests and agendas of groups within and without the country.

As a result of the success at the polls by the NLD and the consequent relentless calls for the transfer of power to it by the 'international community', the NLD and its supporters grew bolder and began to make claims that the NLD represented the legitimate Government of Myanmar. This was a clear gamble for the NLD, for it knew it went against the ground rules that everyone had agreed to, published in public statements made by its own leaders in 1989 and 1990 prior to the elections. And that was: the function of all elected representatives from these elections was to write a new constitution, hold a referendum regarding that constitution; only after that would transfer of power commence.

In other words, that these elections themselves were not meant to initiate a transfer of power was clear to the NLD and all other parties prior to the contest. Daw Aung San Suu Kyi herself was quoted one year earlier as stating that "Whoever is elected will have to draw up a constitution that will have to be adopted *before the transfer of power* [our italics]. They [the Government] haven't said how the constitution will be adopted. It could be through a referendum, but that could be for months and months, if not years."[8] The Western media chose to ignore that statement.

The publishing of the election results by the Election Commission in late May 1990 did not help matters either, as the voting results prompted Western governments to renew pressure on the SLORC to relinquish power to the NLD immediately. Media representatives, many of whom had flown in just prior to the elections, also printed editorials and stories in their respective newspapers that called for the *transfer of power*, not realizing (or choosing not to recognize) that these were Constituent Assembly elections.

Surprised by the sudden media barrage and no doubt also by the election results, the Government restated in July 1990 that power would be transferred only when a constitutionally formed government was established. For the time being the sitting Government would retain all powers of the judiciary, legislature and the executive. Winning the majority of seats was certainly an accomplishment for the NLD but this was just the first step in a much longer process and in the military's view it was its duty to maintain order 'until a government has been formed in accordance with the law'.[9]

In October 1990 some elected representatives who had become impatient with the delays secretly attempted to convene their own Assembly, which only succeeded in drawing the attention of security forces who promptly clamped down on the event. The NLD itself was split over the matter, as some executive members accepted and wished to honour the agreed purpose of the elections, while the rank and file decided they did not want to.

Furthermore, media reports suggested that some within the NLD were not certain about what they should do now that they had a majority of the seats in the Assembly. For participation in it meant legitimizing and endorsing the new Constitution to be written; while boycotting it with a majority of the seats meant others with fewer seats would be drafting what was to become the highest law in the land. For many observers within the region and overseas, these Constituent Assembly elections provided an opportunity to confirm existing world views about legitimate forms of liberal-democratic governments, so that Myanmar joined Tibet, (then) East Timor and Tiananmen Square in the list of 'unfinished' revolutions.

In the end the National League for Democracy gained significant domestic and international support from these events despite the fact that the party decided to boycott the Constituent Assembly when it began the process of writing a new constitution. The NLD's subsequent policy of confrontation with the SLORC (and the latter's inability to respond to these issues in a sophisticated manner to the Western world) not only created an oversimplified perspective of the country's domestic political situation, but also made the contest for 'democracy' – at the expense of socio-economic change – the operating framework through which events in Myanmar *had* to be interpreted.

Two Myanmars

Following the Constituent Assembly elections, two nearly opposite perceptions of Myanmar appeared, partly reminiscent of the period when the British annexed the coastal provinces and the Delta following the First and Second Anglo–Burmese Wars. Only this time the territorial boundaries, the social, economic and religious structures and institutions remained intact and were, in fact, one unit rather than split between British Burma and the Kingdom of Ava. Nonetheless, their representation – one in cyberspace, mostly external and meant for external audiences, the other, 'on the ground' and internal for internal consumption – were quite different.

The more internationally visible 'Burma' was the one created by activists, journalists, students, dissidents, politicians, artists, ex-soldiers, disgruntled monks, sympathetic governments and the so-called 'international community'. They painted a picture of the country as a nation under authoritarian rule opposed by a united people who had spoken in one voice for political change for a system they called 'democracy' via the only political party considered by the west as legitimate: the NLD. To and with this 'Burma', neither international tourism nor doing business was recommended; in fact, economic sanctions were imposed on it that remain today. Its authority, laws, decrees, policies and even its indigenous name that almost went back to the eleventh century were not recognized by proponents of this version of 'Burma'.

The other 'Myanmar' consisted of the SLORC (and later SPDC) along with the majority of the agrarian population; the country's traditional name remained the official and legal national entity in the eyes of the majority of the world's nations represented by the United Nations. This Myanmar attempted to ignore and counteract the 'Burma' of cyberspace by directing its (mainly Burmese-language) messages more internally than externally, using symbols and terms it regarded as authentically Burmese and representative of the people. Despite international sanctions that were levied on the country – a policy that was supported by the hard-liners in the NLD (including Aung San Suu Kyi) – the military Government focused on nation-building infrastructural projects: dams, river pumping stations, railways, roads, airports, bridges, communication services, hydroelectric plants, schools, universities and hospitals.

Many of these accomplishments were broadcast and printed in national newspapers, mostly in Burmese and rarely seen in external media. This 'Myanmar' also engaged in a large public history campaign (as noted above), building heritage theme parks, repairing and/or building anew sacred Buddhist sites and founding new Buddhist universities, all appealing to traditional criteria for legitimacy that were far older and more important to most than ballot-box elections.

One of the most important achievements by this 'on-the-ground' 'Myanmar' was ending the half-century of civil war in the country. Between 1989 and 1997 seventeen armed groups signed ceasefire agreements with the Government.[10] It was an event that would have been considered momentous in any country's history, especially Myanmar's. And that it was accomplished in less than a decade while the Government was being hammered from all sides was also a significant feat. No Government of Myanmar, democratic or authoritarian, had succeeded in that endeavour after nearly half a century of trying. Yet this momentous event was barely mentioned in the 'Burma' of cyberspace, a selective excising tantamount to ignoring the end of the Chinese or American Civil War and all that they entailed.

It appears that 'push' as well as 'pull' factors were responsible for this success. Internal rivalries amongst the various insurgent groups, withdrawal of financial and political support for the Burma Communist Party (BCP) by the Chinese Communist Party and the earlier assassination of the BCP's leader, the growth in strength of the Tatmadaw forces itself, and simple fatigue and disillusionment with the insurgencies that had been ongoing for nearly 50 years, a long time to sustain revolutionary fervour without much to show for it. There also must have been a realization by these groups, especially by the 1990s, that if they did not join the state soon – as some were already doing – they might be left out of the development programmes and plans that were forging ahead with or without them.

Of course, there were and are still a small number of fissiparous groups, many of whom live in the 'autonomous zones', who refused to sign the ceasefire agreements let alone participate in the writing of the Constitution or elections. But representatives from the majority of those who did sign were invited to participate in the writing of the new Constitution and encouraged to form (even ethnic-based) political parties to run in the national elections scheduled for 2010.

The Constitutional Convention

Because the civil war was effectively coming to an end (with the most important of the insurgent groups agreeing to talks with the Government), it could once again focus on national political affairs and restart its long-stated goal of returning the reins of government to civilians. In that endeavour the SPDC was continuing the policy of its predecessor, the SLORC, although it went a step further by devising its own explicit seven-step 'Roadmap to Democracy' beginning with the Constitutional Convention. (A new constitution had to be written because the 1974 Constitution had been abrogated by the military takeover of 1988.)

In 1992 the Government decided to convene the Constitutional Convention. At the time relations had warmed between the Government and the NLD, so the Convention included the then Chairman of the NLD, U Aung Shwe. It also included leaders of the ceasefire groups who had entered into talks with the Government. The first round of sessions was convened between 1993 and 1996. But by 1995 the NLD withdrew from them, citing the 'closed-door' sessions as reason, along with the quota of seats (25 per cent) guaranteed to the military in the yet to be formed Hlutdaw ('parliament').

The Convention adjourned for eight years, in part because of the walk out and disruption of the assembly, but also to complete the final ceasefire agreements with the rest of the insurgent groups (a high priority) and allow the new participants to organize in preparation for the Convention. When it reconvened in 2004 the SPDC's seven-step 'road map' to a constitutional government was announced, which thereafter became part of the 'conversation'. This 'road map' strove to:

1 reconvene the national convention;
2 conduct a 'step-by-step' implementation of a 'disciplined democratic' system;

3 draft a constitution;
4 adopt the constitution via a referendum;
5 hold legislative elections according to the constitution;
6 convene the legislatures;
7 form a government and other constitutional bodies.

During this crucial period of time when the Government was seriously moving towards creating a representative government, relentless external pressure continued for 'regime change', ignoring everything accomplished so far, especially the end of the civil war. Economic sanctions continued to be imposed on the country, affecting mainly ordinary people, while two major events, one domestic and man-made, the other an act of nature, threatened both the completion of the constitutional endeavour and the promulgation of representative government. And once again these events shifted negative international attention on the country, nearly sabotaging the entire process and returning everything accomplished during the past two decades back to 'square one'.

The first was a dramatic march by monks in Yangon in September 2007. The problems began in Upper Myanmar several weeks before when monks held Government officials hostage after some local disputes. That escalated to the internationally publicized event at Yangon where an estimated 2,000 monks (with another 5,000 to 10,000 in Mandalay) belonging to various and myriad monastic establishments marched in protest of specific and personal affronts to their status by authorities in Upper Myanmar during the previous weeks.[11]

The Yangon protests were initially peaceful; for several days security forces simply looked on as people 'protected' the marching monks by holding hands and encircling them. Visually it was most dramatic: a sea of saffron engulfing the television screen. For the outside, especially Western world, it was probably something they had never seen before. Predictably, these demonstrations fell into the Cold War paradigm of 'democracy' versus 'authoritarian rule', so that even the 'non-violent' Buddhist 'church' was now said to be also fighting the Government.

But what few diplomatic observers and even fewer journalists realized was that over 97 per cent of the nearly 400,000 properly ordained *pongyis* (monks) who belonged to the nine sects of the orthodox and officially recognized national Sangha had remained in their monasteries and not participated, prohibited by their vows of non-violence and involvement in secular activities. That means that most of those marching did not belong to the national Sangha, and even if some did they represent no more than 1 to 2 per cent of the total number of monks in the country.

More likely they were novices yet to be properly ordained and/or those who belonged to 'marginalized' and 'outlaw' monasteries not officially recognized as 'orthodox' by the national Sangha. Since people can 'become' monks and enter such monasteries for short periods of time for just about any secular reason without committing themselves to the life of an ortho-dox and permanent member of the Sangha, many are what Prime Minister U Nu once referred to as 'humans in yellow robes'. They do not have to take the required exams, prove their dedication and devotion to the path for twenty *wa* (rainy seasons) or follow any of the vows required of bona fide members of the Sangha. Indeed, their very participation in such sec-ular and violent activity reveals their heterodox and 'bogus' standing. But since their heads are shaved and they wear the saffron robe they are visually indistinguishable from genuine monks.

Subsequently the demonstrations turned violent when politicos hijacked and inflamed the situation.[12] At least four identified political fugitives of the 1988 riots (posing as monks by having shaved their heads and wearing monks' robes) capitalized on the potentially volatile situation and incited a violent confrontation between security forces and hard-core demonstrators. The Government was severely criticized for the manner in which order was restored in the streets, especially when media reports pitted guns and bayonets against alleged non-violent, peaceful, world-renouncing monks.

But that was far from the reality of the situation, as recounted not only by evidence that emerged subsequently from various quarters but by eye-witnesses of those particular days of violence. These news reports had conflated the earlier non-violent phases of the protests (where thousands of monks were involved) with the last week of September when the dem-onstrations turned violent and only a handful of 'rogue' monks (or people dressed up as monks) were left, giving the impression that the entire Buddhist 'church' was being massacred.[13]

In fact, and not surprisingly, it was discovered subsequently that most of these 'rogue' monks belonged to the above-mentioned 'outlaw' sects and monasteries, not recognized as part of the official Sangha by the public nor the national Sangha. Pornography and weapons were also found in one of these monasteries. Involvement of monks in such violent secular activities is not new – in modern Myanmar's history, it goes back at least to the 1920s if not earlier – and should not be construed as reflecting the sentiments of either the majority of *pongyis* in the country or the official Sangha.

Indeed, according to eyewitnesses who watched from the Traders Hotel above the area of confrontation – which occupied about two, at most three, city blocks on Sule Pagoda Road – when the shooting with live ammunition began on 26 and 27 September (rubber bullets were used earlier), there were *no monks* left to be seen, genuine or 'bogus'. The once-peaceful protest had become another confrontation between security forces and rioters, who by then were using metal darts and hard, sun-dried clay balls shot from various types of slings, brickbats trucked in for that purpose (and caught on news video) and other improvised devices.

Outside media reports fanned the flames by making dubious connections between these marching monks of 2007 and the 1988 demonstrations – despite the distance in time of nineteen years and the historically different situation – even going so far as to call it the 'Saffron Revolution'. Of course it was neither. Not only was it not a protest led by the leadership of the Myanmar Sangha, there was no identifiable leadership at all amongst the hodge-podge of demonstrators, no expressed or implied unity of purpose and no agenda articulated by the marchers. Nonetheless, external commentators rushed to 'fill in the blanks', declaring that the event was a 'revolution' for 'democracy' on behalf of the people by their moral arbiters: the *pongyis*.

Socio-economic factors, not 'democratic ideology', were far more likely responsible for this particular social unrest. Natural gas and petrol prices had suddenly gone up just a few days earlier, while regional monasteries had been experiencing overcrowding during the previous two years, as a growing number of lay members were joining the monkhood, straining its resources. Donations to the religious sector had also been declining in recent months, exacerbating the situation. Yet the Western media paid little or no attention to these factors or to the economic sanctions that continued to weigh heavily on society. (This event, like the 1988 riots, will need a more scholarly analysis once emotions have subsided.)

The other event that nearly sabotaged the 'seven step' process towards constitutional government was Cyclone Nargis, which hit the Irrawaddy Delta on 2 May 2008. Once again the Government was criticized for its handling of the event, though the occasion this time was totally an act of Mother Nature. The storm devastated the lower parts of the Irrawaddy delta region killing a maximum of 138,000 people. The cyclone had suddenly shifted direction eastwards from its 'normal' annual northerly path towards Bangladesh. United Nations relief forces and international aid agencies resident in the country were immediately on the scene, while regional neighbours were there with aid or offers of aid within a day or two.

But when three openly hostile countries – France, Britain and the United States – belatedly 'offered' aid from warships sitting on the Gulf of Muttama it was turned down by the Government, wary of the motives of nations that had been for the past twenty years extremely critical of it. Harsh criticism from these governments and their media ensued when entry into the country was denied.

Apart from symbolic and other reasons for the refusal, practically speaking, Myanmar's infrastructure could not have handled any more relief supplies anyway. Yangon's small international airport could not have handled the unloading of more than one (at most two) C-5s (military cargo aircraft) at one time, nor could the Delta sustain any movement of goods by truck, impassable with much of its roads and bridges washed away. The conditions required that only those knowledgeable about the layout of the land, using native means, could potentially help victims. And much of that responsibility fell on the local authorities, local monasteries and relief agencies such as the Myanmar Red Cross and World Vision, already part of the country's domestic relief infrastructure now for several decades. They were on the scene almost immediately helping the victims well before the sensational reports about the warships appeared. And as part of the system, these agencies had the proper papers that allowed them access to local currency, employ people, distribute goods, build relief shelters and so on. These and other NGOs and INGOs were the real 'heroes', coordinating relief operations with Government and local monasteries, doing the most good in helping the victims of Nargis. Yet we heard little about them in English-language media and much more about the Government's refusal to allow entry to members of hostile governments from their warships.

Thus while external political forces interpreted the Government's response to Cyclone Nargis only (or mainly) through an analytical framework of an insensitive Government that had rejected much needed aid for its people, other communities within the Association of Southeast Asian Nations and China took a non-ideological, humanitarian and practical approach, which ultimately turned out to be more accurate in reporting the situation and certainly far more effective in relieving this natural disaster.

It is unfortunate that a devastating event the scope and scale of Cyclone Nargis was politicized by (especially) the Bush White House, using the opportunity to score political points, charging the Myanmar Government as negligent and being more concerned about the referendum (on the Constitution) that continued to be held in parts of the country (not affected by the cyclone), than in addressing the natural disaster, which, of course, was not the case.

It is also revealing when these reports by the 'international media' on Nargis are compared to those concerning the earthquake that hit China just a few days later, Haiti's earthquake of 2010 and Japan's earthquake and tsunami of 2011. Although the human toll of Nargis far outstripped these other natural disasters, none of them was ever politicized; all were reported only as natural disasters that deserved humanitarian concerns. When reporting events in Myanmar during the past twenty years – even devastating natural disasters – there is an obvious double standard.

Since this natural disaster no major outbursts of anti-government political activity (or acts of nature) other than minor incidents have occurred. There was the 'swimmer' affair, the Mormon from Missouri who swam to Aung San Suu Kyi's house, remaining there for a couple of days and creating a diplomatic incident, along with the hoax about Myanmar's 'nuclear equipment' that turned out to be ordinary pipes. The latter was clearly meant to sabotage the upcoming elections.

Like it or not, and despite a relentless effort with millions of dollars financing the 23-year battle to topple the Myanmar Government, the domestic opposition and its 'international' supporters have, to put it frankly, lost the battle, and perhaps also the war.

To summarize, Myanmar's domestic events especially between 1988 and 2008 had become the purview of the world. Initially triggered by the riots of 1988, they included the Constituent Assembly elections of 1990, the years of intermittent meetings to draft the national constitution before and after 2004, the protests of 2007 by Buddhist monks, Cyclone Nargis in 2008 and the new Constitution of 2008. All had become international media events, for internet and other mass communication technologies, heretofore relatively inconsequential, had turned them into universal issues and everyone else's business.

That skewed the images crafted about the country thenceforth, as they described modern Myanmar almost solely from the perspective of 1988 – as if modern Burmese history began with it – thereby giving the event an unwarranted, artificial 'agency' and linking its fundamental causes to certain external ones occurring at the time considered to be 'universal' in nature. Interpreted within this post-Cold War framework of 'freedom' versus 'tyranny', virtually every event in Myanmar became a struggle: between civilian and military classes, authoritarianism and democracy, majority ethnic centre and minority ethnic periphery.

Such conceptual polarization into a 'good and evil' paradigm over-simplified and misrepresented what was in fact a much more complicated situation which overlooked (and therefore 'de-privileged') people, voices and experiences that were *not* considered part of that paradigm. Those with little or no access to the internet or newspapers, those not remembered in textbooks or museums, those who spoke little or no English, and those whose everyday concerns and priorities did not include agonizing over Western theories of governance, were simply left out. And since these comprise the vast majority of the population of Myanmar that meant the modern history of the Burmese people was being analysed, discussed and written without their involvement. It was as if the entire country of Myanmar consisted of only two groups: the army and the NLD.

Perhaps by reconsidering the recent history of Myanmar, at least from Independence onward, as consisting of different experiences of many groups with a shared history, politics and culture, rather than as a single struggle between only two groups with opposite political orientations, lives and values, readers may better understand the situation as much more comprehensive and complex, and based not on what a small group living outside the country *wished* it were, but on the priorities and concerns of the many within Myanmar itself. That internal perspective also helps explain the results of the recent elections, the topic of the following section.

THE CONSTITUTION OF 2008 AND THE ELECTIONS OF 2010

The new Constitution of 2008 was endorsed by national referendum completed at the end of May of 2008; it is now the highest law in the land. Published in book form and sold throughout the country for approximately US $1 each, the Constitution retains some aspects of the two earlier versions of 1947 and 1974 while making some changes of a fairly substantive nature.[14] To quote Robert H. Taylor, the foremost specialist on the state in Myanmar during this period, the Constitution of 2008 'endorses the past and holds out the promise of sharing power with those who currently monopolize state authority. The promise for the future is for the possibility of the army sharing some power with civilian political parties'.[15]

That 'possibility' was realized on 7 November 2010 when national elections were held to implement the provisions of the Constitution, which effectively transformed the Government from a military junta to a multi-party representative system. The latter consists of a *Hlutdaw* ('parliament') at the national level consisting of two 'Houses': the *Pyithu* (peoples') *Hlutdaw* (with 330 seats allotted to it) and the *Amyotha* (national) *Hlutdaw* (with 168 seats). At the state or regional level are *Hlutdaws* for each of the 14 states with a total of 673 seats allotted, based on population, except for the capital, Naypyidaw, which is administered differently, like the District of Columbia in the United States.

The total number of seats in these three bodies is officially put at 1,171. In the elections themselves, however, eight seats assigned to certain state assemblies were not contested since they were in the 'autonomous zones' where elections could not be held for security reasons, while in four others there was only one candidate or none contesting, so that a total of 1,154 seats were actually contested nationwide.

Each eligible voter had three votes to cast (one for each assembly) so that the total number of ballots cast can exceed the number of eligible voters. But not everyone cast all three ballots nor were all ballots cast deemed valid – that is, not lost or cancelled. The best estimate of the total number of ballots cast is 66 million, of which approximately 62 million were counted as valid. If these figures are correct, that suggests most eligible voters cast at least two of their three ballots.

As anticipated the Union Solidarity and Development Party (in English, the USDP) composed of retired military officers and various other non-military supporters affiliated with the Government (SPDC) received approximately 36,161,818 votes, which translates into approximately 59 per cent of the seats in the 'Pyithu Hlutdaw', 57 per cent in the 'Amyotha Hlutdaw' and 489 seats in the state and regional assemblies.[16] In addition, and not unlike provisions in the constitutions of Thailand, Turkey, Pakistan, Bangladesh and (before Suharto) Indonesia as well, a quota is reserved for the military, in effect giving the USDP and its political allies nearly 83 per cent of the total number of seats.

The largest non-USDP party to contest the elections, the National Unity Party (NUP, composed of old BSPP members) received a total of 62 seats (or 5.37 per cent), with a large number of the total valid votes cast: 14,285,043 (or 22.87 per cent of the total). These results are very interesting, for the following reasons.

First, the former politicians and members of the old BSPP, effectively removed from the political scene since 1988 and trounced by the NLD in the 1990 Constituent Assembly elections, actually made an unexpected 'comeback', enough to garner over 14 million valid votes. It suggests that Myanmar's political landscape still contains a range of old interests, factions and allegiances. Similarly, the entry and campaign by the so-called 'three princesses' – two of them daughters of former prime ministers (U Nu and U Ba Swe) – representing the new Democratic Party Myanmar, also suggest the continuing presence of even older elite networks in contemporary Myanmar politics, although they did not attain much success (the party won three seats).

Second, if the votes received by the NUP are combined with those of the USDP, it means the vast majority of ballots cast (50,446,981 out of an estimated 66 million) favoured the two parties that represent the previous two Governments (the BSPP and the SPDC). This is almost exactly the opposite of what happened in 1990 and suggests that the mood of the country has changed dramatically since then. (The probable reasons for that are discussed below.)

The Shan Nationalities Democratic Party came in third nationally, receiving a total of 57 seats or 4.94 per cent of the total. Yet it garnered only 2.69 per cent of the valid votes cast, well below the estimated Shan population of Myanmar at about 9 per cent. That, in itself, is an interesting comment on issues of ethnic identity, which is too large a topic to be dealt with here. There were even 82 independent candidates who ran without any party affiliation, of whom six won seats. The relative distribution of these figures amongst old and new political groups promises a very interesting future in Myanmar politics provided the present system remains intact.

What surprised many international observers, many of whom had anticipated trouble, is that the whole process of transition from military to civilian rule, especially in its final phases, has been largely smooth and calm.[17] Certainly compared to the North African 'Arab Spring' of 2011 and the violent transfer of governments in Egypt and Libya, and the attempts to do the same in Syria and Yemen, Myanmar's transition was a 'walk in the park'.

Some international media organizations, and as much as a year before the elections were even held, had already predetermined the framework for discussion by saying that the *forthcoming* process was not *going* to be inclusive because a single party, the National League for Democracy, was *expected* not to participate. (That despite the fact that 37 other parties were scheduled to participate, representing 1171 constituencies.) As it turned out, the NLD indeed did not participate. But it *chose not* to participate by deliberately not registering as required by election law, hence disqualifying itself. That decision was clearly made at the recommendation of party leader Daw Aung San Suu Kyi and other party hard-liners, consistent with the NLD's position since the 1990s to protest the entire process. It appeared to be a strategic one: it did not want to give tacit legitimacy to either the 2008 Constitution or the elections themselves. Not only would that have gone against two decades of its own political position but it would have incurred the wrath of its hard-line supporters. Perhaps they were also hopeful that 'international' criticism would render the elections null and void, which of course did not happen. (One should note, however, that Suu Kyi was given a voter registration number and along with members of her party *was* eligible to vote as a Burmese citizen.)

The decision not to participate and boycott the elections had internal consequences for the Party, deepening pre-existing rifts within it, to the extent that one faction defected and decided to form a new party called the National Democratic Front. It registered with the Union Election Commission and legally participated in the elections, winning 16 seats (with a total of 3,213,877 valid votes). At least it had secured a place – albeit a modest one – in the future governance of the country; whereas the NLD, because it did not participate, was left out of national governance as well as the 'national conversation' on the future of the country, a rather self-defeating strategy. (And that is precisely why Aung San Suu Kyi and the party announced in November 2011 that it would reverse its twenty-year hard-line position and participate in the next by-elections.)

Two other parties normally aligned with the National League for Democracy – the Shan Nationalities Democratic Party and the Rakhine Nationalities Development Party – also 'defected' and decided to participate and offer candidates. (As noted above, the former won 57 seats, the latter 35 seats or 3.03 per cent.)[18]

In short, by boycotting the elections the NLD ended up with nothing. Yet because it is still considered the *only* legitimate opposition party by certain foreign governments, especially the United States, it can continue to play the role of 'national victim'. But for how long and how effectively it can do that remains to be seen. After more than twenty years of political and personal struggles, with overwhelming financial and political support by the richest nations in the world and private organizations, the NLD has little to show for it; and part of it is of its own making.

Other international observers also complained – again, well before the elections were actually held – that the elections would not be free or fair. Although these criticisms were not, on the whole, borne out by most news reports of on-the-spot and trained foreign and domestic observers on voting day, certain 'rights' groups and others claimed irregularities, while admitting that these problems were not sufficient to have affected the outcome.[19] Myanmar scholars, placing the elections in a longer-term perspective, appear to be more realistic, agreeing that while the elections may not have been perfect they still represent a step in the right direction.[20]

Yet as soon as Daw Aung San Suu Kyi was released on 13 November 2010 from house arrest, criticism of these elections (at least in English-language media) began to dissipate, suggesting that procedural matters were never really a major issue to begin with for some of these groups. Then, when 'parliament' was seated by early 2011 as the legal Government of the country, followed by the dissolution of the SPDC at the end of March officially ending military rule in Myanmar, only the voices of diehard dissidents were left. It is a fait accompli that cannot be easily undone. Historical events had overtaken the debate concerning the 'legitimacy' of the elections.

Given that reality, the main question that needs asking, in our view, is not how 'really democratic' Myanmar is now, but what the election results, both quantitative and qualitative, can tell us? How might one reasonably interpret the fact – beyond the usual (and easy) accusations of 'fraud', intimidation and such – that the USDP received 36 million votes and the NUP 14 million? As historians, moreover, we would like to know how and where these elections 'fit' as an historical event in the modern story of Myanmar. And finally, we hope and wonder whether the peaceful transition of government might help make the country more stable and trouble-free, at least for the majority of its citizens, 75 per cent of whom are rural, agrarian folks.

One of the most important things the results of the elections tell us is the fact that so many people actually participated. When 1,154 seats representing many different constituencies – labour, women, ethnic minorities, intellectuals and academics, peasants, workers, civil servants, ex-military – were contested; when 37 political parties fielded candidates (of which at least 21 won seats) and when nearly 66 million ballots were cast, it is undeniable that a wide spectrum of Burmese society was involved in these elections, regardless of who won and why voters may have voted the way they did.[21] Participation, after all, is the whole point of participatory democracy, so we consider this kind of change to be positive not negative.

Second – and this speaks to the question posed above about the possible reasons the mood of people in 2010 might have been different from 1990 – is that a party that receives nearly 36 million votes – notwithstanding irregularities – in an election held by secret ballot in a country with high literacy rates, suggests or reflects widespread support, if not for any particular party, at least for *incumbency* and *continuity*, rather than *inexperience* and *unpredictability*. In other words, for the majority of voters in Myanmar, *preserving* rather than *changing* the status quo must have been important. If that were *not* the case the voting results would have been vastly different.

Unlike the Constituent Assembly elections of 1990 when change *was* desired and the NLD was that 'party of change', the national elections of 2010 were more about preserving and perpetuating the infrastructural and military-cum-security achievements of the past twenty years. (Indeed, that is precisely the thrust of the platform on which the USDP ran.) Moreover, since 1990, the NLD had taken on the role of 'spoiler' without anything more concrete to offer than boycotts, demonstrations and vague notions of 'democracy'. (Even that thunder has been stolen with the establishment of a new constitution and the completion of these national elections.) Thus while the NLD was still whipping the 'dead horse of democracy' and the technical legality of the 2008 Constitution, the USDP ran on current, practical issues of national security, union integrity, infrastructural achievements and development of the market sector.

The latter's platform, therefore, was far more attuned to the concerns of the majority of the population of Myanmar than the NLD's, which was obsessed with theoretical notions of a foreign political system and its principles of governance. The average farmer is not concerned with such issues but with having: a secure and stable countryside free of banditry and civil war, a continued subsidy for fertilizer and similar 'perks' provided by Government, free or cheap access to state irrigation water, tube wells, one-person tractors and home septic systems, low tax rates on their land and produce, easy and cheap transportation for their goods on improved roads and highways and enough money left to donate to the Religion and pay for their children's most important ear-boring and novitiate ceremonies.

The USDP could legitimately point to the enormous infrastructural development projects completed over the past twenty years which had begun to have a positive impact on rural Burmese, especially in enhanc-ing their ability to produce and distribute agricultural goods.[22] Perhaps most important, ending the half-century of devastating civil war not only enabled such infrastructural development to take place in areas that were once unsecured, but was also concrete demonstration of the Govern-ment's ability to resolve extremely difficult and complicated problems (especially of a military nature) that for decades had plagued all modern Burmese Governments – authoritarian or democratic – an accomplish-ment that no other party contesting the elections could claim.

For those in major urban areas, just ending the political squabbling of the past twenty years and maintaining the current law and order was priority enough, as many are civil servants under government employ or in jobs related to its maintenance. Furthermore, since the demise of the BSPP in 1988 and the end of the Burmese Way to Socialism, the market components of the country's economy have expanded significantly, creat-ing and benefiting a new, very conspicuous, non-military business class with considerable wealth. Certainly they are not about to jeopardize their new material and social standing by voting to change the status quo.

And lest we forget, patron–client relations in Myanmar are still alive and well; indeed, one could call them the normative structure of Burmese society. Obviously, the patron who is considered the most likely to 'deliver the goods' not only for the ordinary Burmese cultivator but for most classes (including the Sangha and military) is the Government and its proxy, the USDP. When, for every military officer, there are nine civilians dependent on him or her for 'perks' – such as subsidized prices on gaso-line and rice, access to public housing and so on – the election results suggest that the majority of the voters neither wanted to change the patron–client structure nor the patron; at least for now.

Why, then, do we expect the average Burmese citizen *not* to vote for the hand that feeds it, and to vote against his/her own self-interest? After all, the saying 'it's the economy, stupid' applies to the average Burmese as well. And when they do not comply with our expectations, we suspect some sinister reason for it – such as Government meddling with the ballots. At the same time we unreasonably expect the average Burmese citizen to vote *for* a political party whose entire platform rests on advo-cating the adoption of a little understood foreign ideology (democracy) without offering any concrete solutions to address the everyday economic needs of most people.

Worse, the political interests of such parties, particularly the NLD, are perceived (real and imagined) to be linked to those of foreign organ-izations and countries. The indirect financial support for the NLD's agenda by entities such as the Soros Foundation and the National Endowment for Democracy has not been lost on the ordinary Burmese voter. Even if the average Burmese farmer may not be aware of these particular organizations and the details of their 'strategic funding' projects, the public is well aware of foreign support for and encouragement of political activities that have contributed to the chaos and disorder of the past two decades.

In this relentless pursuit to affect 'regime change' in Myanmar the United States Congress has been a leader, allocating approximately US $10 million annually (now for about twenty years) to that goal, while continuing the imposition of economic sanctions against the country for nearly as long. These are precisely the kinds of activities that have hurt the ordinary Burmese most. Why, then, do we expect him or her to vote for parties that have for decades publicly endorsed such activities?

At the same time nearly all the issues raised by the so-called 'international community' concerning Myanmar are not only *ideological* in nature but based on Western principles and assumptions about political legitimacy and authority, with little or no relevance to the daily lives of most Burmese. To hope that such a political ideology is so compelling that it would make one vote against one's own way of life, culture, government, religion and family, is not only naive but rather culture-centric.

A vote for the USDP, therefore, was not only a vote for incumbency and continuity but also for one's own material (and psychological) self-interest, while at the same time it was a vote *against* foreign interference in the country's domestic affairs via 'proxies' such as the NLD. These factors are far more likely the basis for the USDP's landslide victory than the alleged manipulation of 66 million ballots by hand.

Between January and March 2011 nearly all the top Government posts and most of the other constitutional bodies had been filled. Former Prime Minister Thein Sein (domestically known as 'Mr Clean') was elected President (along with two vice presidents) by representatives of the two 'Houses' of the *Hlutdaw*. His new cabinet features a mixture of senior ex-military officers and a host of new faces to lead the various ministries. And as noted above, on 30 March 2011 the SPDC was dissolved, marking the official end of military rule in Myanmar and the reinstatement of civilian Government.

This important event barely made the back pages of the major international newspapers. Perhaps it was because an entire year of 'preemptive strikes' on the elections had rendered the conclusions about those elections wrong and the news passé. Perhaps it was because the composition of this new Government at the highest levels had retained some of the same personnel from the previous Government, so that the 'restoration of civilian rule' appeared largely superficial – 'old wine in new bottles'.

But even on a theoretical level that conclusion is not warranted: for the *form* of government has really changed – from a military junta to a parliamentary system; the structure, composition and functioning are different. At an empirical level the change is just as pronounced, for most of the seats in the three *Hlutdaws* are occupied by new faces, as all candidates running for office must, by law, be civilian, so that one assumes only those seriously concerned with public service and willing to resign their military portfolios have actually registered to run.[23]

Although it is true that the military as a corporate unit still has a solid presence with their 25 per cent quota in the *Hlutdaws*, they now must operate in tandem with a host of civilians, in new ways, according to new rules, with new superiors and accountable to new constituencies, especially since the two most senior military officers of the previous Government – U Than Shwe and U Maung Aye – have retired, or are expected to retire; and anyway, are not part of the new 'parliament' in daily deliberations.

Perhaps what bothered most long-time critics about this transition is the fact that the army had kept its word, just as it did in 1960 and 1974, and returned governmental authority to civilians in a representative system; a promise that had been scoffed at for over twenty years by these same critics.

THE ROADMAP: FINAL STEPS

Observers misunderstood the historical relationship between the series of SLORC/SPDC initiatives – the Roadmap to Democracy – and the reformist policies that followed the 2010 elections. Few commentators recognized that the convening of the constitutional convention (1993–6, 2004–7), the securing of major ceasefire agreements (1989–97), the conducting of the constitutional referendum (2008) and the holding of general elections (2010) were essential steps that enabled Thein Sein to come to office in the first place. The widespread 'surprise' over the timing, pace and extent of reforms was due to the lack of confidence in the military Government's policies over the previous two decades. If viewed from a longer historical perspective, the reforms did not 'begin suddenly' in 2011 with the transfer of power: the process had actually started much earlier, in 1993, when the SPDC initiated the process to write a new constitution. The military, though uncomfortable for many to admit, was at the centre of the transformations from the very beginning. With over twenty years of preparation and many of the institutional foundations and procedures finally in place, the new president and parliament hit the ground running.

President Thein Sein's inauguration speech of 31 March 2011 to the national parliament provided a preview of things to come. It had elements of older rhetoric but also referred to new themes that had not been addressed by previous Myanmar heads of state. Predictably, there were familiar statements made on the need for national reconciliation, the threat of Union disintegration and the need to cultivate solidarity, as well as a reminder of the historical importance of the Tatmadaw. There were still hints of older socialist priorities in his pledge to protect the interests of workers, farmers and civil servants. Yet he also spoke of the need to safeguard the fundamental rights of citizens, to review and rewrite policies concerning public health, social security, education and environmental conservation – even to amend some journalism laws to align with the spirit of the new constitution.

In fact, the president began with a statement concerning his commitment to safeguarding the constitution and its broader mission to produce a democratic nation. The speech covered Thein Sein's ambitious domestic agenda and foreign policy but it did so with several references to achieving democracy, preserving equality and governing through the rule of law – a marked difference from the language previous governments had employed to rationalize their policies. He stressed that his administration would focus on economic management and poverty alleviation, but he also elaborated on how such measures taken would connect to his domestic political policies. By building roads, bridges, schools and a national healthcare infrastructure, the president was confident that communication and interaction among the national races would be improved. Finally, he made key remarks that the Government would engage minority interests and those stakeholders with different 'ideas and concepts', even those 'individuals' and 'unlawful organizations' that did not recognize the state's seven-step Roadmap.[24]

Thein Sein expressed his intention to ease the country into the market economy gradually, stressing that this process was one of evolution and management. It would begin with privatization reforms, amendments to finance and tax laws, and creating a stable environment for investors. Immediate measures included reducing export taxes, granting tax exemptions for agricultural produce and providing measures to stabilize the exchange rate. The administration expected an ambitious 8.8 per cent growth in the first year, attributing these figures to the growth of the agricultural and service sectors. While the president spoke of these initiatives as part of a five-year plan, the measures he and his administration took surprised observers, leaving some quite optimistic about the level of change that appeared to be forthcoming.

In the days following the transfer of power, Thein Sein moved briskly to establish his cabinet, appointing 30 members to his inner circle, many of whom had held positions in the SPDC. Five members were civilians and were assigned ministerial posts in Commerce, Tourism, Education, Health and the Vice Presidency. To observers, it was the appointment of key civilians as advisers that signalled a significant change. U Myint, respected economist, former professor at Yangon Institute of Economics and close friend of Daw Aung San Suu Kyi, accepted the offer to be the president's chief economic adviser, surprising many external observers who felt that the new government's changes had until that point been somewhat cosmetic. Between May and June 2011 a series of dignitaries visited the country, including the Special Adviser to the Secretary-General of the UN, Vijay Nambiar; the US Deputy Assistant Secretary of State, Joseph Yun; the former US presidential nominee, Senator John McCain; and the UN special rapporteur on human rights in Myanmar, Tomás Ojea Quintana. Quintana had been critically outspoken with regard to the Government's roadmap but on this visit had admitted that 'a somehow different political context' had emerged.

Yet it was the president's efforts to approach Daw Aung San Suu Kyi in direct talks in August 2011, and later again in a highly visible national workshop on economic development, that seemed to open the door for the renewing of diplomatic ties with Myanmar. That month, the president addressed civil servants, business organizations, social groups and members of civil society to publicly urge political exiles to return home while pledging to establish and uphold the rule of law, fundamental rights, economic development and democracy. In the next few years, members of political opposition groups, advocacy organizations and exiled officials would be welcomed back into the country, with some even taking positions within Government. Domestic and international audiences were surprised and suspicious of the new government, because the political climate had fundamentally changed.

Some of this suspicion was alleviated when, in September, the president made the announcement that the government would be suspending the development of the Myitsone Dam project, a joint initiative with China to harness hydroelectric power from Myanmar to China. Local communities and advocacy groups had petitioned the government to halt the building of the dam for environmental and financial reasons. The president's decision to suspend the project won immediate praise, since it was widely known that the Myanmar Government would normally avoid upsetting such an important strategic partner as China and the lucrative incentives that accompanied such projects. The decision seemed to signal that the government was not only willing to engage new international partners but that it was keen to address the needs of its citizens more directly. The project's suspension astonished both international and domestic stakeholders, drawing both support and criticism from within and without the government. The flurry of activities that followed in the latter months of 2011 would leave little doubt that a genuine transition was taking place.

Later that month, press restrictions were relaxed while bans on exile media and activist websites were lifted. Five genres of media coverage (entertainment, health, children, information technology, sports) were no longer required to submit drafts to state censors ahead of publication, benefiting nearly 178 media publications. Foreign media was invited to cover parliamentary hearings and the domestic press was now allowed to run stories on Daw Aung San Suu Kyi. The BBC and other international news agencies were given greater access to the country. Government-led meetings involving civil society groups, development partners and business associations were now open to the press and featured in the next day's papers, providing the reading public with access to socio-political developments that had previously been limited.

The relaxing of media laws was followed by the establishment of new labour laws, new domestic tax polices, currency reforms, the privatization of state monopolies and the announcement that a new foreign investment law would soon be enacted. Rights activists welcomed the release of nearly 900 political prisoners and new legislation that allowed public demonstrations. The Government continued to approach opposition groups, civil society organizations, NGOs, ethnic leaders, former generals, former BSPP party members and even members of the 88 Generation (those students activists who had led protests against the BSPP in 1988) for advice and consultation. By engaging and (in some cases) offering key advisory posts to recently released prisoners and newly returned exiles, the Government hoped to demonstrate its commitment to a broadly defined reconciliation process. Such actions provided Thein Sein's administration with the opportunity to tap into this existing talent and to neutralize potential opponents (within and without the USDP) while providing the political space for Western nations to modify their official positions towards the country.

Many foreign nations responded in kind. Between September and November 2011, diplomats from the UN, the US, the EU and Britain streamed into Yangon to meet government officials. In September, the US Government's special envoy (and future US Ambassador), Derek Mitchell, arrived in Yangon to encourage the process, meet local stakeholders and to set the foundations for what was being termed 'principled engagement'. Diplomats from Norway and Indonesia followed Mitchell in October 2011, an indication that the European Union and the Association of Southeast Asian Nations (ASEAN) were eager to support the government as well. Following his visit, Indonesia's Foreign Minister, Marty Natalegawa, proposed that sanctions should be lowered and Myanmar be allowed to chair ASEAN on account of the Government's actions. 'The genie is out of the bottle,' he said, 'and this [reform process] should be made irreversible.'[25]

Opposition parties and ethnic groups that had once dismissed the Roadmap were now taking part in the very process, realizing that the prospects of achieving their vision of Myanmar would be improved by engaging Naypyidaw's initiatives. The announcement in November

2011 that the NLD would re-register as a political party marked its tacit recognition that engaging the Roadmap provided options, though the leadership was conflicted about the 2008 constitution and its mandate.

Despite this shift in the political climate, there remained voices in the Myanmar diaspora, in opposition circles and in foreign advocacy groups that continued to reject the 2008 constitution and the elections of 2010. Many of these groups remained abroad and therefore somewhat isolated from the transformations occurring within the country. Support for their activities, which was predicated on a different image of Myanmar, would be reduced, as engagement – rather than isolation – was the new policy of the day. The high-profile visit in December 2011 by Hillary Clinton, then US Secretary of State, marked a change in the way Myanmar would be portrayed by the press and members of the international community. This shift in perception, in marked contrast to earlier decades, provided the Thein Sein administration with important political space within which to pursue its domestic reforms in 2012.

MYANMAR MANIA

In January 2012, the Thein Sein administration secured an important ceasefire agreement with the Karen National Union (KNU), a collection of different Karen political groups and military units that had been fighting Myanmar's central Government since the announcement of independence in 1948. The new Government had finally succeeded in convincing this crucial ethnic minority group, the third largest in the country, to take part in the overall reconciliation process: a remarkable achievement. Bringing the KNU to the table to ink the agreement also enabled Naypyidaw to redirect resources and political energy towards other stakeholders, such as the Kachin, who were still reluctant to build on earlier ceasefires. Significant investment into the region from China, which was interested in developing the country's energy resources, lubricated pre-existing differences between the Government and local ethnic groups, creating complications for broader reconciliation efforts in the years to come.

The news of the KNU ceasefire agreement was overshadowed in the international media by the anticipation that Daw Aung San Suu Kyi and the NLD would contest the by-elections in April 2012. The by-election was conducted to fill seats vacated by MPs who had been appointed to the president's cabinet the previous year. In sweeping fashion, the NLD won 66 per cent of the total votes, taking 43 seats in Parliament and propelling Aung San Suu Kyi into public office. Many foreign governments, including the US and many in the EU, had made her release from house arrest a precondition for the restoration of diplomatic relations; her election into Parliament excited both domestic and international supporters. Thein

Sein's administration was also encouraged by her decision to participate, for doing so added more credibility to its reform initiatives and contained the potential for confrontation with the democracy activist (and her party) at a crucial period in the transition.

Shortly thereafter, the British prime minister David Cameron and a business delegation visited Myanmar and called for the suspension of sanctions in order to 'send a signal' that democracy and freedom were possible in Myanmar. The EU followed suit a few weeks later, stating that the bloc would also suspend sanctions (but retain an arms embargo) in order to ensure that the changes would remain 'irreversible'. The shift in policy by Britain and the EU provided Thein Sein and other reformers with the international support they needed in the perceived struggle with 'hardliners' within Government who might have preferred a return of direct military rule. Although this view ignored the role of the military in establishing the Roadmap in the first place, it was true that international recognition of Thein Sein's reforms could provide important political leverage for the Government.

Both Cameron and the EU, along with supporters inside and outside Myanmar, were likely surprised when Daw Aung San Suu Kyi and her fellow party members chose to boycott the oath-taking ceremony on entering the Parliament. The 43 new MPs found issue with one word in the oath, preferring to use the term 'respect' rather than 'safeguard' the constitution, in order to demonstrate that the 2008 constitution, which the NLD had originally dismissed, could be modified. Given the domestic political changes that had occurred since 2010 and the optimism of the 2012 by-elections, the boycott disappointed domestic and international observers alike.

The party's decision to boycott served two immediate purposes: it signalled the NLD's objections over elements of the constitution that reserved seats in Parliament for the military (25 per cent), and it reminded its constituents that its leader had not compromised her activist principles, even though she was participating in a political system that she and her party had opposed for over two decades. The new NLD had split with its more moderate factions in 2010, and the remaining hardliners were not ready to acquiesce to the Government's management of the reconciliation process. By refusing to take the oath, the NLD was making its stance clear: amending the constitution would be a significant priority of the party. But subtle coaxing from mediators, muted signs of international support and a group of opposition parliamentarians quietly convinced Suu Kyi that the boycott was not in the country's interest, and she eventually took her oath a few weeks later.

Meanwhile, the Thein Sein administration pressed on to stabilize Myanmar's domestic situation as natural disasters, ethnic unrest and communal violence persisted on the eastern and northern borders. Resolving ethnic and communal tensions was at the top of the Government's agenda. While a number of ethnic groups had signed ceasefire agreements, there were several armed groups that maintained control of vital border areas. Fighting in the Kachin State reignited as different factions within the Kachin Independence Organization and its military wings asserted their varying and sometimes conflicting interests. In April the president replaced his negotiating team in Kachin State with senior civilian leaders and military officers to lead the negotiations with the various Kachin groups. In the east a Government peace committee, also led by senior officials of the military, secured an important deal with Shan State leaders and their military wings. In both cases, the presence of senior commanders involved in the negotiations demonstrated to ethnic group leaders that the Government was committed to the peace process and that the terms of the agreements would be passed down to the rank and file.

Establishing political stability with ethnic groups also required securing strategic agreements with foreign governments, who had investments in key ethnic zones. Later in 2012 the president toured China and discussed with its leaders the growth of economic cooperation zones along and within Myanmar's borders, where Chinese businesses were keen to develop hydroelectric power. While in Japan the president secured a crucial agreement to waive Myanmar's multi-billion-dollar debt and obtained guarantees for future Japanese investment into its infrastructure. It was not clear, however, whether local leaders in key ethnic states would cooperate with Myanmar's central Government and its international partners. Nor was it a given that factionalism within ethnic groups and Government could be overcome for the sake of the larger reconciliation process. The threat to the reform process was not necessarily that of conservative members of the Government who favoured a return of military rule, but rather of those within local and central government with competing interests, whose ideas of reform were focused on different priorities, agendas and foreign partners than those favoured by the Thein Sein administration. The persistence of strong patron–client relations, characterized by personal loyalties to an individual or kin group (rather than to broader notions of the national community), continued to act as a barrier to national integration.

For the most part, these deeper challenges were hidden from view as the more public transformation of Myanmar society seemed to be captured in the sudden 'Myanmar-mania' that surrounded the travels of the country's most iconic figures. Senior members of Myanmar's Parliament and key cabinet advisers travelled extensively to promote the reforms internationally as academic institutions and business groups competed for their time. In June 2012, Suu Kyi visited Europe to receive the Nobel

Peace Prize that she had been awarded in 1991, an enormously important ceremony that offered some closure for many of her followers. Her
visit to Norway was followed by a trip to Britain where she addressed
both houses of parliament in Westminster Hall. And in September she
travelled to the United States to receive the Medal of Honor and to speak
to a number of overseas Myanmar communities. President Thein Sein
also travelled there to address the UN and to meet senior officials of the
Obama administration.

The world tours by Daw Aung San Suu Kyi and President Thein
Sein in 2012 were important for Myanmar's international image and
seemed to signal the end of a difficult chapter in the country's history.
From an external perspective, the visits promoted an image of Myanmar
as a nation in transformation – from an isolated nation that was closed off
to the international community to one that was engaged and concerned
with the values and priorities that were held by its international partners.
Although Myanmar had hardly been isolated from its Asian partners, it
did seem as if the old rivalries with the West were in the past. The president's statements concerning the political and economic priorities of
the country and the need to engage the various stakeholders were well
received by his hosts in Europe and America. Suu Kyi's freedom of movement was vital for her supporters, for Western nations and for the Myanmar Government. For many Western countries her release from house
arrest and subsequent election to Parliament met (and exceeded) the
conditions established for the renewal of diplomatic relations and the
lifting of sanctions.

For Thein Sein's administration, Daw Aung San Suu Kyi's tour was
good PR for the country and highlighted the Government's broader initiatives: it demonstrated to those who understood Myanmar only through
Suu Kyi's experiences that she was now part of the broader reconciliation
process, and it complicated her image as a staunch anti-Government
activist. Though she would sometimes struggle with the complexities of
her new role, since it sometimes placed her former views in question, she
was now regarded as an opposition leader *within* the Government. The
president's association with Suu Kyi and his supportive statements about
her role in Myanmar's future also provided him with political capital over
internal rivals, whose own reform agendas threatened the momentum of
the broader process.

Finally, the 2012 visits to Europe and North America by President
Thein Sein and Daw Aung San Suu Kyi also gave foreign governments
the political opening they needed to adjust their own economic and political policies towards Myanmar, which was fast becoming known as the last
viable economic frontier in Asia. The mania surrounding their tours was
matched only by the more problematic wave of investors seeking fortune

in the country. A new foreign investment law was in the works along with other financial reforms to support the growing interest of Western companies that were eager to expand into Myanmar. Jim Rogers, the noted American investor and financial adviser, captured the mania surrounding the country's potential by declaring Myanmar 'the best investment opportunity in the world'.[26]

The surprise visit to Myanmar by President Barack Obama in November 2012 seemed to punctuate the year's Myanmar mania and the Roadmap that had made it all possible. With the words *'Myanmar Naingan, Mingalaba!'*, President Obama greeted both the audience at the University of Yangon and the nation using its preferred nomenclature – a strong signal that Myanmar and the United States had turned a corner and were heading towards a new era of transformation.

THE ROAD AHEAD

By 2013, some of the euphoria and excitement of the previous year was tempered by renewed ethnic and communal tensions in Kachin and Rakhine states, a reminder that Myanmar's multi-ethnic, multi-religious and multi-linguistic population still struggled with the notion of a common national community. Military clashes in Kachin State resumed as different factions fought the central government and each other in order to secure their political autonomy and retain a stake in China–Myanmar energy projects. Bitter violence towards Bengali and Muslim communities in the western Rakhine State highlighted the significant challenges the Government faced on issues of immigration and citizenship. While international attention focused on the plight of the 'Rohingya' minorities, who are not recognized by either Bangladesh or Myanmar, the violence that was directed towards members of immigrant communities and Muslim citizens pointed to the indisputable fact that the recent political-economic reforms had had little effect on the lives of many rural communities. While the Government was quick to assign a series of peace commissions to investigate the escalation of violence, Naypyidaw was certainly aware that underneath these ethnic and religious tensions were socio-economic factors that required time, investment and the capacity to make good on its promises.

The pace and breadth of reforms that were initiated between 2011 and 2013 were among the most ambitious in a generation. General Than Shwe's transfer of power to the Thein Sein Government in late March 2011 was met with scepticism both at home and abroad, despite his earlier assurances that the authorities were still leading the country towards 'disciplined democracy.' But, by 2013, most of the earlier scepticism in the international community had diminished, though some viewed continuing ethnic and communal violence as an indicator of whether the new administration would be able to sustain these reforms. Uncertainty also remained over whether reforms would be 'derailed' by conservatives within the military, a view that overlooked the multifaceted nature of reform and the military's central contribution to the process.

From a broader domestic perspective, there were other challenges to the transition that did not always come into clear view. Members of the president's cabinet stated privately that overcoming popular distrust of the Government and deep political factionalism at all levels would be among the most important challenges facing the reform process. Differing economic and political interests across Government, competing constitutional priorities within Parliament, new foreign investors jostling for economic advantage and security issues along the borders continued to complicate the political landscape. Clearly, the political transition that began in the early 1990s was still a work-in-progress – a somewhat uneven transformation that affected some sectors of Myanmar society and not others, bringing change to some communities while leaving many still wondering whether the changes would affect them at all.

Part of the reason such a transition is possible at all is the 'hybrid' character of Government in Myanmar. Throughout the modern history of the country both military and civilian Governments have operated in a symbiotic relationship, whereby members of one invariably participated in the other, for governing a nation requires experienced hands whether military or civilian. That hybrid character of Government actually goes back to the colonial structure, in which many civilian portfolios were held by military officers. And the main reason for the continued presence of the military in civilian Governments in the post-colonial period was the half-century of civil war that followed the Second World War, placing the country on a perpetual war footing until the late 1990s, much like Vietnam, Cambodia and Israel.

That symbiosis not only made it relatively easy for personnel to move from one to the other, but allowed the Government to be 'both' without having to go through the trauma of a major revolution each time. This has resulted in an oscillation between the two forms of government, so that, between the Second World War and 2011 four military (or authoritarian) forms of government (1945, 1958, 1962 and 1988) were replaced by – or changed places with – four 'civilian' (or representative) forms of government (1948, 1960, 1974 and 2011). And because Burmese society experienced this regularly for six decades – on average, one every fifteen years – that kind of 'change' was never really considered extraordinary.

Although such oscillation has been interpreted as evidence of a 'struggle' between civilian and military rule, we would prefer to regard it more as a 'natural' movement between *stable* (or strong) institutions and *unstable* (or weak) ones. Conditions in Myanmar's recent past – pre-war politics, the Second World War, decolonization and a half-century of civil war – have made representative (and civilian) institutions less stable than authoritarian (and military) ones.

Yet whenever the military has taken over, in time it has invariably created a national political party (AFPFL, BSPP, USDP) and a representative Government through which its national priorities – especially the integrity of the Union – could be effected. Subsequently, the enmeshed character of party and government becomes rigid and inflexible until that stasis is challenged, resulting in anarchy and disorder. At which time the military steps in once more to restore law and order, beginning another oscillation.

Had the military intended to keep power indefinitely rather than return authority to civilians – an oft repeated statement made by them – why would it bother to go through the tedious and time-consuming process of creating a national political party and a representative government? Why not simply retain the power they already had without creating, each and every time, a nominal civilian government?

At the same time, with each new oscillation, representative institutions have become stronger and more stable. The most recent version of both the Constitution of 2008 and the *Hlutdaw* of 2011 is illustrative: they are clearly stronger, more stable and improved versions of their previous incarnations. Thus, for example, although the 2008 Constitution is similar to the 1947 model in its multi-party configuration, it has made the union much stronger, having omitted the kinds of provisions found in the 1947 Constitution that allowed certain states to secede from it, a serious weakness. In fact the 1974 Constitution consciously addressed that weakness. But in so doing it went too far towards central authority, creating a single-party system (the BSPP) and single (socialist) economy (the Burmese Way to Socialism).

The current version of the 2008 Constitution and the 2011 *Hlutdaw* is an attempt to alleviate these earlier problems by bringing the state back towards the middle. Thus although the 2011 *Hlutdaw* is more centralized than the 1947 parliament, it is not as centralized as the 1974 state was. Clearly the writers of the present Constitution, having learned from the weaknesses of both the 1947 and 1974 versions have thought through the issues carefully and addressed them, even though there are still 'contradictions' in it, as would be expected of hybrids.[27]

Civilian or military, weak or strong, unstable or stable, socialist or capitalist, single or multi-party, hybrid or not, similar to the situation in the 1920s with the introduction of dyarchy, 1943 with nominal 'independence' under Japan, 1948 with Independence, 1958–60 with the 'Caretaker Government', 1962 with the Revolutionary Council, 1974 with the BSPP, 1988 with the SLORC/SPDC and now 2011 with the new *Hlutdaw*, incumbents and elites still hold most of the cards.

As throughout Myanmar's history since the eleventh-century Kingdom of Pagan, the competition for the state today is largely between and amongst elites, even if each side invokes 'the people' as part of its legitimacy. With the 'contest' for the state largely in the hands of elites, 'national' leaders drift between establishment and opposition, so that at one time or another many have been in both camps. It is almost as if (at the national level anyway) politics in Myanmar is a game of 'musical chairs' – if it were not so deadly at the street level – and close to being a 'family feud', as most of the top contestants were either kin or at one time, close friends and/or associates. Politics in Myanmar has been very personal. Since elites still dominate politics, one could say with some aplomb that there has been no true revolution in Burmese history, only evolutionary oscillations amongst and between elites.

Now, with some distance separating Independence and the current generation of leaders, with most of the important insurgencies over, with an elected 'parliament' in place, and with the country far more stable now than it has ever been since Independence, the nation can return to focusing on infrastructural and economic development without being interrupted by internecine politics, outside powers and perhaps even Mother Nature.

But Myanmar is not out of the woods yet. If anarchy returns to compel the military to take over and restore order once again – a legal provision written into the 2008 Constitution under the same kind of emergency clauses found in most constitutions in the world – then the pendulum will swing back again to begin another oscillation. For that to happen, however, the kinds of conditions that triggered such disorders in the past must reappear as well. That means the economy, especially, must remain virtually moribund without making any meaningful progress from now on, while politics must also return to 'business as usual'. Both are unlikely prospects, although one can never tell with Myanmar.

For the present, in this phase of reintegration and reconstruction of the nation, the main question remains much the same as it was during most of the twentieth century. And that is: whether the current leaders of the Government, members of the religious orders, dissident groups, political parties, private foundations and foreign governments will become part of the solution or continue to be part of the problem?

Conclusion

Given the history of Myanmar as described in this book and given that the demographic, geographic, part of the political, most of the ethno-linguistic and much of the socio-cultural environment in which that history occurred is also likely to persist for some time – what might the country's future look like, particularly compared to its neighbours who have experienced some of the same region-wide historical events?

Although historians are ordinarily loath to predict – we usually leave that to political scientists who are eager to do so – in this case, we feel that the reader might appreciate a discussion of that issue stemming from a perspective based on the country's documented history, rather than from one that is only a theoretical exercise commensurate with one's personal political philosophy. We should remind the reader from the outset, therefore, that expectations, or more accurately, *wishing* that the country take a path contrary to its historical trajectory is not only unrealistic but romantic (even harmful) and not likely to happen in any case. With that in mind, which countries in the region might Myanmar look like in the future, if any?

It certainly will not resemble Singapore, the most modern and secular nation in Southeast Asia today, whose legitimacy and perception of itself is based on 'newness' and 'modernity' while Myanmar's is based on 'oldness' and 'tradition'. Part of the reason, and to Singapore's advantage, is that as a nation it began with a near clean slate only in 1965, without the kind of historical 'baggage' that has burdened Myanmar, and with extremely competent leaders. Also, *as a nation*, Singapore in its albeit brief time as a *republic* has never experienced colonialism or decolonization, particularly decolonization's invariably violent aftermath, civil war, which every other country in Southeast Asia that was colonized went through, and which in Myanmar was to last over half a century. Furthermore, Singapore is only a city-state with a little over five million people covering 270 square miles, comprised of only three main ethno-linguistic communities who all speak the *de facto* 'national' language (English) while

Myanmar has approximately 59 million people, 260,000 square miles and over a dozen major languages. And, finally, Singaporeans unabashedly share a common 'ideology' and vision for the future – making money.

Although Malaysia's rural areas appear to typify an indigenous Southeast Asia that looks much like Myanmar, the two countries are fundamentally quite different. Not only is Malaysia Muslim, it is also a maritime and commerce-oriented society and has been for most of its history. Both its colonial and decolonizing experiences have been relatively mild compared to Myanmar's. As a result its post-colonial era was relatively stable (despite the so-called 'Emergency'), allowing its competent leadership to focus on forging a modern society without insurmountable hindrance. Although not as secular as Singapore, nonetheless its religion and (decentralized) religious organization has long been attuned to being very much part and parcel of the socio-economic fabric of the country while its ethno-linguistic configuration is much like Singapore's. This enabled the state to pursue economic and political modernization and nation-building as a whole without being seriously hampered by the kind of armed and violent opposition from within that Myanmar faced, giving Malaysia an earlier start that allows it to remain ahead today. Myanmar's modern history could not have been more different and its future is unlikely to resemble Malaysia's.

Compared to the Philippines' long colonial past with Spain and the depth to which that history has penetrated the country's culture, particularly its religion (Catholicism), Myanmar's relatively short colonial experience (and its impact) is even more dissimilar. Add to that the Philippines' island and maritime geo-political configuration, its adoption of American values and institutions when it became a United States colony, the widespread knowledge and use of English, and its emotional sentiments that favour Western culture in general – notwithstanding the antipathy towards the centre in the southern regions – and it makes the chasm with Myanmar even wider. Although the underlying indigenous foundations of both countries are also (like Malaysia's) recognizably Southeast Asian, and the ethno-linguistic make-up of the Islands is as diverse as Myanmar's, the latter's future is *least* likely to look like the Philippines'.

Myanmar resembles Thailand in certain ways, such as Theravada Buddhism's (sometimes eager, sometimes reluctant) 'accommodation' with the modern world and the focus on rural development and agrarian concerns that stem from their similar geo-political setting. In contrast, however, the ethno-linguistic make-up in Thailand is not nearly as diverse as that found in Myanmar: those whose 'mother-tongue' is T'ai comprise nearly the entire population of the country, constituting an overwhelming ethno-linguistic majority. That common language and culture, cemented around the stabilizing presence of a respected (if not beloved) monarch who has been a symbol (and actual focus) of unity for many decades, have enhanced the making of a viable modern Thai nation-state. And, finally, because Thailand was not colonized it never experienced the decolonizing civil war that devastated Myanmar. As a result the two countries are fundamentally different in their views of certain Western powers, hence their current power alignments and different foreign policies. China's influence in Myanmar today and the United States' in Thailand promise to make things interesting for the two neighbours.

In terms of a traumatic colonial history, an ambivalent experience in the Second World War with the Japanese, a contentious post-war struggle for independence and especially a *military solution* to post-independence problems, Myanmar resembles Indonesia. Indeed, the similarity of their modern historical experience may be part of the reason the Myanmar Constitution of 2008 adopted a crucial component of Indonesia's original Constitution (before Suharto), which reserved a percentage of seats for its military in 'parliament'. Myanmar's 'disciplined democracy' also appears to be an echo of Indonesia's 'guided democracy', so that there is more ideological empathy between the two countries than meets the eye. There are other similarities that are uncanny: both the daughters of the 'fathers' of modern Myanmar and Indonesia came to assume leadership roles in national politics in recent years. Despite these similarities, however, Indonesia's island configuration and non-contiguous land mass, Islam and its formal and informal place in the state, the nation's proximity and increasing ties to Australia rather than China, its geo-political position on the Straits of Malacca rather than Myanmar's on the Bay of Bengal, Yunnan and the old Silk Road to and from China, all suggest a different economic future for Myanmar.

The half-century of civil war in Myanmar, although devastating and immobilizing in terms of nation-building, palls in comparison to Cambodia's 'Killing Fields' and Vietnam's French and American Wars. Nonetheless, the violent and traumatic decolonizing experiences of all three instilled a common fear of anarchy and disorder in the psyches of their people. That experience also left a deep suspicion amongst them of certain Western powers, although Cambodia's holocaust appears to be mainly of its own making, even if the conditions for it were created by the interference of Cold War superpowers. And whereas the Vietnamese usually celebrate their history of resistance against its big neighbour to the north, that is not a cause célèbre in Myanmar's history. On the contrary its future is more closely tied to extending the current alliance with and reliance on China. Even though neither Vietnam nor Cambodia is likely to be a model for Myanmar's future, chances are it will probably look more like them than like any other nation in Southeast Asia.

Whether or not Myanmar's historical trajectory continues to shape its future, of course, depends on what intersects and interferes with it. As noted in the previous chapter, if extreme disorder recurs (for whatever reason), the new 'disciplined democracy' may be tested and shelved. Even so, chances are that this will be temporary and the nation will return to a representative Government eventually, for not only has that oscillation been the historical pattern but too much has happened historically and structurally to put 'Humpty Dumpty' back together again in its original form.

The present Government is also likely to continue down the present path towards a larger market component in the economy, rather than retain any (or many) of the previous near-total Socialist features. However, Government is still likely to continue to play a prominent role in shaping it, as in China. It matters little, perhaps except symbolically, what happens to the much celebrated or maligned economic sanctions imposed on the country, for Myanmar can get much of what it needs and wants from Asia and elsewhere. And if these political and economic transformations are given a chance to be properly installed and institutionalized, parallel socio-cultural changes are likely to follow. Lest we become too starry eyed, however, Myanmar probably will not look like present day Taiwan, South Korea or Singapore in all their manifestations even within the next 50 years.

In the end, Myanmar's future will be shaped by its own past, its historical patterns, its own human and material contexts, its own beliefs; not someone else's. Indeed, that Myanmar's priorities will remain mainly agrarian and domestic; its Government a centralized hybrid of mainly indigenous and foreign ideas and realities; and its society steadfastly devoted to Theravada Buddhism and native supernaturalism, are all safe bets. In short, for the foreseeable future Myanmar's past will continue to remain an indelible part of its present.

References

Prologue: A Synthesis of Old and New

1 The paste is made by rubbing a piece of the bark of a special tree on a whetstone with some water. It is used as sun-screen, moisturizer and for other cosmetic reasons.

2 The United Nations Weather Agency in Geneva tracks and reports such information. See 'WHO praises Burma cyclone response', *Bangkok Post* (5 September 2008).

3 Michael Aung-Thwin, 'Of Monarchs, Monks, and Men: Religion and the State in Myanmar', *Asia Research Institute Working Paper Series*, 127 (2009), pp. 2–31. For other sources on this event, see the following: *Myanmar Information Committee, Yangon* (7 October 2007), p. 1; 'Monks – being used to smuggle porn CDs across the border from Myanmar', *Asian Tribune* (4 May 2003), p. 1; F. William Engdahl, 'Myanmar's "Saffron Revolution": The Geopolitics behind the Protest Movement', *Global Research* (15 October 2007), pp. 1–16; Denis D. Gray, 'Myanmar Monks, 1988 Activists Linked', *USA Today* (26 October 2007), p. 1.

4 The official Government rate (of 6 kyats to US $1) does not apply to individuals who visit the country. Rather it is meant for other sectors, such as landing and docking fees for international airlines and ships. If it were the market rate the stronger economies would pay next to nothing in Myanmar while others must pay huge, unaffordable fees. That difference would have to be made up by the Myanmar farmer (as the GDP stems largely from agriculture and related industries) who, in effect, would then be subsidizing Silk Air and Japanese freighters when they land and dock in Myanmar airports and piers.

5 The most recent example is the bogus charge of developing nuclear weapons that stopped US Senator Jim Webb's planned visit to the country for more talks. These are not mere coincidences.

Introduction: A Different Perspective

1 See James C. Scott's arguments in *The Art of Not Being Governed: An Anarchist History of Upland Southeast Asia* (New Haven, CT, 2009).

2 Michael Aung-Thwin, 'Ava and Pegu: A Tale of Two Kingdoms', *Journal of Southeast Asian Studies*, XLII/1 (2011), pp. 1–16.

3 Jean Gelman Taylor, *Indonesia: Peoples and Histories* (New Haven, CT, and London, 2003), p. xvii.
4 The notion and analysis of 'autonomous history' comes from John Smail's seminal article on the subject: 'On the Possibility of An Autonomous History of Modern Southeast Asia', *Journal of Southeast Asian History*, II/2 (1961), pp. 72–102.
5 Michael Aung-Thwin, 'Spirals in Burmese and Early Southeast Asian History', *Journal of Interdisciplinary History*, XXI/4 (1991), pp. 575–602.
6 The phrase comes from James C. Scott's *Weapons of the Weak: Everyday Forms of Peasant Resistance* (New Haven, CT, 1985).
7 To our knowledge, only one person was reported to have been killed.
8 Jon Wiant, 'Tradition in the Service of Revolution: The Political Symbolism of *Taw-hlan-ye-khit*', in *Military Rule in Burma Since 1962: A Kaleidoscope of Views*, ed. F. K. Lehman (Singapore, 1981), pp. 59–72.
9 Michael Aung-Thwin, 'Parochial Universalism, Democracy *Jihad*, and the Orientalist Image of Burma: The New Evangelism', *Pacific Affairs*, LXXIV/4 (2001/2), pp. 483–505.

Chapter 1 The Setting

1 Michael Aung-Thwin, 'Principles and Patterns of the Precolonial Burmese State', in *Tradition and Modernity in Myanmar: Proceedings of an International Conference held in Berlin from May 7th to May 9th, 1993*, ed. Uta Gartner and Jens Lorenz (Berlin, 1994), pp. 15–44; Michael Aung-Thwin, 'Debate', *Bijdragen tot de Taal-, Land- en Volkenkunde*, CLXVII/1 (2001), pp. 86–99.
2 Michael Adas, *The Burma Delta: Economic Development and Social Change on an Asian Rice Frontier, 1852–1941* (Madison, WI, 1974).
3 As early as 1993, if not earlier, this event was predicted. See Aung-Thwin, 'Principles and Patterns', p. 37. That the new capital lay adjacent to Pyinmana is also no surprise, as we shall see below.
4 W. Donald MacTaggart, 'Myanmar, or Burma' (unpublished paper), pers. comm., 21 July 1992.
5 Adas's *The Burma Delta* is perhaps the best book on this process.
6 Frank M. LeBar, Gerald Cannon Hickey and John K. Musgrave, eds, *Ethnic Groups of Mainland Southeast Asia* (New Haven, CT, 1964).
7 This is an area of study that needs much more research. But on current available evidence, not a single stone inscription in Shan has been found in Myanmar other than these two which likely belonged to the T'ai speakers of Ayuthaya.
8 For a more detailed analysis of this argument, see Michael Aung-Thwin, *The Mists of Ramanna: the Legend that was Lower Burma* (Honolulu, HI, 2005), ch. 5, pp. 112–13.
9 All the figures cited in this chapter can be found in public domain sources such as the United States Census Bureau, International Programs Center, International Data Base (IDB), WHO, UNESCO and UNHCR, along with a host of other databanks such as the CIA's *World Factbook*, *Europa World Yearbook* and International Monetary Fund publications.
10 Union of Myanmar, *Fundamental Principles and Detailed Basic Principles Adopted by the National Convention in Drafting the State Constitution* (Yangon, 2007).

Chapter 2 Prehistory

1 Peter Bellwood, 'Southeast Asia before History', in *The Cambridge History of Southeast Asia. Volume One: From Early Times to c. 1800*, ed. Nicholas Tarling (Cambridge, 1992), pp. 55–136.
2 Ba Maw, 'Research on the Early Man in Myanmar', *Myanmar Historical Research Journal*, 1 (1995), pp. 213–20.
3 Michael Aung-Thwin, 'Origins and Development of the Field of Prehistory in Burma', *Asian Perspectives Special Issue: The Archaeology of Myanma Pyay (Burma)*, ed. Miriam T. Stark and Michael Aung-Thwin, XL (2002), pp. 6–34.
4 Helmut de Terra and H. L. Movius, Jr, 'Research on Early Man in Burma. I – The Pleistocene of Burma by H. de Terra. II – The Stone Age of Burma by H. L. Movius, Jr', *Transactions of the American Philosophical Society*, XXXII (1943), pp. 271–393.
5 Wilhelm G. Solheim II, 'New Light on a Forgotten Past', *National Geographic*, CXXXIX/3 (1971), pp. 330–39.
6 Aung Thaw, 'The "Neolithic" culture of the Padah-lin Caves', *Asian Perspectives*, XIV (1973), pp. 123–33.
7 Aung Thaw, 'The "Neolithic" culture'.
8 Bellwood, 'Southeast Asia before History'.
9 Pamela Gutman and Bob Hudson, 'The Archaeology of Burma, from the Neolithic to Pagan', in *Southeast Asia: from Prehistory to History*, ed. Ian Glover and Peter Bellwood (Abingdon & New York, 2004), pp. 149–76.
10 Michael Aung-Thwin, 'Burma before Pagan: The Status of Archaeology Today', *Asian Perspectives*, XXV (1982–3), pp. 1–21.
11 Bob Hudson, 'Iron in Myanmar', *Enchanting Myanmar*, V (2006), pp. 6–9; also, Elizabeth Moore and Pauk Pauk, 'Nyaung-gan: A Preliminary Note on a Bronze Age Cemetery Near Mandalay, Myanmar (Burma)', *Asian Perspectives Special Issue: The Archaeology of Myanma Pyay (Burma)*, ed. Miriam T. Stark and Michael Aung-Thwin, XL (2002), pp. 35–47.
12 Elizabeth Moore, 'Bronze and Iron Age Sites in Myanmar: Chindwin, Samon, and Pyu', *SOAS Bulletin of Burma Research*, I (2003), pp. 24–39.

Chapter 3 The Urban Period

1 Michael Aung-Thwin, 'Principles and Patterns of the Precolonial Burmese State', in *Tradition and Modernity in Myanmar: Proceedings of an International Conference held in Berlin from May 7th to May 9th, 1993*, ed. Uta Gartner and Jens Lorenz (Berlin, 1994), pp. 15–44.
2 Paul Wheatley, *Nagara and Commandery: Origins of the Southeast Asian Urban Traditions* (Chicago, IL, 1983), ch. I.
3 Aung Thaw, *Excavations at Beikthano* (Rangoon, 1968). See also Janice Stargardt, *The Ancient Pyu of Burma* (Cambridge, 1990); Elizabeth Moore, *Early Landscapes of Myanmar* (Bangkok, 2007).
4 Michael Aung-Thwin, 'A New/Old Look at "Classical" and "Post-Classical" Southeast Asia/Burma', in *New Perspectives on the History and Historiography of Southeast Asia: Continuing Explorations*, ed. Michael Aung-Thwin and Kenneth R. Hall (London, 2011), pp. 25–55.
5 Bob Hudson, 'The Origins of Bagan' (PhD, University of Sydney, 2004).

6 Michael Aung-Thwin, 'Heaven, Earth and the Supernatural World: Dimensions of the Exemplary Center in Burmese History', in *The City As a Sacred Center: Essays on Six Asian Contexts*, ed. Holy Baker Reynolds and Bardwell Smith (Leiden, 1987), pp. 88–102.

7 Myint Aung, 'The Excavations at Halin', *Journal of the Burma Research Society*, LIII (1970), pp. 55–64.

8 Michael Aung-Thwin, 'Burma before Pagan, the Status of Archaeology Today', *Asian Perspectives*, XXV (1982–3), pp. 1–21.

9 Myint Aung, 'The Development of Myanmar Archaeology', *Myanmar Historical Research Journal*, 9 (2002), pp. 11–29, and 'The Excavations of Ayethama and Winka (?Suvannabhumi)', in *Essays Given to Than Tun on his 75th Birthday: Studies in Myanma History* (Yangon, 1999), pp. 17–64.

10 Robert S. Wicks, 'The Ancient Coinage of Mainland Southeast Asia', *Journal of Southeast Asian Studies*, XVI (1985), pp. 195–225.

11 G. H. Luce, *Phases of Pre-Pagán Burma: Languages and History*, 2 vols (Oxford and New York, 1983).

12 Tha Mya, *Pyu Reader* (Rangoon, 1963).

13 Michael Aung-Thwin, *The Mists of Ramanna: the Legend that was Lower Burma* (Honolulu, HI, 2005), ch. 2.

14 Pierre Pichard, 'A Distinctive Technical Achievement: The Vaults and Arches of Pagan', in *The Art of Burma: New Studies*, ed. Donald M. Stadtner (Mumbai, 1999). See also G. H. Luce, *Old Burma – Early Pagan*, 3 vols (New York, 1969–70).

15 Michael Aung-Thwin, *Pagan: the Origins of Modern Burma* (Honolulu, HI, 1985).

Chapter 4 Pagan: The Golden Age of Myanmar

1 Michael Aung-Thwin, *Pagan: the Origins of Modern Burma* (Honolulu, HI, 1985).

2 At the time, the Burmese were fighting for independence from Britain, which surely inspired this theory.

3 Peter Grave and Mike Barbetti, 'Dating the City Wall, Fortifications, and the Palace Site at Pagan', *Asian Perspectives Special Issue: The Archaeology of Myanma Pyay (Burma)*, ed. Miriam T. Stark and Michael Aung-Thwin, XL (2002), pp. 75–87.

4 Michael Aung-Thwin, 'Heaven, Earth and the Supernatural World: Dimensions of the Exemplary Center in Burmese History', in *The City As a Sacred Center: Essays on Six Asian Contexts*, ed. Holy Baker Reynolds and Bardwell Smith (Leiden, 1987), pp. 88–102.

5 For a detailed study of this issue, see Michael Aung-Thwin, *The Mists of Ramanna: the Legend that was Lower Burma* (Honolulu, HI, 2005).

6 Melford E. Spiro, *Buddhism and Society: A Great Tradition and Its Burmese Vicissitudes* (New York, 1970).

7 The primary evidence in the history of Myanmar does not support this contention by James C. Scott in *The Art of Not Being Governed: An Anarchist History of Upland Southeast Asia* (New Haven, CT, 2009).

8 Sergey S. Oshegov (U Kan Hla), 'Pagan: Development and Town Planning', *Journal of the Society of Architectural Historians*, XXXVI/1 (1977), pp. 15–29.

9 Michael Aung-Thwin, *Irrigation in the Heartland of Burma: Foundations of the*

Pre-Colonial Burmese State (DeKalb, IL, 1990).

10 Mabel Haynes Bode, *The Pali Literature of Burma* (London, 1909).

11 Aung-Thwin, *Pagan*, ch. 6.

12 Michael Aung-Thwin, 'The Role of *Sasana* Reform in Burmese History,
Economic Dimensions of a Religious Purification', *Journal of Asian Studies*,
XXXVIII (1979), pp. 671–88.

13 Michael Aung-Thwin, *Myth and History in the Historiography of Early Burma:
Paradigms, Primary Sources, and Prejudices* (Athens and Singapore, 1998),
ch. 3.

14 Aung-Thwin, *Pagan*, ch. 9.

15 Michael Aung-Thwin, 'Spirals in Burmese and Early Southeast Asian
History', *Journal of Interdisciplinary History*, XXI/4 (1991), pp. 575–602.

Chapter 5 Ava and Pegu: A Tale of Two Kingdoms

1 A facsimile of this chapter was published by Michael Aung-Thwin, 'A Tale of
Two Kingdoms: Ava and Pegu in the Fifteenth Century', *Journal of Southeast
Asian Studies*, XLII/1 (2011), pp. 1–16.

2 G. E. Harvey, *A History of Burma: From the Earliest Times to 10 March 1824:
The Beginning of the English Conquest* (London, 1925), pp. 73, 106; D.G.E.
Hall, *Burma* (London and New York, 1950), p. 32; Sao Saimong Mangrai,
'The Shan States and the British Annexation', *Cornell Southeast Asia Program
Data Papers*, 57 (Ithaca, NY, 1965), p. 49; Than Tun, 'History of Burma: A.D.
1300–1400', *Journal of the Burma Research Society*, XXXXII (1959), pp. 131, 133;
Victor B. Lieberman, *Burmese Administrative Cycles: Anarchy and Conquest,
c. 1580–1760* (Princeton, NJ, 1984), p. 15.

3 Michael Aung-Thwin, *The Mists of Ramanna: The Legend that was Lower
Burma* (Honolulu, 2005).

4 Hall, *Burma*; Sir Arthur Phayre, *History of Burma Including Burma Proper,
Pegu, Taungu, Tenasserim, and Arakan* (London, 1883); Harvey, *History*, and
Maung Htin Aung, *History of Burma* (New York, 1967).

5 For the problematization of this issue see Michael Aung-Thwin, 'The Myth
of the "Three Shan Brothers" and the Ava Period in Burmese History',
Journal of Asian Studies, LV (1996), pp. 881–901.

6 Hall, *Burma*, p. 32. It is not that Pagan did not produce good literature; it did,
and indeed surpassed Ava's in several respects. Only, literature at Pagan was
dominated by Pali (the 'classical' language of the clergy and the Buddhist
scriptures), its subject-matter was mainly religious in nature, and its structure
was decidedly taken from Indic forms. In contrast, although Ava retained
many religious themes, especially those taken from the *Jatakas* (birth stories
of the Buddha), almost all its literature was written in Old Burmese, much
of which was conspicuously secular and expressed in new forms of verse
heretofore not evident in the records.

7 The information for this reconstruction of Ava is contained in Michael Aung-
Thwin's yet unpublished book-length manuscript, 'Ava and Pegu: A Tale of
Two Kingdoms' from which the synopsis for the article cited in note 1 is
taken. The original sources used in this reconstruction are cited and explained
in the manuscript. They are also found in Aung-Thwin's *Myth and History in
the Historiography of Early Burma: Paradigms, Primary Sources, and Prejudices*

(Athens and Singapore, 1998) and *The Mists of Ramanna* and *Pagan: the Origins of Modern Burma*. If one reads Old Burmese, these can be found in G. H. Luce and Pe Maung Tin, eds, *Selections From the Inscriptions of Pagan* (Rangoon, 1928), *Inscriptions of Burma*, 5 vols (Rangoon, 1933–56) and *She Haung Myanma Kyauksa Mya* [Ancient Stone Inscriptions of Myanmar], 6 vols (Yangon, 1972–present). One of the most important 'chronicles' for the reconstruction of Pegu is Amatgyi Bannya Dala's *Yazadarit Ayedawpon* [The Royal Crisis Account of Yazadarit] (Yangon, 1974) in Burmese.

8 Harvey, *History*, p. 107.

9 For an elaboration of this analysis, see Michael Aung-Thwin, 'Mranma Pran: When Context Encounters Notion', *Journal of Southeast Asian Studies*, XXXIX/2 (2008), pp. 193–217.

10 The myth concerning Ramanna and Lower Burma is explained in Aung-Thwin, *The Mists of Ramanna*.

11 But as noted previously the new state temple is one foot lower than the Shwedagon, not mere coincidence, but a deliberate attempt at acknowledging the latter's stature.

12 Victor B. Lieberman, 'Excising the "Mon Paradigm" from Burmese Historiography', *Journal of Southeast Asian Studies*, XXXVIII (2007), pp. 377–83.

13 Although this 'upstream–downstream' paradigm has been for long an important part of the historiography of Southeast Asia, it has not been part of Myanmar's until recently. See Michael Aung-Thwin, 'Lower Burma and Bago in the History of Burma', in *The Maritime Frontier of Burma: Exploring Political, Cultural and Commercial Interaction in the Indian Ocean World, 1200–1800*, ed. Jos Gommans and Jacques Leider (Leiden, 2002).

14 Sun Laichen, 'Ming-Southeast Asian Overland Interactions, 1368–1644', (PhD, University of Michigan, 2000).

Chapter 6 The 'Early Modern' Experiment

1 Depending on how one counts, Rangoon was de facto 'capital' for at most a century, but formally only since 1948; hence the nearly 60 years.

2 Anthony Reid, *Southeast Asia in the Age of Commerce: 1450–1680, Volume One: The Lands below the Winds* (New Haven, CT, 1988).

3 For the central role of the Malay speakers in the commercial history of maritime Southeast Asia, see Leonard Andaya's recent work, *Leaves of the Same Tree: Trade and Ethnicity in the Straits of Melaka* (Honolulu 2008).

4 A Portuguese adventurer wrote that Martaban's (Muttama's) annual revenues were '3 million of Gold'. He also noted that 100 million in gold was taken and another 12 million left for Tabinshwehti's soldiers to plunder. The king reportedly also received 6,000 cannon and 100,000 *quintals* (100 base units) of pepper. See Manuel de Faria e Sousa, *The Portugues Asia: Or, the Discovery and Conquest of India by the Portugues*, trans. Captain John Stevens, vol. III (Farnborough, 1971), pp. 350–1.

5 Although Faria e Sousa recorded that this event took place in 1544, most of the record fits the 1541 event.

6 G. E. Harvey, *A History of Burma: From the Earliest Times to 10 March 1824: The Beginning of the English Conquest* (London, 1925), p. 161.

7 It is interesting that precisely the opposite tactic was used in the 2007 so-called

'Saffron Revolution' when laymen *donned the robe* to do much the same thing.

8 Harvey, *History*, p. 162.

9 Faria e Sousa, *The Portugues*, pp. 359–60.

10 Sunait Chutintaranond, '"Cakravartin": The Ideology of Traditional Warfare in Siam and Burma, 1548–1605' (PhD, Cornell University, 1990).

11 Michael Aung-Thwin, 'Heaven, Earth and the Supernatural World: Dimensions of the Exemplary Center in Burmese History,' in *The City As a Sacred Center: Essays on Six Asian Contexts. International Studies in Sociology and Social Anthropology*, ed. Holy Baker Reynolds and Bardwell Smith (Leiden, 1987), pp. 88–102.

12 Ava, however, is a bit of a puzzle. The original rectangular citadel that housed the innermost square in which stood the palace had nine gates instead of the usual twelve. Thereafter an additional walled area was added to the central citadel on its south and west sides that enlarged the city itself, wherein presumably lived much of the population. This formed an additional defensive perimeter which most likely followed the contour of the land than any particular cosmological pattern. The larger city is most likely a seventeenth-century addition by the Second Ava Dynasty, whereas the smaller original citadel is the product of the First Ava Dynasty, which experienced increased Chinese influences which may account for the nine gates.

13 There are some problems with some of this information, however. First, the recent reconstructions made during the 1990s and early 2000s changed the original direction that both the Lion Throne and the *Myenan* faced; they now face east. Why this was done is not entirely clear. But apparently there was some controversy in the early and mid-1990s regarding the inauspicious (Western) direction these structures originally faced, which created a rift between some Myanmar historians, the Ministry of Culture and certain segments of the Pegu Sangha. As a result the Government stepped in to force a compromise amongst the contending parties, resulting in the changes noted above. At least this is the way the controversy was (subtly) presented in the Burmese language newspapers, the *Thuriya*, *Myanma Alin* and particularly the *Kye Hmon* (*The Mirror*). The latter published a series of articles between August of 1993 and September 1995 and again subsequently when the palace was opened to the public.

14 Cesar Frederick, *Voyages and Travels of Cesar Frederick in India* (Edinburgh, 1811). Most easily accessible is the downloadable version reproduced in the *SOAS Bulletin of Burma Research*, II/2 (2004).

15 The Burmese calendar has eight days in a week, Wednesday being divided into two, a dark (inauspicious) side and a light (auspicious) side. However, U Kala puts Bayinnaung's birth date at 7 am (on the auspicious side), so that issue remains controversial. See his *Mahayazawingyi* [Great Royal Chronicle], vol. III, ed. Saya Pwa (Yangon, 1960), p. 65.

16 For an extensive analysis of this dynasty as well as the next, see Victor B. Lieberman's *Burmese Administrative Cycles: Anarchy and Conquest, c. 1580–1760* (Princeton, NJ, 1984). U Thaw Kaung's 'Accounts of King Bayinnaung's Life and *Hanthawady Hsinbyu-myashin Ayedawbon*, a Record of his Campaigns', *Myanmar Historical Research Journal*, 11 (June 2003), pp. 23–42 is a more recent analysis of the most important existing historical sources on Bayinnaung.

17 Other interpretations of Pegu's decline can also be found in Victor B.

Lieberman, *Strange Parallels: Southeast Asia in Global Context, c. 800–1830* (Cambridge, 2003).

18 Harvey, *History*, pp. 183–4.

19 This issue of tyranny versus anarchy is elaborated in Michael Aung-Thwin, 'Parochial Universalism, Democracy *Jihad*, and the Orientalist Image of Burma: The New Evangelism', *Pacific Affairs*, LXXIV/4 (2001/2), pp. 483–505.

Chapter 7 Return to the 'Heartland'

1 Much of the story for this chapter is taken from U Kala's *Mahayazawingyi*, vol. III. The closest rendition in English to the Burmese narrative is G. E. Harvey's *A History of Burma*. For a modern analysis and interpretation of this dynasty see the reconstruction by Victor B. Lieberman, *Burmese Administrative Cycles: Anarchy and Conquest, c. 1580–1760* (Princeton, NJ, 1984).

2 D.G.E. Hall calls it the 'Later Toungoo Dynasty' and Lieberman, the 'Restored Toungoo Dynasty'.

3 Hla Pe, *Burma: Literature, Historiography, Scholarship, Language, Life, and Buddhism* (Singapore, 1985), p. 11.

4 W. O. Dijk, *Seventeenth-century Burma and the Dutch East India Company, 1634–1680* (Singapore, 2006).

5 By the time this palace was built, its configuration may have returned to a traditional form whereby the women's quarters were once again on the west side, rather than on the east as in Bayinnaung's palace.

6 Aung-Thwin, 'Spirals in Burmese and Early Southeast Asian History', *Journal of Interdisciplinary History*, XXI/4 (1991), pp. 575–602.

7 Hla Pe, *Burma*, pp. 12–13.

8 This stems from an older (sixteenth-century) story which was used to legitimate the thirteenth-century Wagaru Dynasty.

Chapter 8 The Last Myanmar Dynasty

1 A detailed narrative of this period and its implications to the broader history of the country can be found in Victor B. Lieberman's *Burmese Administrative Cycles: Anarchy and Conquest, c. 1580–1760* (Princeton, NJ, 1984), ch. 5. For a treatment of the general structure of the patron–client system see Michael Aung-Thwin, '*Athi, Kyun Taw, Hpaya Kyun*: Varieties of Commendation and Dependence in Pre-Colonial Myanmar', in *Slavery, Bondage and Dependency in Southeast Asia*, ed. Anthony Reid (New York, 1983).

2 Michael Aung-Thwin, 'Prophecies, Omens, and Dialogue: Tools of the Trade in Burmese Historiography', in *Moral Order and the Question of Change: Essays on Southeast Asian Thought*, ed. David K. Wyatt and Alexander Woodside (New Haven, CT, 1982), pp. 78–103.

3 Lieberman, *Burmese Administrative Cycles*.

4 Victor B. Lieberman, 'Ethnic Politics in Eighteenth-Century Burma', *Modern Asian Studies*, XII/3 (1978), pp. 455–82.

5 For example, see D.G.E. Hall, *Burma* (London and New York, 1950), pp. 41, 43, 94.

6 The *Chronicle of Ayutthaya: A Translation of the Yodaya Yazawin* (Yangon,

2005), p. 122, ed. Tun Aung Chain, simply stated that Ayutthaya 'fell'. The Burmese chronicle that contains this narrative, the *Konbaungset Mahayaza-windawgyi* [The Great Royal Chronicle of the Konbaung Dynasty], ed. Maung Maung Tin (Yangon, 1969), vol. I, pp. 411–15, also stated that many cannon and firearms were taken, but those they could not take with them were either destroyed or thrown into the ocean. No conflagration is recorded, although the 'moat' and walls were said to have been destroyed. The details in the latter record are supported by the Thai 'chronicle' written by Prince Damrong of the present dynasty whose account was translated into English by U Aung Thein in a series of articles in the *Journal of the Burma Research Society* between 1938 and 1957 (listed in the Bibliography). However, there are French reports that the Portuguese and French quarters of Ayuthaya were burned down. (Pers. comm., Kennon Breazeale, 10 May 2010.)

7 *Konbaungset*, I, pp. 459–86. Although both the Burmese and Chinese accounts provided their perspective of things, the *Konbaungset* was rather matter-of-fact, while the Chinese accounts, at least according to Parker's interpretation, were less so. It seems obvious that the Burmese won this particular campaign as the Chinese generals were executed for failure upon their return. Moreover, the Chinese Emperor was said to have instructed his forces to withdraw because of the heavy losses, but reportedly stated that he 'out of sheer compassion . . . had decided not to annihilate them [the Burmese] as they deserved'. See Edward Harper Parker, *Burma: With Special Reference to her Relations With China* (Rangoon, 1893), p. 72.

8 Prime Minister U Nu of the Union of Burma and President Ne Win of the Socialist Republic of the Union of Myanma built their respective works of merit during their tenure as heads of state. Their successors continue to do likewise.

9 D.G.E. Hall refers to the collection of these inquests as the 'Doomesday Book' in *Burma*, p. 67. Many of the edicts have been translated into English and published in Than Tun, *The Royal Orders of Burma, A.D. 1598–1885*, 10 vols (Kyoto, 1983–90).

10 For the complex of factors involved in the most recent move, see Michael Aung-Thwin, 'Shift of Capital in Burma', *Asian Studies Newsletter* (2006), p. 9.

11 Michael Aung-Thwin, 'Divinity, Spirit, and Human: Conceptions of Classical Burmese Kingship', in *Centers, Symbols and Hierarchies: Essays on the Classical States of Southeast Asia*, ed. Lorraine Gesick (New Haven, CT, 1983), pp. 45–86.

12 Many of these depositions remain in the original Burmese. One of the earliest collections published was J. S. Furnivall and Pe Maung Tin's edition of *Zambudipa Okhsaung Kyan* (Yangon, 1960). Yi Yi translated some of these records into English in Frank N. Trager and William J. Koenig's edition of *Burmese Sit-tans 1764–1826: Records of Rural Life and Administration* (Tucson, AZ, 1979).

13 Father Sangermano, *A Description of the Burmese Empire Compiled chiefly from Burmese documents by Father Sangermano*, trans. William Tandy (New York, 1969), p. 75.

14 G. E. Harvey, *A History of Burma: From the Earliest Times to 10 March 1824: the Beginning of the English Conquest* (London, 1925), p. 276.

15 For an interpretation different from most English-language press accounts of

the so-called 'saffron-revolution' of 2007, see Michael Aung-Thwin, 'Of Monarchs, Monks, and Men: Religion and the State in Myanmar', *Asia Research Institute Working Paper Series* (2009), pp. 2–31.

16 Hiram Cox, *Journal of a Residence in the Burmham Empire and More Particularly at the Court of Amarapoorah* (London, 1821).

17 Aung-Thwin, 'Divinity, Spirit, and Human', pp. 45–86.

18 Michael Aung-Thwin, 'Principles and Patterns of the Precolonial Burmese State', in *Tradition and Modernity in Myanmar: Proceedings of an International Conference Held in Berlin from May 7th to May 9th, 1993*, ed. Uta Gartner and Jens Lorenz (Berlin, 1994), p. 32.

19 Thant Myint U, *The Making of Modern Burma* (New York, 2001), pp. 58–9; D.G.E. Hall, *Burma*, pp. 106, 108.

20 Harvey, *History*, p. 294.

21 Dorothy Woodman, *The Making of Burma* (London, 1962) is an exhaustive and scholarly treatment of all three wars, particularly the role that Commodore Lambert played in single-handedly starting the Second Anglo–Burmese War, but for which Mindon was ultimately held accountable.

22 Reverend Marks, *Forty Years in Burma* (London, 1917).

23 Woodman, *Making of Burma*, ch. 11, pp. 231–5.

24 Pagan U Tin, *The Royal Administration of Burma*, trans. Euan Bagshawe (Bangkok, 2001), p. 26.

25 Pe Maung Tin, ed., *Kinwun Mingyi's London Diary*, 2 vols (Rangoon, 1953–4).

26 Yi Yi, 'Burmese Sources for the History of the Konbaung Period 1752–1885', *Journal of Southeast Asian Studies*, VI (1965), pp. 48–66.

Chapter 9 Disintegration of the Burmese Kingdom, 1824–1886

1 See Dorothy Woodman, *The Making of Burma* (London, 1962) and Oliver Pollack, *Empires in Collision: Anglo-Burmese Relations in the Mid Nineteenth-Century* (Westport, CT, 1979).

2 Dalhousie explicitly instructed Phayre to include these teak forests as part of the spoils of war. See D.G.E. Hall, *The Dalhousie–Phayre Correspondence, 1852–1856* (London, 1932).

3 Michael Aung-Thwin, 'A Tale of Two Kingdoms: Ava and Pegu in the Fifteenth Century', *Journal of Southeast Asian Studies*, XLII/1 (2011), pp. 1–16.

4 Parimal Ghosh, *Brave Men of the Hills: Resistance and Rebellion in Burma, 1825–1932* (London, 2000).

5 John Cady, *A History of Modern Burma* (Ithaca, NY, 1958).

Chapter 10 Reintegration and British Burma, 1886–1942

1 Ian Brown, *A Colonial Economy in Crisis: Burma's Rice Cultivators and the World Depression of the 1930s* (London, 2005).

2 Bernard S. Cohn, *An Anthropologist among the Historians and Other Essays* (New York, 1987).

3 Thomas R. Metcalf, *Imperial Connections: India in the Indian Ocean Arena, 1860–1920* (Berkeley, CA, 2007).

4 Mandy Sadan, 'Constructing and Contesting the Category of "Kachin" in the

Colonial and post-Colonial Burmese State', *Exploring Ethnic Diversity in Burma*, ed. Mikael Gravers (Copenhagen, 2007).

5 John Cady, *A History of Modern Burma* (Ithaca, NY, 1958).

6 Robert H. Taylor, *The State in Myanmar* (Honolulu, 2009).

7 E. Michael Mendelson, *Sangha and State in Burma: A Study of Monastic Sectarianism and Leadership*, ed. John P. Ferguson (Ithaca, NY, 1975). See also Michael Aung-Thwin, 'Of Monarchs, Monks, and Men: Religion and the State in Myanmar', *Asia Research Institute Working Paper Series*, 127 (2009), pp. 2–31.

8 Michael Adas, *The Burma Delta: Economic Development and Social Change on an Asian Rice Frontier, 1852–1941* (Madison, WI, 1974).

9 Siok-hwa Cheng, *The Rice Industry of Burma, 1852–1940* (Kuala Lumpur, 1968).

10 Chie Ikeya, *Refiguring Women, Colonialism, and Modernity in Burma* (Honolulu, HI, 2011).

11 Taylor, *The State in Myanmar*.

12 Cady, *A History of Modern Burma*.

13 Taylor, *The State in Myanmar*.

14 James C. Scott, *The Moral Economy of the Peasant: Rebellion and Subsistence in Southeast Asia* (New Haven, CT, 1976).

15 Maitrii Aung-Thwin, *The Return of the Galon King: History, Law, and Rebellion in Colonial Burma* (Athens, OH, 2011).

Chapter 11 Fragmentation and the Union of Myanmar, 1942–1962

1 John Cady, *A History of Modern Burma* (Ithaca, NY, 1958).

2 Mary P. Callahan, *Making Enemies: War and State Building in Burma*, (Ithaca, NY, 2003). For the Japanese occupation of the country and the BIA's role, see Dorothy Hess Guyot, 'The political impact of the Japanese occupation of Burma' (PhD, Yale University, 1966).

3 Robert H. Taylor, *The State in Myanmar* (Honolulu, HI, 2009).

4 Theippan Maung Wa, *Wartime in Burma: A Diary, January to June 1942*, trans. and ed. L. E. Bagshawe and Anna Allot (Athens, OH, 2009).

5 Journal Kyaw U Chit Maung, *A Man Like Him: Portrait of the Burmese Journalist Journal Kyaw U Chit Maung*, trans. Ma Thanegi (Ithaca, NY, 2008).

6 Callahan, *Making Enemies*.

7 Taylor, *The State in Myanmar*, pp. 229–31.

8 Cady, *A History of Modern Burma*.

9 Angelene Naw, *Aung San and the Struggle for Burmese Independence* (Chiang Mai, 2001), p. 215 has a detailed account of the assassination.

10 Taylor, *The State in Myanmar*.

11 D.G.E. Hall, *Burma* (London and New York, 1950), pp. 187–9.

12 Callahan, *Making Enemies*, pp. 187–8.

13 Taylor, *The State in Myanmar*, p. 250.

14 Michael Aung-Thwin, 'Introduction', in Ma Ma Lay, *Blood Bond*, trans. Than Than Win, ed. Michael Aung-Thwin, University of Hawai'i Center for Southeast Asian Studies Translation Series (Honolulu, 2004), p. 9.

Chapter 12 Reconstruction and Nation-Building, 1962–2011

1 Robert H. Taylor, *The State in Myanmar* (Honolulu, HI, 2009).
2 Ma Ma Lay, *Not out of Hate: A Novel of Burma*, trans. Margaret Aung-Thwin (Athens, OH, 1991).
3 Michael Aung-Thwin, '1948 and Burma's Myth of Independence', in *Independent Burma at Forty Years: Six Assessments*, ed. Josef Silverstein (Ithaca, NY, 1989), pp. 19–34.
4 Although Dr Maung Maung's *The 1988 Uprising in Burma* (New Haven, CT, 1999) goes far to describe those events from the 'inside' – that is, from the view of the most important people in Government who were involved – there is still no scholarly treatment of that important year.
5 Local media reports on these decapitations are extensive and graphic, although only some of them reached the outside world. See, for example, the AP report in the *Los Angeles Times* for 10 August 1988 with the headline, '3 Policemen Beheaded in Burma Riots'; and *Asiaweek: Eyewitness Reports*, for 26 August 1988.
6 For this incident, see Dr Maung Maung's *Uprising in Burma*, p. 172, and chs 10–11. Many of these events have been documented in the domestic and even international media for the months of July and August 1988.
7 See Aung San Suu Kyi, *Freedom from Fear and Other Writings* (New York, 1991).
8 As quoted in Derek Tonkin, 'The 1990 Elections in Myanmar: Broken Promises or a Failure of Communication?', *Contemporary Southeast Asia*, XXIX/1 (2007), pp. 33–54. Her original interview with Dominic Faulder can be found in *Asiaweek*, 21 July 1989.
9 Ibid.
10 The State Peace and Development Council (SPDC) had replaced SLORC in terms of most personnel, some policies and name by 15 November 1997, so that the credit for these ceasefires must go to both.
11 Reuters, 22 September 2007.
12 For a short treatment of this event within a larger context of the history of the Sangha, see Michael Aung-Thwin, 'Of Monarchs, Monks, and Men: Religion and the State in Myanmar', *Asia Research Institute Working Paper Series*, 127 (2009), pp. 2–31, esp. Appendix 1, p. 25 which showed that the National Endowment for Democracy, an alleged non-partisan organization, gave approximately US $15,000 in 2006 (the year before the 2007 protests) to 'educate' monks within 'Burma' about non-violent 'struggle for democracy'. This information, found in the public domain, is given below verbatim. It was accessible on the website of the National Endowment for Democracy. The relevant part reads: 'The 2006 Budget of the National Endowment for Democracy. $15,000: A. Internal Organizing and Coalition-Building. To monitor the human rights situation in Burma and educate monks and Buddhist lay people about the nonviolent struggle for democracy in Burma. The organization will produce and distribute material, including pamphlets, stickers, and calendars, on human rights and democracy and support efforts to organize the Buddhist community inside Burma.' The question, of course, is how was that US $15,000 converted into Burmese kyats, for the NED does not have a license to do so in the country?
13 It was reported that monks' robes were sold out during that week in Yangon, something that has not happened even during the 'robe giving' season.

14 The text of the published version is bilingual (Burmese and English) as is the title, which reads: *Constitution of the Republic of the Union of Myanmar (2008) Pyidaungzu Thamada Myanma Naingnandaw Phwesipon Achekhan Upade* (Yangon, Ministry of Information, 2008). Electronic versions are readily available at various websites, including *Network Myanmar*, one of the most credible, run by Derek Tonkin, former British Ambassador to Vietnam and Thailand. See www.networkmyanmar.org.

15 Taylor, *The State in Myanmar*, p. 487.

16 There are numerous analyses and reports, each counting the votes in different ways. But the Union Election Commission's final report in the *Myanma Alin* of Wednesday 8 December 2010, pp. 1, 9 has the most detailed set of figures, including the number of votes cast, invalid votes, and valid votes on each of the three *Hlutdaws*. See also Richard Horsey, 'Outcome of the Myanmar Elections', *SSRC Conflict Prevention and Peace Forum* (17 November 2010). When this report was compiled, not all the data was yet available from the Union Election Commission and so it may have a few minor discrepancies. Most of the information on the elections is archived at *Network Myanmar*, cited in note 14 above.

17 See Horsey, 'Outcome of the Myanmar Elections', p. 1: 'Election day itself was peaceful, and the voting took place in an overwhelmingly calm (even subdued) atmosphere'. Irregularities, of course, were also reported by others, cited elsewhere.

18 It is interesting to note that whereas less than one quarter of the Shan population in the country voted with the 'Shan' party about two-thirds of the Arakanese population voted with the 'Arakanese' (Rakhine) party.

19 For example, see Burma Fund– UN Office, *Burma's 2010 Elections: A Comprehensive Report* (New York, 2011) whose political agenda is clear, and also International Crisis Group, 'Myanmar's Post-Election Landscape', *Crisis Group Asia Briefing*, 118 (Jakarta/Brussels, 2011) which tried to be objective but the biases are obvious.

20 David I. Steinberg, 'Is Burma Finally Poised for Change?', *Pacific Forum*, 3 (Honolulu, HI, 2011).

21 Horsey, 'Outcome of the Myanmar Elections', p. 8, has 1,157 although the *Crisis Group Asia Briefing* report gives 1,154, p. 171.

22 Most illustrative of this development, described in an earlier chapter, is the building of bridges across the 1,100 mile Irrawaddy. Before 1988 there was one that traversed it, the Sagaing Bridge. Today there are well over a dozen that link the River's west and east banks. For more detailed figures on this infrastructural development see Michael Aung-Thwin with Carl Hefner, 'Making of Modern Burma', CD-ROM (2001).

23 Pers. comm., Robert H. Taylor, 13 June 2011.

24 'President U Thein Sein Delivers Inaugural Address to Pyidaungsu Hluttaw', *The New Light of Myanmar* (31 March 2011).

25 Eric Bellman, 'Indonesia Minister Proposes Rewarding Myanmar', *The Wall Street Journal* (8 November 2011).

26 Steven Orlowski, 'Jim Rogers: "Myanmar Best Investment Opportunity in the World"', *Emerging Money* (16 July 2012).

27 This does not surprise us, since we know some of the academics involved in the writing of the 2008 Constitution, most of whom are highly respected historians and well known in the country.

Bibliography

Adas, Michael, *The Burma Delta: Economic Development and Social Change on an Asian Rice Frontier, 1852–1941* (Madison, WI, 1974)

Andaya, Leonard Y., *Leaves of the Same Tree: Trade and Ethnicity in the Straits of Melaka* (Honolulu, HI, 2008)

Aung Myint, *Kaung Kin Dat Pon Mya Hma Myanma She Haung Myo Taw Mya* [Ancient Royal Cities of Myanmar from Aerial Photographs] (Yangon, 1998)

Aung San, *Burma's Challenge* (Yangon, 1974)

Aung San Suu Kyi, *Freedom from Fear and Other Writings* (New York, 1991)

Aung Thaw, *Excavations at Beikthano* (Rangoon, 1968)

——, 'Expert team conducting research on ancient objects unearthed in Budalin Township', *Myanmar Alin* (1999), pp. 5, 12

——, *Historical Sites in Burma* (Rangoon, 1972)

——, 'The 'Neolithic' culture of the Padah-lin Caves', *Asian Perspectives*, XIV (1973), pp. 123–33

Aung Thein (Phra Phraison Salarak), 'Intercourse between Siam and Burma', *Journal of the Burma Research Society*, XXV/2 (1935), pp. 49–108

——, 'Intercourse between Siam and Burma', *Journal of the Burma Research Society*, XXVIII/2 (1938), pp. 109–76

——, 'Our Wars with the Burmese', *Journal of the Burma Research Society*, XL/2 (1957), pp. 135–238

——, 'Our Wars with the Burmese', *Journal of the Burma Research Society*, XL/2(a) (1957), pp. 241–345

——, 'Our Wars with the Burmese', *Journal of the Burma Research Society*, XXXVI–II/2 (1955), pp. 121–96

Aung-Thwin, Maitrii, 'British Counter-Insurgency Narratives and the Construction of a Twentieth-Century Burmese Rebel' (PhD, University of Michigan, 2001)

——, *The Return of the Galon King: History, Law, and Rebellion in Colonial Burma* (Athens, OH, 2010)

——, 'Structuring Revolt: Communities of Interpretation in the Historiography of the Saya San Rebellion', *Journal of Southeast Asian Studies*, XXXIX/2 (2008), pp. 297–317

Aung-Thwin, Michael, '1948 and Burma's Myth of Independence', in *Independent Burma at Forty Years: Six Assessments*, ed. Josef Silverstein (Ithaca, NY, 1989), pp. 19–34

——, 'A New/Old Look at "Classical" and "Post-Classical" Southeast Asia/Burma', in *New Perspectives on the History and Historiography of Southeast Asia: Continuing Explorations*, ed. Michael Aung-Thwin and Kenneth R. Hall (London, 2011), pp. 25–55

——, '*Athi, Kyun Taw, Hpaya Kyun*: Varieties of Commendation and Dependence in Pre-Colonial Burma', in *Slavery, Bondage and Dependency in Southeast Asia*, ed. Anthony Reid (New York, 1983), pp. 64–89

——, 'Ava and Pegu: A Tale of Two Kingdoms', unpublished manuscript

——, 'A Tale of Two Kingdoms: Ava and Pegu in the Fifteenth Century', *Journal of Southeast Asian Studies*, XLII/1 (2011), pp. 1–16

——, 'The British "Pacification" of Burma: Order without Meaning', *Journal of Southeast Asian Studies*, XVI (1985), pp. 245–61

——, 'Burma', in *Encyclopedia of Asian History*, ed. Ainslie T. Embree (New York, 1988), pp. 202–4

——, 'Burma before Pagan: The Status of Archaeology Today', *Asian Perspectives*, XXV (1982–3), pp. 1–21

——, 'Burmese Historiography-Chronicles (*Yazawin*)', in *Making History: A Global Encyclopedia of Historical Writing*, ed. D. R. Woolf (New York, 1997), pp. 119–22

——, 'The "Classical" in Southeast Asia: The Present in the Past', *Journal of Southeast Asian Studies*, XXVI/1 (1995), pp. 75–91

——, 'Divinity, Spirit, and Human: Conceptions of Classical Burmese Kingship', in *Centers, Symbols and Hierarchies: Essays on the Classical States of Southeast Asia*, ed. Lorraine Gesick (New Haven, CT, 1983), pp. 45–86

——, 'Heaven, Earth and the Supernatural World: Dimensions of the Exemplary Center in Burmese History', in *The City As a Sacred Center: Essays on Six Asian Contexts*, ed. Holy Baker Reynolds and Bardwell Smith (Leiden, 1987), pp. 88–102

——, '*Hmannan Mahayazawindawgyi* [The Great Royal Chronicle of the Glass Palace]', in *Making History: A Global Encyclopedia of Historical Writing*, ed. D. R. Woolf (New York, 1998), pp. 417–19

——, *Irrigation in the Heartland of Burma: Foundations of the Pre-Colonial Burmese State* (DeKalb, IL, 1990)

——, 'Jambudipa: Classical Burma's Camelot', *Contributions to Asian Studies*, XVI (1981), pp. 38–61

——, 'Kingship in Southeast Asia', in *Encyclopedia of Religion*, ed. Mircea Eliade (New York, 1987), pp. 333–6

——, 'The Legend that Was Lower Burma', in *International Conference on Texts and Contexts* (Yangon, 2001)

——, 'Lower Burma and Bago in the History of Burma', in *The Maritime Frontier of Burma: Exploring Political, Cultural and Commercial Interaction in the Indian Ocean World, 1200–1800*, ed. Jos Gommans and Jacques Leider (Leiden, 2002), pp. 25–57

——, *The Mists of Ramanna: The Legend that Was Lower Burma* (Honolulu, 2005)

——, 'Mranma Pran: When Context Encounters Notion', *Journal of Southeast Asian Studies*, XXXIX/2 (2008), pp. 193–217

——, *Myth and History in the Historiography of Early Burma: Paradigms, Primary Sources, and Prejudices* (Athens and Singapore, 1998)

——, 'The Myth of the "Three Shan Brothers" and the Ava Period in Burmese

History', *Journal of Asian Studies*, LV/4 (1996), pp. 881–901

——, 'Of Monarchs, Monks, and Men: Religion and the State in Myanmar', *Asia Research Institute Working Paper Series*, 127 (2009), pp. 2–31

——, 'Origins and Development of the Field of Prehistory in Burma', *Asian Perspectives Special Issue: The Archaeology of Myanma Pyay (Burma)*, XL/1 (2001), pp. 6–34

——, *Pagan: the Origins of Modern Burma* (Honolulu, 1985)

——, 'Parochial Universalism, Democracy *Jihad*, and the Orientalist Image of Burma: the New Evangelism', *Pacific Affairs*, LXXIV/4 (2001/2), pp. 483–505

——, 'Principles and Patterns of the Precolonial Burmese State', in *Tradition and Modernity in Myanmar: Proceedings of an International Conference Held in Berlin from May 7th to May 9th, 1993*, ed. Uta Gartner and Jens Lorenz (Berlin, 1994), pp. 15–44

——, 'The Problem of Ceylonese–Burmese Relations in the Twelfth Century and the Question of an Interregnum in Pagán: 1165–1174 A.D.', *Journal of the Siam Society*, LXIV (1976), pp. 53–74

——, 'Prophecies, Omens, and Dialogue: Tools of the Trade in Burmese Historiography ', in *Historical Essays in Honor of Kenneth R. Rossman*, ed. Kent Newmyer (Lincoln, NE, 1980), pp. 171–85

——, 'A Reply to Lieberman', *Journal of Asian Studies*, XL/1 (1980), pp. 87–90

——, 'The Role of *Sasana* Reform in Burmese History, Economic Dimensions of a Religious Purification', *Journal of Asian Studies*, XXXVIII/4 (1979), pp. 671–88

——, 'Shift of Capital in Burma', *Asian Studies Newsletter* (2006), p. 9

——, 'Spirals in Burmese and Early Southeast Asian History', *Journal of Interdisciplinary History*, XXI/4 (1991), pp. 575–602

——, 'Toungoo and Burma in Southeast Asian History', *Journal of Southeast Asian Studies*, XVI (1985), pp. 150–8

Aung-Thwin, Michael with Carl Hefner, 'Making of Modern Burma', CD-ROM (2001)

Ba Maw, 'Research on the Early Man in Myanmar', *Myanmar Historical Research Journal*, I (1995), pp. 213–20

Ba Maw *et al.*, 'Artifacts of Anyathian Cultures Found in a Single Site', in *Essays Given to Than Tun on His 75th Birthday: Studies in Myanma History* (Yangon, 1999), pp. 7–15

Ba Shin, ed., *Essays offered to G. H. Luce by His Colleagues and Friends in Honour of His Seventy-Fifth Birthday*, 2 vols (Ascona, 1966)

Bannya Dala, *Yazadarit Ayedawpon* [The Royal Crisis Account of Yazadarit] (Yangon, 1974)

Bellwood, Peter, 'Southeast Asia before History', in *The Cambridge History of Southeast Asia. Volume One: From Early Times to c. 1800*, ed. Nicholas Tarling (Cambridge, 1992), pp. 55–136

Benda, Harry J., 'The Structure of Southeast Asian History: Some Preliminary Observations', *Journal of Southeast Asian History*, III (1962), pp. 106–38

Bennett, Paul J., 'The "Fall of Pagan": Continuity and Change in 14th Century Burma', in *Conference Under the Tamarind Tree: Three Essays in Burmese History* (New Haven, CT, 1971), pp. 3–53

Bode, Mabel Haynes, *The Pali Literature of Burma* (London, 1909)

Burma Fund – UN Office, *Burma's 2010 Elections: A Comprehensive Report* (New York, 2011)

Cady, John, *A History of Modern Burma* (Ithaca, NY, 1958)

Callahan, Mary Patricia, 'The Origins of Military Rule in Burma' (PhD, Cornell University, 1996)

——, *Making Enemies: War and State Building in Burma* (Ithaca, NY, 2003)

Chhibber, Harbans Lal and R. Ramamirtham, *The Geology of Burma* (London, 1934)

Chutintaranond, Sunait, '"Cakravartin": The ideology of traditional warfare in Siam and Burma, 1548–1605' (PhD, Cornell University, 1990)

——, 'King Bayinnaung in Thai Perception, Historical Writings and Literary Works', in *Traditions in Current Perspective* (Yangon, 1996), pp. 59–67

Cooler, Richard M., *British Romantic Views of the First Anglo–Burmese War, 1824–1826* (Dekalb, IL, 1977)

Cox, Hiram, *Journal of a Residence in the Burmham Empire and More Particularly at the Court of Amarapoorah* (London, 1821)

Dalrymple, A., *Reprint from Dalrymple's Oriental Repertory, 1891–7 of Portions Relating to Burma*, vols I–II (Rangoon, 1926)

de Terra, Helmut and H. L. Movius, Jr, 'Research on Early Man in Burma. I – The Pleistocene of Burma by H. de Terra. II – The Stone Age of Burma by H. L. Movius, Jr', *Transactions of the American Philosophical Society*, XXXII (1943), pp. 271–393

Dijk, W. O., *Seventeenth-century Burma and the Dutch East India Company, 1634–1680* (Singapore, 2006)

Duroiselle, Charles, ed., *A List of Inscriptions Found in Burma*, Archaeological Survey of Burma (Rangoon, 1921)

Faria e Sousa, Manuel de, *The Portugues, Asia: Or, the Discovery and Conquest of India by the Portugues*, trans. Captain John Stevens, 3 vols (Farnborough, 1971)

Federici, Cesare, *Voyages and Travels of Cesar Frederick in India* (Edinburgh, 1811), pp. 142–211

Furnivall, J. S. and Pe Maung Tin, eds, *Zambudipa Okhsaung Kyan* (Yangon, 1960)

Goh, Geok Yian, 'Cakkravatiy Anuruddha and the Buddhist Oikoumene: Historical Narratives of Kingship and Religious Networks in Burma, Northern Thailand, and Sri Lanka (11th–14th Centuries)' (PhD, University of Hawaii, 2007)

Grave, Peter and Mike Barbetti, 'Dating the City Wall, Fortifications, and the Palace Site at Pagan', *Asian Perspectives*, XL/1 (2001), pp. 75–87

Gutman, Pamela, 'Ancient Arakan: With Special Reference to its Cultural History between the 5th and 11th Centuries' (PhD Australian National University, 1976)

Gutman, Pamela and Bob Hudson, 'The Archaeology of Burma, from the Neolithic to Pagan', in *Southeast Asia: from Prehistory to History*, ed. Ian Glover and P. Bellwood (Abingdon and New York, 2004), pp. 149–76

Hall, D.G.E., *Burma* (London and New York, 1950)

——, 'The Daghregister of Batavia and Dutch Trade with Burma in the Seventeenth Century', *Journal of the Burma Research Society*, XXIX/2 (1939), pp. 139–56

——, *Early English Intercourse with Burma 1587–1743* (London, 1968)

——, *Europe and Burma: A Study of European Relations with Burma to the Annexation of Thibaw's Kingdom, 1886* (London and New York, 1945)

——, *A History of South-East Asia*, 3rd edn (London, Melbourne and New York, 1968)

——, *Hanthawady Hsinbyumyashin Ayedawbon*, trans. Thaw Kaung and San Lwin, *Myanmar Min Mya Ayedawbon* (Yangon, 1967), pp. 319–95

Harvey, G. E., *A History of Burma: From the Earliest Times to 10 March 1824: The Beginning of the English Conquest* (London, 1925)

Herbert, Patricia M., *The Hsaya San Rebellion (1930–1932) Reappraised* (London and Clayton, Australia, 1982)

Hla Pe, *Burma: Literature, Historiography, Scholarship, Language, Life, and Buddhism* (Singapore, 1985)

Horsey, Richard, 'Outcome of the Myanmar Elections', *SSRC Conflict Prevention and Peace Forum* (17 November 2010)

Htin Aung, *History of Burma* (New York, 1967)

Hudson, Bob, 'The King of "Free Rabbit" Island: A GIS-Based Archaeological Approach to Myanmar's Medieval Capital, Bagan', in *Myanmar Two Millennium Conference* (Yangon, 2000), pp. 10–20

——, 'Iron in Myanmar', *Enchanting Myanmar*, V (2006), pp. 6–9

——, 'Myanmar's Early Urban Centres: Some Proposals for Computer Mapping and Analysis of Archaeological Data', in *Traditions of Knowledge in Southeast Asia* (Yangon, 2003)

——, 'The Nyaungyan "Goddesses": Some Unusual Bronze Grave Goods from Upper Burma', *Journal of the Asian Arts Society of Australia*, X/2 (2001), pp. 4–7

——, 'The Origins of Bagan' (PhD, University of Sydney, 2004)

——, 'The Origins of Bagan: New Dates and Old Inhabitants', *Asian Perspectives Special Issue: The Archaeology of Myanma Pyay (Burma)*, XL/1 (2002), pp. 48–74

——, 'A Pyu Homeland in the Samon Valley: A New Theory of the Origins of Myanmar's Early Urban System', in *Myanmar Historical Commission Conference Proceedings* (Yangon, 2005), pp. 59–79

Hudson, Bob and Nyein Lwin, 'Archaeological Excavations and Survey, Yon Hlut Kyun, Bagan, Myanmar: A Preliminary Report', in *Report to Director General of Archaeology* (Yangon, 1999)

Hudson, Bob, Nyein Lwin and Win Maung (Tanpawady), 'Digging for Myths: Archaeological Excavations and Surveys of the Legendary Nineteen Founding Villages of Pagan', in *Asian Perspectives Special Issue: The Archaeology of Myanma Pyay (Burma)*, ed. Miriam T. Stark and Michael Aung-Thwin (Honolulu, 2002)

Huxley, Andrew, ed., *Religion, Law and Tradition: Comparative Studies in Religious Law* (London and New York, 2002)

——, 'Sanction in the Theravada Buddhist Kingdoms of S.E. Asia', *Transactions of the Jean Bodin Society for Comparative Institutional History*, LVIII/4 (1991), pp. 335–70

——, 'Thai, Mon, and Burmese Dhammathats – Who Influenced Whom?' in *Thai Law, Buddhist Law: Essays on the Legal History of Thailand, Laos, and Burma*, ed. Andrew Huxley (Bangkok, 1996)

Ikeya, Chie, *Refiguring Women, Colonialism, and Modernity in Burma* (Honolulu, 2011)

International Crisis Group, 'Myanmar's Post-Election Landscape', *Crisis Group*

Asia Briefing, 118 (Jakarta/Brussels, 2011)

Kala, U., *Mahayazawingyi* [Great Royal Chronicle], ed. Saya Pwa, 3 vols (Yangon, 1960)

Koenig, William J., 'The Burmese Polity, 1752–1819: A Study of Kon Baung Politics, Administration, and Social Organization', *Michigan Papers on South and Southeast Asia*, 34 (Ann Arbor, MI, 1990)

Lach, Donald F., *Southeast Asia in the Eyes of Europe: The Sixteenth Century* (Chicago and London, 1968)

Laichen, Sun, 'Chinese Historical Sources on Burma: A Bibliography of Primary and Secondary Works', *Journal of Burma Studies*, II (1997), pp. 1–116

——, 'Ming–Southeast Asian Overland Interactions, 1368–1644' (PhD, University of Michigan, 2000)

LeBar, Frank M., Gerald Cannon Hickey and John K. Musgrave, eds, *Ethnic Groups of Mainland Southeast Asia* (New Haven, CT, 1964)

Letwe Nawyahta and Twinthintaik Wun, *Alaungmintaya Ayedawpon*, ed. Hla Tin, 2 vols (Yangon, 1961)

Levenson, Joseph R., ed., *European Expansion and the Counter-Example of Asia, 1300–1600* (Englewood Cliffs, NY, 1967)

Lieberman, Victor B., 'An Age of Commerce in Southeast Asia? Problems of Regional Coherence – A Review Article', *Journal of Asian Studies*, LIV/3 (1995), pp. 796–807

——, *Burmese Administrative Cycles: Anarchy and Conquest, c. 1580–1760* (Princeton, NJ, 1984)

——, 'The Burmese Dynastic Pattern, circa 1590–1760: An Administrative and Political Study of the Taung-ngu Dynasty and the Reign of Alaung-phaya' (PhD, University of London, 1976)

——, 'Ethnic Politics in Eighteenth-Century Burma', *Modern Asian Studies*, XII/3 (1978), pp. 455–82

——, 'Excising the "Mon Paradigm" from Burmese Historiography', *Journal of Southeast Asian Studies*, XXXVIII (2007), pp. 377–83

——, 'How Reliable is U Kala's Burmese Chronicle? Some New Comparisons', *Journal of Southeast Asian Studies*, XVII/2 (1986), pp. 236–55

——, 'A New Look at the Sasanavamsa', *Bulletin of the School of Oriental and African Studies*, XXXIX (1976), pp. 137–49

——, 'Reinterpreting Burmese History', *Comparative Studies in Society and History*, XXIX (1987), pp. 162–94

——, *Strange Parallels: Southeast Asia in Global Context, c. 800–1830* (Cambridge, 2003)

——, 'The Transfer of the Burmese Capital from Pegu to Ava', *Journal of the Royal Asiatic Society of Great Britain and Ireland*, 1 (1980), pp. 64–83

Luce, G. H., 'The Ancient Pyu', in *Burma Research Society Fiftieth Anniversary Publications* (Rangoon, 1960), pp. 307–21

——, 'A Cambodian(?) Invasion of Lower Burma – A Comparison of Burmese and Talaing Chronicles', *Journal of the Burma Research Society*, XII/1 (1922), pp. 39–45

——, 'The Career of Htilaing Min (Kyanzittha)', *Journal of the Royal Asiatic Society*, I–II (1966), pp. 53–68

——, 'Countries Neighbouring Burma: Parts 1 & 2', *Journal of the Burma Research Society*, XIV/2 (1924), pp. 137–205

——, 'Dvaravati and Old Burma', *Journal of the Siam Society*, LIII/1 (1965), pp. 9–26

——, 'The Early *Syam* in Burma's History: A Supplement', *Journal of the Siam Society*, XLVII/1 (1959), pp. 59–101

——, 'Economic Life of the Early Burman', in *Burma Research Society Fiftieth Anniversary Publications* (Rangoon, 1960), pp. 323–75

——, 'Mons of the Pagan Dynasty', *Journal of the Burma Research Society*, XXXVI/1 (1953), pp. 1–19

——, 'Note on the Peoples of Burma in the 12th–13th Century AD', *Census of India*, XI/1 (1931), pp. 296–306

——, *Old Burma–Early Pagan*, 3 vols (New York, 1969–70)

——, 'Old Kyaukse and the Coming of the Burmans', *Journal of the Burma Research Society*, XLII/1 (1959), pp. 75–109

——, *Phases of Pre-Pagán Burma: Languages and History*, 2 vols (Oxford and New York, 1983), vol. I

——, 'Sources of Early Burma History', in *Southeast Asian History and Historiography: Essays Presented to D.G.E. Hall*, ed. C. D. Cowan and O. W. Wolters (Ithaca, NY, 1976)

Luce, G. H. and Pe Maung Tin, eds, *Inscriptions of Burma*, 5 vols (Rangoon, 1933–56)

——, *Selections from the Inscriptions of Pagan* (Rangoon, 1928)

Ma Ma Lay, *Not Out of Hate: A Novel of Burma*, trans. Margaret Aung-Thwin (Athens, OH, 1991)

Marks, John E., *Forty Years in Burma* (London, 1917)

Maung Maung, *Burma's Constitution* (The Hague, 1959)

Maung Maung Tin, ed., *Konbaungset Mahayazawindawgyi* [The Great Royal Chronicle of the Konbaung Dynasty], 3 vols (Yangon, 1967)

Mendelson, E. Michael, 'The King of the Weaving Mountain', *Royal Central Asian Journal*, XLVIII (1961), pp. 229–37

——, 'A Messianic Buddhist Association in Upper Burma', *Bulletin of the School of Oriental and African Studies*, XXIV (1961), pp. 560–80

——, 'Observations on a Tour in the Region of Mount Popa, Central Burma', *France-Asie*, XIX/179 (1963), pp. 786–807

——, *Sangha and State in Burma: A Study of Monastic Sectarianism and Leadership* (Ithaca, NY, 1975)

Ministry of Information, Myanmar, 'Hsinbyushin Ayedawbon', in *Myanmar Swai-Son Kyan* [Myanmar Encyclopaedia] (Yangon, 1960)

Moore, Elizabeth, 'Bronze and Iron Age Sites in Myanmar: Chindwin, Samon, and Pyu', *SOAS Bulletin of Burma Research*, I/1 (2003), pp. 24–39

——, *Early Landscapes of Myanmar* (Bangkok, 2007)

Moore, Elizabeth and Aung Myint, 'Finger-Marked Designs on Ancient Bricks in Myanmar', *Journal of the Siam Society*, LIIIX/2 (1991), pp. 81–102

Moore, Elizabeth and U. Pauk Pauk, 'Nyaung-gan: A Preliminary Note on a Bronze Age Cemetery Near Mandalay, Myanmar (Burma)', *Asian Perspectives Special Issue: The Archaeology of Myanma Pyay (Burma)*, XL/1 (2002), pp. 35–47

Morris, T. O., 'Copper and Bronze Antiquities from Burma', *Journal of the Burma Research Society*, XXVIII (1938), pp. 95–9.

——, 'The Konbyin Terrace of the Irrawaddy at Thayetmyo', *Journal of the*

Burma Research Society, XXVI (1936), pp. 163–9

——, 'A Palaeolith from Upper Burma', *Journal of the Burma Research Society*, XXII (1932), pp. 19–20.

——, 'A Palaeolith from Yenangyaung', *Journal of the Burma Research Society*, XXVI (1936), pp. 119–21

——, 'The Prehistoric Stone Implements of Burma', *Journal of the Burma Research Society*, XXV (1935), pp. 1–39

Movius, H. L. Jr, 'Palaeolithic Cultures of the Far East', *Transactions of the American Philosophical Society*, XXXVIII/4 (1948), pp. 335–411

——, 'The Stone Age of Burma', *Transactions of the American Philosophical Society*, Part II, XXXII (1943), pp. 271–393

Myanma Alin (Wednesday, 8 December 2010), pp. 1, 9

Myint Aung, 'The Capital of Suvannabhumi Unearthed?' *Shiroku*, 10 (1977), pp. 41–53

——, 'The Development of Myanmar Archaeology', *Myanmar Historical Research Journal*, 9 (2002), pp. 11–29

——, 'The Excavations at Halin', *Journal of the Burma Research Society*, LIII/2 (1970), pp. 55–64

——, 'The Excavations of Ayethama and Winka (?Suvannabhumi)', in *Essays Given to Than Tun on his 75th Birthday: Studies in Myanma History* (Yangon, 1999), pp. 17–64

Naw, Angelene, *Aung San and the Struggle for Burmese Independence* (Chiang Mai, 2001)

Ni Ni Myint, *Burma's Struggle against British Imperialism: 1885–1895* (Rangoon, 1983)

Nyi Nyi, 'Old Stone Age of Burma', *Working Peoples Daily* (1988)

Nyunt Han, Win Maung (Tanpawady) and Elizabeth Moore, 'Prehistoric Grave Goods from the Chindwin and Samon River Regions', in *Burma: Art and Archaeology*, ed. Alexander Green and T. Richard Blurton (Chicago, 2002)

Okudaira, Ryuji, 'The Burmese Dhammathat', in *Laws of South-East Asia. Volume 1: The Pre-Modern Texts*, ed. M. B. Hooker (Singapore, 1986), pp. 23–142

Oshegov, Sergey S. (U Kan Hla), 'Pagan: Development and Town Planning', *Journal of the Society of Architectural Historians*, XXXVI/1 (1977), pp. 15–29

Parker, Edward Harper, *Burma: With Special Reference to Her Relations with China* (Rangoon, 1893)

Pe Maung Tin, ed., *The Glass Palace Chronicle of the Kings of Burma*, trans. Ehrhardt Exp MTPe Maung Tin and G. H. Luce (New York, 1976)

——, *Myanma Sapei Thamaing* [History of Burmese Literature] (Yangon, 1948)

Phayre, Sir Arthur, *History of Burma Including Burma Proper, Pegu, Taungu, Tenasserim, and Arakan* (London, 1883)

——, 'History of Pegu', *Journal of the Asiatic Society of Bengal*, XLII/1 (1873), pp. 23–57

Pichard, Pierre, 'A Distinctive Technical Achievement: The Vaults and Arches of Pagan', in *The Art of Burma: New Studies*, ed. Donald M. Stadtner (Mumbai, 1999)

——, *Inventory of Monuments at Pagan*, 8 vols (Gartmore, 1992–2000)

——, *The Pentagonal Monuments of Pagan* (Bangkok, 1991)

Pinto, Ferdinand Mendez, *The Voyages and Adventures of Ferdinand Mendez Pinto, The Portuguese*, trans. Henry Cogan (London, 1891)

Pires, Tomâe, Armando Cortesäao and Francisco Rodrigues, *The Suma Oriental of Tome Pires: An Account of the East, from the Red Sea to Japan, Written in Malacca and India in 1512–1515; and, The Book of Francisco Rodrigues: Rutter of a Voyage in the Red Sea, Nautical Rules, Almanack and, Maps, Written and Drawn in the East before 1515*, Hakluyt Society 2nd ser., 89–90 (Nendeln, Liechtenstein, 1967)

Pranke, Patrick Arthur, 'The "Treatise on the Lineage of Elders" (*Vamsadipani*): Monastic Reform and the Writing of Buddhist History in Eighteenth-Century Burma' (PhD, University of Michigan, 2004)

Reid, Anthony, *Southeast Asia in the Age of Commerce – 1450–1680, Volume One: The Lands below the Winds* (New Haven, CT, 1988)

Sangermano, Father, *A Description of the Burmese Empire Compiled Chiefly from Burmese Documents by Father Sangermano*, trans. William Tandy (New York, 1969)

Scott, James C., *The Art of Not Being Governed: An Anarchist History of Upland Southeast Asia* (New Haven, CT, 2009)

——, *Weapons of the Weak: Everyday Forms of Peasant Resistance* (New Haven, CT, 1985)

Sithu Gamani Thingyan, *Zimme Yazawin* [Chronicle of Chiang Mai], trans. Thaw Kaung and Ni Ni Myint, ed. Tun Aung Chain (Yangon, 2003)

Smail, John, 'On the Possibility of an Autonomous History of Modern Southeast Asia', *Journal of Southeast Asian History*, II/2 (1961), pp. 72–102

Solheim, Wilhelm G., 'Early Bronze in Northeastern Thailand', *Current Anthropology*, IX (1968), pp. 59–62

——, 'New Light on a Forgotten Past', *National Geographic*, 139 (1971), pp. 330–39

Spiro, Melford E., 'Buddhism and Economic Action in Burma', *American Anthropologist*, LXVIII/5 (1966), pp. 1163–73

——, *Buddhism and Society: A Great Tradition and Its Burmese Vicissitudes* (New York, 1970)

——, *Burmese Supernaturalism* (Englewood Cliffs, NJ, 1967)

Stargardt, Janice, *The Ancient Pyu of Burma* (Cambridge, 1990)

——, *Tracing Thought through Things: The Oldest Pali Texts and the Early Buddhist Archaeology of India and Burma* (Amsterdam, 2000)

Stark, Miriam T. and Michael Aung-Thwin, eds, *Asian Perspectives Special Issue: The Archaeology of Myanma Pyay (Burma)*, XL (Honolulu, 2001)

Strachan, Paul, *Pagan: Art & Architecture of Old Burma* (Whiting Bay, Scotland, 1989)

Steinberg, David I., 'Is Burma Finally Poised for Change?', *Pacific Forum*, 3, (Honolulu, 2011)

——, *Burma/Myanmar: What Everyone Needs to Know* (New York, 2009)

Symes, Michael, *An Account of an Embassy to the Kingdom of Ava, Sent by the Governor-General of India, in the Year 1795* (London, 1800)

Tarling, Nicholas, ed., *The Journal of Henry Burney in the Capital of Burma 1830–1832* (Auckland, 1995)

Taylor, Jean Gelman, *Indonesia: Peoples and Histories* (New Haven, CT, and London, 2003)

Taylor, Robert H., 'Perceptions of Ethnicity in the Politics of Burma', *Southeast Asian Journal of Social Sciences*, X/1 (1982), pp. 7–22

——, *The State in Myanmar* (Honolulu, 2009)

Tha Myat, Thiripyanchi, *Mon Myanma Ekaya Thamaing* [History of the Mon–Myanma Alphabet] (Yangon, 1956)

——, *Myazedi Khaw Gubyauk Kyi Pyu Kyauksa* [The Pyu Inscription of the So-Called Myazedi] (Rangoon, 1958)

——, *Pyu Phat Ca* [Pyu Reader] (Rangoon, 1963)

Than Tun, 'Administration Under King Thalun (1629–1648)', *Journal of the Burma Research Society*, LI/2 (1968), pp. 173–88

——, 'The Buddhist Church in Burma During the Pagan Period: 1044–1287' (PhD, University of London, 1955)

——, 'Emperor without [an] Empire', *English for All*, 62 (1992), pp. 71–4

——, 'Hanthawady Sinbyushin: An Autobiogaphy', *Golden Myanmar*, 1/4 (1994), pp. 13–15

——, 'History of Buddhism in Burma: A.D. 1000–1300', *Journal of the Burma Research Society*, LXII/1 and 2 (1978), pp. 1–266

——, 'History of Burma: A.D. 1300–1400', *Journal of the Burma Research Society*, XLII/2 (1959), pp. 119–33

——, *The Royal Orders of Burma, A.D. 1598–1885*, 10 vols (Kyoto, 1983–90)

Thant Myint U, *The Making of Modern Burma* (New York, 2001)

——, *The River of Lost Footsteps* (New York, 2006)

Thaw Kaung, 'Accounts of King Bayinnaung's Life and Hanthawady Hsin-byu-myashin Ayedawbon, a Record of his Campaigns', *Myanmar Historical Research Journal*, 11 (2003), pp. 23–42

——, 'Ayedawbon Kyan, An Important Myanmar Literary Genre Recording Historical Events' (unpublished paper, Bangkok, 2000)

Thin Kyi, 'The Old City of Pagan', in *Essays Offered to G. H. Luce by His Colleagues and Friends in Honour of His Seventy-Fifth Birthday*, ed. Ba Shin (Ascona, 1966), pp. 179–88

Tin Hla Thaw, 'History of Burma: A.D. 1400–1500', *Journal of the Burma Research Society*, XLII/2 (1959), pp. 135–51

Tin Shein, ed., *Hmannan Mahayazawindawgyi* [Great Royal Chronicle of the Palace of Mirrors], 3 vols (Yangon, 1967)

Tonkin, Derek, 'Network Myanmar', www.networkmyanmar.org

Trager, Frank N., William J. Koenig and Yi Yi, eds, *Burmese Sit-táans 1764–1826: Records of Rural Life and Administration* (Tucson, 1979)

Tun Aung Chain, 'Pe Maung Tin and Luce's Glass Palace Revisited', *Journal of Burma Studies*, IX (2004), pp. 52–69

——, ed., *Chronicle of Ayutthaya: A Translation of the Yodaya Yazawin* (Yangon, 2005)

Universities Historical Research Centre, *Proceedings of the Workshop on Bronze Age Culture in Myanmar* (Yangon, 1999)

Vink, M., 'Seventeenth-Century Burma and the Dutch East India Company, 1634–1680', *Journal of the Economic and Social History of the Orient* (2008)

Wales, H. G. Quaritch, 'Dvaravati in South-East Asian Cultural History', *Journal of the Royal Asiatic Society*, I–II (1966), pp. 40–52

Wheatley, Paul, *Nagara and Commandery: Origins of the Southeast Asian Urban Traditions* (Chicago, 1983)

Wiant, Jon, 'Tradition in the Service of Revolution: The Political Symbolism of Taw-hlan-ye-khit', in *Military Rule in Burma Since 1962: A Kaleidoscope of Views*, ed. F. K. Lehman (Singapore, 1981), pp. 59–72

Wicks, Robert S., 'The Ancient Coinage of Mainland Southeast Asia', *Journal of Southeast Asian Studies*, XVI/2 (1985), pp. 195–225

Woodman, Dorothy, *The Making of Burma* (London, 1962)

Wyatt, David K., 'Relics, Oaths and Politics in Thirteenth-Century Siam', *Journal of Southeast Asian Studies*, XXXII/1 (2001), pp. 3–65

Yi Yi, 'Burmese Sources for the History of the Konbaung Period 1752–1885', *Journal of Southeast Asian Studies*, VI (1965), pp. 48–66

Yule, Henry, *A Narrative of the Mission to the Court of Ava in 1855 Compiled by Henry Yule together with the Journal of Arthur Phayre, Envoy to the Court of Ava, and Additional Illustrations by Colesworthy Grant and Linnaeus Tripe with an Introduction by Hugh Tinker* (New York, 1968)

Acknowledgements

The Bibliography acknowledges the authors and their works to whom we owe much, particularly the historians and other scholars who have preceded us by over a century. But as most are published academic works in Western languages (mainly English), our Burmese friends and colleagues who do not publish in English are left out of that bibliography by default. And yet, it is from the latter that we have learned some of the most important things about Myanmar and its people: what makes them 'tick', what makes them happy or angry, what they respond to most eagerly, which institutions they most cherish, who and what they remember most about their history and legends: in other words, their inner thoughts and the kinds of things that they value most. Precisely because these are not the basis of most recent Western-language accounts of the country, we feel it is about time their 'voices' are acknowledged. This voice is not particularly loud, neither is it pushy, demanding, self-righteous, sanctimonious, confrontational or, perhaps most important, fleeting. And that 'voice' seldom 'speaks' in English. It is largely that of secure, confident and often cautiously optimistic people, although not without awareness of the larger world. It is these Burmese friends and acquaintances that we thank for enabling us to write, with some understanding, what is largely *their* history from *their* perspective.

We are also deeply indebted to our home institutions for their support, without which this book would not have been possible. Over the years, the Asian Studies Program at the University of Hawai'i, the Department of Southeast Asian Studies and the Department of History at the National University of Singapore provided indispensable time and funding for travel and research in Myanmar.

Throughout the years we have been fortunate to work closely with a number of scholars who have helped shape our approach to the writing and interpretation of Myanmar history. Among them (and in no particular order) we are especially grateful to Ian Brown, F. K. Lehman, Victor B. Lieberman, Robert H. Taylor, David I. Steinberg, U Saw Tun, Catherine Raymond, Mary Callahan, Patricia Herbert, Kyaw Yin Hlaing, Chie Ikeya, Ardeth Thawnghmung, Patrick Pranke, Alicia Turner, Elizabeth Moore, Jane Ferguson, Sun Laichen, Dr Maung Aung Myoe, John Miksic, Lily Handlin, John O'Kell, Juliane Schober, Ward Keeler, Jacques Leider, D. Christian Lammerts, Yoshihiro Nakanishi, Mandy Sadan, James Scott, Goh Geok Yian, Will B. Womack, Penny Edwards, Michael Adas, Don Swearer, Park Jang Sik, Michio Takatani, Tamura Katsumi, Alexey Kirichenko, Toshihiro Kudo, Guillaume Rosenberg, Pat McCormick and Julian Wheatley.

Within Myanmar numerous friends and colleagues continually and unconditionally offered their friendship and advice. Many provided key sources, made invaluable introductions, or took the time to share with us their experiences and expertise. We are forever grateful to: U Thaw Kaung, Dr Myo Myint, Dr Khin Maung Nyunt, U Tun Aung Chain, U Toe Hla, U Sai Aung Tun, Daw Ni Ni Myint, Daw Kyan, U Hla Shain, Nanda Hmun, U Aung Myo, U Myint Aung, U Kyi Saw Tun, U Than Oo, U Win Maung, Dr Myo Oo, Dr Thant Thaw Kaung, Dr Nyunt Nyunt Shwe, Dr Khin Hla Han, U Aung Kyaing, Dr Htwe Htwe Win, Troy Tun, U Than Ohn, U Tin Saung, U Nyein Lwin, U Aung Myo Nyunt, Ko Soe Moe and Ma Win Win.

Finally, we thank our immediate families – especially Maria and Eileen – who patiently listened to numerous conversations about Myanmar history that always seemed to occur at the most inappropriate occasions.

Photo Acknowledgements

The authors and publishers wish to express their thanks to the below sources of illustrative material and/or permission to reproduce it:

Michael Aung-Thwin, *Pagan: The Origins of Modern Burma* (Honolulu, HI, 1985): p. 92; courtesy of the authors: pp. 11, 12, 17, 19, 21, 22, 39, 68, 70, 72, 88, 89, 93, 100, 102, 104, 114, 119, 121, 150, 157, 161, 168, 169, 185, 214, 226, 227, 229, 243; from Google Earth: pp. 69 (© 2011 Cnes / Spot Image, © 2011 Mapabc.com, image © 2011 Digital-Globe, © 2011 Google), 110 (image © 2011 GeoEye, © 2011 Europa Technologies, image © 2011 DigitalGlobe, © 2011 Google), 130 (© 2011 Mapabc.com, image © 2011 GeoEye, © 2011 Google); photos courtesy of Bob Hudson: pp. 58, 61; maps courtesy of Lee Li Kheng: pp. 36, 46, 57, 78, 79; from Victor B. Lieberman, *Burmese Adminis trative Cycles: Anarchy and Conquest, c. 1580–1760* (Princeton, NJ, 1984): p. 135; from V. C. Scott O'Connor, *Mandalay and Other Cities of the Past in Burma* (London, 1907): p. 172; map © One World – Nations Online, OWNO, nationsonline.org: p. 24; photo courtesy of Dr Robert H. Taylor: p. 20.

Index

McCain, John 285
Maharattathara, Shin 112
Mahayazawingyi (Great Royal
   Chronicle) 151
Maitreya 73, 84, 176
Malabari 131
Malay 29, 117, 119, 129, 181
Malaysia 13, 117, 296
Mandalay 8, 14, 15, 16, 18, 19, 32, 37,
   49, 50, 67, 164, 168, 169, 170, 171,
   178, 188, 189, 190, 191, 198, 199,
   205, 211, 233, 271
Mandela, Nelson 259, 265
Martaban 7, 8, 42, 94, 144, 145, 146,
   154, 164, 184, 206 *see also*
   Muttama
Maung Aye, General 283
Maung Maung, Dr 260, 266
Melaka 119, 129, 146
Mello, Soarez de 131, 132, 133
Mergui (Myeik) 45, 47, 48, 91, 94, 146
Mindon, King 169, 170, 171, 186, 188
Mingaung the First, King 111, 112
Mingaung the Second, King 114
Mingyiswa Sawke, King 111, 112
Mitchell, Derek (UN Ambassador to
   Myanmar) 286
Mon 30, 31, 32, 33, 44, 45, 46, 47, 48,
   50, 64, 83, 88, 96, 117, 118, 119,
   120, 126, 132, 137, 153, 154, 158,
   171, 172, 182, 184, 194, 239, 250
Mongols 99, 102, 105, 109, 143, 172
monks 11, 12, 19, 30, 84, 89, 91, 92, 95,
   96, 98, 99, 102, 103, 104, 112, 124,
   148, 151, 165, 183, 199, 202, 203,
   204, 212, 216, 220, 222, 225, 245,
   253, 257, 268, 271, 272, 273, 275
Moors 131
Moulmein 8, 147, 206, 232
Mountbatten, Lord 236
Mranma 7
Mrauk-U 31, 138, 139
Mu 16, 29, 38, 60, 78, 79, 94, 95, 101,
   109, 115, 133, 156, 158
Mumbai 8
Muslim 47, 99, 125, 129, 291, 296
Muttama 7, 42, 44, 67, 68, 94, 105, 117,
   118, 119, 131, 132, 134, 136, 137,
   144, 180, 273 *see also* Martaban

Myanma 7, 8, 64, 198
Myanma Pyay (Pyi) 7, 8
Myitnge River 16, 29, 60, 110, 163
Myitsone Dam 285
myosa ('town eater') system 32, 87, 111,
   113, 114, 140, 143, 147, 148, 156,
   170
myo-thu-gyi (township headman) 181,
   183, 186, 202

Nambiar, Vijay 285
Nanchao kingdom 77, 78, 108, 143
Nandabayin, King 137, 138
Narapatisithu, King 87, 88, 90, 99, 117,
   124
Narathihapade, King 99, 100
Nat Shin Naung, Prince 145
Natalegawa, Marty (Foreign Minister,
   Indonesia) 286
National Democratic Front 278
National League for Democracy (NLD)
   260, 263, 264, 265, 266, 267, 268,
   269, 270, 275, 277, 278, 279, 280,
   281, 282, 287, 288
National Unity Party (NUP) 277, 279
nationalism 31, 209, 216, 252
Natonmya, King 99
Nats (spirits) 50, 85, 86, 87, 145, 165
Naypyidaw (capital of Myanmar) 16,
   17, 18, 19, 20, 40, 49, 73, 123, 129,
   232, 276, 286, 287, 291
Ne Win, General 20, 34, 223, 231, 235,
   239, 241, 242, 246, 248, 249, 252,
   253, 254, 255, 262, 266
Neolithic 29, 38, 45, 55, 56, 57, 58, 59,
   60, 65, 66
North Korea 246
Norway 286, 290
Nyaungyan Min, King 143

oil 43, 84, 125, 197, 206, 223, 229, 240
Obama, Barack 291
Ojea Quintana, Tomás (UN Special
   Rapporteur on Human Rights)
   285

Padethayaza 152, 153, 154
Pagan 8, 11, 15, 16, 17, 19, 25, 29, 30,
   31, 32, 37, 64, 67, 71, 73, 74, 77,